MECHANICAL DESIGN
FOR THE STAGE

D1451985

MECHANICAL DESIGN
FOR THE STAGE

Alan Hendrickson

Colin Buckhurst

LIBRARY
FRANKLIN PIERCE UNIVERSITY
RINDGE, NH 03461

AMSTERDAM • BOSTON • HEIDELBERG • LONDON
NEW YORK • OXFORD • PARIS • SAN DIEGO
SAN FRANCISCO • SINGAPORE • SYDNEY • TOKYO

Focal Press is an imprint of Elsevier

Acquisitions Editor: Cara Anderson
Publishing Services Manager: George Morrison
Project Manager: Mónica González de Mendoza
Marketing Manager: Christine Degon Veroulis
Cover Design: Karen O'Keefe Owens

Focal Press is an imprint of Elsevier
30 Corporate Drive, Suite 400, Burlington, MA 01803, USA
Linacre House, Jordan Hill, Oxford OX2 8DP, UK

Copyright © 2008, Elsevier, Inc. All rights reserved.

The information presented in this text, while believed to be accurate, should not be used or relied upon for any specific application without professional examination and verification of its accuracy, suitability, and applicability by a competent licensed engineer, or other qualified professional. Publication of the material contained herein is not intended as a representation or warranty on the part of Alan Hendrickson or Colin Buckhurst that this information is suitable for any general or particular use, or that it is free from infringement of any patent or copyright. Anyone using this information assumes all risk and liability arising from such use.

No part of this publication may be reproduced, stored in a retrieval system, or transmitted in any form or by any means, electronic, mechanical, photocopying, recording, or otherwise, without the prior written permission of the publisher.

Permissions may be sought directly from Elsevier's Science & Technology Rights Department in Oxford, UK: phone: (+44) 1865 843830, fax: (+44) 1865 853333, e-mail: permissions@elsevier.co.uk. You may also complete your request online via the Elsevier homepage (http://elsevier.com), by selecting "Customer Support" and then "Obtaining Permissions."

 Recognizing the importance of preserving what has been written, Elsevier prints its books on acid-free paper whenever possible.

Library of Congress Cataloging-in-Publication Data
Hendrickson, Alan.
  Mechanical design for the stage / Alan Hendrickson, Colin Buckhurst.
    p. cm.
  Includes bibliographical references and index.
  ISBN-13: 978-0-240-80631-0 (pbk. : alk. paper)
  1. Stage machinery. 2. Machine design. I. Buckhurst, Colin. II. Title.
  PN2091.M3H46 2008
  792.02'5--dc22
                              2007031303

British Library Cataloguing-in-Publication Data
A catalogue record for this book is available from the British Library.

ISBN: 978-0-240-80631-0

For information on all Focal Press publications visit our website at www.books.elsevier.com

08 09 10 11 12 13 10 9 8 7 6 5 4 3 2 1

Printed in the United States of America

Working together to grow
libraries in developing countries

www.elsevier.com | www.bookaid.org | www.sabre.org

ELSEVIER   BOOK AID International   Sabre Foundation

Table of Contents

Table of Contents . . . . *v*

Preface . . . . *xiii*

Part I: The Physics of Stage Machinery . . . *1*

1   *Basic Concepts & Definitions* *3*

Fundamentals 3
Displacement 4
Definition of Translational Displacement 5
Speed and Velocity 7
Acceleration. 9
Graphical Relationships Between x, v, and a 9
Problems 12

2   *The Equations of Constant Acceleration* . . *13*

Constant Acceleration. 13
Equations of Constant Acceleration 14
Moves with a Given Time and Distance 18
The Acceleration Due to Gravity 20
Problems 22

3   *The Force to Accelerate Mass: $F_{acceleration}$* . *23*

Overview. 23
Newton's Laws of Motion 23
Mass and Force. 24
Conversion Table – Mass and Force 25
Weight 26
The Force Needed to Accelerate Mass 27
Problems 28

4   *The Friction Force, $F_{friction}$* *29*

Friction—Complex and Simplified 29
Definitions 30
Sliding Friction 32
Static Friction 33
Kinetic Friction 35
Measuring Coefficients of Friction 36
Rolling Friction 38
Friction of Ropes on Cylinders 40
Problems 43

5   *The Lifting Force, $F_{lifting}$* *45*

Gravity, Weight, and the Lifting Force 45
The Lifting Force 45
Counterweighting 46
Problems 48

6   *Maximum Power and Force* *49*

Power 49
Maximum Power 51
Maximum Force 55
Problems 57

7   *Basic Concepts of Rotational Motion*   . . .*59*

Definition of Rotational Motion 59
Coordinate Systems 59
Angular Displacement 60
Angular Speed 62
Angular Acceleration 63
Converting Between Linear and Rotational 63
An Aside: Centripetal Acceleration 64
The Equations of Constant Angular Acceleration 65
Torque 66
Problems 68

8   *The Torque to Accelerate Mass, T_{accel}*   . . .*71*

Overview 71
Moment of Inertia 72
Transferring the Axis of Rotation 75
An Aside: WK^2 77
The Torque to Accelerate Mass 78

Rolling Objects 84
Problems 86

9   *The Torque to Overcome Friction, $T_{friction}$*   **.** **87**

Rotation and Friction 87
The Torque Due to Friction, $T_{friction}$ 88
Caster Friction and Turntables 89
Rotational Bearing Friction 95
Problems 100

10   *The Lifting Torque, T_{lift}* **.** **.** **.** **.** **.** **.** **.** ***103***

Overview 103
The Center of Mass 104
The Lifting Torque 106
Problems 110

11   *Maximum Power and Torque* **.** **.** **.** **.** **.** ***113***

Power 113
Maximum Power 115
Maximum Torque 124
An Important Caveat—Mass and Spring Vibrations 126
Problems 127

12   *Combining Multiple Motions*   **.** **.** **.** **.** **.** ***129***

Overview 129
Combining Linear and Rotational Power 129
Converting Terms within the Power Formula 133
Combining Multiple Speed Effects 136
Problems 141

Part II: Stage Machinery Components **.** **.** ***143***

13   *Safety*   **.** **.** **.** **.** **.** **.** **.** **.** **.** **.** **.** ***145***

General Concepts 145
Risk Assessment 146
Hazard Abatement 146
Single Failure Proof Design 147
Design Factor and Factor of Safety 148
Emergency Stop 150
Codes and Standards 150
Formalized Procedures 152

Inspection and Maintenance 153
Additional Information Sources 154

14   *Actuators* *155*

Electric, Hydraulic or Pneumatic 155
Powering the Actuator 155
Electric Motors 155
Common Motor Types 156
Sizes and Configurations 157
The Speed/Torque Curve 159
Enclosures 160
Service Factor 160
Choosing an Electric Motor 160
Hydraulic Actuators 161
Pneumatic Actuators 161
Cylinders 162
Stop Tube 165
Cylinder Selection 166
Counterbalance Valves 167
Additional Information Sources 168

15   *Speed Reduction* *169*

Speed Reduction 169
Speed Reduction Methods 171
Gear Reducers 173
Terms Used in Gear Reducer Selection 174
Using the Reducer Ratings 178
Gear Motor Selection 180
Roller Chain 181
Roller Chain Strength 182
Roller Chain Sprockets 184
Roller Chain Guidelines 185
V-belts and Sheaves 185
Toothed Belts 186
Additional Information 186

16   *Shafting* *187*

Shaft Basics 187
Shaft Strength 187
Shaft Diameter and Torsional Stiffness Rule of Thumb 189
Other Shaft Stress Sources 190
Combined Torque and Bending Shaft Analysis 191
Resonant Speed 193

Stress Concentrations 193
Keys and Keyways 194
Practical Shaft Design Considerations 195
Jaw Couplings 196
Roller Chain Couplings 197
Universal Joints 197
Types of Bushings 199
Additional Information 200

17   *Bearings and Wheels* *201*

Bearings 201
Rolling Element Bearings 202
Plain Bearings 203
Calculating Pressure and Velocity 204
Mounted Bearings 205
Linear Bearings 207
Slewing Rings, or Turntable Bearings 208
Cam Followers 209
Track Capacity 210
Bearing Selection Considerations 211
Wheels and Casters 212
Wheel and Caster Terminology 212
Specialty Wheels 213
Additional Information 214

18   *Wire Rope and Sheaves* *215*

Wire Rope 215
Wire Rope Terminology 215
Inspection 219
Sheave Terminology 219
Additional Information Sources 222

19   *Cable Drums* *223*

Grooved Cable Drums 223
Drum Types 223
Drum Sections 224
Drum Materials 226
Groove Dimensions 226
Drum Diameter 227
Drum Width 227
Drum Groove Threads per Inch Values 227
Cable Anchors 229
Drum Construction 229

Drum Reeving 230
Additional Information Sources 231

20   *Screw Mechanisms* *233*

Screw Mechanism Basics 233
Sliding Contact Screws: Acme Screws 234
Rolling Contact Screws: Ball Screws 235
Common Screw Mechanism Uses 236

21   *Brakes* *239*

Spring-Set Brakes 239
Brake Noise 240
Brake Placement 242
Manual Release 243
Orientation 244
Fluid Power Brake Circuits 244
Overspeed Braking 245
Brake Engage and Release Speed 245
Additional Information 246

22   *Control Components* *247*

External Sensors 247
Position Sensing 248
Limit Box Ratios 250
Disconnects 251
Connectors 252
Additional Information Sources 253

23   *Frames and Framing* *255*

General Concepts 255
Open vs. Enclosed Frames 255
Stock Shapes vs. CNC Plates 256
Steel vs. Aluminum 258
Mounting and Handling Options 258
Structural Design Considerations 259

Part III: A Mechanical Design Process . *263*

24   *Mechanical Design in Theatre* *265*

Overview 265
Five Key Points 266

Mechanical Design in Industry and Theatre 269
Influences on an Individual's Design Abilities 272
A Brief Overview of the Mechanical Design Process 274

25   *Developing a Design Specification* . . . *279*

Overview. 279
When a Written Specification Is Useful 281
Elements of a Complete Specification. 282
Summary 296

26   *Concept Design* . . . . *26* *297*

Overview. 297
Concept Generation Techniques 298
Concept Evaluation 304
An Evaluation Matrix 305
Freedom and Constraint 306
Degrees of Freedom 306
Some Diverse Constraint Issues 309

27   *Detail Design* *311*

Overview. 311
Analysis 311
Failure Modes and Effects Analysis, FMEA. 313
Parts and Materials List 315
Drafting 315

28   *Design for Manufacture* *317*

Overview. 317
Design for Fabrication 318
Design for Fabrication Issues 318
Outside Part Fabrication 322
Design for Assembly 325
Conclusion 330

Part IV: A Compendium of Stage Machinery . 331

29   *A Compendium of Stage Machinery* . . . *333*

Overview. 333
Machine Details Common to Many Machines 334
Backup Needs and Techniques 336

30   *Winches* **341**

Overview 341
Typical Applications 341
Cable Drum Winch Concepts 344
Chain Drive Winch Concepts 344
Direct Drive Winch Concepts 346
Zero Fleet Angle Winch Concepts 350
Machine Details 355
Winch Specification Issues 355

31   *Turntable Drives* **359**

Overview 359
A Typical Application 360
Turntable Drive Concepts 367
Limited Rotation Turntable Drive Concepts 376
Machine Details 379
Turntable Drive Specification 381

32   *Lifts* **385**

Overview 385
A Typical Application 386
Lift Concepts 393
Hydraulic Cylinder Run Lifts and Leveling Techniques 401
Lift Specification 404

33   *Tracked Scenery* **407**

Overview 407
Typical Applications 408
Deck Track Drive Concepts 417
Electric Dogs 420

Bibliography **423**

Index **427**

Preface

The use of machinery on stage is staggering in its variety. A machine may move a load in excess of 100,000 pounds, or drop a feather on cue. An effect may be as simple as a pneumatic cylinder closing a door, or as complex as a whole system of synchronized winches assembling the pieces of a chandelier into a single unit over the audience's heads. There have been battery powered wirelessly controlled boats, hydraulically elevated flying cars, and over one hundred years ago, chariot races complete with real horses running on treadmills, and locomotives racing along belching smoke, sparks, and steam. All of the machinery used for these effects share one thing in common, they were all designed and built specifically for use in one production to realize the artistic vision of a director and a set designer.

This book is about this type of machinery, and it is written for the theatre technicians who design, construct, install, and often operate it. These technicians, and their employers, are a highly diverse group too. Their level of formal education in machine design runs the gamut from none to degrees in mechanical engineering, their experience with such equipment may be limited or extensive, and their employment may be in educational or regional theatres, in opera houses, or in commercial scene shops serving the Broadway, Las Vegas, touring or theme park markets. Not surprisingly, given the breadth of both the topics that could be covered, and the diversity of the potential audience for this book, it will never satisfy anyone all the time—that is an impossible goal. This book does however provide a solid base to start from, and its main intent is as a text and reference book for theatre technicians interested in this area.

It has been designed to be a companion to Alys Holden's and Bronislaw Sammler's *Structural Design for the Stage*, since structural and mechanical design are so often intertwined. At the Yale School of Drama, the material in that book is presented over three semesters of graduate level classes, two of which occur in the first year of the three year program. Parts I and II of this book, *The Physics of Stage Machinery* and *Stage Machinery Components* are covered in a first semester second year course. Students in that class will therefore have had two semesters of work by that time covering wood and steel structures, and considerable problem solving experience with the mathematics involved. A separate third year elective class on mechanical design uses the information in Parts III and IV, *A Mechanical Design*

Process and *A Compendium of Stage Machinery,* as a reference for machine design projects.

Another essential companion to this book is the vast amount of information available on the Internet concerning the specifications, dimensions, and suggested uses of the components that are a part of every machine. It was not that long ago that printed catalogs were a collected and carefully guarded part of a technician's reference library, but today all that information, and more, is available instantly virtually anywhere in the world via the web. Finding it is not hard, since any search engine will find hundreds of hits for "pillow blocks" or "gearmotors", so instead reducing the choices becomes the issue, and here the brands offered by parts distributors you often use can be the key to limiting what you look at.

Since there is so much information needed for mechanical design, no one book could ever contain it all, and so this book should be seen as only a beginning. I have considered many times amending the title to be ***An Introduction to*** *Mechanical Design for the Stage.* Entire books have been written on each of the major machine components alone: roller chain, gear reducers, bearings, and electric motors. One book entitled *An Introduction to the Design and Behavior of Bolted Joints* runs a mere 950 pages long—an introduction indeed!

From the inception of this book, its illustrations were seen as key. I have been frustrated looking at small black and white photos reproduced in the few existing books that cover anything near to this topic. They often do not show enough to make the operation of the device depicted clear. So what has been done here are line drawings, some made strictly as illustrations, and some pulled from construction drawings of existing machines. Throughout, the intent is to convey the concept of the depicted device, not to provide plans that can be built without thought. A major theme of this book is that you are in charge of every decision that goes into the design of a machine, and these generic un-dimensioned depictions never let you off easy. Now whether these are any clearer at conveying the concepts than photos would have been is something you the readers will have to judge.

Another choice made here that may cause comment is the mix of units used. In the United States, we are still entrenched in what are called the U.S. customary units (long ago based on, but now somewhat different from, the English Imperial system of units). The rest of the world, of course, is metric. Many machine components sold in the United States are manufactured in Europe or Asia, and so motor power will be listed in Watts, tapped holes may require metric hardware, and weights are given in kilograms. This is a world we must be familiar with. The examples and problems in Chapters 1–6 alternate between customary and metric units. This works, I feel, because the underlying concepts there are simple enough that the potential for confusion due to the use of varying units is minimal. In the later chapters, formulas will be introduced with both systems of units, but the examples and problems will all be in customary units. This is not ideal, but the complexity of the material and the length of the examples preclude continuing the mix. This unfortunately also reduces the convenience of using this book in the solely metric world.

One major and essential topic not covered here is the subject of any control equipment needed to operate this machinery, since that is a whole other topic deserving book length coverage in itself. Machinery control systems, and this very much includes the operator, share responsibility with the mechanical system design for overall machine safety.

This text has a number of warnings and disclaimers. Heed them. Even with every part of a stage automation system working correctly, moving scenery is inherently hazardous. Safety can be compromised at any point along the path from design, to construction, installation, and the use of a machine on stage in tech and performance conditions. Be thorough and methodical in your work. Seek out the services of an engineer to verify your work, or to develop a machine that is not in your area of competence. Be ready to assert your authority to say no to potentially unsafe uses of your machines, since no one will know better than you what they can and cannot do. Mechanical design requires a certain mind-set, a certain personality—study and experiment to gain knowledge and experience, be observant, be realistic, be rigorous, be conservative, be safe.

I would like to thank a number of people who have helped make this work what it is. First and foremost, Colin Buckhurst, of Adirondack Studios, wrote Part II, Chapters 13 through 23, from a jumble of notes and illustrations I had been using as class handouts for years. Without his considerable and capable work this book would not yet be done. Chuck Adomanis, of Hudson Scenic Studio, while a student at Yale, brought to my attention the topic of engineering design and the design process. Its inclusion here is directly attributable to him. Neil Mazzella, the owner of Hudson Scenic, and Corky Boyd have given me a number of opportunities to work on projects for Broadway productions, and those experiences have provided validation for the information presented here.

I would also like to thank Bob Goddard, Loren Schreiber, and Fritz Schwentker who read drafts of this book and offered many useful suggestions for correction and improvement. Were it not for my procrastination and painfully slow writing, many of their ideas could have been more fully explored and implemented, undoubtedly enriching the end result.

I must thank all of those at the Yale School of Drama who have worked to create a program that expects a consistent investigation into what constitutes the state of the art in technical theatre. Ben Sammler, chairman of the Technical Design and Production department, has led this effort in the areas of technical management and structural design, and he encourages others to excel in their specific areas. Nearly 30 years of technical students at the Drama School have put up with this material in an everevolving form. Their questions and comments have shaped this material profoundly, and I thank them for their patience, their knowledge, and their inquisitiveness.

Alan Hendrickson
New Haven, Connecticut
August 2007

Part I: The Physics of Stage Machinery

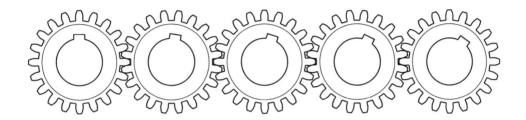

Mechanical design in the broadest sense involves the process of developing a machine to meet an identified set of goals. Mechanical design, as it relates to a production to be developed for theatre, involves the conversion of a director's and set designer's vision for the production into the reality of a machine that will move scenery as they imagine. An essential and early part of this process is quantifying the relevant aspects of the scenery and its move. Numerous questions need to be asked and answered. For instance, what is the top speed of the fastest move? How much does the scenery weigh? What exactly is the move: a wagon traveling 25 feet straight down a raked deck, a turntable spinning half a turn, a lift rising 2.2 meters? Does it roll on casters riding on a smooth stage floor, or does it just slide? From the answers to these and other questions, estimates of the power, force, and speed needed to perform a given move can be determined. These values become the loading conditions for the machine that can then be designed.

In Part I of this book, comprising Chapters 1 through 12, each of the component terms of a formula describing the maximum power needed by scenery for a given move will be methodically defined and described. This occurs twice, once for scenic effects that move in straight lines, such as wagons, lifts, or flown units, and once for those things that rotate, mainly turntables. To provide an overview of what is to come, a brief qualitative description of the terms in these two formulas will prove useful.

During linear motion, the maximum power required by the scenic unit being moved is:

$$P_{max} = (F_{acceleration} + F_{friction} + F_{lifting})\, v_{max}$$

In words this says that the maximum power equals the sum of three forces times the top speed. The three forces are:
- the force needed to accelerate, or speed up, the mass of the scenery,
- the force needed to overcome the resistance to movement imposed by friction,
- and any force needed to lift the piece if its motion has any vertical component.

The underlying logic of this relationship may appear evident from our experiences outside of theatre, driving around in cars.
- A sports car, with a relatively powerful engine in a light weight body, is capable of much greater acceleration than either a heavier or less powerful vehicle.
- Roads are paved, and tires pressurized correctly to reduce frictional resistance. Driving on sand or in deep mud involves much more force to overcome the friction involved, and so these surfaces make poor roads.
- It is obvious from the sound of the engine that driving up a steep mountain road involves more effort than coasting downhill on that same road.

Not surprisingly, the same basic relationships hold true for simple circular rotation:

$$P_{max} = (T_{acceleration} + T_{friction} + T_{lifting})\, \omega_{max}$$

Here the basic formula is the same, but force has been replaced by its rotational equivalent torque, and speed by angular speed (denoted by the Greek letter lower-case omega). The same everyday example of the car given above actually applies here too, because everything providing or transmitting power there, from the engine to the tires, is actually rotating. It is only where the tires contact the road that torque is converted to force.

These formulas, as presented in the following chapters, are not universal. They are in fact case formulas, applicable only to certain very specific situations, but since most scenery moves either in straight lines or rotates, these two find continual use.

Basic Concepts & Definitions

Fundamentals

There are concepts, called fundamentals, that form the base of all of physics. Anything that physics describes can be expressed in terms made up only of fundamentals. The fundamentals are not reducible to anything more basic, and are undefinable by definition. The fundamentals therefore are the starting point for our development of a mathematics of motion.

There is a certain element of arbitrary choice in picking what to use for fundamentals. Science seeks simplicity where possible, and fundamentals should be concepts commonly understood as obvious. Also the fundamentals should be as few in number as possible, while still as a group remaining a complete base for the physics built upon them. The fundamentals needed to cover all the material in this book are: time, length, and one of either mass or force. The choice between mass or force as a fundamental is an arbitrary one, and in the past each have had their advocates. Mass and force are related to each other through Newton's 2nd law, a topic of a later chapter—so discussion is deferred until then.

Time is perhaps the most intangible of the fundamentals, yet everyone has a sense of what time is. Einstein notwithstanding, the rate and direction of the passage of time are invariant. Time moves forward; only its passing may be measured. The units of time are the most universal of any of the fundamentals. Throughout this book the units of seconds, minutes, and hours will be freely mixed. Such mixing is justified by the variety displayed in common usage: feet per second, revolutions per minute, kilometers per hour.

The fundamental length provides a measure of space. With length, the position of a object in space can be specified. A fixed origin is needed, but can be anything that is appropriate to the problem. A judicious choice of an origin can often simplify a problem right from the start. An exaggerated example relating to origin choice involves measuring the width of a flat. A perfectly valid measurement could be obtained by starting with an origin at some prominent location, say the center of town. Surveyor-like measurements and trig calculations in three dimensions could yield the flat's width, but this would not be quick, accurate, or easy. Reducing the task down to one dimension helps by eliminating all trigonometry from the problem. Careful alignment of the flat's edges relative to a straight line from the flat to the origin could occur before taking two measurements to the flat; one to each edge. By taking the absolute value of the result of the subtraction of one measurement from another, the answer would be found. Mathematically:

$$\textit{flat width} = |x_1 - x_2|$$

where: x_1 and x_2 are the two length measurements (feet or meters)

If, though, we had assumed one edge of the flat as the origin, just temporarily, then our two measurements of lengths from origin to edges would always include one measurement of zero. This has two benefits. We do not need to measure anything from the center of town, and performing the same absolute value of the result of the subtraction of two measurements would now be trivial because of the one zero value measure. Of course when using a tape measure, the act of defining an origin by placing the tape end on an edge is rarely considered, we just do it.

Origins for length measurements can be points, the center of a spherically shaped dome, lines, the plaster line of the stage, or planes, the stage floor with respect to the height of battens. In all three cases, measurements of position must involve more than a length specification alone. This is because the expression of position by length alone does not resolve the ambiguity of what direction from the origin the measurement is being made. This ambiguity is commonly eliminated by direction indicating specifiers. For instance, in the case of one dimensional, or straight line movement systems, say a flysystem, position is indicated both by a length between object and origin, and a direction specified by any two-state indicator: up, down, in, out, +, –, etc. Because quantities, like position, that require both direction and size are common in physics, a special set of mathematical rules and notations has developed. Any quantity that requires a size, or magnitude, component and a directional component is called a vector. Position is therefore a vector. In most texts a vector quantity is, by convention, indicated by a bold letter: **x** . The magnitude, or the size component of a vector, is notated: x. In a one-dimensional system, a system where all movement occurs along a straight line, the magnitude of a position vector is simply the distance from the origin in the units being used (meters, feet, or inches for instance), and the direction is indicated with a + or – sign.

Assigning a sign of + or – to a position is an arbitrary choice that needs to be made once for a given situation, and then followed consistently from then on. Some choices seem obvious, assume the stage floor is the origin or zero point, and then straight up into the flytower is positive, and down into the trap room is negative, but the opposite assumption is just as valid. In other situations there may be no clear convention. Is stage right + or – relative to the centerline? Ultimately it does not matter what you choose, just pick one and stick with it.

Displacement

If an object moves, its position changes. The change of position is called displacement. To describe displacements mathematically, they are usually broken up into two distinct components, translational and rotational. Any movement, the rolling of a wheel or the trajectory of a thrown ball, for example, can be described with a sum of translational and rotational components. While accurate and complete, this is far more complex than we need for 99% of stage scenery moves. From here on, through Chapter 6, we will assume all moves are linear, i.e., motion confined to straight lines; in later chapters all moves will be rotational, or spinning around a fixed axis of rotation. These assumptions are acceptable because flying scenery, wagons, and lifts usually move only in straight lines, and turntables spin around a point that remains stationary. So in summary, and for emphasis:

 Assumption: In Chapters 1-6, all moves will be in straight lines.

Definition of Translational Displacement

If the position of an object is recorded at two different times, with x_1, a position at an arbitrary time t_1, and x_2 the objects position at a later time t_2, then the displacement of the object is defined as:

$$\Delta x = x_2 - x_1 \qquad \qquad 1.1$$

The Δ is the capital Greek letter delta, and its meaning is "the change of." So for instance, Δx is "the change of x," or "the change of position." The Δ implies a subtraction of two measurements taken of some variable, with the value of the measurement taken first always subtracted from the value of the one taken second. It is the number subscripts that imply a time sequence. Lower number subscripts always refer to times earlier than higher numbered subscripts. Therefore x_1 is a position measurement taken before x_2 which likewise refers to a measurement taken before x_3.

As was mentioned earlier, simplification of calculations can result by proper origin choice. If x_1 is considered an origin or zero point, then the displacement simply becomes:

$$\Delta x = x_2 - x_1 = x_2 - 0$$

$$or: \qquad \Delta x = x_2$$

Position and displacement are both forms of the length fundamental. Units for length in common use are the meter throughout most of the world, and feet, inches, and miles within the United States. Though this book is primarily aimed at a U.S. audience, the metric system is far too prevalent to ignore. We purchase machinery made in Europe or Asia to metric specifications, and so we must be familiar with both systems of measure. In the examples that follow, the units used will be a mix between metric units (specifically SI units, or *Système international d'unités*), and the units used in the United States, which are called U.S. customary units. Throughout the book some examples will be presented in metric units, and they will be denoted in the example heading with the term "(SI)".

EXAMPLE: A wagon sits directly on center stage. It then is moved to a position 10 ft stage right of center, and then again later it is moved to a position 2 ft stage left of center. What was its displacement during the first move? the second move? and the total displacement from start to finish?

SOLUTION: There are three positions of note in this problem:

$$\mathbf{x}_1 = \text{the position at time } t_1, \text{ the start of the problem}$$

$$\mathbf{x}_2 = \text{the position at time } t_2, \text{ after the first move}$$

$$\mathbf{x}_3 = \text{the position at time } t_3, \text{ after the second move}$$

Values need to be assigned to these variables. Magnitudes are given in the statement of the problem, a zero origin of center stage seems logical (though zero could be a stage right wall, or the center of town if you wanted), and a direction convention can easily be set. For this problem let's assume (and it truly is an arbitrary assumption) that stage right of center is positive, and stage left of center is negative. So then:

$$\mathbf{x}_1 = 0 \, ft \qquad \mathbf{x}_2 = +10 \, ft \qquad \mathbf{x}_3 = -2 \, ft$$

With these values, the questions asked can now be answered. The displacement during the first move would be:

$$\Delta \mathbf{x}_{first\ move} = \mathbf{x}_2 - \mathbf{x}_1 = (+10) - 0 = +10 \, ft$$

The displacement during the second move would be:

$$\Delta \mathbf{x}_{second\ move} = \mathbf{x}_3 - \mathbf{x}_2 = (-2) - (+10) = -12 \, ft$$

And the total displacement from start to finish would be:

$$\Delta \mathbf{x}_{total} = \mathbf{x}_3 - \mathbf{x}_1 = (-2) - 0 = -2 \, ft$$

Note the use of descriptive subscripts, "first move" for instance. These are always a good idea to help clarify exactly what is being determined.

EXAMPLE (SI): A batten flies out from 3.65 meters off the stage floor to 16.25 meters. What is the displacement of the batten?

SOLUTION: In this problem a zero position has already been assumed, as is implied in the words "off the stage floor". A direction needs to be assumed, and defining positions above the stage floor as being positive is conventional (though not necessary). The two positions therefore become:

$$\mathbf{x}_1 = \text{the position at time } t_1, \text{ the start of the problem} = +3.65 \, m$$

$$\mathbf{x}_2 = \text{the position at time } t_2, \text{ after the first move} = +16.25 \, m$$

The displacement during the move therefore would be:

$$\Delta \mathbf{x}_{batten\ flies\ out} = \mathbf{x}_2 - \mathbf{x}_1 = (+16.25) - (+3.65) = +12.60 \, m$$

The positive result of this calculation indicates that the batten moves up.

Speed and Velocity

If an object undergoes a displacement during some time interval, it is easy to calculate the average speed of the movement.

$$average\ speed\ =\ displacement\ per\ time\ =\ \frac{\Delta \mathbf{x}}{\Delta t}$$

The units of both distance and time determine the units of speed: miles per hour, meters per second, feet per second, or furlongs per fortnight. Speed alone specifies no direction, yet any movement has both speed and direction. Another vector quantity, involving speed and direction has been defined as velocity. Mathematically:

$$\bar{\mathbf{v}}\ =\ \frac{\Delta \mathbf{x}}{\Delta t}\ =\ \frac{\mathbf{x}_2 - \mathbf{x}_1}{t_2 - t_1} \qquad 1.2$$

Where $\bar{\mathbf{v}}$ = average velocity (ft/sec, m/sec)
  $\mathbf{x}$ = position (feet, meters)
  t = time (seconds)

The bar over the $\mathbf{v}$ is the mathematical notation for average, a value also obtainable by the typical averaging process of adding two numbers together and dividing the result by two:

$$\bar{\mathbf{v}}\ =\ \frac{\mathbf{v}_1 + \mathbf{v}_2}{2}$$

If the position, $\mathbf{x}_1$, at time t_1 is the same as the position, $\mathbf{x}_2$, at time t_2, then the result of formula 1.2 would be zero. Because of the finite time interval of Δt, the position of the object at any point in time between t_1 and t_2 is not known. The object may have been constantly oscillating back and forth during Δt and only happened to be in the same place when position measurements were taken. Formula 1.2 gives us only the average velocity.

If the time interval Δt were made very small, then it is more likely that any movement of the object would be caught during Δt and as a result reflected in $\mathbf{v}$. The time interval Δt cannot be made zero because division by zero is not allowed. However through the mathematics of calculus Δt can become infinitesimally small. This book requires no use of calculus mainly because the movements we analyze are simple, and our needs are for quickly obtained reasonably close estimates of powers and forces. The formulas below for instantaneous velocity and acceleration are given because they provide completeness, and for those who do understand them and may find them illuminating, they may be skipped over without harm.

When the change in time does become infinitesimally small the resultant velocity figure obtained is the true velocity at that instant in time, called instantaneous velocity. Mathematically:

$$\mathbf{v}\ =\ \lim_{\Delta t \to 0} \frac{\Delta \mathbf{x}}{\Delta t}\ =\ \frac{d\mathbf{x}}{dt}$$

If the speed and direction of movement of an object is constant, then average and instantaneous velocities are equal:

$$\bar{v} = v = \frac{\Delta x}{\Delta t} = \frac{dx}{dt} \qquad \textit{true only if velocity is constant}$$

Velocity is a displacement per unit of time, and so the units used in theatre are typically feet per second, feet per minute, and meters per second. Outside of theatre, miles per hour, kilometers per hour, and furlongs per fortnight are common.

EXAMPLE: A drop flies in a distance of 40 feet in 8 seconds. What is its average velocity?

SOLUTION: A direction convention must first be assumed, so pick "in" as + (a completely arbitrary choice, "out" could have been called +). Now assign values to variables:

$$\Delta x_{total} = +40 \, ft \qquad \Delta t_{total} = 8 \, sec$$

Using these numbers, calculate the average velocity:

$$\bar{v} = \frac{\Delta x}{\Delta t} = \frac{40}{8} = 5 \, ft/sec$$

Since the direction of our vector quantities is represented by the sign of a value, the positive result for average velocity means only that displacement and speed are in the same direction. This is, in this case, an intuitively obvious result.

EXAMPLE (SI): The top speed a given winch can produce is 1.2 m/sec. How far will scenery move at this speed over a time of 5.5 seconds?

SOLUTION: If the winch runs at an unchanging speed for the full 5.5 second time period, the average speed value over this time equals the speed at any instant. The knowns become:

$$\bar{v} = v = 1.2 \, m/sec \qquad \Delta t = 5.5 \, sec$$

The average velocity formula can be solved for change of position:

$$\bar{v} = \frac{\Delta x}{\Delta t} \qquad so: \quad \Delta x = \bar{v} \Delta t$$

Inserting the knowns gives the final answer:

$$\Delta x = \bar{v} \Delta t = (1.2)(5.5) = 6.6 \, m$$

The formula above might be familiar to you in a different form, that of the commonly stated phrase "distance equals rate times time."

Acceleration

The rate at which an object's position changes with time relates to its velocity. The rate at which velocity changes with time is important too, and this is called acceleration. Average acceleration is defined as:

$$\bar{a} = \frac{\Delta v}{\Delta t}$$

Where $\bar{a}$ = average acceleration (ft/sec^2, m/sec^2)
        v = velocity (ft/sec, m/sec)
        t = time (seconds)

Using the same logic as was used earlier in the discussion on velocity, because the finite time interval Δt is involved, this is an average acceleration. Instantaneous acceleration will be obtained only if Δt is infinitesimally larger than zero.

$$a = \lim_{\Delta t \to 0} \frac{\Delta v}{\Delta t} = \frac{dv}{dt}$$

If there is no change in velocity, meaning that velocity is constant, or stated mathematically $\Delta v = 0$, then $a = 0$.

Acceleration is the ratio of velocity change to time. The units of acceleration are therefore the units of velocity divided by the unit of time. This is expressed one of two ways, displacement per time per time, or displacement per time squared. Commonly this would be stated as "feet per second per second" or "feet per second squared", and written as ft/sec/sec or ft/sec^2 (or likewise m/sec/sec, or m/sec^2).

The rate at which acceleration changes with respect to time is somewhat amusingly called jerk. This quantity is rarely used but deserves mention because its presence is very perceptible. Jerky motion can result from elastic or springy elements within a mechanical system. Any blockage of movement is temporarily allowed by the springy element, but eventually forces build up and overcome the blockage and the springs stored force is released, causing the load to surge ahead. The rapid changes in acceleration and deceleration that are expressed as jerk should be avoided, not only because they are visually distracting, but because the forces developed by this motion will cause higher stress on moving parts and more rapid mechanical wear.

Graphical Relationships Between x, v, and a

A qualitative feeling for the relationships between position, velocity, and acceleration, or x, v, and a, is very useful for proceeding through the rest of this text. If, as is true for many people, the mathematical formulas given above do not convey this feeling, then some other approach is needed. A graphic presentation is usually helpful.

Consider the following graph of the position of a batten plotted versus time (Figure 1.1). At first, before time $t = 3$ sec, the position remains constant while time changes. In other words:

$$\Delta x = 0 \qquad therefore: \quad v = \frac{\Delta x}{\Delta t} = \frac{0}{\Delta t} = 0$$

Velocity is zero, so the batten is not moving.

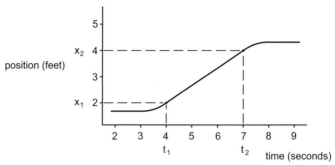

Figure 1.1   Batten position versus time

During the time between t_1 and t_2 the position of the batten changes at a constant rate. The slope of the line is constant. Mathematically, slope is defined as the ratio of vertical change to horizontal change between two given points on the graph. Since a vertical change represents a change of position, and a horizontal change a change in time, the slope of the line as taken here equals the change of position divided by the change in time, which equals average velocity. On the example graph, the slope of the line between times t_1 and t_2 is:

$$slope = \frac{\Delta\ vertical}{\Delta\ horizontal} = \frac{\Delta \mathbf{x}}{\Delta t} = \bar{\mathbf{v}} = \frac{\mathbf{x}_2 - \mathbf{x}_1}{t_2 - t_1} = \frac{4 - 2}{7 - 4} = 0.67\ ft/sec$$

The slope of a line on a graph of speed versus time also has significance. As before, the slope is the change of vertical units per change of horizontal, or:

$$slope = \frac{\Delta\ vertical}{\Delta\ horizontal} = \frac{\Delta \mathbf{v}}{\Delta t} = \bar{\mathbf{a}}$$

This says that acceleration equals the slope of a speed versus time plot.

The slope of any curved line on a graph varies from point to point, but the slope at a specific point is the slope of a line tangent to the curve at that point. Taking the slope of a line at a point is equivalent to the differentiation process of calculus. The instantaneous values of velocity and acceleration can be determined from graphs as well as mathematically. For example see Figure 1.2a, which could be a graph of a batten's position as it is flown out. At time t_1, the slope of the tangent line is slightly positive. The slope at time t_2 is more positive. Finally, the slope at t_3 is the maximum slope that this line attains. Times t_4 and t_5 yield similar slope values respective to t_2 and t_1. The horizontal portions of the plotted line at the left and right of the graph have zero slope ($\Delta \mathbf{v}/\Delta t = 0$) indicating no movement. Since these slope values relate to the velocities of the moving object, they can be plotted on a graph of velocity (Figure 1.2b).

A procedure exactly like that above can now be used on this graph of velocity to determine approximate magnitudes of acceleration at given times. The slope at t_1 is slightly positive, at t_2 is more positive. The tangent at t_3 is now horizontal indicating zero slope, and so zero acceleration. Points t_4 and t_5 have values similar to t_2 and t_1 respectively, but their slopes are negative. A negative slope

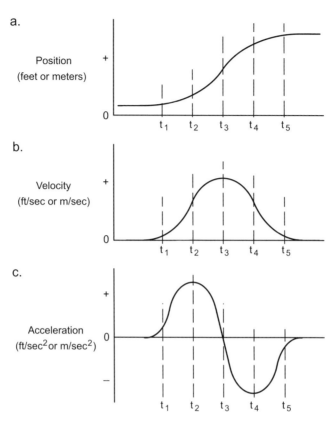

Figure 1.2 Position, velocity, and acceleration motion profiles

always indicates that the direction of the quantity involved is 180° from what is was when slope was positive. In the example here acceleration switches direction, but velocity does not. This indicates deceleration, or slowing down. The third graph, Figure 1.2c displays the results of the acceleration estimates obtained from the slope of the velocity graph.

Whenever you plot these rough graphs be aware of the shape of the lines that result. Corners, or abrupt changes in a plotted line indicate instantaneous changes in position, velocity, or acceleration which are rare in real movements. Normally the plots should be smooth curves. Check your work if this is not true.

This is one of the few places where easily justifiable comments can be made about the ultimate use of the material presented in this book. To serve the needs of a theatre production, the movement of scenery, be it driven by people or machines, must be in harmony with all other elements of the stage picture. The successful mechanization of scenery involves more than just moving something within distance and time constraints. The look of the movement, and the noise involved are factors which the audience will experience with the rest of the show. These elements should be weighed no less heavily than other directorial and design decisions. The rough graphic analysis presented in this chapter can be used as a starting point to determine critical events – rapid accelerations or high speeds for instance – that may affect the choice of devices that will ultimately move the scenery. A solid sense of the relationships between position, velocity, and acceleration will greatly assist in recognizing the interplay between the dry facts of some specific machine and its potential as a very perceptible element within a show.

Problems

1. A batten moves at a constant 6 ft/sec. How long will it take to cover 40 feet? (6.7 sec)

2. A stage weight is dropped from a grid 64 feet above stage level. It takes 2 seconds to hit the floor. What is the average velocity over this 2 second time interval? If acceleration is assumed to be constant, and the weight was not thrown down (i.e., velocity at grid = 0), what velocity does the weight have as it reaches the stage floor? Given the velocities at the start and end of this 2 second move, what is the average acceleration? (32 ft/sec, 64 ft/sec, 32 ft/sec^2)

3. Position at time $t_1 = 0$ is 42 meters. Position at time $t_2 = 12$ seconds is 36 meters. What is Δx and $\bar{v}$?

4. For each of the motion profiles shown below, develop the two missing graphs that will make each part of a set of three that includes position versus time, velocity versus time, and acceleration versus time.

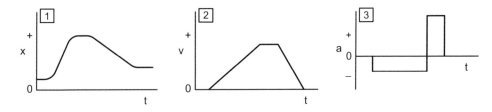

2

The Equations of Constant Acceleration

Constant Acceleration

Acceleration is a measure of how rapidly an object speeds up or slows down, or more specifically, how much its velocity changes over some given interval of time. Acceleration can be measured both at a point in time, the result being called instantaneous acceleration, or over some finite time interval, called an average acceleration. *Constant* acceleration exists whenever both measures of acceleration remain the same for some period of time. During these time periods, average acceleration, $\bar{a}$, and instantaneous acceleration, a, are equal, and both hold at one value regardless of the length of the time interval chosen for Δt:

$$a = \bar{a} = \frac{\Delta v}{\Delta t} \quad \textit{if acceleration is constant}$$

In a typical scenery move, there are three key periods where acceleration can be considered constant: during acceleration from zero on up to top speed, during travel at a constant top speed, and during deceleration to a stop (see motion profiles in Figure 2.1). During the constant velocity portion, acceleration, a, will be zero because velocity does not change. (True too before and after the move, but since nothing is moving then, it is of no interest to us here.) During a constant

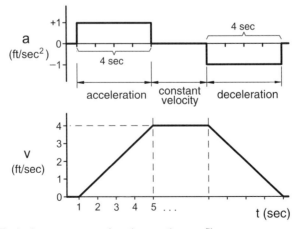

Figure 2.1 Typical constant acceleration motion profiles

acceleration or deceleration, the change of velocity versus time is a fixed number regardless of the value chosen for Δt. For three arbitrary values of t_1 and t_2 in the example in Figure 2.1, acceleration calculates out to the same value:

$$for\ t_1 = 1\ and\ t_2 = 2 \qquad \bar{a} = \frac{v_2 - v_1}{t_2 - t_1} = \frac{1 - 0}{2 - 1} = 1\ ft/sec^2$$

$$for\ t_1 = 1\ and\ t_2 = 5 \qquad \bar{a} = \frac{v_2 - v_1}{t_2 - t_1} = \frac{4 - 0}{5 - 1} = 1\ ft/sec^2$$

$$for\ t_1 = 1.5\ and\ t_2 = 3.5 \qquad \bar{a} = \frac{v_2 - v_1}{t_2 - t_1} = \frac{2.5 - 0.5}{3.5 - 1.5} = 1\ ft/sec^2$$

Acceleration certainly does not need to be constant, any function of speed versus time is possible, but assuming that acceleration will always be constant is both useful and reasonable. Useful because it keeps the mathematics of motion solely in the realm of algebra, rather than the more complex calculus. Reasonable because most moves on stage do occur with constant accelerations. Many theatre automation control systems generate a trapezoidal velocity motion profile for the scenery they move. Most motor drives, if not following the commands of an external control system, will themselves give a constant acceleration/deceleration motion to the motors they run. Even a flyman running a line-set by hand will provide a good approximation of such a move.

The goal of any technique presented in an engineering book is to model the behavior of the real world as accurately as is needed for the situation being analyzed. For the movement of scenery on stage, there is no particular need for the mathematics to model a move to an accuracy beyond a tolerance of perhaps ±5%. If the calculated top speed of a wagon is 3 ft/sec, and the actual machine runs at 2.9 ft/sec, will anyone notice? Probably not. The balance between the accuracy of a mathematical model and its simplicity is always worth weighing. And so here, with constant acceleration, we have an acceptably accurate simple mathematical model of what happens in typical moves involving real scenery.

 Throughout this book, constant acceleration is assumed.

Equations of Constant Acceleration

Given the simple equations that define average velocity and average acceleration:

$$\bar{v} = \frac{\Delta x}{\Delta t} \qquad \bar{a} = \frac{\Delta v}{\Delta t}$$

four frequently used equations may be derived. These equations give valid answers only when acceleration is constant, or in other words when average and instantaneous accelerations are equal, $\bar{a} = a$. Given the three parts of a typical move: acceleration, constant velocity, and deceleration, each with their own unique value of acceleration, the constant acceleration equations can only be applied individually to each of these parts to determine the times, distances, velocities, and accelerations that occur within them. If acceleration is not constant, the movements of an object that occur between the t_1 and t_2 limits of Δt are unknown, and these formulas will give incorrect answers.

The four equations of constant acceleration are:

$$\boldsymbol{v}_2 = \boldsymbol{v}_1 + \boldsymbol{a}\Delta t \qquad\qquad 2.1$$

$$\Delta\boldsymbol{x} = \frac{\boldsymbol{v}_1 + \boldsymbol{v}_2}{2}\Delta t \qquad\qquad 2.2$$

$$\Delta\boldsymbol{x} = \boldsymbol{v}_1\Delta t + \frac{1}{2}\boldsymbol{a}\Delta t^2 \qquad\qquad 2.3$$

$$\boldsymbol{v}_2^2 = \boldsymbol{v}_1^2 + 2\boldsymbol{a}\Delta\boldsymbol{x} \qquad\qquad 2.4$$

Where $\boldsymbol{v}$ = velocity (ft/sec, m/sec)
  $\boldsymbol{a}$ = acceleration, which here must be constant (ft/sec^2, m/sec^2)
  t = time (sec)
  $\boldsymbol{x}$ = position (ft, m)

There are five variables in these formulas: $\Delta\boldsymbol{x}$, $\boldsymbol{a}$, $\boldsymbol{v}_2$, Δt, and $\boldsymbol{v}_1$. $\boldsymbol{v}_1$ is called the initial velocity, because it represents the speed and direction the object under question has at the start of the time interval being investigated. The initial velocity appears in all four equations because it is a basic condition at the start of the move being analyzed, and it is what the constant acceleration acts on over the time interval Δt. Of the remaining four variables, three are found in each of the four equations of constant acceleration:

Equation:	has the variables:					and lacks:
2.1	-	$\boldsymbol{a}$	$\boldsymbol{v}_2$	Δt	$\boldsymbol{v}_1$	$\Delta\boldsymbol{x}$
2.2	$\Delta\boldsymbol{x}$	-	$\boldsymbol{v}_2$	Δt	$\boldsymbol{v}_1$	$\boldsymbol{a}$
2.3	$\Delta\boldsymbol{x}$	$\boldsymbol{a}$	-	Δt	$\boldsymbol{v}_1$	$\boldsymbol{v}_2$
2.4	$\Delta\boldsymbol{x}$	$\boldsymbol{a}$	$\boldsymbol{v}_2$	-	$\boldsymbol{v}_1$	Δt

Table 2.1 Variables in the Equations of Constant Acceleration

The equation to use in any given situation will depend on what you know, and what you need to determine. The following examples should illustrate the equation selection process.

EXAMPLE: A scene change requires a piece to move onstage a distance of 28 feet in 8 seconds. Assume the velocity motion profile is symmetric, with the object accelerating while covering half the travel distance, and decelerating while covering the other half. Find the required acceleration, and the maximum velocity.

SOLUTION: Given $\Delta \boldsymbol{x}_{total} = 28\,ft$ (a positive number which implies off-stage is 0 and onstage is +), $\Delta t = 8\,sec$, and half the total time is spent accelerating, half decelerating. The position, velocity, and acceleration motion profiles shown below can be used to help illustrate this move.

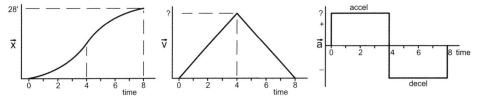

Figure 2.2   Motion profiles for this example

The motion profiles show that the problem has two distinct halves, the 4 seconds of acceleration, and the 4 seconds of deceleration. The equations of constant acceleration are only valid during time intervals when acceleration remains unchanged, and so they cannot apply to the whole move as a major change occurs 4 seconds into the move when acceleration changes to deceleration. The equations can be applied though to the acceleration portion of the move, and then again to the deceleration portion.

During acceleration, the initial velocity is zero, or $\boldsymbol{v}_1 = 0$, the change of position is half the total move distance, $\Delta \boldsymbol{x}_{acc} = 14\,ft$, and the change of time is $\Delta t_{acc} = 4\,sec$. Both acceleration and maximum velocity are unknowns, and either could be determined first. The arbitrary choice of finding $\boldsymbol{a}$ first will be made here. Given these parameters, use Equation 2.3 to determine acceleration.

$$\Delta \boldsymbol{x} = \boldsymbol{v}_1 \Delta t + \frac{1}{2}\boldsymbol{a}\Delta t^2$$

$$14 = (0)(4) + (0.5)\boldsymbol{a}(4)^2$$

$$\boldsymbol{a} = 1.75\,ft/sec^2$$

The positive sign of the result means acceleration is in the positive, or onstage direction, which in this case is an intuitively obvious result. The calculation of maximum velocity can now be done using both what was known before, and the just determined acceleration. Any of the four equations of constant acceleration will work except 2.3, which does not include final velocity, $\boldsymbol{v}_2$. For its simplicity choose Equation 2.1:

$$\boldsymbol{v}_2 = \boldsymbol{v}_1 + \boldsymbol{a}\Delta t$$

$$\boldsymbol{v}_2 = 0 + (1.75)(4)$$

$$\boldsymbol{v}_2 = \boldsymbol{v}_{maximum} = 7\,ft/sec$$

EXAMPLE: A winch will be used to move a wagon a distance of 30 feet, at a top speed of 4 ft/sec. A motion control system running the winch will set the acceleration and deceleration times to 2 and 4 seconds respectively. How long will the whole move take?

SOLUTION: The situation implied in the statement of this problem is a common one. All winches have top speed limits, and no scenery run by a particular winch will move faster than its maximum. Also, most theatre automation control systems will allow an operator to set accel/decel times in some way. The velocity motion profile takes on a trapezoidal shape that represents the majority of moves on stage.

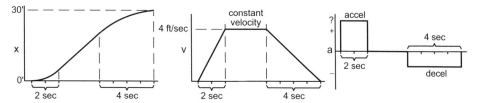

Figure 2.3   Motion profiles

The move has three distinct parts, delineated by the acceleration, constant velocity, and deceleration portions of the move. Given this, the total distance traveled during the whole move is the sum of the distance traveled during acceleration, during constant velocity, and during deceleration. Mathematically:

$$\Delta \mathbf{x}_{total} = \Delta \mathbf{x}_{accel} + \Delta \mathbf{x}_{convel} + \Delta \mathbf{x}_{decel}$$

The same is true of time:

$$\Delta t_{total} = \Delta t_{accel} + \Delta t_{convel} + \Delta t_{decel}$$

Some of these terms are part of the givens of the problem:

$$30\,ft = \Delta \mathbf{x}_{accel} + \Delta \mathbf{x}_{convel} + \Delta \mathbf{x}_{decel}$$

$$\Delta t_{total} = 2\,sec + \Delta t_{convel} + 4\,sec$$

Since the total move time is the question to be answered, the time spent at constant velocity needs to be found, and that value will come out of the numbers found in the change of position equation.

Using the equations of constant acceleration, determine the distance traveled during acceleration and during deceleration. The givens are:

$$\Delta t_{accel} = 2\,sec \qquad \Delta t_{decel} = 4\,sec \qquad \mathbf{v}_1 = 0 \qquad \mathbf{v}_2 = 4\,ft/sec$$

With these values, the distance traveled during acceleration can be calculated using Equation 2.2:

$$\Delta \mathbf{x}_{accel} = \frac{\mathbf{v}_1 + \mathbf{v}_2}{2}\Delta t_{accel}$$

$$\Delta \mathbf{x}_{accel} = \frac{0 + 4}{2}2$$

$$\Delta \mathbf{x}_{accel} = 4\,ft$$

The distance traveled during deceleration is calculated in an identical manner, the result being:

$$\Delta \mathbf{x}_{decel} = 8\,ft$$

The distance traveled during constant velocity is:

$$\Delta x_{total} = \Delta x_{accel} + \Delta x_{convel} + \Delta x_{decel}$$

$$30 = 4 + \Delta x_{convel} + 8$$

$$\Delta x_{convel} = 18\,ft$$

During the constant velocity portion of the move, acceleration is zero. An acceleration of zero is a valid value for a in the equations of constant acceleration, and this simplifies Equation 2.3 into the familiar "distance = rate times time" form:

$$\Delta x = v_1 \Delta t + \frac{1}{2} a \Delta t^2$$

$$\Delta x_{convel} = v_{max} \Delta t_{convel} + \frac{1}{2}(0) \Delta t^2$$

$$\Delta x_{convel} = v_{max} \Delta t_{convel}$$

Inserting the known values, Δt_{convel} can be determined:

$$\Delta x_{convel} = v_{max} \Delta t_{convel}$$

$$18 = (4) \Delta t_{convel}$$

$$\Delta t_{convel} = 4.5\,sec$$

Finally now, the problem's answer is the sum of acceleration, constant velocity, and deceleration times:

$$\Delta t_{total} = \Delta t_{accel} + \Delta t_{convel} + \Delta t_{decel}$$

$$\Delta t_{total} = 2 + 4.5 + 4 = 10.5\,sec$$

Moves with a Given Time and Distance

In theatre, no director or designer ever speaks technically of the moves they want to see. You will never hear the director say "The moon should rise with a trapezoidal velocity motion profile using equal accels and decels of 2.4 ft/sec^2!" Time and distance are, at best, the information you will get, "The piece moves about 20 feet in 10 seconds." But even given these two values, there are an infinite number of possible combinations of acceleration, constant velocity, and deceleration that will accomplish the needed move. Two velocity motion profiles though define the extremes of all these possible move combinations, and they can quickly be calculated to give you some numbers that will begin to describe the feasibility of a move. One profile is triangular in shape, with half the move being acceleration and half deceleration. The other profile assumes acceleration and deceleration is infinite, and the whole move occurs at a constant velocity. The following example will illustrate these calculations.

EXAMPLE (SI): A batten needs to travel a distance of 9.5 m over a time of 10 sec. Determine the range of velocities and accelerations that will allow this move to occur.

SOLUTION: To determine the triangular velocity motion profile, the problem is broken in halves, with symmetric acceleration and deceleration portions of the move. Given this assumption:

$$\Delta t_{accel} = \frac{10}{2} = 5 \; sec \qquad \Delta \mathbf{x}_{accel} = \frac{9.5}{2} = 4.75 \; m \qquad \mathbf{v}_1 = 0$$

Now use Equation 2.3 to determine acceleration:

$$\Delta \mathbf{x} = \mathbf{v}_1 \Delta t + \frac{1}{2}\mathbf{a} \Delta t^2$$

$$4.75 = (0)(5) + (0.5)\mathbf{a}(5^2)$$

$$\mathbf{a} = 0.38 \; m/sec^2$$

The maximum velocity reached by the batten using this acceleration can be found with Equation 2.1:

$$\mathbf{v}_2 = \mathbf{v}_1 + \mathbf{a}\Delta t$$

$$\mathbf{v}_2 = 0 + (0.38)(5)$$

$$\mathbf{v}_2 = \mathbf{v}_{max} = 1.9 \; m/sec$$

The velocity motion profile that uses these values is shown below.

If acceleration and deceleration are infinite, it would take no time to reach any given speed, and the entire move would occur at a constant velocity. This situation is not possible in reality, infinite acceleration would require infinite force, but it does define an extreme of the range of all possible moves. Since the entire move time is spent at one speed, $\mathbf{a} = 0$, $\Delta \mathbf{x} = 9.5 \; m$, and $\Delta t = 10 \; sec$. Equation 2.3 can be used to find velocity:

$$\Delta \mathbf{x} = \mathbf{v}_1 \Delta t + \frac{1}{2}\mathbf{a} \Delta t^2$$

$$9.5 = \mathbf{v}_1(10) + 0.5(0)(10^2)$$

$$\mathbf{v}_1 = 0.95 \; m/sec$$

The velocity motion profile showing the results of both these situations is shown below. The triangular profile represents the move with the gentlest acceleration, the least abrupt speed-ups and slow-downs. It spends no time at a constant velocity, but its maximum velocity is exactly twice that for the other move.

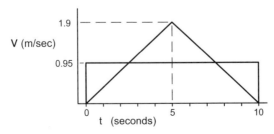

Figure 2.4   Velocity motion profiles for lowest top speed and lowest accel/decel

Those of you familiar with calculus may have noticed that the area under each of these profiles is identical. The area of the rectangular profile is:

$$area = width \times height$$

$$area = 10 \; sec \times 0.95 \; m/sec = 9.5 \; m$$

and the area under the triangular profile would be the same. The area under any graph of velocity versus time equals the travel distance. The basic shapes of the motion profiles here allow easy calculation of area, but the area under any shaped graph of velocity versus time would equal the distance traveled. To do this involves using integration (this is *not* a technique you need to know, it is included only as a glimpse into the mathematics beyond the equations of constant acceleration):

$$\Delta \mathbf{x} = \int_{0}^{\Delta t_{total}} \mathbf{v} \; dt$$

Any combination of just acceleration and deceleration, illustrated at the left below, must reach 1.9 m/sec to cover the 9.5 meters in 10 seconds. All combinations that involve one period of constant acceleration, constant velocity, and deceleration, as is illustrated at the right, will have a maximum velocity somewhere between 0.95 and 1.9 m/sec (equal accelerations and decelerations are shown on this graph, but this is not a requirement).

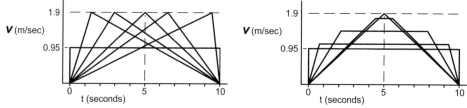

Since the triangular motion profile's maximum velocity is always exactly twice the velocity found if the move occurred all at one speed, calculating either alone essentially gives you both answers.

The Acceleration Due to Gravity

Gravity causes unsupported objects to fall, and the rate at which they accelerate can be measured. For a given spot on Earth, the acceleration due to gravity is constant. At different places though, there are slight variations in this acceleration depending mainly on latitude and elevation. The spinning Earth has a slight tendency to throw objects off its surface, and this effect is greatest at the equator and nil at the poles. Elevation alters acceleration because the gravitational attraction between objects depends on the distance between their centers of mass. At high altitude, the centers are further apart, and both the attraction and acceleration are less. For most uses, and undoubtedly all theatre uses, the acceleration due to gravity can be assumed to be 32.2 ft/sec^2 (9.81 m/sec^2). Even this is often reduced to simply 32 ft/sec^2 (9.8 m/sec^2) with a loss of accuracy of less than 1%. For the trivia enthusiast, the acceleration due to gravity is greatest at the North Pole at sea level, approximately 32.26 ft/sec^2 (9.833 m/sec^2), and lowest on the tops of the highest mountains near the equator, in Equador and Kenya, approximately 32.04 ft/sec^2 (9.766 m/sec^2).

EXAMPLE: If an object is dropped, what is its speed after falling 10 feet? Assume no friction.

SOLUTION: Assume that the object not given an initial velocity, but simply let go, and that down is the positive direction. With this assumption the givens become:

$$\textbf{\textit{a}}_{gravity} = 32.2\ ft/sec^2 \qquad \Delta \textbf{\textit{x}}_{accel} = 10\ ft \qquad \textbf{\textit{v}}_1 = 0$$

Since the velocity, $\textbf{\textit{v}}_2$, at the end of the 10 foot travel is to be determined, equation of constant acceleration 2.4 is appropriate.

$$\textbf{\textit{v}}_2^2 = \textbf{\textit{v}}_1^2 + 2\textbf{\textit{a}}\Delta\textbf{\textit{x}}$$

$$\textbf{\textit{v}}_2^2 = 0 + 2(32.2)(10)$$

$$\textbf{\textit{v}}_2 = 25.4\ ft/sec$$

Since a rule-of-thumb value for a typical top speed of flown scenery is 6 ft/sec, dropped objects quickly attain speeds well beyond that of typical moves. A wrench inadvertently dropped from a 75 ft high grid will hit the floor at roughly 70 ft/sec, or 47 mph. "Heads!"

EXAMPLE: A ball is thrown upward with an initial velocity of 45 ft/sec. How high will it go before it slows to a stop and falls back down?

SOLUTION: The given in this problem is initial velocity, with final velocity and the acceleration due to gravity being implied. The initial velocity is in the upwards direction, while the acceleration due to gravity is always down. The sign of $\textbf{\textit{v}}_1$ and $\textbf{\textit{a}}_{gravity}$ will be opposite. It does not matter whether up is assumed the positive or negative direction, but once a choice is made, the sign on all variables must indicate the proper direction. As a demonstration, this problem will be solved both ways.

• First assume up is the positive direction. The givens are:

$$\textbf{\textit{v}}_1 = 45\ ft/sec \qquad \textbf{\textit{a}}_{gravity} = -32.2\ ft/sec^2 \qquad \textbf{\textit{v}}_1 = 0$$

Find $\Delta\textbf{\textit{x}}$. Equation 2.4 can be used:

$$\textbf{\textit{v}}_2^2 = \textbf{\textit{v}}_1^2 + 2\textbf{\textit{a}}\Delta\textbf{\textit{x}}$$

$$0 = (45)^2 + 2(-32.2)(\Delta\textbf{\textit{x}})$$

$$\Delta\textbf{\textit{x}} = 31.4\ ft$$

The answer is positive, indicating the ball moved in the upward direction, an obvious answer.

• Now assume that up is the negative direction, and that down is positive. The givens are:

$$\textbf{\textit{v}}_1 = -45\ ft/sec \qquad \textbf{\textit{a}}_{gravity} = 32.2\ ft/sec^2 \qquad \textbf{\textit{v}}_1 = 0$$

Find Δx. As above, Equation 2.4 can be used:

$$v_2^2 = v_1^2 + 2a\Delta x$$

$$0 = (-45)^2 + 2(32.2)(\Delta x)$$

$$\Delta x = -31.4 \, ft$$

The answer is negative, indicating again that the ball moved in the upward direction.

Problems

1. An object is dropped from a height of 55 ft above the stage floor. How long will it take to hit the floor? Write down any assumptions made.

2. A motorized winch system is capable of a maximum speed of 4 ft/sec, and a constant acceleration and deceleration of 1 ft/sec². How long will it take to fly out a batten 40 feet? Assume the batten is stationary at the start and end of the move. (14 sec)

3. A wagon is traveling offstage at 1.5 m/sec. What deceleration is needed to stop it over a distance of 4 m?

4. A lift is to lower a distance of 10 feet from stage level into the trap room in 8 seconds. What top speed is reached if a triangular motion profile of one half acceleration, on half deceleration is used? (2.5 ft/sec)

5. A control system will set up a trapezoidal velocity motion profile such that 2 seconds is spent accelerating, constant velocity occurs for 4.5 seconds, and the move slows to a stop with 3 seconds of deceleration. What value of constant velocity is needed if the total distance covered during the move is 22 feet?

6. A designer wants a move to take 12 seconds, with 3 seconds of that time allotted to acceleration, and 2 seconds to deceleration. The total distance traveled by the piece is 34 feet. What top speed is needed to accomplish this move?

3

The Force to Accelerate Mass: $F_{acceleration}$

Overview

Mass is a measure of the quantity of matter in an object. Mass could be related directly to the number of electrons, protons, and neutrons in an object (or whatever fundamental particles are appropriate today), if those could easily be counted. The mass of a given object is a fixed value, a constant, completely independent of its location: on earth, on the moon, in outer space. In contrast, the weight of an object depends on the action of gravity on its mass, and this very much changes as it travels around the universe. Theatre of course is still earthbound, and the distinction between mass and weight might seem to be unimportant, but these differences are at the heart of both Newton's second law of motion, which equates force with the acceleration of mass, and between the fundamental base units of the U.S. customary and metric systems.

The force needed to accelerate just the mass of an object is one of three force components in the maximum power formula. The maximum power needed to move an object can be found by multiplying the object's maximum velocity times the sum of the acceleration, friction, and lifting forces:

$$P_{max} = (\boldsymbol{F}_{accel} + \boldsymbol{F}_{friction} + \boldsymbol{F}_{lifting}) \, \boldsymbol{v}_{max}$$

The force needed to accelerate a given object due to its mass alone, or $\boldsymbol{F}_{accel}$, is the main topic of this chapter.

Newton's Laws of Motion

Despite the inaccuracy of ascribing the following laws to just one person, Sir Isaac Newton's publication of one of the milestones of science, *Philosophiae Naturalis Principia Mathematica* (*Mathematical Principles of Natural Philosophy*, 1687), has since caused his name to be connected with three laws of motion. Stated here without the full mathematical rigor they would receive in a physics text, they are:

> 1. If a mass is stationary it will remain stationary, or if a mass is moving with a constant velocity it will continue to do so, until any net force acts on the mass.

Put another way, velocity will not change unless a force is present to make the change. When a net force exists on an object, a force in excess of those needed to overcome friction and to provide whatever lifting force is needed to counteract gravity, then that object will accelerate. The exact amount of acceleration obtained for a given force is spelled out in Newton's second law:

> 2. When a force acts on a mass, that mass will accelerate in the direction of the force. The magnitude of the acceleration will be directly related to the magnitude of the force, and inversely related to the magnitude of the mass. Mathematically:

$$F_{accel} = ma$$

> Where F_{accel} = the force needed to accelerate a mass (lb, N)
> m = mass of the material upon which the force acts (slug, kg)
> a = acceleration of the mass (ft/sec^2, m/sec^2)

This simple formula defines the force needed to accelerate a given mass, and defines the first of the three force components summed in the maximum power formula. Before the implications of this law are discussed at length though, Newton's third law is:

> 3. A force can exist only as one of an equal in magnitude but oppositely directed pair of forces. Traditionally this is worded as "action equals reaction."

This law is not stated as one formula, but rather it is a basic assumption that was used in developing the whole branch of physics called mechanics that itself encompasses the mechanical engineering topics of static structures and machine design.

Mass and Force

Newton's second law now allows a discussion of the third fundamental, mass or force. Because the second law relates the two quantities, $F_{accel} = ma$, and acceleration is already the ratio of two fundamentals, length and time, there is a certain arbitrary choice to be made in which one is called a fundamental. Indeed, throughout the past several hundred years there have been proponents on each side. This has resulted in a considerable mire of units, and these various units would be only a historical curiosity but for the stubborn resistance of the United States to adopt the metric system.

The U.S. customary system of units is based largely (but not entirely) on the British Imperial system of units, and in that force was chosen as the fundamental, and it was given the unit name of the pound, abbreviated as lb. With this choice made, mass can be defined through use of Newton's second law:

$$F_{accel} = ma \qquad so, \qquad m = \frac{F_{accel}}{a}$$

$$m = \frac{1\ pound}{1\ foot/second^2} = 1\ \frac{lb\ sec^2}{ft} = 1\ slug$$

This means that a mass of 1 slug will accelerate at a rate of 1 ft/sec^2 when pushed by a force of 1 pound (assuming friction and gravity are not present):

$$\boldsymbol{F}_{accel} = m\boldsymbol{a}$$

$$1 \; lb = 1 \; slug \times 1 \; ft/sec^2$$

The slug is a dead unit, little used in any science, and almost unheard of any more. It will however appear throughout this book. Fortunately, as will be explained below, a conversion between the weight of an object and its mass is a trivial calculation.

In the metric SI system, in the past called the MKS (meter-kilogram-second) system, mass was chosen as the fundamental, with units of kilograms. The defined unit therefore becomes force, and it is given units of newtons, which is abbreviated as N (the abbreviation is capitalized, and the unit name is not):

$$\boldsymbol{F}_{accel} = m\boldsymbol{a} = 1 \; kilogram \left(1 \; \frac{meter}{sec^2} \right) = 1 \; \frac{kg \; m}{sec^2} = 1 \; newton = 1 \; N$$

In both of these cases, the defined units are given names, the slug and the newton, just to simplify reference to these quantities. It is far easier, for instance, to refer to 43 N than 43 kg m/sec^2. Do not forget though that they are just names representing a specific arrangement of fundamentals.

Conversion Table – Mass and Force

Multiply ...	by ...	to convert to ...
MASS:		
slugs	32.2*	pounds (lb)
	143.2*	newtons (N)
	14.59	kilograms (kg)
kilogram (kg)	2.205*	pounds (lb)
	9.81*	newtons (N)
	0.0685	slugs
FORCE:		
pounds (lb)	4.448	newtons (N)
	0.0311*	slugs
	0.4536*	kilograms (kg)
newtons (N)	0.2248	pounds (lb)
	0.00698*	slugs
	0.102*	kilograms (kg)

* These conversion multipliers assume $a_{gravity} = g = 32.2 \; ft/sec^2$ or $9.81 \; m/sec^2$.

Weight

The choice of fundamentals has little direct impact on our use of terms and formulas, but a distinction does arise when referring to weight. If an object with a mass of one slug is weighed on a scale calibrated in pounds, it is found to weigh around 32.2 pounds. This is because the slug of material is under the influence of the gravitational field of the Earth which will pull down on it with a force of 32.2 pounds. If the acceleration due to gravity, $\boldsymbol{g}$, is used as the acceleration term in Newton's second law, the weights of masses can be calculated:

$$\boldsymbol{F}_{accel} = m\boldsymbol{a} = m\boldsymbol{g} = (1\ slug)(32.2\ ft/sec^2) = 32.2\ lb$$

Therefore 1 slug would weigh roughly 32.2 lb at any point on earth.

Scales used to weigh objects are, unfortunately, confusingly calibrated in force units, pounds, in the U.S. customary system, and mass units, kilograms, in the metric system. So strictly speaking, a person that weighs say 154.0 lb has a mass of 69.85 kg.

Since weight is a force, and it has magnitude and direction, it is a vector. Rather than use a symbol different from the $\boldsymbol{F}$ already assigned to force, weight in this text will use the symbol $\boldsymbol{F}_w$. The direction of the force vector that is weight is always straight down (ignoring the minor effects of nearby mountains, location of the moon, and the Earth's crust density variations).

The mass term in Newton's second law is just that, mass. When using the customary system of units, a conversion from weight to mass (pounds to slugs) is needed for the mass term. The conversion comes from:

$$\boldsymbol{F}_{accel} = m\boldsymbol{a}$$

$$\boldsymbol{F}_w = m\boldsymbol{g}$$

$$\boldsymbol{F}_w = m\,(32.2\ ft/sec^2)$$

$$m = \frac{\boldsymbol{F}_w}{32.2} \qquad or \qquad m = 0.0311\boldsymbol{F}_w$$

Not having to convert mass in the metric system offers no overall advantage though because whenever weight is needed, as for friction formulas, kilograms will have to be converted to newtons in a similar manner:

$$\boldsymbol{F}_{accel} = m\boldsymbol{a}$$

$$\boldsymbol{F}_w = m\boldsymbol{g}$$

$$\boldsymbol{F}_w = m(9.81\ m/sec^2)$$

EXAMPLE: A platform weighs 1350 lb. What is its mass?

SOLUTION: Using the U.S. customary units formula above:

$$m = \frac{\boldsymbol{F}_w}{32.2} = \frac{1350}{32.2} = 41.9\ slugs$$

The Force Needed to Accelerate Mass

The end goal of a typical problem analysis is what power, force, and speed is involved in a move:

$$P_{max} = (F_{accel} + F_{friction} + F_{lifting}) v_{max}$$

The F_{accel} component of this equation is Newton's second law of motion:

$$F_{accel} = ma$$

With it, calculations can be made of the force needed just to accelerate the mass of a piece of scenery, totally separately and independent from any concerns about friction and lifting. This is an important point. If a mass is to be accelerated at a given rate, then the force needed to do that is F_{accel}. This is true whether the mass moves left and right, or up and down, easily on wheels, or plowing through a dirt covered deck, and on planet Earth, or out in empty space. Other terms, dealt with separately, will take into account forces due to friction and gravity.

EXAMPLE: A stage wagon weighing 2400 lb accelerates to a top speed of 2.5 ft/sec in 2 sec. Determine F_{accel}.

SOLUTION: The givens for this problem, specifically stated, are:

$$F_w = 2400\ lb \qquad v_{max} = v_{2_{accel}} = 2.5\ ft/sec \qquad \Delta t_{accel} = 2\ sec$$

Now since $F_{accel} = ma$, values for mass and acceleration need to be determined from the givens. One of the equations of constant acceleration will give a value for acceleration:

$$v_2 = v_1 + a\Delta t$$

$$2.5 = 0 + a(2)$$

$$a = 1.25\ ft/sec$$

The mass of the wagon can be obtained from its weight:

$$m = \frac{F_w}{32.2} = \frac{2400}{32.2} = 74.5\ slugs$$

So the force needed just to accelerate the mass of the platform is:

$$F_{accel} = ma$$

$$F_{accel} = (74.5)(1.25) = 93.1\ lb$$

In other words, if a 2400 lb platform sat on a perfectly horizontal frictionless floor, pushing it with 93.1 lb of force would accelerate it at 1.25 ft/sec^2, reaching the desired 2 ft/sec top speed in 2 seconds.

EXAMPLE (SI): A large drop, with a mass of 422 kg, flies out 9 m in 10 sec. Determine F_{accel}. Assume that the velocity motion profile is one half acceleration, one half deceleration.

SOLUTION: Given:

$$m = 422\ kg \qquad \Delta x_{total} = 9\ m \qquad \Delta t_{total} = 10\ sec$$

Since the mass of the unit is a given, the problem here is mainly to determine acceleration. During acceleration, the drop moves 4.5 m in 5 sec from an initial velocity of zero. Using an equation of constant acceleration:

$$\Delta \boldsymbol{x} = \boldsymbol{v}_1 \Delta t + \tfrac{1}{2} \boldsymbol{a} \Delta t^2$$

$$4.5 = (0)(5) + \tfrac{1}{2} \boldsymbol{a} (5)^2$$

$$\boldsymbol{a} = 0.36 \; m/sec^2$$

The final answer of the force needed to accelerate the drop's mass is:

$$\boldsymbol{F}_{accel} = m\boldsymbol{a}$$

$$\boldsymbol{F}_{accel} = (422)(0.36) = 152 \; N$$

Problems

1. What force is needed to accelerate a 450 lb platform at a rate of 2.5 ft/sec²? Ignore friction and lifting.   (34.9 lb)

2. A wagon of mass 1550 kg is pushed with a force of 500 N. What is its acceleration rate? Assume no friction or lifting.   (0.323 m/sec²)

3. A platform weighing 4800 lb is supported on air bearings (assume them to be frictionless) and sits stationary on a level floor. A stagehand pushes it with 35 lb for 5 seconds. What is the platform's speed at the end of the push?

4. During an emergency stop, the velocity of a scenic piece goes from 6 ft/sec to stopped over a distance of $\Delta \boldsymbol{x}_{decel} = 3 \; ft$. What is the deceleration, $\boldsymbol{a}_{decel}$?

4

The Friction Force, $F_{friction}$

Friction—Complex and Simplified

Friction occurs between all matter in contact. Any combination of two materials, whether gaseous, liquid, or solid, will have unique friction characteristics dependent on many factors: the materials themselves, their surface finish, their speed relative to each other; the presence of any lubricant or impurities (dust and dirt); the direction of movement relative to any grain-like structure in a material; the pressure between the materials; temperature, and on and on. Because of all these factors, accurate mathematical models of frictional effects are extremely complex, and this is especially so for fluids. Fortunately, for the rough predictions of the loads imposed by friction on scenery movement, the complexity can be reduced considerably. Scenery movement speeds and "sail" area are usually low enough that air resistance can be considered nil. The flow of liquids, and of solids through liquids, is likewise beyond 99.9% of scenic situations (friction does affect oil flow in any hydraulic systems that we may use, but that topic is beyond the scope of this book). So for our needs here, *friction will be considered only between solid materials, that can either slide against or roll over each other, in two states of motion—static, or not moving relative to each other, and dynamic, when movement does occur.*

The effect of friction on a move fits into the general formula for the maximum power needed to move an object as the friction force, $F_{friction}$:

$$P_{max} = (F_{accel} + F_{friction} + F_{lifting})\, v_{max}$$

Friction always opposes motion, and it never creates it. The term will never be zero (though it is sometimes small enough to be negligible), and so even in the absence of acceleration and lifting, power will be required to keep something moving because friction is always present.

Friction during motion wastes power, and is usually minimized as much as possible, by using wheels rather than sliding, by using ball bearings instead of plain bearings, and through the use of lubricating oils for instance. The friction that exists in the absence of motion between materials is on the other hand primarily beneficial. The pull on a rope from a hands grip, or the traction between your shoes and the floor are instances of the usefulness of this aspect of friction.

Scenery does not move around in the controlled environment of a laboratory, but in the changeable environment of the stage. A director might alter a scene's blocking in tech and three more actors than ever anticipated will load down a wagon, the designer may choose a thicker carpet than her first choice and a wagon rolling across it would then become harder to move, a bobby pin could fall out of a hairdo and lodge under a caster, or humidity could swell a wood deck pinching the wagon's drive dog more tightly. These everyday events will not automatically be accommodated by any formula. It is the technical designer's job to estimate loads and friction coefficients, and choose contingencies all based on the worst case conditions under which an effect must run. Questions the technician should ask include is this effect similar to others successfully done before, or is it unusual or ill-defined? What are the consequences of failure, not being able to run that effect, or not being able to run the show? Are there financial penalties or press and public relations issues to keep in mind? On a small college show probably not, on a Broadway show absolutely yes. Certainly these types of questions are not unique to friction, but friction is by far the hardest of the three power formula forces to estimate accurately, and so the technician will always have to make a decision on how conservative to be to attain the power overhead appropriate to the situation.

Definitions

Plane of contact – Whenever two solid materials are pressed together, a surface forms where the two meet. The shape of this surface will depend on the shape of the two objects involved, and their elasticity relative to each other. In another attempt to simplify a potentially complex situation, it is assumed that whenever any two objects touch, the area of contact forms a plane surface, called here the plane of contact. This plane is obvious in most situations on stage. If anything rests on the stage floor, the plane of contact is the plane of the floor. For anything on wheels, the plane of contact is defined by the surface the wheels touch.

Normal Force – The normal force, or $\boldsymbol{F}_n$, is the force acting perpendicular to the plane of contact pressing two materials together. There are two main sources for this force, weight and externally applied forces.

The weight of an object always acts straight down, and so in every case except where the plane of contact is vertical, some part of the object's weight will contribute to the normal force. Mathematically, the component of weight that contributes to the magnitude of the normal force is:

$$F_{nw} = F_w \cos\theta_{rake}$$

Where F_{nw} = the normal force due to weight (lb, N). The direction of the vector $\boldsymbol{F}_{nw}$ is always perpendicular to the plane of contact.

F_w = the weight of the object above the plane of contact (lb, N)

θ_{rake} = the rake angle, with a horizontal plane of contact being defined as 0° (degrees)

The most common situation in theatre involves things moving about on the stage floor. By definition, the rake angle here would be 0° (assuming we are not in an

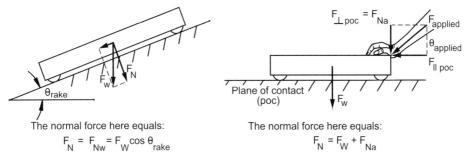

The normal force here equals:
$$F_N = F_{Nw} = F_W \cos \theta_{rake}$$

The normal force here equals:
$$F_N = F_W + F_{Na}$$

Figure 4.1   Two common normal force situations

older European theatre). Since the cosine of 0° equals 1, the normal force due to weight equals the weight of the object on a flat horizontal floor.

In a similar manner, an applied force—a push by a stagehand, or a pull from a wire rope connected to a winch—can add to, or subtract, from the normal force. Mathematically:

$$F_{na} = F_{applied} \sin \theta_{applied}$$

Where F_{na} = the normal force due to an applied force (lb, N) The direction of the vector $\boldsymbol{F}_{na}$ is always perpendicular to the plane of contact.

$F_{applied}$ = the applied force (lb, N)

$\theta_{applied}$ = the angle between the plane of contact and the applied force (degrees)

The illustrations in Figure 4.1 above show two possible normal force situations. On the left, a wagon rolls on a raked stage. The normal force in the absence of any other applied force would be just the component of weight that is perpendicular to the plane of contact. On the right, a platform sits on a level stage floor, with a stagehand pushing the wagon at an angle. The normal force here would equal the sum of the weight of the platform shown acting from the platform's center of mass, with the component of the applied push that is perpendicular to the plane of contact. To generalize these two situations into all others, the normal force always equals the sum of forces acting perpendicular to the plane of contact pressing the two materials in question together.

EXAMPLE: A platform weighing 450 lb sits on a stage raked at a half inch to the foot. A stagehand using a push stick applies 75 lb of force toward the platform at an angle of 30° up from the plane of contact. What is the normal force?

SOLUTION: The rake angle is a given, but it needs to be converted into an angle in degrees to be usable in a formula.

$$\tan \theta_{rake} = \frac{rise}{run} = \frac{0.5}{12} = 0.0417$$

$$\theta_{rake} = 2.39°$$

The other givens include:

$$F_w = 450 \; lb \qquad F_{applied} = 75 \; lb \qquad \theta_{applied} = 30°$$

The normal force will equal the sum of the appropriate components of both weight and applied force.

$$F_n = F_{nw} + F_{na}$$

$$F_n = F_w \cos\theta_{rake} + F_{applied} \sin\theta_{applied}$$

Inserting the givens into the equation will give the normal force:

$$F_n = (450)\cos 2.39 + (75)\sin 30$$

$$F_n = 450 + 37.5 = 487.5 \; lb$$

The direction of F_n is, by definition, always perpendicular to the plane of contact.

EXAMPLE (SI): Two identical wagons run on a 4° rake, one straight up and down it, the other running exactly across it. Each wagon has a mass of 250 kg. What is the normal force on each one? Assume their drive cables add no forces in the normal direction.

SOLUTION: Both wagons would have the same angle between the plane of contact and their weight, the always straight down F_w. Therefore the normal force would be the same for both. Do not forget that metric mass, kilograms, must be converted to force, newtons, for the weight term by multiplying mass times the acceleration due to gravity, $g = 9.81 \; m/sec^2$:

$$F_{nw} = F_w \cos\theta_{rake}$$

$$F_{nw} = (250)(9.81)\cos 4° = 2450 \; N$$

Sliding Friction

Friction occurs between any two objects in contact: a shoe on the sidewalk, a hand on a rope, or a chair on the stage floor for instance. Friction allows the shoe to gain traction on the floor, the hand to pull the rope, and the chair to stay in place even if it is put on a shallow rake. When the objects are stationary relative to each other, a situation defined as static, the friction tends to hold the objects in place. If motion exists between the objects—the shoe, hand, or chair slips—then one material is sliding against the other, and the situation is called kinetic. These two simple categories, static and kinetic, and the two corresponding formulas used to describe friction within them, attempt to predict the resistance to movement caused by sliding friction.

It is worth repeating here again, for emphasis, that friction is not simple. It should, for instance, not be too surprising that in experiments performed at very low speeds, in the inch per year range, that materials in this "kinetic" situation behaved nearly as they would in a static one. Strange things can also happen. Two extremely flat polished surfaces of clean gas-free steel pressed together in a vacuum can weld on contact, the two pieces become one, and they will then obviously not slide against each other at all. Is this friction, or something else? Fortunately theatre operates in the messy real world, with dirt, air, and reasonable speeds. Here the static and kinetic categories offer useful approximations of the complex interactions that occur between two surfaces.

Static Friction

Static friction is that aspect of sliding friction that exists when there is no movement between two objects in contact. (The objects under consideration here are in contact, but not connected. Nails, glue, bolts, or screws cannot be involved.) The static friction force is what opposes you when you begin to slide something across the floor, but movement has not started yet. If you apply a force parallel to the plane of contact, static friction will resist you with a force equal in magnitude and opposite in direction to your push. As motion becomes imminent, the force due to static friction reaches its maximum value, and as the object begins to move, the situation changes over to kinetic.

An approximate value of the maximum force due to static friction can be found using:

$$F_{fs} = \mu_s F_n$$

Where F_{fs} = the magnitude of the maximum force due to static friction, in a direction parallel with the plane of contact (lb, N)

μ_s = the coefficient of static friction for the materials in contact (unitless)

F_n = the normal force, the sum of all forces perpendicular to the plane of contact. (lb, N)

The direction of the friction force vector is not given by this formula, as it is not necessarily related to the direction of the normal force. Since friction always opposes motion, the force due to static friction will always be opposite in direction to the force that is trying to slide the object. To be more specific, the static friction force is a force equal in magnitude and opposite in direction to the sum of all weight and applied force components that are parallel to the plane of contact, as long as no movement occurs between the two objects. This is all more intuitively obvious than the wording makes it sound. The three examples shown in Figure 4.2 will attempt to clarify. In Figure 4.2a, a cable pulls on a platform sitting on a level floor. The platform's weight, F_w, is perpendicular to the plane of contact formed by the platform and floor, and so there is no component of weight parallel to the

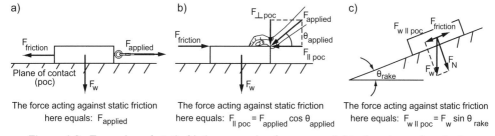

Figure 4.2   Examples of static friction opposing forces parallel to the plane of contact

plane of contact. The cable pull, $F_{applied}$, acts parallel to the plane of contact and is the sole force capable of sliding the platform along the floor. The force due to friction, $F_{friction}$, and specifically here the force due to static friction, F_{fs}, will exactly oppose the cable's pull. In Figure 4.2b a hand pushes a block across a level floor. Only the component of the hand push that is parallel to the plane of contact will be opposed by friction. The weight of the block, and the component of the push perpendicular to the plane of contact will sum to equal the normal force.

The coefficient of static friction is a unitless number, unique in large part to the materials in contact, their surface finish, and presence or absence of any lubricant. The coefficient defines the relationship between the force pushing the two materials together, the normal force, F_n, and the maximum resistance to movement the setup will offer, the force due to static friction, F_{fs}. The coefficients for a wide variety of pairs of materials in contact are listed in tables in many physics reference books, but these values are nearly useless for theatre because they are for materials we will never use, glass on nickel, or zinc on cast iron for instance. Table 4-1 does give a very short list of potentially useful coefficients, and these can be used to estimate the coefficients for similar materials and situations, but in general the most accurate coefficients for our use come from measurements using a mock-up of the actual materials to be used. This will be discussed in the **Measuring Coefficients of Friction** section below.

The formula for the maximum force due to static friction does not include any term for the area of contact. This is because within wide limits the force due to friction is independent of the area of contact. For example, if a number of stage weights is used to hold open a door, it should not matter whether the weights are piled one atop the other, or placed side by side. Only when the area becomes small enough that the forces involved cause the one material to dig into the other will this area independence vanish.

A material's surface finish or texture has a major impact on its coefficient of friction. A smooth steel block will slide more easily across another material than will

Materials	Static		Kinetic	
	dry	lubricated	dry	lubricated
hard steel on hard steel	0.75	0.15	0.45	0.10
oil-impregnated nylon on steel	0.15	-	0.08-0.13	-
soft rubber tire on painted wood	0.8	-	-	-
steel on UHMW [a]	0.22	0.1	0.10-0.22	0.05-0.08
teflon on teflon or steel	0.04-0.20	-	0.04-0.10	-
wire rope on steel	0.17	0.07	-	-

Table 4.1 Coefficients of Static and Kinetic Friction

a.   Ultra-high molecular weight polyethylene, an inexpensive plastic often used for guides.

an identically loaded steel file. The file's teeth dig into the other surface, forcing a shearing action on that surface rather than a sliding action. Wood grain can have a similar interlocking interaction. Two wood blocks with their grains parallel to each other but perpendicular to the direction of movement will generally have higher coefficients than if their grains are perpendicular. Painted, stained, waxed, or rosined surfaces behave much differently than would the original unpainted materials. Certainly even the cure time to complete hardness of the finish will impact friction.

Lubrication is a huge factor altering the friction between materials. In some cases lubricants will decrease friction nearly ten times from its dry value. Lubricants are materials with high compressive strength, which is necessary to support the loads placed on them, but with very low strength in shear, which means motion perpendicular to the compressive support is easy. Highly viscous liquids, for instance mineral oil, and some solids, such as graphite, are common lubricants that exhibit these behaviors. Lubricants can provide a separating layer of incompatibility between like materials that may otherwise be inclined to stick together. Lubricants will also remove or more evenly distribute the heat friction generates, also reducing the tendency of materials to seize up. The "lubricated" values in Table 4.1 are only approximate as the exact lubricant used will affect the actual performance.

All these factors play into the potential for major differences between a friction coefficient listed in this or any other table, and that found using the two real objects. If an accurate value of the friction force is needed for some specific situation, test a realistic mock-up of the system. There is no other choice.

Kinetic Friction

From everyday experiences we generally have the sense that it is easier to keep something moving than it is to start it. Part of this sense comes from the effort needed to overcome the inertia of the piece and accelerate it. The force required to accelerate mass is taken into account with the $\boldsymbol{F}_{accel}$ term, and this is not due in any way to friction. But in general, the force due to static friction is larger than the force due to kinetic friction, and so because of this it is harder to start movement than it is to continue it.

Mathematically, kinetic friction is found in the same way as static friction, only the coefficient used is different. The force due to kinetic friction is:

$$F_{fk} = \mu_k F_n$$

Where F_{fk} = the maximum force due to kinetic friction (lb, N). The vector $\boldsymbol{F}_{fk}$ will be in a direction parallel with the plane of contact.

μ_k = the coefficient of kinetic friction for the materials in contact (unitless)

F_n = the normal force, the sum of all forces perpendicular to the plane of contact (lb, N)

As was true in the static situation, the direction of the friction force vector is not given by this formula. Friction always opposes motion, and so the direction of the friction force will always be opposite to $\Delta\boldsymbol{x}$, which itself must be some direction along the plane of contact to maintain a sliding movement.

EXAMPLE: A platform weighing 265 lb travels across a stage raked at a half inch to the foot. If $\mu_s = 0.42$ and $\mu_k = 0.33$, what is F_{fs} and F_{fk}? Assume only weight affects the normal force, and that there are no other applied forces.

SOLUTION: Knowing the coefficients of friction means that only the normal force must be determined. Since the platform sits on a rake, the normal force will be a function of the rake angle, which from the rise and run information given, can be calculated to be:

$$\tan \theta = \frac{rise}{run} = \frac{0.5}{12} = 0.0417$$

$$\theta = 2.39°$$

With this angle, and the weight of the platform, the normal force can be found:

$$F_{nw} = F_w \cos \theta_{rake} = 265(\cos 2.39°) = 264.8 \ lb$$

On such a shallow rake, the normal force essentially equals the object's weight. The two friction forces can now be found:

$$F_{fs} = \mu_s F_n = 0.42(264.8) = 111 lb$$

$$F_{fk} = \mu_k F_n = 0.33(264.8) = 87.4 lb$$

These results imply that any force parallel to the plane of contact up to and including 111 lb will be resisted by the force due to static friction, preventing the object from moving. Once 111 lb has been exceeded, the object will move, and it will require a push of 87.4 lb continuously during movement just to overcome the force due to kinetic friction. The forces needed to accelerate the object, and to overcome any lifting (zero here as the problem stated the movement is across the rake) would need to be determined separately and summed in with the friction force, as is done in the maximum power formula:

$$P_{max} = (\boldsymbol{F}_{accel} + \boldsymbol{F}_{friction} + \boldsymbol{F}_{lifting}) \boldsymbol{v}_{max}$$

Measuring Coefficients of Friction

Determining by experiment either a friction coefficient or the friction force itself is necessary if anything beyond the rough estimates are needed. The coefficients of friction for materials we are likely to use in theatre simply will not appear in standard engineering references, and the great variety that exists in materials and the finishes we might put upon them makes it pointless to attempt to list them all here.

One straightforward method of estimating friction is to assemble a model of the setup being considered, load it down with some weight, and use a spring scale to measure the force needed to move it (see Figure 4.3a). The sliding surface materials must be exactly the ones the full scale setup will use, sanded smooth or painted in the model if the real object will be sanded smooth or painted. The closer the model is in size to the to-be-built setup the better. Do not expect a 1 pound model to give useful answers about the behavior of a 1000 pound pallet. The floor the model is placed on should be level, and the spring scale should be as close to and parallel with the plane of contact as practical, as this will insure that the normal force simply equals the weight of the moving piece. Increase the pull force slowly while watching the scale. The highest number reached just before movement starts will be F_{fs} for that model. Using the static friction formula, the coefficient can be calculated:

$$F_{fs} = \mu_s F_n \qquad so \qquad \mu_s = \frac{F_{fs}}{F_n} = \frac{F_{fs}}{F_w} = \frac{spring\ scale\ reading}{weight}$$

An attempt could be made to measure the force needed to keep the object moving, and that is then used to calculate μ_k, but since the static force is generally higher, it is an easy to measure conservative choice to use.

A different experimental technique uses a variable angle rake to alter the ratio between the normal force and the component of the weight that is parallel to the plane of contact (see Figure 4.3b). The same type of model is needed as in the previous method, but here it is set up on a platform or sheet of plywood that can be tilted. As the angle of tilt, θ, increases, the normal force decreases, and the component of the weight down the rake increases. At some angle of tilt, the decreased normal force pressing the two materials together no longer develops enough friction force to resist the increased component of the weight down the rake, and the pallet will slide. Mathematically, at the rake angle where sliding just begins, the magnitudes of the two forces in the static friction equation are:

$$F_n = F_{nw} = F_w \cos\theta$$

$$F_{fs} = F_w \sin\theta$$

Substituting these into the static friction equation, solving for μ_s, and using a trigonometric equality gives:

$$F_{fs} = F_n \mu_s$$

$$F_w \sin\theta = (F_w \cos\theta)\mu_S$$

$$\mu_s = \frac{F_w \sin\theta}{F_w \cos\theta} = \frac{\sin\theta}{\cos\theta} = \tan\theta$$

This derivation aside, the result is simple. Make a model of the system, tilt it to the point where it just begins to slide (gentle taps help get somewhat more consistent

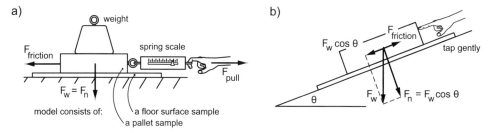

Figure 4.3 Two techniques to measure friction

results), and take the tangent of the angle of the rake. The number obtained is the coefficient of static friction for those materials. There is no need to weigh anything, nor to have a spring scale to measure anything.

Heavy objects sliding across a stage are rare. This in part is a reason why there is little to look up in any references concerning coefficients. When something large needs to be moved, we use wheels. Sliding contact does commonly occur in guides on lifts and counterweight arbors, and in the knives and dogs in deck tracks. The normal forces in these situations are generally low and so the forces due to friction are often considered negligible. Friction drives, which might use a motorized tire to push a wagon across a floor or an endless loop of cable wrapped v-belt-like around a turntable and drive sheaves, are instances where easy sliding is not wanted, and considerable forces need to be developed between the two materials involved. Here conservative estimates of the coefficients, or careful testing of mock-ups is wise to insure a successful final product.

Rolling Friction

Wheels, of course, allow things to be moved more easily than by sliding. As was the case for sliding friction, a full description and accounting of all friction effects in rolling situations is quite complex. Friction affects wheels in at least the following ways.

- at their bearings (devices with numerous complexities themselves). Bearing lubrication is a major player here too, as it was in sliding friction,
- at the contact surface between the wheel and the material it rides on, which takes into account surface material, its roughness, and the amount of dirt or debris present,
- in proportion to the wheel's width of contact with the floor (only an issue on a curved travel path, because the distance traveled at a wheel's outer edge is greater than that at the inner edge),
- in the air's resistance to the movement of the wheel (negligible at low speeds),
- in proportion to wheel diameter, as a larger wheel generally rolls over a given rough surface more easily than does a smaller diameter one,
- at their mounting frames, where tire bulging due to loading could cause the wheel to bind,
- in proportion to the alignment of a swivel caster to the direction of motion, and
- within the materials of wheel and floor as they deform under load and spring back.

Each of these effects could be mathematically modeled, computed for a particular situation, and summed to give the force required to overcome rolling resistance. Even in engineering in general this is rarely done. Simpler techniques are used.

From the point of view of a person or a motor moving an object on wheels, the individual component friction effects are not apparent, only the total sum of them all. Given this, perhaps the simplest formula to predict the affects of friction on rolling, and the one presented here, is one analogous to the sliding friction formulas covered above.

$$F_{fr} = \mu_r\, F_n$$

Where F_{fr} = the force due to rolling friction, in a direction parallel with the plane of contact (lb, N)

μ_r = the coefficient of rolling friction for the wheel and rolling surface combination (unitless)

F_n = the normal force, the sum of all forces perpendicular to the plane of contact (lb, N)

The coefficient of rolling friction is, like its sliding counterparts, the percentage, in decimal form, of the normal force needed to move a rolling object. Distinctions could be made between static and kinetic situations, but this is not generally done. Finding rolling coefficients, even from the manufacturers of casters, is often a futile effort. Surprisingly, wheel and caster manufacturers provide little information on the performance of their products. This is probably because they have no control over one half the rolling system, the floor, and do not want to claim a level of performance their customers may not get. If they do give information, any of a variety of terms might be used, "rollability" or "rolling effort" for example. Data is usually in the form of a graph of normal force versus rolling friction force for a particular wheel construction running on a smooth clean concrete floor, rather than as a coefficient and a formula. This information might be useful if you can get it, but it will still need to be tested through experience before its worth is proven.

Experimental measurements with full size wagons can of course be done. The exact same techniques described above can be applied to rolling systems too, and the results of these tests are unquestionably the best information you can get, related as they are to the very components being used. The caveats given earlier apply here too. Make the models as large as practical, and load the setup down with enough weight that the wheels are loaded to at least half their capacity. Make sure the surface the wheels roll over is what you plan to use on stage. The same caster will roll much differently over plywood than carpet, Homosote™, or sand. If the set design calls for a floor with routed grooves or planking, or has a lift or traps with their inevitable gaps, mock up a section of that floor for the tests, and make sure at least one wheel sits in a groove or gap for some of the measurements. Swivel or "zero-throw" casters should be tested with their starting wheel alignment off the axis of movement. The starting force needed to spin the swivels can easily be three times the force needed to move them once they are all aligned.

Table 4.2 is a very short list of coefficients found to work well in practice on stage. Always use your best judgment as to whether these values should be altered up or down given the specifics of your application, and recall that tests on mockups are always an option if need to be sure your estimates are accurate.

The number of wheels does not show up in the equation, nor does it have a significant effect in reality unless a castor becomes so grossly overloaded that they deflect out and rub against their frames, or a wheel fails by fracturing apart (all of

Wheel type and surface	Coefficient of rolling friction
Generic 3″ soft rubber straight castor, with roller bearings, on plywood	0.04
Zero-throws with 3.5″ polyurethane wheels on plywood, wheels aligned to the direction of movement	0.03
Zero-throws with 3.5″ polyurethane wheels on plywood, wheels aligned 90° to the direction of movement	0.06

Table 4.2 Coefficients of Rolling Friction (all values found by testing)

which I have seen happen). Never just assume castors can be distributed evenly under a wagon, but note instead the location of heavier loads that will need to be supported by more, or higher capacity, wheels.

EXAMPLE: A wagon weighing 665 lb travels across a level stage floor decked in medium density fiberboard. The wagon is supported on 3″ diameter soft rubber castors found to have a coefficient of rolling friction of 0.04. What force parallel with the plane of stage floor is needed just to overcome rolling friction?

SOLUTION: Because the stage floor is level, and there are no other forces contributing to the normal, the normal force equals the weight of the wagon, 665 lb. The rolling friction force equals:

$$F_{fr} = F_n \mu_r = 665(0.04) = 26.6 \; lb$$

Friction of Ropes on Cylinders

The act of taking a wrap of rope around a fixed pipe to control the descent of a heavy object is a common trick of the trade. The friction between rope and pipe absorbs some of the tension on the line due to the weight of the object being lowered, and this makes the person's job much easier. Capstan winches use the friction between a few wraps of rope around a motor driven smooth drum to amplify the operator's pull on the rope. The motor supplies the power to lift the load, the person merely supplies a minimal tension needed to control whether the rope slips or grabs the capstan drum. Another similar use of the friction between a cylinder and a rope is in an endless-loop cable drive unit, often used to drive turntables (see page 367). Friction between a wire rope and the edge of a turntable is the only connection converting cable tension into turntable torque.

All of these examples are instances of sliding friction between a flexible tension-member, most often a fiber or wire rope, but sometimes a belt or chain, and a

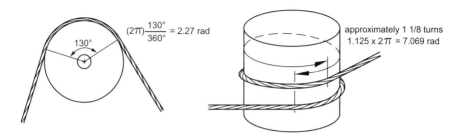

Figure 4.4   Two example of wrap angle calculation

cylindrical surface of contact: a drum, sheave, or a piece of plain pipe. The behavior of this situation is described mathematically by the following equation:

$$F_{slack} = \frac{F_{tensioned}}{e^{\mu\theta}}$$

Where F_{slack} = the magnitude of the smaller of the two tensions involved (lb, N)
   $F_{tensioned}$ = the magnitude of the larger of the two tensions involved (lb, N)
   e = the base of the natural logarithms, 2.71828 ... (inverse "ln" on some calculators)
   μ = the appropriate coefficient of sliding friction, static or kinetic (unitless)
   θ = the wrap angle, defined as the angle between where the rope first touches the cylinder, to where it leaves (radians). See Figure 4.4.

   The coefficient of friction you use will depend on the answer you want. If the rope remains stationary relative to the cylinder, the situation between the materials is static, and the tensioned and slack numbers will reflect the maximum difference possible without the rope slipping. If the rope does slip, a kinetic friction situation exists, and the difference between tensioned and slack numbers will be lower. In a turntable drive for instance, using a kinetic coefficient will be conservative, because it will represent the worst case, or the least possible difference in tension between tensioned and slack ropes. If a winch is being designed for an effect that requires ropes being pulled over pieces of pipe, use the coefficient of static friction as that will be the worst case for that setup.

EXAMPLE: A simple effect involves a 5 lb piece of muslin draped over props on stage. A single manila line tied to the muslin runs up over three fixed pipes as shown, and down off stage. What pull will be needed on the line off-stage to fly out the muslin? Assume the coefficient of static friction of manila rope on steel is 0.25, and that the rope itself is of negligible weight.

SOLUTION: To pull the muslin out, a pull greater than the 5 lb weigh of the goods will be needed. In this situation, at the first pipe, 5 lb is F_{slack},

Illustration

and $F_{tensioned}$ is to be determined. At the second and third pipes, the pull needed past the pipe to lift the goods will be greater than tension on the line coming into it, so the $F_{tensioned}$ out of the first pipe equals the F_{slack} into the second, and likewise for the third. At the first pipe:

$$F_{slack} = \frac{F_{tensioned}}{e^{\mu\theta}} = 5 = \frac{F_{tensioned}}{e^{(0.25)(1.57)}}$$

$$F_{tensioned} = 7.40 \; lb$$

At the second pipe:

$$F_{slack} = \frac{F_{tensioned}}{e^{\mu\theta}} = 7.40 = \frac{F_{tensioned}}{e^{(0.25)(0.785)}}$$

$$F_{tensioned} = 9.01 \; lb$$

And finally at the third:

$$F_{slack} = \frac{F_{tensioned}}{e^{\mu\theta}} = 9.01 = \frac{F_{tensioned}}{e^{(0.25)(0.785)}}$$

$$F_{tensioned} = 11.0 \; lb$$

The final result is not a large number, but it is over twice the weight being lifted. Sheaves would of course normally be used to greatly reduce this effect of friction, and the wear and tear on the rope due to sliding.

   This is also just an example of how this sort of situation could be analysized. No one would ever actually calculate out this particular problem, but instead rely on their intuition that a tug on a rope could lift a small piece of fabric.

   An endless-loop type turntable drive, sometimes called a grommet drive, uses an end-to-end spliced loop of wire rope as the power transmission medium between the turntable and a motorized drive (see the rotary motion chapters for more information on turntables). The turntable is built to be a large diameter cable sheave, with the cable resting in a slot or channel built into the outer edge of the table. The drive uses two sets of stacks of sheaves, or multi-groove sheaves, to form drive and idler shafts (see Figure 4.5). A motor with gear reduction spins the drive shaft,

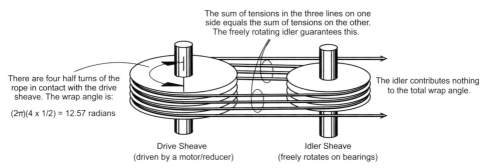

The sum of tensions in the three lines on one side equals the sum of tensions on the other. The freely rotating idler guarantees this.

There are four half turns of the rope in contact with the drive sheave. The wrap angle is:

$(2\pi)(4 \times 1/2) = 12.57$ radians

The idler contributes nothing to the total wrap angle.

Drive Sheave
(driven by a motor/reducer)

Idler Sheave
(freely rotates on bearings)

Figure 4.5   Endless-loop drive

while the undriven idler functions only to lift the cable out of one groove at the driver and shift it down into the next groove. The wrap angle in one of these setups is not as obvious as in other simpler systems. A cable that wraps around any freely rotating idler sheave never becomes part of the wrap angle because the rope tension on either side of the sheave will be identical (ignoring the typically negligible friction of the sheave's bearings). If the tensions ever tried to become different, the sheave would just spin and equalize them. So in this setup, the tension on the wire rope as it leaves the drive sheave equals the tension into and out of the idler, and the tension as the rope re-engages the drive. As far as tension is concerned, it is as if the rope never left the drive sheave.

For the setup depicted, the wrap angle, in turns, equals four half turns, which totals two full turns, or *2 turns × 2π radians/turn = 12.57 radians.* With a wrap angle this large, huge differences can be developed between $F_{tensioned}$ and F_{slack} minimizing the likelihood of the cable slipping. Turntable drives with two, three, and four grooves on the drive shaft have been built. As in any friction drive type system, the greater the friction, the less likely slipping will occur, and so the four groove setup will provide the most slip-free performance. This drive technique is used outside of theatre in some ski lifts, traction drive elevators, and for the San Francisco cable cars.

Problems

1. A platform weighing 165 lb sits on a level stage floor. How much force parallel to the plane of the floor needs to be provided just to overcome friction and allow the platform to start moving? The coefficients of static and kinetic friction in this case are 0.63 and 0.47 respectively.

2. A wagon with a mass of 955 kg rolls on a rake angled at 3.5° on casters with a coefficient of rolling friction of 0.04. What is $F_{friction}$?

3. A large thin pallet is to be built for a show using wheels made from 1.5″ diameter polyurethane rollers. A test pallet weighing 134 lb is built and pulled across the stage with a spring scale reading roughly 5.5 lb. What is μ_r for this setup?

4. A capstan winch is being used to haul counterweight up to the loading rail. If the arbor and weight being hauled weighs 400 lb, and there are exactly 2.25 full wraps of rope around the capstan drum, what force does the operator have to provide to get the weight lifted? The worst case coefficient of friction between rope and drum is 0.20. Ignore all other friction, and the force needed for acceleration.

5

The Lifting Force, $F_{lifting}$

Gravity, Weight, and the Lifting Force

Gravitational attraction acts on the mass of all matter, pulling any two objects together. Normally, we perceive only the pull of one close-by massive object, the earth, but in fact all objects attract all others gravitationally (trivia: two 10 lb objects 1 foot apart exert a gravitational attraction force of about 1 billionth of a pound on each other). By convention, the force developed due to the gravitational pull of the Earth is called weight, and many texts therefore give it the symbol *w*. In this book, a force is a force regardless of its origin, and so for consistency weight will be expressed as F_w.

Every person has learned through experience to gauge how hard it might be to move something by hand. An object's apparent weight and the direction it needs to be moved affects this assessment. Lowering is easier than lifting, rolling something up a ramp can seem more practical than lifting that thing straight up the same vertical distance, and moving anything across a level floor is simple once friction is reduced. While this intuition is useful, it provides no precise values that would allow, for instance, a motor horsepower to be picked with confidence. A formulaic approach is needed.

The Lifting Force

Part of the maximum power formula sums three distinct forces: the force needed to accelerate the mass of the system, the force needed to overcome friction, and the force needed for any lifting against the pull of gravity:

$$P_{max} = (F_{accel} + F_{frict} + F_{lifting})\, v_{max}$$

The lifting force relates to both the weight of the object being moved, and its direction of movement relative to the always down direction of weight, F_w. Mathematically, the lifting force is:

$$F_{lifting} = -F_w \sin\theta$$

Where $F_{lifting}$ = the lifting force (lb, N)
  F_w = the weight of the object (lb, N)
  θ = the rake angle, defined as the angle between Δx and horizontal (deg)

As the minus sign in the formula implies, the directions of the lifting force and weight are always opposite. It does not matter whether you assume up is positive or negative, as long as you are consistent in assigning appropriate signs for all the other terms: displacement, velocity, etc. Since the maximum power needed for a move that involves any lifting will occur during acceleration while the direction of movement is up against the direction of gravity, it is usually easiest to assume up is positive. With this, a and therefore F_{accel} will be positive, F_w will be negative which will make $F_{lifting}$ positive, and as will be shown in the friction chapter, $F_{friction}$ will be positive.

EXAMPLE: A wagon weighing 1300 lb rolls up and down a stage raked at 1″ in 12″. What is the lifting force, $F_{lifting}$?

SOLUTION: The designer's specification for the rake needs to be converted into a rake angle in degrees.

$$\tan\theta = \frac{opposite}{adjacent} = \frac{1}{12}$$

$$\theta = 4.76°$$

Assume up is the positive direction, which means F_w is negative. The lifting force is:

$$F_{lifting} = -F_w \sin\theta = -(-1300)\sin 4.76$$

$$F_{lifting} = 108 \; lb$$

EXAMPLE (SI): A platform with a mass of 245 kg rolls up and down a stage raked 1 in 10. What is the lifting force, $F_{lifting}$?

SOLUTION: Two conversions need to occur, one to find the rake angle, one to find the weight in newtons of the given mass:

$$\tan\theta = \frac{opposite}{adjacent} = \frac{1}{10} \qquad so: \quad \theta = 5.71°$$

$$F_w = mg = (245)(9.8) = 2401 \; N$$

If up is assumed to be the positive direction, then F_w is negative. $F_{lifting}$ becomes:

$$F_{lifting} = -F_w \sin\theta = -(-2401)\sin 5.71$$

$$F_{lifting} = 239 \; N$$

Counterweighting

A dead hauled load is the name given to describe a load hauled directly, without the assistance of counterweight. A stagehand can dead haul maybe 30 to 50 lb without too much effort, and chain hoists are dead haul machines rated by their weight lifting capacity. Since stagehands lack capacity, and chain hoists lack speed, purpose built dead haul winches are often considered to fly heavy scenery quickly. The motors needed for these machines can however become prohibitively large.

EXAMPLE: A main drape weighing 1000 lb is to be dead hauled out by a winch. The top speed of the piece is 6 ft/sec, the maximum acceleration rate will be 2 ft/sec^2, and assume the friction force equals 60 lb. What is the maximum power required by this setup?

SOLUTION: The maximum power formula is:

$$P_{max} = (F_{accel} + F_{frict} + F_{lifting}) v_{max}$$

Since values for the friction force and top speed have been given, only the acceleration and lifting forces need to be determined. The acceleration force is:

$$F_{accel} = m a = \left(\frac{1000}{32.2}\right)(2)$$

$$F_{accel} = 62.1 \ lb$$

The lifting force formula includes the rake angle term, θ. Flown scenery travels perpendicularly to the horizontal stage floor, and so the rake angle equals 90°. The lifting force equals (using the assumption that up is positive):

$$F_{lifting} = -F_w \sin\theta = -(-1000)\sin 90°$$

$$F_{lifting} = 1000 \ lb$$

The maximum power needed to dead haul out this drape is therefore:

$$P_{max} = (F_{accel} + F_{frict} + F_{lifting}) v_{max}$$

$$P_{max} = (62.1 + 60 + 1000) \ 6$$

$$P_{max} = 6733 \ ftlb/sec \qquad or: \quad 12.2 \ hp$$

The power formula gives answers in units of *ft-lb/sec*. To obtain the more commonly used unit of horsepower, divide *ft-lb/sec* by 550, the number of *ft-lb/sec* per *hp*.

One advantage of the power formula in this format is to allow you in a glance to see the relation of the three force components to each other. In this situation, 89% of the power needed for this move is used just for lifting, the acceleration and friction components are relatively negligible. If there is no possibility of getting a winch capable of providing this power, then there are only two possible choices that will significantly reduce the drapes power needs, run it slower, decreasing v_{max}, or decrease $F_{lifting}$ in some manner.

Counterweighting can be used to reduce or eliminate the consequences of a large lifting force by having the lifting force of the load be partially or totally countered by the lifting force of a counterweight. There are several penalties to doing this. One, there will be an increase in F_{accel} because the mass of both the load and the counterweight would now need to be accelerated. Two, the force to overcome friction, $F_{friction}$, would probably increase because of the inevitable added rigging. And three, there is the very practical question of whether there is an available space to rig a counterweight system. Traditional fly houses have been designed with this in mind, but other stage forms may not be so accommodating.

EXAMPLE: Given the same 1000 lb drape as in the problem above, but now counterweighted with 1000 lb, what is the maximum power required? Assume the added rigging doubles the friction.

SOLUTION: If both drape and counterweight are exactly 1000 lb, there is no net lifting force, or $\boldsymbol{F}_{lifting} = 0$. The acceleration force needs to be recalculated using the doubled mass of the system:

$$\boldsymbol{F}_{accel} = m\boldsymbol{a} = \left(\frac{1000 + 1000}{32.2}\right)(2)$$

$$\boldsymbol{F}_{accel} = 124 \ lb$$

The maximum power needed to fly the counterweighted drape out is:

$$P_{max} = (\boldsymbol{F}_{accel} + \boldsymbol{F}_{frict} + \boldsymbol{F}_{lifting}) \, \boldsymbol{v}_{max}$$

$$P_{max} = (124 + 120 + 0) \, 6$$

$$P_{max} = 1464 \ ftlb/sec \qquad or: \quad 2.66 \ hp$$

By using counterweight, the power required is only 22% of what it was for the dead haul setup.

Problems

1. What lifting force is needed for a 486 lb wagon tracking straight up and down a rake built with a rise/run ratio of 3/4″ to the foot?

2. What rake angle sets the lifting force to 10% of the weight of an object on the rake?

3. A flat weighing 122 lb flies straight up. What is the lifting force for the flat during acceleration? Constant velocity? Deceleration?

4. A counter-raked platform with a mass of 223 kg slides up and down the side of a pyramid raked at 45°. What is the lifting force for this platform?

6

Maximum Power and Force

Power

Force without movement does not require power. A column holding up a building does not need a battery or gas engine to keep it standing. Movement without force also does not require power. No examples of that exist here on Earth because friction always presents a resistance to be overcome, but in deep space, a rocket initially propelled forward may then travel for decades with no further push. It is the combination of force and movement, or more specifically force and velocity, that requires power.

Power is a scalar quantity, which means that it has magnitude, but not a direction. So there is no left power versus right power, or offstage power versus onstage, but power does have a sign associated with it, and that is because supplying power is much different than absorbing power. In mathematics, an operation known as the dot product was developed to allow vector multiplication with a signed scalar result.

$$P = \mathbf{F} \cdot \mathbf{v} = |F||v| \cos\theta$$

Where P = power (ft-lb/sec, w)

$\mathbf{F}$, F = force, in vector and magnitude form respectively (lb, N)

$\mathbf{v}$, v = velocity, in vector and magnitude form respectively (ft/sec, m/sec). Instantaneous velocity is shown, but average velocity, $\bar{v}$, can be used too, with the result being average power, $\bar{P}$. (The bars surrounding both $|F|$ and $|v|$ indicate absolute value, or that those quantities are always positive.)

θ = the angle between $\mathbf{F}$ and $\mathbf{v}$ (degrees). This angle is 0° if force and velocity are in the same direction, 180° if they are opposite.

Both customary and metric units for power are in common use today, even in the USA. In the U.S., the formulas give power in foot pounds per second, or ft-lb/sec, but these units are almost always instantly converted to the more familiar horsepower:

$$1 \; hp = 550 \; ft\text{-}lb/sec$$

In the metric SI, the unit for power is the newton meter per second, or Nm/sec. This is not converted to anything else, but it is given a unique name, the watt. So

$$1W = 1 \ Nm/sec$$

Conversion between customary and metric power units is often performed:

$$1 \ hp = 746 \ watts$$

This is usually rounded to give an easier to remember, but now only approximate value:

$$1 \ hp \cong 750 \ watts = 0.75 \ kilowatts = 0.75 \ kW$$

Throughout these linear motion chapters an assumption has been made that all movement will follow straight lines. To simplify the dot product calculation of the power formula, one further assumption will be made. *During the calculation of power, the forces acting to move an object will always be parallel with the direction of motion.* This is not actually new, as the acceleration, friction and lifting force formulas described in previous chapters where all defined as forces parallel with the direction of movement. Neither is it a severe limitation on our application of this mathematical model to real situations. Wagons run along deck tracks are pulled by cables paralleling the direction of movement. Lifts are most commonly pulled or pushed straight up (scissor lifts are an exception, but their arms actually rotate, so they are covered in the rotational motion chapters). The cables rigged to flown scenery pull parallel to the direction of movement in all but the rarest instances.

What this allows here is an easy way around the cosine term in the dot product definition of power. If force and velocity are always parallel, then the only possible angles between them, θ, are 0°, when they are both in the same direction, and 180°, when they are opposite. The cosine of 0° equals 1, and the cosine of 180° equals -1. The cosine term will—with this **F** and **v** must be parallel assumption—only ever affect the sign of the power, never its size.

The direction of vectors in the straight line motion world of these chapters has been represented with plus and minus signs. Regardless of which direction along the line from the origin is chosen as positive, if force and velocity are both in the same direction relative to each other, their signs will be the same, and the outcome of their multiplication will be positive: $(+F) \times (+v) = +P$, or $(-F) \times (-v) = +P$. If they are in opposite direction from each other, one term will be positive and the other negative, and the outcome will always be negative: $(+F) \times (-v) = -P$, or $(-F) \times (+v) = -P$. This behavior is identical to the results that would be obtained using the cosine in the definition of the dot product, and so if the force and velocity vectors will always be parallel, the sum of three power components:

$$P_{max} = (\boldsymbol{F}_{accel} \cdot \boldsymbol{v}_{max}) + (\boldsymbol{F}_{frict} \cdot \boldsymbol{v}_{max}) + (\boldsymbol{F}_{lift} \cdot \boldsymbol{v}_{max})$$

will equal the sum of three component forces times velocity:

$$P_{max} = (\boldsymbol{F}_{accel} + \boldsymbol{F}_{frict} + \boldsymbol{F}_{lift}) \boldsymbol{v}_{max}$$

Passed by quickly above was the notion that power, a scalar having magnitude but not direction, has a sign. Power can be positive or negative, and the implication of these signs is very important. Imagine a car driving up and then down a steep hill. While going up, the driver will have to press the accelerator to give the engine gas for sufficient power. The velocity of the car up the hill and the push from the tires are both in the same direction. In the power formula, if force and velocity are in the same direction, the result is a positive value for power. When going down the hill, the brakes will have to be applied, and the force developed at the tires on the road retards motion down the hill. Force and velocity here are in opposite directions, and the power that would result would be negative.

A positive power corresponds to any situation where a power source (a motor, a stagehand, or a hydraulic cylinder) has to supply power to the load to move it—power flows from actuator to the load. A negative power occurs whenever the load tries to drive the power source, or in other words whenever the load's power must be absorbed to keep the movement under control. Here power flows from the load to the actuator. A car's brakes are perhaps the most familiar power absorbing mechanism, but far more common in electric motor driven machines is the fact that most motor types can absorb power by becoming a generator as needed, and they then push electric current back out onto the power lines. If it were not for all the unavoidable electrical and mechanical losses, mainly from resistance and friction, a chain hoist would use the exact same amount of power from the electric lines in lifting a load as it would supply back to the lines on lowering it.

Finally, the value for power given by

$$P_{max} = (F_{accel} + F_{frict} + F_{lift})\, v_{max}$$

is the power needed at the effect to move it as was modeled in the calculations. It is **not** the power of the motor needed to run the effect. Power transmission systems—gear reducers, roller chains, or a cable and sheaves, for instance—are never 100% efficient, and so power losses will occur between motor and effect. Motors are available only in certain increments of power: 1, 1.5, 2, 3, 5, 7.5 hp for example, and so rounding up to the next available size will always be necessary. And finally, the mechanical designer may want a power contingency to allow for changes between the assumptions made early on during these calculations, and the reality of the effect as used on stage. It is common for a motor to be 1.5 to 2 times as large as the value this formula gives, and not unusual in commercial theatre work for it to be 4, or more, times as large.

Maximum Power

In order to design a machine that will successfully run an effect, the maximum power that the effect requires must be determined. The maximum power formula includes three force terms and velocity, and they all interact in such a way that one situation is always the worst case for power needed to run an effect:

- F_{accel} will be zero while the effect is at rest, or moving at a constant velocity. It will be in the same direction as v_{max} during acceleration, and opposite in direction during deceleration. Therefore, the power needed just to accelerate mass will always be at its positive maximum during the acceleration portion of the move.

- $F_{friction}$ is the force that must be applied to overcome the effects of friction. It is always present during movement, and is always in the same direction as v_{max}. The power needed to overcome friction is at its positive maximum throughout all portions of a move, regardless of the move's direction.
- $F_{lifting}$ will be zero if the effect moves horizontally. In any other situation, $F_{lifting}$ will equal some component of the effect's weight in magnitude, and in the direction that, given the travel path followed, is in the upwards direction— straight up for a lift, angled gently up from horizontal for a wagon on a shallow rake. Given this, the power due just to lifting will be at a positive maximum whenever v_{max} represents a move with any upward component.

If the worst case situation for power needed to move a load is distilled out of these three statements, it occurs, simply, at the end of acceleration, while traveling up.

EXAMPLE: A 250 lb weight is hauled up and down by a winch mounted on the grid directly above it. Given motion parameters are: $v_{max} = 4 \, ft/sec$, $a = 2.5 \, ft/sec^2$, and $F_{friction} = 12 \, lb$. There is no counterweight. Analyze the power needed to do the acceleration, constant velocity, and deceleration portions of the move, for both moves up and down.

SOLUTION: There are six results to this problem corresponding to the three portions of a typical move and the two directions. Assume up is positive.

• Moving up, accelerating

$$P_{max} = (F_{accel} + F_{frict} + F_{lift})v_{max}$$

$$P_{max} = \left(\frac{250}{32.2}(2.5) + 12 + 250\right)4$$

$$P_{max} = (19.4 + 12 + 250)4 = 1126 \, ft\text{-}lb/sec \ or \ 2.05 \, hp$$

• Moving up, constant velocity

$$P_{max} = (0 + 12 + 250)4 = 1048 \, ft\text{-}lb/sec \ or \ 1.91 \, hp$$

• Moving up decelerating, the value of acceleration is now negative

$$P_{max} = \left(\frac{250}{32.2}(-2.5) + 12 + 250\right)4$$

$$P_{max} = (-19.4 + 12 + 250)4 = 970.4 \, ft\text{-}lb/sec \ or \ 1.76 \, hp$$

Not surprisingly the maximum power needed for a move traveling upwards occurs during the acceleration portion of the move. The power needed during the move does not change much in this example because the lifting force predominates throughout, common for dead-hauling situations.

• Now for the move down. During the acceleration portion of the move, with up still being the positive direction, velocity and acceleration both in the down direction will be negative.

$$P_{max} = (F_{accel} + F_{frict} + F_{lift})v_{max}$$

$$P_{max} = \left(\frac{250}{32.2}(-2.5) - 12 + 250\right) - 4$$

$$P_{max} = (-19.4 - 12 + 250)4 = -874.4 \; ft\text{-}lb/sec \;\; or \; -1.59 \; hp$$

• Moving down, constant velocity.

$$P_{max} = (0 - 12 + 250) - 4 = -952 \; ft\text{-}lb/sec \;\; or \; -1.73 \; hp$$

• Moving down, decelerating. The acceleration value is now positive, as a deceleration must be opposite from the direction of velocity.

$$P_{max} = \left(\frac{250}{32.2}(2.5) - 12 + 250\right) - 4$$

$$P_{max} = (19.4 - 12 + 250) - 4 = -1030 \; ft\text{-}lb/sec \;\; or \; -1.87 \; hp$$

All the powers for the move down are opposite in sign from those obtained for the move up. This means power must be absorbed by the winch rather than supplied. The motor and its electrical supply, and the gear reducer in the winch will usually perform this task, but a brake may sometimes be used. (The ability of a variable speed motor drive to absorb power is always something that must be considered. This is a control issue, and unfortunately well beyond the topics here.) The maximum value of this braking power occurs, again not surprisingly, during deceleration to a stop.

The three graphs shown here give a visual representation of the move up. At the top, the typical trapezoidal velocity motion profile is shown, with speed increasing and decreasing linearly with time during acceleration and deceleration respectively, and with an unchanging top speed during the middle of the move. The center graph shows the sum of the three component forces, F_{accel}, $F_{friction}$, and $F_{lifting}$ versus time. Before the move the tension on the line between the winch and weight is 250 lb. Both F_{accel} and $F_{friction}$ are zero because there is no movement. During acceleration, all three component forces are in the same direction, so they sum to the largest value for this move. During the constant velocity portion of the move, F_{accel} drops to zero, but

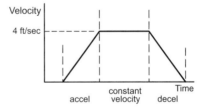

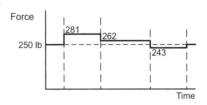

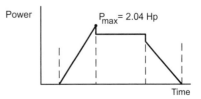

$F_{friction}$ and $F_{lifting}$ remain present. During deceleration, F_{accel} reappears, but now in the opposite direction from the still present $F_{friction}$ and $F_{lifting}$. The bottom graph plots power versus time, and shows the result of multiplying, at each instant of time, force times velocity. The peak power needed occurs just at the end of the acceleration period.

Finally, one last comment about this example. If you could measure and plot the three graphs from the behavior of a real winch lifting a weight, the results would look similar, but all the sharps corners of the graphs above would be rounded off. The response of real systems is never as instantaneous as this simple model would predict.

EXAMPLE: A castered wagon with a mass of 1300 kg (which includes all live and dead loads) travels up and down a stage raked at 5 cm per meter. The wagon's castors have a coefficient of rolling friction of 0.035. During acceleration the wagon's speed goes from 0 to 1 m/sec in 2 seconds. What maximum power must be supplied to this effect?

SOLUTION: Assuming up is the positive direction, the givens are:

$$m = 1300kg \qquad V_{max} = 1 \; m/sec \qquad \mu_r = 0.035 \qquad \Delta t_{accel} = 2 \; sec$$

The rake angle can be found from the rise and run information:

$$\tan\theta_{rake} = \frac{rise}{run} = \frac{5}{100} = 0.05$$

$$\theta_{rake} = 2.86°$$

Acceleration can be determined from the givens using one of the equations of constant acceleration:

$$V_2 = V_1 + a\Delta t$$

$$1 = 0 + a(2)$$

$$a = 0.5 \; m/sec^2$$

At this point the maximum power formula could be written out with the appropriate equations inserted for the force components, but this is often confusing, and prone to errors. (Outside of class use, most mechanical designers set up a spread sheet programs to quickly get accurate answers without the tedium of hand calculations.) A better approach is to figure out each of the three force components separately, and then use them in the power formula to get a final result.

• Find the force needed just to accelerate the mass of the wagon, or F_{accel}:

$$F_{accel} = ma = 1300(0.5) = +650 \; N$$

• Find the force needed just to overcome the effects of friction, or $F_{friction}$:

$$F_{friction} = F_n\mu_r = (F_w\cos\theta_{rake})\mu_r = (mg\cos\theta_{rake})\mu_r$$

$$F_{friction} = (1300(9.81)\cos2.86°)0.035 = +446 \; N$$

• Find the lifting force, $F_{lifting}$:

$$F_{lifting} = F_w \sin\theta_{rake} = mg\sin\theta_{rake}$$
$$\boldsymbol{F}_{lifting} = 1300(9.81)\sin 2.86° = +636 \ N$$

And finally, use the power formula to determine the answer:

$$P_{max} = (\boldsymbol{F}_{accel} + \boldsymbol{F}_{frict} + \boldsymbol{F}_{lift})\boldsymbol{v}_{max}$$
$$P_{max} = (650 + 446 + 636)1 = 1730 \ watts \quad or \quad 1.73 \ kw \ (2.31 \ hp)$$

Maximum Force

The three component forces, acceleration, friction, and lifting, sum to equal the force needed to accomplish a particular portion of a move: acceleration, constant velocity, or deceleration. Certainly all the parts of the machine powering the move, and the scenery being moved, have to be designed to be able to withstand (with appropriate margins for safety) the worst case value of this sum of forces. Within a particular problem, the friction and lifting forces are, given the simplified assumptions made here, fixed values. They are completely independent of the specific speeds and accelerations of the move. It is the acceleration force that can differ significantly between the calculations done to determine what power motor is needed to run a particular move, and what worst case force might be developed during an emergency stop.

A typical move during the run of a show will involve relatively gentle transitions from stopped to full speed and back to stopped. These accelerations and decelerations, under the control of the automation control system, might take two to four seconds. The goal is to make the scene changes either visually smooth from the audience's point of view, or if in black-out, gentle on the actors, props, and scenery. All this concern is abandoned during an emergency stop or E-stop. These should occur whenever something serious seems to be going wrong, an actor stands out of place in the path of a wagon, when a poorly placed prop is about to hit the stage floor as a lift goes up through a trap opening, or even just if an odd mechanical noise is heard. Triggered either by the automation operator, the stage manager, or stagehands pressing strategically placed red "mushroom" switches, or automatically by sensors placed to sense abnormal conditions, E-stops most commonly involve the complete shutdown of power to all the actuators in the show. Spring-set brakes engage when power is cut, and hydraulic valves center themselves into a stopped position. The deceleration that can occur with an E-stop might take as little as a tenth of a second, which means that the force to decelerate an effect which was potentially traveling at top speed when the E-stop was hit will easily exceed the acceleration force supplied during a move. The net result of this is that while a motor is usually chosen with enough power to run the effect as envisioned, all the other components in the system must be designed with the forces involved in an emergency stop in mind.

Brakes acting on motors act to decelerate the rotation of the motor's shaft, and so an analysis of that will appear later, in Chapter 12, but an example of a hydraulic cylinder directly running a lift can be given here.

EXAMPLE: A lift run by hydraulic cylinders travels a total of 4.5 feet. The weight of lift bed and all anticipated loads equals 1850 lb, and there is no counterweight. The lift's top speed is 1.5 ft/sec, and assume friction will be only 25 lb in this setup. The hydraulic valve running this lift has a manufacturer's specified response time from full open to closed of 0.095 seconds. What is the worst case total force developed by this setup?

SOLUTION: The worst case total force for this lift will occur if an E-stop is hit during full speed travel, because the corresponding rapid deceleration caused by the valve shutting down will create a large F_{accel}. Since it is not instantly obvious whether this worst case will occur during a move up or down, an analysis of both directions will be performed.

The givens are:

F_w = 1850 lb v_{max} = 1.5 ft/sec $F_{friction}$ = 25 lb Δt_{decel} = 0.095 sec

• First find the value for deceleration.

$$v_2 = v_1 + a\Delta t$$

$$0 = 1.5 + a(0.095)$$

$$a = -15.8 \, ft/sec^2$$

• Find the force needed to decelerate the lift, or F_{accel}:

$$F_{accel} = ma = \frac{1850}{32.2}(-15.8) = -908 \, lb$$

Since the force needed to overcome friction is a given, and the lifting force on a vertically running lift simply equals F_w, the three component forces can now be summed appropriately for the two directions the lift moves. The signs of the components must reflect their directions and they will always be:

• F_{accel}, the force needed to accelerate (or decelerate) a mass, will be same sign as velocity during acceleration, the opposite sign from velocity during deceleration.

• $F_{friction}$, the force opposing frictional resistance, will always have the same sign as velocity.

• $F_{lifting}$, the force needed to overcome the tendency of weight to fall, will always have the same sign as the up direction.

Assuming that up is the positive direction, if an E-stop is hit during movement at full speed up, the three forces would sum to:

$$F_{total} = (F_{accel} + F_{frict} + F_{lift})$$

$$F_{total} = (-908 + 25 + 1850) = 967 \, lb$$

Assuming that up is still the positive direction, if an E-stop is hit during movement at full speed down, the three forces would now sum to:

$$\boldsymbol{F}_{total} = (\boldsymbol{F}_{accel} + \boldsymbol{F}_{frict} + \boldsymbol{F}_{lift})$$
$$\boldsymbol{F}_{total} = (+908 - 25 + 1850) = -2733 \; lb$$

The total force during deceleration while moving down is almost three times that during the move up, and it is nearly 900 lb more than the weight of the lift. All parts of the machine would have to be designed with this force in mind.

Problems

1. A small pallet guided by a track in a level stage floor is pulled across stage at speeds reaching a maximum of 3 ft/sec. The pallet and its load weigh 300 lb. The pallet and floor combination has a coefficient of static and kinetic friction of 0.42 and 0.30 respectively. If accelerations will occur no more rapidly than over 1.5 seconds, what maximum power will be needed?

2. A lift with a mass of 850 kg travels a distance of 2.5 m, at fastest, in 8 seconds. If friction is assumed to be negligible, make reasonable assumptions to estimate the power needed to move this lift.

3. A wagon travels up and down a deck raked at 3/4″ to the foot. The wagon and its load weigh 1448 lb, and it is castered on wheels with $\mu_r = 0.035$. If acceleration occurs over 2 seconds, and top speed is 3.5 ft/sec:
   a. What is $\boldsymbol{F}_{accel}$?
   b. What is $\boldsymbol{F}_{fricition}$?
   c. What is $\boldsymbol{F}_{lifting}$?
   d. What is P_{max}?

7

Basic Concepts of Rotational Motion

Definition of Rotational Motion

Rotating machine parts are everywhere: the shaft on an electric motor, a gear inside a reducer, or a winch drum and shaft on its bearings, are all common examples. A wide variety of rotating scenery is less obvious beyond the turntables that might first come to mind, but pivoting panels, doors, *periaktoi*, and jack-knife stages for instance all turn about a single stationary axis of rotation. As was true in the linear motion section, the complexity of the mathematics describing rotation can be considerably reduced by a number of assumptions. In the following chapters, rotation will be assumed to involve only rigid solid materials traveling in a simple circular motion around a single fixed axis of rotation. Rigid solids insures that all points on that material are spinning at the same speed around the same axis. This is not true in fluids and elastic solids, but we do not make liquid doors, or turntables with sheets of rubber. The circular motion assumption is similar to restriction of movement to a straight line made earlier, as this confines all moves to changes in a single dimension. Wheels alone will be the one exception to these assumptions that will be covered here as wheels do both rotate *and* translate, but that discussion will wait until a later chapter.

Coordinate Systems

Two systems of coordinates are commonly used to specify the position of points in space. One is the Cartesian system which, in two-dimensional space, uses a pair of perpendicular axes commonly labeled x and y. The crossing point of these axes is called the origin. Any point on the plane defined by these axes can be specified by two numbers, x and y, each of which relates to the distance between the origin and

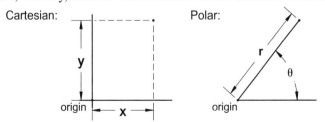

Figure 7.1 Cartesian and polar coordinates

the point in a direction parallel to the corresponding axis (graph on the left of Figure 7.1). The other coordinate system, polar coordinates, describes the position of a point by specifying the length of a line between an origin and the point, and the angle between this line and a given reference direction (shown on the right of Figure 7.1). Polar coordinates are more useful than Cartesian when purely circular rotation occurs because only the angular coordinate changes with time, the length of the radial line remains constant. Given this, polar coordinates will be assumed for all the rotational motion chapters.

Angular Displacement

Since the rotational quantities of angular displacement, angular speed, and angular acceleration are analogous to their linear counterparts, much of the information in this chapter will appear familiar, albeit with different variables. For instance, angular displacement, denoted with the Greek characters "delta theta," $\Delta\theta$, represents the change of angular position over the time interval between t_1 and t_2:

$$\Delta\theta = \theta_2 - \theta_1$$

Where $\Delta\theta$ = the change of angular position (radians, degrees)
        θ_1, θ_2 = angular positions at different times (radians, degrees)

In everyday use angles are expressed in degrees, and everyone is familiar with the fact that one full revolution or turn amounts to a rotation of 360°. Angle measurement in radians however is what must be used in most of the rotational motion formulas presented here. An angular measurement in radians is, by definition, the result of a ratio between arc length and radial distance (left side of Figure 7.2). Regardless of the units used to measure the radius and arc length—feet, meters, or light years—the ratio cancels those units out and the result is a dimensionless number. So, for instance, angular speed will be described in terms of "radians per second" to unambiguously state how the angles are measured, but the true units of angular speed are simply "per second" or "1/sec".

One full revolution, or 360°, in radian measure is the ratio of the circumference of a circle of radius r to that radius, r. Since the circumference is $2\pi r$, the ratio of arc length to radius for one revolution becomes (see right side of Figure 7.2)

$$1\ revolution\ =\ 1\ turn\ =\ 360° = \frac{circumference}{radius}\ =\ \frac{2\pi r}{r}\ =\ 2\pi\ radians$$

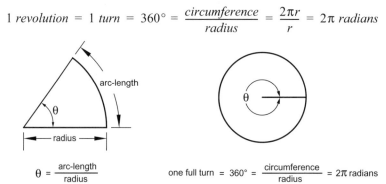

Figure 7.2   Radian angle measurement

This value allows two common conversions to be developed—degrees to radians and turns to radians

$$degrees \times \frac{2\pi \; radians \; per \; revolution}{360 \; degrees \; per \; revolution} = degrees \times 0.0175 = radians$$

$$turns \times 2\pi = turns \times 6.28 = radians$$

EXAMPLE: During a scene change, a turntable rotates 110° (the direction of rotation is intentionally being left out, for reasons to be explained below). What is its angular displacement in radians?

SOLUTION: Since displacement is the subtraction of one position from another, or, stated differently, the difference between two positions, the exact value of the initial position at time t_1 is unimportant as it gets subtracted out in the calculation. So the initial position can be assumed to be anything, and 0° is both a logical choice, and a simple one to use. So then, the givens are:

$$\theta_1 = 0° \qquad \theta_2 = 110°$$

Using the conversion for degrees to radians:

$$\theta_1 = 0° = 0 \; radians \qquad \theta_2 = (0.0175)110° = 1.93 \; radians$$

The angular displacement therefore is:

$$\Delta\theta = \theta_2 - \theta_1 = 1.93 - 0 = 1.93 \; radians$$

Angular displacement is a vector quantity because it has both a magnitude, 25° for example, and a direction, commonly expressed as clockwise or counter-clockwise. Unfortunately, in three dimensional space, angles of finite size do not add commutatively, $A + B \neq B + A$, and this is an unacceptable violation of the rules set up for vector addition (see Figure 7.3). Only infinitesimal angles, those that are not zero but not finite either, add commutatively and this forces the generalized approach to rotation into the world of calculus. If rotation is assumed to always occur around one fixed axis, as it will be assumed here, the addition of finite sized angles does work correctly, though what now do you call these directional finite angles? Different physics or engineering texts use different approaches. Some books use the fully generalized infinitesimal angle calculus approach, some define "pseudo-vectors" that only work in certain situations, and some treat the angles as scalars with signs. The latter approach will be used here, as it meshes perfectly with the conventions used in the linear motion sections. Ultimately this means that every variable, despite not being a true vector, will have a magnitude and a positive or negative sign to denote direction.

The association of a positive or negative sign to a clockwise or counterclockwise rotation is as arbitrary as the analogous situation is in linear problems. As long as a choice is made and then consistently applied throughout the analysis of a move, it does not matter which choice is made. Typically though, for the convenience of slightly simpler math, moves can be considered to begin at zero and progress in the positive direction. If any lifting is involved, the positive direction is

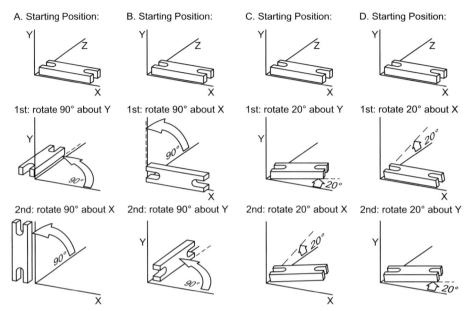

Figure 7.3   Addition of finite angles is not commutative, in other words $A + B \neq B + A$. The top row shows identical starting positions of four different situations. The two left columns demonstrate that $90^\circ_Y + 90^\circ_X \neq 90^\circ_X + 90^\circ_Y$. As angles become smaller, the end results are closer, as shown in the right two columns, but it is only infinitessimal angles that are truly commutative.

the one where power will have to be supplied to accomplish the move. With this, the three torque terms in the maximum power formula, T_{accel}, $T_{friction}$, and $T_{lifting}$ will all be positive.

Angular Speed

How rapidly something changes position over time is a measure of its speed. The angular displacement that occurs over some interval of time is used to define average angular speed as:

$$\bar{\omega} = \frac{\Delta\theta}{\Delta t} = \frac{\theta_2 - \theta_1}{t_2 - t_1}$$

Where $\bar{\omega}$ = average angular speed (rad/sec) The character used is a lower case Greek omega.

θ = angular displacement (rad)

t = time (seconds)

This formula describes *average* angular speed because the exact position of the object being measured is known only at the two times, t_1 and t_2. Between those times it is possible, for instance, that any number of revolutions first clockwise and then identically counterclockwise occurred. The formula, knowing only the positions at the two times, would be blind to the speed required to do those additional rotations.

Instantaneous angular speed, the speed at one point in time, is measured using the formula above only when the time increment, Δt, is infinitesimally small, but not zero. This involves, as it did in the analogous linear world, the use of calculus.

$$\omega = \lim_{\Delta t \to 0} \frac{\Delta \theta}{\Delta t} = \frac{d\theta}{dt}$$

The most common unit for angular speed on equipment such as motors and gear reducers is revolutions per minute, abbreviated rpm. To convert rpm to rad/sec

$$rpm \times \frac{2\pi \; radians \; per \; revolution}{60 \; seconds \; per \; minute} = rpm \times 0.105 = rad/sec$$

Angular Acceleration

The rate at which angular speed changes over time is a measure of angular acceleration.

$$\bar{\alpha} = \frac{\Delta \omega}{\Delta t} = \frac{\omega_2 - \omega_1}{t_2 - t_1}$$

Where $\bar{\alpha}$ = average angular acceleration (rad/sec^2). The character used is a lower case Greek alpha.

ω = angular speed (rad/sec)

t = time (seconds)

For exactly the same reasons as above, this formula provides only an average value for acceleration, and so like instantaneous angular speed, a true measure of angular acceleration at one instant in time will be determined only when the time interval Δt is infinitesimally small.

$$\alpha = \lim_{\Delta t \to 0} \frac{\Delta \omega}{\Delta t} = \frac{d\omega}{dt}$$

To keep the mathematics involved in describing rotational motion exclusively in the realm of algebra, the same assumption about constant acceleration will be made here as it was in the linear section. And so, repeating for emphasis:

Throughout this book, constant acceleration is assumed.

Converting Between Linear and Rotational

Converting linear displacement, speed, and acceleration into their angular counterparts or *vice versa* is often necessary while solving problems, and useful for "reality checks" by converting the less intuitive rotational terms into more familiar linear ones. The simple conversion formulas each involve both a pair of linear and rotational counterparts—x and θ, v and ω, or a and α—and a radial distance at which the conversion is to be done.

$$x = r\theta$$

$$v = r\omega$$

$$a = r\alpha$$

Where x = arc length between the line defining the angle measure origin and the point in question (ft, m)

 v = velocity along a tangent to the circle defined by radius r (ft/sec, m/sec)

 a = acceleration along a tangent to the circle defined by radius r (ft/sec^2, m/sec^2)

 θ, ω, α = as they have been previously defined, but to emphasize, the angles used must be measured in radians.

 r = the distance from the axis of rotation to the point at which the linear term is to be determined (ft, m)

EXAMPLE: What is the linear speed of a point on the edge of a 22 foot diameter turntable spinning at 0.195 rad/sec?

SOLUTION: The givens are:

$$r = 11\ ft \qquad \omega = 0.195\ rad/sec$$

Using the linear to angular speed conversion formula, the speed at the edge of this turntable is:

$$v = r\omega = (11)(0.195) = 2.15\ ft/sec$$

An Aside: Centripetal Acceleration

Newton's first law states, in part, that a moving object will have a constant velocity unless acted on by some net force. Constant velocity implies a constant speed *and* a constant direction—in other words perfectly straight line motion. Whenever rotation occurs, all points on a spinning object, except those directly on the axis of

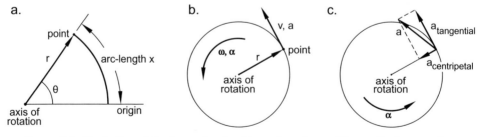

Figure 7.4   Illustration of the terms involved in: a. Angular and linear displacement, b. Angular and linear speed and acceleration, c. Tangential and centripetal acceleration. (In both b. and c. rotational speed and acceleration are indicated in an easily understood way. The actual vectors for rotational velocity and acceleration would be shown by arrows along the axis of rotation, straight out of the page.)

rotation, constantly change direction. Change, be it in the speed of an object or in the direction of its travel, requires an acceleration. Centripetal acceleration is the name given to the always-directed-inward acceleration that must occur during rotation to keep an object spinning in a circle (see Figure 7.4c). Mathematically, centripetal acceleration equals

$$a_{centripetal} = \frac{v^2}{r} = r\omega^2$$

Newton's second law states that force is required to accelerate mass, and so a centripetal force can be defined.

$$F_{centripetal} = ma_{centripetal} = mr\omega^2$$

If you were to tie a weight to a string and spin it around above your head, the tension in the line would equal $F_{centripetal}$. The cohesive forces within the steel of a shaft supply $F_{centripetal}$, keeping the shaft from flying apart as it spins (though there are limits to the speed it can withstand). And a free-standing prop set on a turntable could slide outward, or away from the axis of rotation, if the turntable spins fast enough so that $F_{centripetal}$ exceeds $F_{static\ friction}$.

The Equations of Constant Angular Acceleration

Since it is assumed that acceleration will only take on constant values during the acceleration, constant velocity, and deceleration portions of a typical move, it follows that average and instantaneous accelerations will always be the same within these portions, or $\bar{\alpha} = \alpha$. This implies that the potential for ambiguity in a move between the two times t_1 and t_2 vanishes, and all the aspects of a move can be described by four equations of constant angular acceleration. They are derived by rearranging and combining the simple definitions of average angular velocity and acceleration given earlier. For example, using the equation defining average angular acceleration and the fact that $\bar{\alpha} = \alpha$, we can write:

$$\bar{\alpha} = \alpha = \frac{\Delta\omega}{\Delta t} = \frac{\omega_2 - \omega_1}{\Delta t}$$

Solve this for final angular velocity, ω_2, and one of the equations of constant acceleration is the result:

$$\omega_2 = \omega_1 + \alpha\Delta t$$

In rotational terms the four equations of constant angular acceleration are:

$$\omega_2 = \omega_1 + \alpha\Delta t \qquad \qquad 7.1$$

$$\Delta\theta = \frac{\omega_1 + \omega_2}{2}\Delta t = \bar{\omega}\Delta t \qquad \qquad 7.2$$

$$\Delta\theta = \omega_1\Delta t + \frac{1}{2}\alpha\Delta t^2 \qquad \qquad 7.3$$

$$\omega_2^2 = \omega_1^2 + 2\alpha\Delta\theta \qquad \qquad 7.4$$

Where ω_1, ω_2 = angular speed, at times t_1 and t_2 respectively (rad/sec)
        α = constant angular acceleration (rad/sec^2)
        Δt = the time interval being investigated (sec)
        $\Delta\theta$ = the change of angular position (rad)

EXAMPLE: A 22 foot diameter turntable is to be used for scene change that requires a turn of 180° in 10 seconds. Assume that the total time is split equally between acceleration and deceleration, or in other words that there is a symmetric triangular angular velocity motion profile. What will the top angular speed of the turntable need to be, and what does this equal in linear speed (ft/sec) at the edge of the turntable?

SOLUTION: Since the move is in halves, the top angular speed will occur at the end of the acceleration portion of the move. During acceleration:

$$\Delta t_{accel} = 5 \ sec \qquad \Delta\theta_{accel} = 90° \qquad \omega_1 = 0$$

The angular displacement must be converted to radians for use in any of the equations. The conversion formula could be looked up and used, but it never hurts to have simple techniques memorized for quick use. Since 360° is one full turn, and there are 2π radians per turn, the displacement is:

$$\frac{90°}{360°} \, 2\pi = \frac{1}{4}(2\pi) = 1.57 \ radians$$

Now use Equation 7.2, and solve for top speed.

$$\Delta\theta = \frac{\omega_1 + \omega_2}{2} \Delta t$$

$$1.57 = \left(\frac{0 + \omega_2}{2}\right) 5$$

$$\omega_2 = 0.628 \ rad/sec$$

As is true of many of the rotational quantities, answers like this have little intuitive meaning, so the conversion of an angular to linear speed, for example, can help better show what these numbers really mean. For this problem, the linear speed at the edge of this 22 ft diameter turntable is:

$$v = r\omega = (11)(0.628) = 6.91 \ ft/sec$$

This is roughly double the typical top speed of deck winch, so this is fast, but so long as actors do not need to gracefully step onto or off of the turntable as it is moving, it could be acceptable. If it is not, the problem's givens will have to change to reduce this speed.

Torque

The rotational equivalent of force is torque. Torque is a twisting force, the action a screwdriver applies to a woodscrew, or a wrench applies to a nut. In machinery, motor's and gear reducer's shafts provide torque to drive their loads, and both roller chain sprockets and cable drums convert easily between a torque on a shaft and a force (in the form of chain or cable tension).

Torque results from force acting at some angle and at some distance from an axis of rotation. Mathematically it is defined as:

$$T = r \times F$$

$$T = rF\sin\theta$$

Where T, T = torque, vector and scalar respectively (ft-lb, in-lb, Nm)
        r, r = radius, or the distance from axis of rotation to the point where force is applied (ft, in, m)
        F, F = force (lb, N)
        θ = the angle between the vectors r and F (deg, or rad)

Vectors appear here briefly because they are an essential part of the definition of torque, but they will soon vanish again because the movements of scenery we need to describe are generally simple enough as to be done without the full vector treatment. The bold $\times$ indicates a "cross product", an operation between two vectors with a vector result that follows the "right hand rule" illustrated in Figure 7.5. Basically, the mathematics has to differentiate between the clockwise and counter-clockwise twists that are the directions of torque, and this is accomplished with the direction convention that is a part of the cross product. If, as was done in the linear section, we confine all our problems to one dimension, or one axis of rotation, the direction of torque can only take on two directions, easily represented mathematically as + and – signs.

The scalar component of torque, that is its magnitude or size, involves a sine term to account for the effect that the angle between radius and force has on the value of torque. Forces acting directly through an axis of rotation create no torque, and we all know this from our experience using a wrench (see Figure 7.6a). Forces acting at angles to a radii of other than 0° or 180° will create torque, but for a given radius, the most efficient angle for torque production is 90° (see Figure 7.6b, c).

The units for torque come out of the multiplication of a force times a length, so foot-pounds, abbreviated as ft-lb, and newton-meters, Nm, are common, but so too are inch-pounds used when discussing shafts and gear reducer outputs, and inch-ounces for very small machine components. The order of the American units

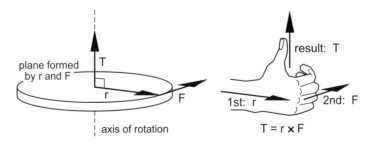

Figure 7.5   The right hand rule helps to determine the direction of T

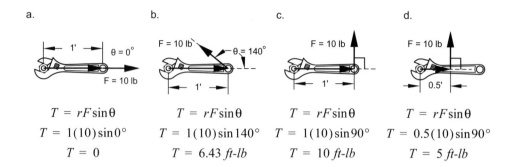

Figure 7.6   Four examples of the interaction of force, radius, and the angle between them to create torque

is not standardized, and so they may appear reversed—lb-ft, lb-in, or oz-in—not really different, just confusing.

EXAMPLE: A winch with a drum 1 foot in diameter is to be designed to pull 1/4″ 7 ×19 aircraft cable to a tension of 700 lb (10% of its rated breaking strength). What torque, in inch-pounds, will be needed on the drum shaft to achieve this?

SOLUTION: The givens are:

$$r_{drum} = 6 \; in \qquad F_{cable} = 700 \; lb$$

A cable coming off a cylindrical drum inherently makes an angle of 90° with the drum radius, and so $\theta = 90°$. The torque needed at the drum shaft is therefore:

$$T = rF \sin\theta$$
$$T = (6)(700)\sin 90° = 4200 \; in\text{-}lb$$

Problems

1. A turntable rotates 1/3 of a revolution in 10 seconds. What is its average angular speed?

2. A motor accelerates from stopped to a speed of 1750 rpm in 0.5 second. What is its average angular acceleration?

3. A door is to be automated with a motor that will open it 110° in 3 seconds. Assuming equal acceleration and deceleration times, what maximum angular speed, in units of both rad/sec and rpm, is needed?

4. A turntable outer edge moving at 2 ft/sec will allow an actor to step relatively seamlessly onto and off of it. Given an 18 foot diameter turntable, what angular velocity is associated with this edge speed?

5. A rotating wall turns half a turn in 10 seconds. The acceleration and deceleration portions of the move each occur in 2 seconds. What top speed, in rad/sec, is needed?

6. A gearmotor output is rated by the manufacturer at a torque of 4450 in-lb. If a drum 10″ in diameter is directly connected to this shaft, what cable pull will result?

8

The Torque to Accelerate Mass, T_{accel}

Overview

In linear motion, all parts of an object, or put more specifically all of its component masses, are accelerated at the same rate. Mass in Newton's second law, $\boldsymbol{F} = m\boldsymbol{a}$, is simply the mass of the object being moved, regardless of how that mass is distributed into, for instance, wagon structure, walls, props, or performers. When an object rotates however, the spacial distribution of mass relative to the axis of rotation has a major impact on the torque needed to accelerate it. Mass on or near the axis moves slowly compared with mass further out. A given angular acceleration on a compact, tight-to-the-axis piece will require much less torque than will a piece of the same mass that is much more spread out (see the box below). So instead of just mass, moment of inertia is the term used to describe the twofold effect of mass *and* its distribution relative to the axis of rotation on the acceleration of rotating objects. The calculation of moment of inertia, while not difficult, is usually more time consuming than finding mass alone, and so rotational problems often take considerably longer to complete than their linear counterparts.

Newton's second law of motion, in rotational terms, uses moment of inertia and angular acceleration to define the torque needed to accelerate mass, T_{accel}. This torque then becomes one of the three component torques that are added together in the rotational version of the maximum power formula:

$$P_{max} = (T_{accel} + T_{friction} + T_{lifting})\,\omega_{max}$$

- Someday when you have a roughly 2 or 3 foot piece of pipe nearby do this simple demonstration. Spin the pipe back and forth quickly with your hand, maybe a quarter of a turn or so, first with the axis of rotation running down the center of the pipe, and second with your hand in the center of the length, baton-twirler-like (goggles, steel-toed shoes, and a safety barrier please.). Same piece of pipe, same mass, but a very different distribution of mass relative to the axis of rotation in the two situations. The first should be quite easy to do, the second much harder to get anywhere near the same accelerations.

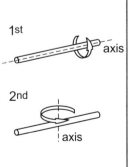

Moment of Inertia

The moment of inertia of an object is the rotational equivalent of mass, and it relates to both the mass of an object, and how that mass is distributed relative to the axis of rotation. Just as the force to accelerate a mass along a straight line path is proportional to mass and acceleration, $F_{accel} = ma$, the torque it takes to angularly accelerate an object is proportional to its moment of inertia and angular acceleration, $T_{accel} = I\alpha$. Since the major difference between m and I occurs in having to account for the location of mass, a brief derivation of moment of inertia will show how this is done.

Any given object can be divided into many small individual pieces that are each of insignificant size compared to the whole. These small pieces will have some mass and therefore would require some force to linearly accelerate them. Newton's second law says that, for piece number 1, that force would be:

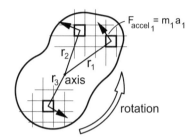

$$F_{accel_1} = m_1 a_1$$

Since the mass is part of a rotating object, a conversion can be made between linear and rotational acceleration. Assuming that a_1 is perpendicular to r_1:

$$a_1 = r_1 \alpha$$

Angular acceleration, α, needs no subscript because the angular acceleration of a rigid solid object is the same everywhere on the object. By using this formula, a substitution can be made in Newton's law for linear acceleration

$$F_{accel_1} = m_1 r_1 \alpha$$

The force to accelerate this one piece could be developed from a torque acting at the axis of rotation. This torque, just for piece number 1, would be

$$T_{accel_1} = r_1 F_{accel_1} = r_1 (m_1 r_1 \alpha) = m_1 r_1^2 \alpha$$

This equation describes the torque needed to angularly accelerate one small piece of the whole object. A number of mr^2 terms, unique to each of the other pieces of the object, can be summed together to account for all the other small masses that make up the spinning object with the result being

$$T_{accel} = \left(\sum_{i = 1 \, to \, ...} m_i r_i^2 \right) \alpha = I\alpha$$

The summation term in parentheses is called the mass moment of inertia (to distinguish it from the completely different area moment of inertia used in structural calculations), and it is given the symbol I. Due to its r^2 component, moment of inertia has a dependence on the distribution of mass relative to the axis of rotation, not just the total amount of mass, and this is the fundamental difference between m and I.

Fortunately, the summation of hundreds of mr^2 terms is unnecessary for us as the moment of inertia of many basic shapes has been worked out into case formulas, the most commonly used of which are shown in Figure 8.1 below. The axes of rotation in all these cases both pass through the object's center of mass, and have a particular orientation to the shape that is important to note. A typical turntable would use the upper left hand DISK formula for instance, the middle left DISK spins differently, perhaps like some round revolving door. Lastly, these formulas

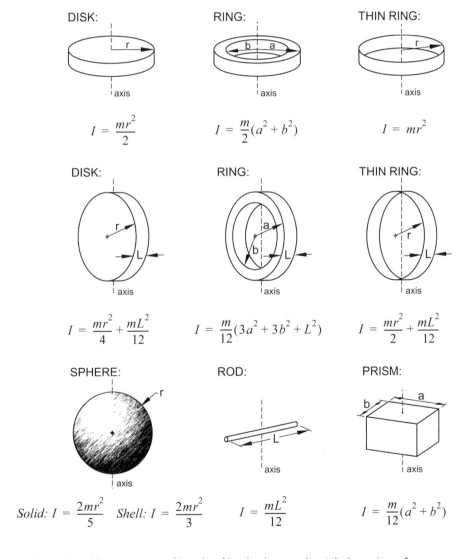

Figure 8.1 Mass moment of inertia of basic shapes about their centers of mass

assume a homogenous distribution of mass, meaning similar construction through-out the shape, with no heavy or light areas of any significance.

The units for moment of inertia are mass times length squared, so in the U.S. they are slug-feet^2, and in the metric world kilogram-meter^2. Neither of these offer any intuitive meaning since we have no daily experience with what, for instance, 426.2 slug-ft^2 means, so be careful and methodical in your calculations, and trust your results.

EXAMPLE: A simple 16 foot diameter turntable consists of just three layers of 1/2″ plywood (1.5 lb/ft^2) thoroughly glued and screwed together. Its casters attach to the floor, wheel-up, and so their mass does not spin with the table. What is the moment of inertia of this disk?

SOLUTION: From Figure 2.1, the moment of inertia of a homogeneous disk spinning around its center point is

$$I = \frac{mr^2}{2}$$

The radius is a given, so only the mass needs to be determined. The weight of the plywood per square foot is known, and that times the area of a 16′ diameter circle times 3 for the three ply layers will give the disk's weight.

$$F_w = layers \times weight/ft^2 \times area$$

$$F_w = (3)(1.5)(\pi 8^2) = 905 \; lb$$

This weight, converted to mass, can be inserted into the formula for moment of inertia to get the desired answer.

$$I = \frac{mr^2}{2} = \frac{(905/32.2)8^2}{2} = 899 \; slug\text{-}ft^2$$

The definition of moment of inertia involves summation, or the adding up of many separate moments. This implies that the moments of inertia of objects more complex than the simple shapes in the case formulas can be obtained by summing —or subtracting to remove material for a hole—the moments of various parts.

EXAMPLE (SI): A 5 meter diameter turntable has a 2 meter square hole in its center. The mass of the turntable is 36.5 kg/m^2. What is the moment of iner-tia of this object?

SOLUTION: Conceptually, this turntable could be constructed by build-ing the full disk first, and then sawing out and discarding the material in the square hole (a ridiculously wasteful way to do it in reality). Mathe-matically the process is identical. Determine the moment of inertia of a full 5 meter diameter disk, and then subtract from that the moment of the square section that is removed.

$$I_{turntable} = I_{full\ disk} - I_{hole}$$

$$I_{turntable} = \left(\frac{m_{full\ disk}\ r^2}{2}\right) - \left(\frac{m_{hole}}{12}(a^2 + b^2)\right)$$

The masses of the full disk and the square section to be removed are

$$mass = 36.5\ kg/m^2 \times area$$

$$m_{full\ disk} = 36.5(\pi)(2.5^2) = 717\ kg$$

$$m_{hole} = 36.5(2^2) = 146\ kg$$

The moment of inertia of this turntable is therefore

$$I_{turntable} = \frac{mr^2}{2} - \frac{m}{12}(a^2 + b^2) = \frac{717(2.5^2)}{2} - \frac{146}{12}(2^2 + 2^2) = 2140\ kgm^2$$

Transferring the Axis of Rotation

In every case shown in Figure 8.1, the axis of rotation passes through the shape's center of mass. While this is almost always true for the disk that makes up a typical turntable, other rotating pieces—jackknife wagons, drawbridges, and doors for example—rotate around axes that do not pass through their centers of mass. Also objects found on turntables, from furniture to flats, are rarely sited with their centers of mass along the axis of rotation. The simple formula below allows the calculation of moments of inertia for these situations.

$$I_{tr} = I_{c\ of\ m} + mr_{tr}^2$$

Where I_{tr} =   the moment of inertia of the object about an axis of rotation not passing through its center of mass (slug-ft^2, kgm^2)

$I_{c\ of\ m}$ = the moment of inertia of the object relative to an axis of rotation that passes through its center of mass (typically from one of the formulas in Figure 8.1). Both the actual axis of rotation and the axis implied by the $I_{c\ of\ m}$ formula used must be parallel. (slug-ft^2, kgm^2)

m =   the mass of the object (slugs, kg)

r_{tr} =   the transfer distance, or the perpendicular distance between the objects axis of rotation and its center of mass (ft, m)

The two terms in this formula imply that an object's moment of inertia will always start with a value related to it spinning around its center of mass (when $r_{tr} = 0$), and it will only grow larger from there as the axis of rotation moves away from that center (when $r_{tr} > 0$). The interaction of these two terms has several implications, and they are best illustrated with examples.

EXAMPLE: What is the moment of inertia of a 3′ by 7′-6″ solid core door that weighs 96 lb? Assume that the door is 1-3/4″ thick, and that its hinges locate the axis of rotation 1″ off one of the corners of a long edge.

SOLUTION: This door does not rotate about its center of mass, but about the hinge pins that form an axis of rotation roughly a foot and a half away. This distance is the transfer distance, r_{tr}, in the transfer of axis formula. Using the Pythagorean theorem, this distance can be calculated accurately. (A perfectly valid alternate approach to finding this distance would be to use a CAD program's dimension or ruler on a drafting of the door.)

$$hypotenuse = \sqrt{a^2 + b^2} = \sqrt{18^2 + (1.75/2 + 1)^2} = 18.1 \ in \ \ or \ \ 1.51 \ ft$$

The moment of inertia for this door, using the formula for a prism for $I_{c \, of \, m}$, can now be determined. Never forget to convert as needed, weights to mass, inches to feet.

$$I_{door} = I_{c \, of \, m} + mr_{tr}^2$$

$$I_{door} = \left(\frac{m}{12}(a^2 + b^2)\right) + mr_{tr}^2 = \left(\frac{(96/32.2)}{12}[3^2 + (1.75/12)^2]\right) + (96/32.2)1.51^2$$

$$I_{door} = 2.24 + 6.80 = 9.04 \ slug\text{-}ft^2$$

Note that the moment of inertia of the door about its center of mass accounts for less than one third of the result. The relative proportions between the $I_{c \, of \, m}$ and mr_{tr}^2 terms will vary depending on the shape of the object and the translation distance, but often when the axis of rotation is located outside of the object, the mr_{tr}^2 term predominates. As r_{tr} gets even larger, you may not even need to determine $I_{c \, of \, m}$ as it becomes a negligible part of the sum (as will be shown in the next example).

Also, it is very easy to get into trouble when doing a problem such as this by sketching the elevation of the door, labeling in the dimensions, here 3′ by 7′-6″, and then using those in the $I_{c \, of \, m}$ of a prism formula. The resulting answer would be wrong though, because the axis of rotation implied by those dimensions would be perpendicular to that formed by the hinges. The actual and through-the-center-of-mass axes must be parallel.

EXAMPLE: As part of a set on a turntable, a grand piano sits near the edge, with its center of mass 14 feet from the axis of rotation. What moment of inertia will this piano add to the whole set? Assume the piano weighs 520 lb.

SOLUTION: The shape of a grand piano does not match any of the simple shapes shown in Figure 8.1, nor is it even closely a sum of several simple shapes. This means that any shape we might use in calculating the piano's $I_{c\,of\,m}$ term could result in a value far from the piano's actual moment. To demonstrate that, in this case, this is not a concern, assume the piano is just a disk 6 feet in diameter, and calculate the transferred moment of inertia.

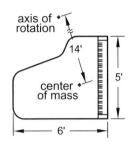

axis of rotation

center of mass

14'

5'

6'

$$I_{piano} = I_{c\,of\,m} + mr_{tr}^2$$

$$I_{piano} = \frac{mr_{disk}^2}{2} + mr_{tr}^2 = \frac{(520/32.2)3^2}{2} + (520/32.2)14^2$$

$$I_{piano} = 72.7 + 3170 = 3240 \; slug\text{-}ft^2$$

Here the $I_{c\,of\,m}$ term is just a bit more than 2% of the total moment of inertia. It is unlikely that the simplification of the grand piano shape into a disk shape is off by anywhere near a factor of two, but even if it is, the resulting moment of inertia would still fall within 3240 slug-ft^2 ±5%. This is a much closer tolerance result than can be expected for any of the estimates involving friction used elsewhere in most problems. This crude estimate of $I_{c\,of\,m}$ is possible here, of course, because the transfer distance, r_{tr}, is large relative to the size of the piano. There are no hard and fast guidelines indicating when quick approximations are acceptable, but a first pass run of the numbers will show the relative balance between the $I_{c\,of\,m}$ and mr_{tr}^2 terms, and it will then be apparent whether more exacting work needs to be done.

This type of situation is a very common one. Furniture, sculpted scenic pieces, and even actors are not the simple shapes commonly found in mass moment of inertia charts. The mechanical designer will constantly have to make choices that approximate reality, and that will lead them quickly to an answer that ultimately results in a successful machine.

An Aside: WK^2

Most of the engineering world uses the mass moment of inertia presented here (albeit in metric units of course), but you will find, primarily in the reference sections of American machinery manufacturers catalogs, a weight based moment of inertia. Usually expressed as wk^2, or weight times the something called the mass radius of gyration squared. By definition, this radius of gyration is

$$k = \sqrt{\frac{I}{m}}$$

Charts of case formulas exist for radius of gyration just as they do for moment of inertia, but in order to demonstrate the relationship between I and wk^2, just substitute this square root term for k, use this book's variable symbol for weight, F_w, in place of w, and simplify the resulting equation (Customary units are assumed here, as wk^2 appears to be unused in the metric world.):

$$wk^2 = F_w\left(\sqrt{\frac{I}{m}}\right)^2 = F_w\frac{I}{m} = F_w\frac{I}{F_w/32.2} = 32.2\,I$$

So this says simply that wk^2 is just 32.2 times as large as I, which follows logically from the often used conversion from weight to mass

$$m = \frac{F_w}{32.2}$$

which basically says weight is 32.2 times as large as mass.

Ultimately there is no difference in results between the mathematics set up to use wk^2 and that presented in this chapter using I. Just be aware that there is another variation out there.

The Torque to Accelerate Mass

To accelerate a spinning object, some amount of torque must be supplied at the axis of rotation just to accelerate the mass of the object. The exact amount of angular acceleration obtained for a given torque is defined in Newton's second law, written here in rotational form:

> When a torque acts on an object, that object will angularly acceler-
> ate in the direction of the torque. The magnitude of the angular
> acceleration that results will be directly related to the magnitude of
> the torque, and inversely related to the magnitude of the moment
> of inertia of the object. Mathematically:
>
> $$T_{accel} = I\alpha$$

Where T_{accel} = the torque needed for angular acceleration (ft-lb, Nm)
         I = the moment of inertia of the object (slug-ft^2, kgm^2)
         α = angular acceleration of the object (rad/sec^2)

Newton's law defines, as it did in the linear chapters, the first of the three torque components in the maximum power formula.

$$P_{max} = (T_{accel} + T_{friction} + T_{lifting})\,\omega_{max}$$

The torque needed to accelerate mass, T_{accel}, is in all ways analogous to its linear counterpart, F_{accel}. The torque to accelerate is independent of both the orientation of the spinning piece, and of any friction involved, as the effects of those conditions are covered with the friction and lifting torque terms.

The units involved in this formula, as is common for rotation, have little intuitive meaning. It may not even appear that the units on one side of the equation could possibility equal those on the other, but by using a process called dimensional analysis, it can be proven that this is true. Start with the given units:

$$T_{accel} = I\alpha$$

$$ft\text{-}lb = slug\text{-}ft^2 \times rad/sec^2$$

Using the units from the linear motion version of Newton's second law solved for mass, an equivalent is found for slugs:

$$m = \frac{F}{a}$$

$$slugs = \frac{lb}{ft/sec^2} = \frac{lb\text{-}sec^2}{ft}$$

Finally recall that radian angle measurement has no units, the "rad" listed is there merely to describe the angular measurement technique used. So finally, writing out these new versions of the units, and canceling out as appropriate yields matching units on both sides of the equals sign:

$$T_{accel} = I\alpha$$

$$ft\text{-}lb = \left(\frac{lb\text{-}\cancel{sec^2}}{\cancel{ft}}\right)\cancel{ft^2} \times \frac{1}{\cancel{sec^2}} = ft\text{-}lb$$

EXAMPLE: Calculate T_{accel} for a typical winch drum assembly that runs to a top speed of 1 rev/sec in 2 seconds. The dimensions are as shown, and assume that all the parts are steel, with a density of 0.282 lb/in^3. Chapter 20 on drums shows typical drum construction in greater detail than the simplified view used here.

SOLUTION: The angular acceleration can be determined using the givens and one of the equations of constant angular acceleration. First convert the top speed to the units needed in the formulas.

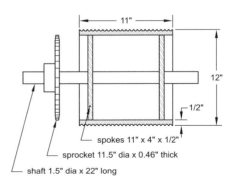

spokes 11" x 4" x 1/2"
sprocket 11.5" dia x 0.46" thick
shaft 1.5" dia x 22" long

$$\omega_{max} = 1\ rev/sec \times 2\pi\ rad/rev = 2\pi\ rad/sec$$

The other givens are:

$$\Delta t_{accel} = 2\ sec \qquad \omega_1 = 0\ rad/sec$$

Equation 7.1 works with these givens and will provide the needed answer.

$$\omega_2 = \omega_1 + \alpha \Delta t$$

$$2\pi = 0 + \alpha(2)$$

$$\alpha = 3.14 \ rad/sec^2$$

The moment of inertia for the drum will equal the sum of the moments of inertia of its parts: drum, spokes, shaft, and sprocket. Since the weight of these parts is needed to find their masses, and the density of steel is given, the volumes of these parts must be calculated.

$$V_{drum} = (area_{od} - area_{id}) \times length = (\pi r_{od}^2 - \pi r_{id}^2)l = (\pi 6^2 - \pi 5.5^2)11 = 199 \ in^3$$

$$V_{spokes} = 2 \times length \times width \times height = 2(11)(4)(0.5) = 44.0 \ in^3$$

$$V_{shaft} = area \times length = (\pi r^2)l = \pi(0.75^2)22 = 38.9 \ in^3$$

$$V_{sprocket} = area \times length = (\pi r^2)l = \pi(5.75^2)0.46 = 47.8 \ in^3$$

The weights, which comes from volume times density, and masses, from weight divided by g, of these parts are:

$$F_{w \ drum} = 199(0.282) = 56.1 \ lb \qquad m_{drum} = 56.1/32.2 = 1.74 \ slugs$$

$$F_{w \ spokes} = 44.0(0.282) = 12.4 \ lb \qquad m_{spokes} = 12.4/32.2 = 0.385 \ slugs$$

$$F_{w \ shaft} = 38.9(0.282) = 11.0 \ lb \qquad m_{shaft} = 11.0/32.2 = 0.342 \ slugs$$

$$F_{w \ sprocket} = 47.8(0.282) = 13.5 \ lb \qquad m_{sprocket} = 13.5/32.2 = 0.419 \ slugs$$

This list slightly simplifies the real parts. Both the sprocket and spokes have a hole where the shaft passes through them. This material was not removed in these calculations. The outer edges of the spokes are rounded to fit inside the drum, not square as the calcs assume. The sprocket has a hub (as the spokes would too on a real drum), and it was not considered. All of these things are small relative to the masses that were accounted for, and to some extent the extras left in account for the hub's omission. The end result should still be sufficiently accurate for typical show estimates, and this is what is most important. Nothing except time, and perhaps sanity, stops you from calculating extremely accurate values for mass and moment of inertia, but always weigh the time spent for the value of the accuracy obtained.

The moments of inertia are calculated from the part's given dimensions, here converted to feet, and their just determined masses.

$$I_{drum} = \frac{m}{2}(a^2 + b^2) = \frac{1.74}{2}(0.5^2 + 0.458^2) = 0.400 \ slug\text{-}ft^2$$

$$I_{spokes} = 2\left(\frac{m}{12}(a^2 + b^2)\right) = 2\left(\frac{0.385}{12}(0.333^2 + 0.917^2)\right) = 0.0611 \ slug\text{-}ft^2$$

$$I_{shaft} = \frac{mr^2}{2} = \frac{0.342(0.0625^2)}{2} = 0.000668 \; slug\text{-}ft^2$$

$$I_{sprocket} = \frac{mr^2}{2} = \frac{0.419(0.479^2)}{2} = 0.0481 \; slug\text{-}ft^2$$

Summing the moments of inertia of these parts gives the moment of the whole assembly.

$$I_{total} = 0.400 + 0.0611 + 0.000668 + 0.0481 = 0.510 \; slug\text{-}ft^2$$

The last step to answer this problem is to calculate T_{accel}:

$$T_{accel} = I\alpha = (0.510)(3.14) = 1.60 \; ft\text{-}lb$$

The answer is a small value when compared to the hundreds of foot-pounds typical winch gear-motors put out. In short, after all this, the torque needed to accelerate just a winch drum is often negligible relative to the torque needed to accelerate the much more massive scenery run by the winch.

Since moment of inertia is generally proportional to the square of the radius, moments up into the tens of thousands of slug-ft^2 easily come about from turntables with radii of 10, 15, or even as at the Met in New York, 29 feet. Unlike the winch drum in the problem just completed, the torque needed to accelerate these massive objects, even with relatively low accelerations, is considerable.

EXAMPLE: A turntable 30 feet in diameter is to be capable of a top speed of one full turn every 20 seconds. Its control system will set the shortest acceleration time to this speed at 1.5 seconds. Scenery on the turntable will consist mainly of a wall and two platforms, with dimensions and weights as shown. Up to ten actors might be on the table during a move, and so their weight should be considered. What torque will be needed just to accelerate the mass of this turntable, or what is T_{accel}?

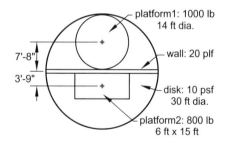

SOLUTION: A typical order of solution will be followed here:
- Determine acceleration based on the problem requirements. A check of the maximum linear edge speed is worth doing here too if you are concerned that at top speed it might be excessively high.
- Break up the object into a logical collection of parts, and then find their weights, masses, and moments of inertia.
- Sum all the values of inertia, and using acceleration find T_{accel}.

With this process in mind, the givens relating to acceleration are:

$$\omega_{max} = 1 \text{ turn every } 20 \text{ sec} = 3 \text{ rpm} \qquad \omega_1 = 0 \qquad \Delta t_{accel} = 1.5 \text{ sec}$$

Convert the given maximum speed into rad/sec.

$$\omega_{max} = 3 \text{ rpm} \qquad \omega_{max} = \frac{3(2\pi)}{60} = 0.314 \text{ rad/sec}$$

Next use an equation of constant angular acceleration to determine α.

$$\omega_2 = \omega_1 + \alpha \Delta t$$
$$0.314 = 0 + \alpha(1.5)$$
$$\alpha = 0.209 \text{ rad/sec}^2$$

Check the linear speed at the edge of the turntable, mainly to get an intuitive sense of how fast the move will feel.

$$v_{max} = r\,\omega_{max} = 15(0.314) = 4.71 \text{ ft/sec}$$

A typical walking speed of 3 mph equals 4.4 ft/sec, so the turntable edge will be moving somewhat faster, and actors will probably not be able to make visually graceful moves onto and off of the turntable. The question of what an actor might look like getting up onto a turntable is so subjective that it is impossible to give a "yes it will work"/"no it won't work" answer. The look of the action, the skill of the actor, the audience's focus on the actor or elsewhere, the lighting of the moment, and on and on will ultimately set whether it is acceptable. Here assume that this speed is acceptable.

Now the weights, masses, and moments of inertia of the various parts of the turntable need to be determined. Everything but the ten actors is very straightforward.

$$F_{w\,disk} = \pi(15^2)(10) = 7070 \text{ lb} \qquad m_{disk} = 7070/32.2 = 220 \text{ slugs}$$
$$F_{w\,wall} = 30(20) = 600 \text{ lb} \qquad m_{wall} = 600/32.2 = 18.6 \text{ slugs}$$
$$F_{w\,plat1} = 1000 \text{ lb} \qquad m_{plat1} = 1000/32.2 = 31.1 \text{ slugs}$$
$$F_{w\,plat2} = 800 \text{ lb} \qquad m_{plat2} = 800/32.2 = 24.8 \text{ slugs}$$

The weights of the actors will be an on-the-high-side estimate of an average for the cast. Usually some number between 150 and 200 pounds is used. This may sound high, but costumes and hand props can add significant weight, and there is little penalty for slightly overestimating weight, especially when compared to the potential of a non-functioning effect. So here assume 175 lb per actor.

$$F_{w\,actor} = 175 \text{ lb} \qquad m_{actor} = 175/32.2 = 5.43 \text{ slugs}$$

The moments of inertia of the four scenic components are, at worst, merely tedious to figure. The disk is the easiest:

$$I_{disk} = \frac{mr^2}{2} = \frac{220(15^2)}{2} = 24800 \; slug\text{-}ft^2$$

The wall can be considered either a prism, with some estimated dimension given to the wall thickness, or, and this will require some explanation, a rod. If one dimension of the prism shape is zero, meaning in reality simply that it is of negligible size compared to the other, then that term vanishes from the formula, leaving a result identical to that of the rod. So the rod shape formula can also represent a flat, or a sheet of plywood, or any other plane shape as long as the axis of rotation runs through the center of mass, and parallel with the surface of the plane.

The moment of inertia of the wall, figured both as a prism and as a rod, with the answers in this case not rounded to the typical three significant figures is:

$$I_{wall} = \frac{m}{12}(a^2 + b^2) = \frac{18.6}{12}(30^2 + 1^2) = 1396.55 \; slug\text{-}ft^2$$

$$I_{wall} = \frac{mr^2}{12} = \frac{18.6(30^2)}{12} = 1395.0 \; slug\text{-}ft^2$$

Both these values are effectively the same, implying that, in this case, the exact thickness of the wall has no great bearing on the final answer.

The centers of mass of both platforms are offset from the turntable's axis of rotation, so their axes will have to be transferred. For platform 1

$$I_{plat1} = I_{c\,of\,m} + mr_{tr}^{\;2} = \frac{mr_{plat1}^2}{2} + mr_{tr}^{\;2}$$

$$I_{plat1} = \frac{31.1(7^2)}{2} + 31.1(7.67^2)$$

$$I_{plat1} = 762 + 1830 = 2590 \; slug\text{-}ft^2$$

The moment of inertia of platform 2 is found in a similar way.

$$I_{plat2} = I_{c\,of\,m} + mr_{tr}^{\;2} = \frac{m}{12}(a^2 + b^2) + mr_{tr}^{\;2}$$

$$I_{plat2} = \frac{24.8}{12}(6^2 + 15^2) + 24.8(3.75^2)$$

$$I_{plat2} = 539 + 349 = 888 \; slug\text{-}ft^2$$

And finally to the self-mobile chunks of mass, the actors. Since the blocking for the scene changes would normally be a complete unknown during the technical design period, a worst case situation will have to be imagined. Assume here that all 10 actors are standing out near the edge of the turntable, somewhere along a 13 foot radius circle. Since this 13 feet will far exceed the dimensions of a person, the $I_{c\,of\,m}$ in the transfer axis formula need not be all that accurate. And so, assuming a person is a disk 1.5 ft in diameter:

$$I_{actors} = 10(I_{c\,of\,m} + mr_{tr}^2) = 10\left(\frac{mr_{actor}^2}{2} + m\,r_{tr}^2\right)$$

$$I_{actors} = 10\left(\frac{5.43(0.75^2)}{2} + 5.43(13^2)\right)$$

$$I_{actors} = 10(1.53 + 918) = 9200\ slug\text{-}ft^2$$

The moment of inertia about the center of mass term is mere tenths of a percent of the transferred axis inertia, and so in this case the accuracy of the person-is-a-disk assumption is acceptable.

Lastly, the moments of inertia can be summed and multiplied by the angular acceleration to get the torque needed just to accelerate the mass of this turntable.

$$T_{accel} = (I_{disk} + I_{wall} + I_{plat1} + I_{plat2} + I_{actors})\alpha$$

$$T_{accel} = (24800 + 1400 + 2590 + 888 + 9200)\,0.209$$

$$T_{accel} = (38878)0.209 = 8130\ ft\text{-}lb$$

Fully writing out the final formula helps show the relative proportion of the moments of the different parts, something that is easily missed if the numbers are spread across multiple pages, or just passed through a calculator unrecorded. Notice here that the actors, who would not appear on the set designer's drawings of this effect, exceed by far everything but the disk. Never forget those actors!

Rolling Objects

Anything that rolls on a surface—a wheel, a ball, or a piece of pipe—moves both linearly and rotationally. A wheel, for instance, spins around its axle as it simultaneously moves some distance across the floor. To accelerate rolling objects, some amount of power will have to go toward each of these motions, and the formulas involved need information on both the mass and moment of inertia of the rolling object. In addition, since rolling can be driven by either a torque applied to the wheels, as an engine does to the wheels in a car, or by a force, as in pushing the car when it's run out of gas, there are two formulas to account for these two possibilites.

$$T_{accel\,roll} = (I_{c\,of\,m} + mr_{wheel}^2)\,\alpha$$

$$F_{accel\,roll} = \left(\frac{I_{c\,of\,m}}{r_{wheel}^2} + m\right)a$$

Where $T_{accel\,roll}$ = the torque needed at a wheel's axle for acceleration (ft-lb, Nm)
$I_{c\,of\,m}$ = the moment of inertia of the wheel about its center of mass (slug-ft^2, kgm^2)
m = mass of the wheel (slug, kg)

r_{wheel} = radius of the wheel (ft, m)

α = angular acceleration of the wheel (rad/sec^2)

$F_{accel\ roll}$ = the force needed, parallel to the direction of acceleration, a, to accelerate the wheel (ft-lb, Nm)

a = acceleration of the wheel (ft/sec^2, m/sec^2)

EXAMPLE: The wheel of a typical 3″ diameter caster weighs approximately 1 pound, and is basically a homogeneous disk rotating about its center of mass. What force is needed to accelerate it as a rolling wheel, and, just for comparison, to accelerate its mass linearly as if it were a sliding piece? Assume $a = 3\ ft/sec^2$.

SOLUTION: Two results are needed, both forces. The force needed to roll a disk can be found by inserting its moment of inertia formula into the-force-to-roll-a-wheel formula

$$F_{accel\ roll} = \left(\frac{I_{c\ of\ m}}{r^2_{wheel}} + m \right) a = \left(\frac{(mr^2)/2}{r^2_{wheel}} + m \right) a = \left(\frac{m}{2} + m \right) a = 1.5ma$$

Of course the force needed to linearly accelerate something is just

$$F_{accel} = ma$$

and so even without any specific values put in to the formulas yet, these show that the force needed to accelerate a disk-like wheel is exactly 50% more than what is needed just to accelerate it linearly. The mass of the caster's wheel is

$$m = \frac{1}{32.2} = 0.0311\ slugs$$

And so finally the force needed to accelerate this wheel, both rolling and sliding is

$$F_{accel} = ma = 0.0311(3) = 0.0933\ lb$$

$$F_{accel} = 1.5ma = 1.5(0.0311)(3) = 0.140\ lb$$

The end result implies two things. The first is that despite the fact that it does take more force to accelerate a rolling wheel than slide it, the considerably greater friction during sliding (not accounted for here), would far outweigh this rolling acceleration penalty. Second the force to accelerate a rolling is not a large number in the grand scheme of things, so unless the weight of the wheels on a unit are a significant percentage of the whole weight, say 10%, then this extra force due to rolling can be ignored.

Problems

1. What is the moment of inertia of an 8 foot diameter turntable disk constructed entirely of just 2 laminated layers of 3/4″ plywood? Assume the turntable spins around its center in a conventional manner, and that 3/4″ ply weighs 2.2 lb/ft^2.

2. A drawbridge, 11 ft wide by 15 ft high pivots along its lower narrow edge. It weighs 550 lb and will move 110° in 10 seconds. What torque is needed just to accelerate it?

3. A model of planet Earth, 2 m in diameter, is constructed as a hollow sphere using plaster and wire reinforcing mesh. It has a mass of 108 kg. What is its moment of inertia?

4. A jackknife stage is made from a 15 by 30 ft platform that pivots around an axis located at one of its corners. The platform weighs an average of 11 psf. What torque is needed to accelerate it if it spins 1/4 of a turn with 2 second acceleration and deceleration times, and a top speed of 0.4 rad/sec?

5. A *periaktos* is built by forming three identical 1 m wide flats into a triangular column 5.5 m tall. The axis of rotation runs the long length of the column, through the exact center of the triangular shape. If each flat has a mass of 24 kg, what torque is needed to accelerate this assembly if it must turn 120° in 4 seconds? Assume a triangular velocity motion profile (i.e., 2 seconds each for acceleration and deceleration), and that the mass of any framing beyond the flats is negligible.

6. A turntable is to be built for a car show as shown in the illustration. What is the approximate worst case moment of inertia for this setup if up to three people (assume they weigh 175 lb each) are scheduled to appear on the turntable with the car?

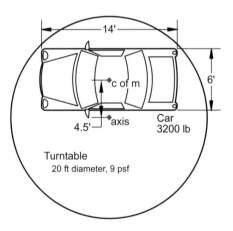

9

The Torque to Overcome Friction, $T_{friction}$

Rotation and Friction

There is nothing different in the behavior of friction due to the differences between linear and rotational motion—friction is friction—but how it is taken into account does differ, since friction will appear as a torsional rather than linear resistance to movement. Some component of the total torque applied to rotate an object will be the torque needed just to overcome friction, and this component, $T_{friction}$, is found in the rotational version of the formula used to estimate the maximum power needed by a given effect:

$$P_{max} = (T_{accel} + T_{friction} + T_{lifting})\, \omega_{max}$$

There is also nothing about rotational motion that negates the complexity involved in accurately predicting friction. The interaction of different materials, in sliding or rolling situations, with or without a lubricant, at different speeds, temperatures, and loads, will all affect the frictional losses of a particular setup. Add in the everyday possibilities of dirt, wear, overloading, and misalignment and accurate predictions become even harder. Fortunately the same rough approximations made in Chapter 4 relative to linear friction will serve us well here too. So then:

Friction will be considered only between solid materials, that can either slide against or roll over each other, in two states of motion—static, or not moving relative to each other, and dynamic, when movement does occur. Lubricants will reduce the coefficients of friction, but speeds will be assumed to be low enough that hydrodynamic effects can be ignored.

These assumptions will lead to conservative, worst case values for the situation being analyzed, but as always with friction other not easily quantified factors might completely throw off your best made estimates. For example, fixed mounted casters are used for most turntables, but on a turtle (a scenic unit that both spins and tracks) swivel casters might be used. As the unit goes from tracking to rotating, or as it changes its direction of rotation, the wheels will scrub against the floor as they swivel to align to the new direction of movement. This can take a surprising amount of effort for both the sliding friction of the wheel pivoting in place, and for the swivelling action as some casters spin clockwise, and others counterclockwise.

Triple-swivels (see Chapter 17, page 213) succeed somewhat in eliminating this problem, but even they have more resistance to reversing direction than a fixed caster. And so during an analysis of friction, always pause to consider if any part of the setup being considered falls outside the basic assumptions inherent in the formulas being used. If you suspect differences, either build and test a mock-up to get real measured values of force or torque due to friction, or increase the calculated value of $T_{friction}$ by some percentage based on your best estimate of the potential impact your particular setup's differences will have on that number. Usually these percentages would usually be in the range of perhaps 20 to 50 percent, but one mechanical designer, creating effects used in the high pressure rarefied world of on-location movie shoots in New York City, applied 400 percent (or a multiplier of 4) to whatever he did. The economic penalties and reputation harm that would come from a failure of a machine to move so outweighed the cost of building it essentially four times more powerful than needed, that it was seen as the proper path to take.

Finally, before the mathematics begin, one observation relative to friction in the context of typical rotating scenery bears mention. Beyond the very major effect caster friction often has on the power needed to spin a turntable, it is relatively rare that friction from any other source will create a $T_{friction}$ component significant enough to be worth including in the maximum power formula. Sliding friction, for instance, will occur in such places as in a door's hinges, or between a shaft and a plastic bearing supporting a pivoting panel, but as will be demonstrated in several examples, the friction losses in these situations are usually negligible in comparison to the torques needed to cause acceleration or lifting. Rolling friction beyond casters occurs mainly in ball and roller bearings, but here too, given the torques generally needed for acceleration and lifting, the friction losses in these bearings is relatively small. This is mainly because the radius at which $F_{friction}$ acts in bearings, whether door hinge or ball bearing, is generally small and so the resulting $T_{friction}$ is small too. This does not eliminate our responsibility to determine friction, for it is only after an estimate has been made that insignificance can be proven, but it does reduce our need to calculate highly accurate results.

The Torque Due to Friction, $T_{friction}$

The basis of $T_{friction}$ is torque, which is in general the result of a force acting at some distance from an axis of rotation, or mathematically

$$\boldsymbol{T} = \boldsymbol{r} \times \boldsymbol{F}$$
$$T = rF\sin\theta$$

To take into account friction, the radius term in this formula could refer to the distance between a turntable's axis of rotation and a particular caster, while the force would relate to that caster's rolling friction. Since friction always opposes motion, the friction force, $\boldsymbol{F}_{friction}$, will act in a direction parallel to the linear instantaneous velocity that occurs out at each caster. Because only perfectly circular motion is assumed throughout this book, linear instantaneous velocity is always perpendicu-

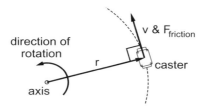

Figure 9.1   Radius, **r**, and **F**$_{friction}$ are perpendicular in simple circular motion.

lar to the radius that runs from pivot to wheel, and because of this the angle in the torque formula sine term is always 90°. Since the sine of 90° equals 1, the torque formula for a single caster can be written simply as

$$T_{friction} = r F_{friction}$$

This formula represents the torque needed to overcome friction at a point located at a distance of r from the axis of rotation, which models the effect of one caster mounted at some distance from the axis of rotation. Sliding friction does not act at a point, so that discussion will be deferred until later.

Caster Friction and Turntables

Turntables are the most common rotating scenic element, and casters are used almost exclusively to support them. Each wheel carries some portion of the total load, generally proportional to the tributary area it supports. This load, in conjunction with the coefficient of rolling friction, implies a certain force is needed to overcome the effects of friction, which from Chapter 5 is defined as:

$$F_{friction} = \mu_r F_n$$

For one wheel located at some distance from an axis of rotation, the torque needed to overcome that wheel's friction is:

$$T_{friction} = r_c F_{friction} = r_c (\mu_r F_n)$$

Where $T_{friction}$ = the torque needed to overcome the friction of one specific wheel (ft-lb, Nm)

r_c =   the caster radius, or the perpendicular distance from the axis of rotation to the center of the wheel's area of contact with the surface it rolls along (ft, m)

μ_r =   the wheel's coefficient of rolling friction (unitless)

F_n =   the normal force on the wheel (lb, N). This is identical to what it was in the linear chapters: $F_n = F_w \cos \theta_{rake}$.

This formula is most useful when you know the placement of each caster and want a reasonably exact accounting of friction. If the loads on the turntable are relatively evenly distributed, the load on each wheel can be approximated from the tributary area it supports and an estimate of the per square foot weight of both the turntable and the scenery and actors it carries. A light-weight turntable construction, for example, might use 1×2 steel tube framing, a 3/4″ plywood structural decking, and a 3/8″ medium density fiberboard (MDF) top skin for a smooth paintable surface. The weight of this construction would fall somewhere in the 6 to 8 lb/ft^2 range, mainly depending on the spacing of the framing steel. Loads placed on top of this may add another 15 lb/ft^2, for a total of say 22 lb/ft^2.[1] If the casters to be used on this setup are rated to support 250 lb each, for example, they would need to be placed so that they supported an area no more than:

$$castor\ load\ rating\ =\ tributary\ area\ \times weight/ft^2$$
$$250\ =\ tributary\ area \times 22$$
$$tributary\ area \leq 11.4\ ft^2$$

or, roughly the area of a square 3′-4″ on a side. (This area-per-caster number could also be divided into the area of the turntable being designed to estimate the approximate number of casters needed to support it.)

Even if a turntable carries loads that are unevenly spread about on it, the sum of weights supported by each wheel will probably still include some component to account for evenly distributed loads, with the additional weight added onto the particular casters that support an individual object. Whether the weight of any individual piece, be it scenery, structure, a prop, or an actor, is considered as part of an even distribution of weight, or as an separate load on a few specific casters depends both on how confident you are that the design in hand now closely represents the final product that will be on stage, and how accurate you need that answer to be. Neither of these questions can be answered generically here, but it is common to start with simplified calculations early on in the budgeting and technical design periods of a show, and either refine the numbers as a design becomes more certain, or plan on using drive motors some percentage larger than you think will be needed to maintain a contingency or cushion between what is expected and what really happens.

EXAMPLE: A 4 foot by 8 foot platform forms a small jackknife stage by pivoting about one corner while sitting on a level stage floor. Three casters, with coefficients of rolling friction of 0.03, are mounted in the other three corners. The platform structure and the loads placed on it can be considered to be an evenly distributed 840 lb. The pivot point, a good ball bearing flange block, is both weight bearing, and has negligible friction. What torque is needed just to overcome the effects of caster friction, or what is $T_{friction}$?

---

1. This is a discussion of the load that the turntable is being designed to move. There is also the additional concern of what loads its structure must withstand in a static situation. Show specific temporary decking is often designed to a 50 psf live load value, and a permanent stage floor load rating of 150 psf is generally required by building codes. It is common for stage machinery to have two load ratings, one defining its structural capacity while stationary, and one relating to what it has been designed to move.

SOLUTION: Since the pivot is to be considered frictionless (a reasonable assumption here because the caster friction will predominate), all of $T_{friction}$ will arise from the three casters, which is therefore made up of the sum of three individual torques:

$$T_{friction} = r_{c1}(\mu_r F_{n1}) + r_{c2}(\mu_r F_{n2}) + r_{c3}(\mu_r F_{n3})$$

The unknowns to be determined are the three radii from pivot to wheels, and the normal force loads on those wheels.

The radii could be measured off a drawing, or simply assumed to be a few inches inside the corners of the 4 by 8 platform. Following the latter technique, the distances between the axis of rotation—the pivot point— and the three casters are:

- the closest wheel to the pivot is 4' away, minus a bit, or roughly 3'-9",
- the caster diagonally across the platform from the pivot is at

$$r_{c2} = \sqrt{4^2 + 8^2} = 8.94 \; ft \qquad assume \; 8'\text{-}9''$$

- and the final wheel is approximately 7'-9" away from the pivot.

Since it is given that the platform sits on a level stage floor, the normal force on the wheels will simply equal the weight they support. Because the platform load is stated to be evenly distributed, and the pivot bears weight, the pivot and three wheels can each be assumed to support one quarter of the total weight, or $840/4 = 210 \; lb$.

The torque needed to overcome friction is therefore:

$$T_{friction} = 3.75(0.03(210)) + 8.75(0.03(210)) + 7.75(0.03(210))$$

$$T_{friction} = 23.6 + 55.1 + 48.8 = 128 \; ft\text{-}lb$$

Just as a check on this answer in the more familiar linear terms, convert this torque into the push force needed just to overcome friction at the platform corner 8' away from the pivot point. If the push is assumed to be perpendicular to the 8' edge of the platform, then:

$$T = rF$$

$$T_{friction} = r_{pivot \; to \; corner} \; F_{push} = 128 = 8 \, F_{push}$$

$$F_{push} = 16 \; lb$$

This is a believable result, and so the solution is acceptable.

Dealing with each caster as an individual, with its own potentially unique load and radius to the axis of rotation is an accurate approach to take, but it is very slow and tedious, especially if there are many casters. It is also impossible to do this if these calculations are being done early on in the technical design process, and no caster placements have been set yet. Symmetry in caster layout can help shorten the calculation process in those situations where it exists. For instance, one common turntable construction technique is to use a number of identical pie-wedge shaped segments that when joined together form the full turntable. Provided that weight can be assumed to be evenly distributed across the whole area of the table, then caster radii and the weights of tributary areas will need to be figured for only one segment, with the resultant $T_{friction}$ then being multiplied by the number of segments.

A variation on this individual caster technique exists that will lead in many instances to a much quicker determination of $T_{friction}$. It involves finding two numbers, the average caster radius, $r_{avg\,c}$, or literally the mathematical average of all the distances between pivot and wheel for every caster on the unit, and the total normal force on the wheels.

$$T_{friction} = r_{avg\,c}(\mu_r F_n)$$

Where $T_{friction}$ = the torque needed to overcome the friction of a number of wheels (ft-lb, Nm)

$r_{avg\,c}$ = the average caster radius, calculated from an average of the radii to each caster (ft, m). The average is simply the sum of all the radii divided by the number of casters:

$$r_{avg\,c} = \frac{(r_{c1} + r_{c2} + r_{c3} + \ldots + r_{cn})}{n}$$

If the pivot point bears weight, it counts as a caster in the variable n, and it has a radius of zero

μ_r = a wheel's coefficient of rolling friction (unitless). All wheels must have the same coefficient.

F_n = the total normal force supported by all of the wheels (lb, N)

The derivation of this formula assumes that each wheel carries exactly the same load, but as long as a revolving unit is supported by wheels that carry roughly the same loads, then this formula can be used.

EXAMPLE: Using the same 4 foot by 8 foot jackknife platform from the previous example, use the average caster radius concept to determine the torque needed just to overcome the effects of caster friction, $T_{friction}$.

SOLUTION: The equal load on each wheel and identical coefficients of rolling friction criteria are met by this setup, so the average caster distance technique will work. Some values obtained from the earlier problem:

$$\mu_{friction} = 0.03$$

$$F_n = 840\ lb$$

$$r_{c1} = 3'\text{-}9'' = 3.75' \qquad r_{c1} = 8'\text{-}9'' = 8.75' \qquad r_{c1} = 7'\text{-}9'' = 7.75'$$

The weight bearing pivot will count in n, but it has a radius of zero, so the average caster distance is therefore:

$$r_{avg\,c} = \frac{(r_{c1} + r_{c2} + r_{c3})}{n} = \frac{(3.75' + 8.75' + 7.75')}{4} = 5.063'$$

The torque needed to overcome friction is therefore:

$$T_{friction} = r_{avg\,c}(\mu_r F_n) = (5.063)(0.03)(840) = 128\ ft\text{-}lb$$

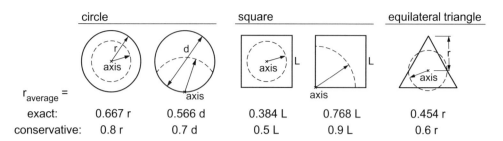

Figure 9.2   The average caster radius for five turntable types

> The answer is exactly the same as before (which is a result not always to be expected if the tributary area caster load estimates are not as straight forward as they are here). This process is not appreciably faster to calculate when there are only 3 casters as here, but if there are say 53 casters, then the calculation time savings could be considerable.

One further refinement of the average caster radius concept can be made, which is to replace the step of taking the average of all the individual radii with a radius found by using a simple case formula (see Figure 9.2). Early on in the technical design period the exact placement of casters is probably unknown, so the average caster distance calculation just described cannot be made. In most cases though, the distribution of casters will follow a pattern that roughly assigns equal tributary areas per caster, and this is usually true even if the layout is done only intuitively rather than with any mathematical precision.

For example, on a conventional circular turntable 24 ft in diameter, it would not be unusual to use a weight bearing center pivot and three rings of casters at radii of 4, 8, and 12 feet (shown in Figure 9.3). If the radial distance from the pivot to each of the casters is added together and then divided by the total number of casters, the result is the average caster radius, which for this example turns out to

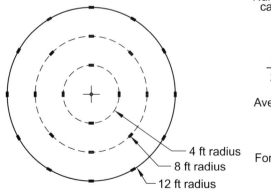

Number of casters: Radius:

1	at	0 ft	=	0 (center pivot)
4	at	4 ft	=	16
8	at	8 ft	=	64
12	at	12 ft	=	144

25 casters total   224 ft sum of all radii

Average caster distance:

$$\frac{224}{25} = 8.96 \text{ ft}$$

— 4 ft radius
— 8 ft radius
— 12 ft radius

For this turntable:

$$\frac{r_{avg\,c}}{r_{turntable}} = \frac{8.96 \text{ ft}}{12 \text{ ft}} = 0.747\, r_{turntable}$$

Figure 9.3   Example of typical caster distribution and average caster radius

be 8.96 ft (the pivot is a valid "caster" here, with a radius of 0 ft). If the case formula for a circle spinning about its center from Figure 9.2 is used, the conservative average caster distance is:

$$conservative: \qquad r_{avg\,c} = 0.8r_{turn} = (0.8)12 = 9.60\,ft$$

The result here is about 7% larger than the actual distance calculated from known caster positions, not a large difference, and acceptable in light of the unknowns involved in predicting friction.

The case formulas can be derived from either a somewhat complex calculation involving the ratio of two integrals, or by conceptually marking out the turntable being analyzed with a fine grid of equal area shapes, and by then finding the average of all the radii taken between the centers of these shapes and the table's axis of rotation. (The calculations for these formulas were done in MathCad using up to 250,000 radii.) The exact average radius values listed are more for reference than practical use, the rounded up conservative values are the ones that should be used as $r_{avg\,c}$ in the torque due to friction formula.

$$T_{friction} = r_{avg\,c}(\mu_r\,F_n)$$

As was true earlier, this formula assumes that all casters have the same coefficient of friction, and that each caster carries roughly the same load. If this is not true, then the calculations involving each caster as an individual must be used.

EXAMPLE: A conventional turntable 28 ft in diameter sits on a level stage floor. It has an evenly distributed combined dead and live load weight of 11,000 lb. Casters, having a coefficient of rolling friction of 0.03, will be installed under the table in locations that will support areas of roughly equal size. What torque is needed just to overcome the effects of caster friction, or what is $T_{friction}$?

SOLUTION: Since this turntable meets the requirements of evenly distributed loading and caster placement, and it matches one of the cases given in Figure 9.2, a simplified friction estimate based on average caster distance can be used.

$$T_{friction} = r_{avg\,c}(\mu_r\,F_n) = 0.8(14)(0.03)(11000)$$

$$T_{friction} = 3700\,ft\text{-}lb$$

This method of estimating average caster radius is fast, but not universally applicable. If the turntable is not *exactly* like one of those depicted in the five case formulas, a doughnut or ring shaped one for instance, then this method cannot be used. If the casters are not going to be distributed more or less evenly underneath the table, but instead perhaps all out at the edge, then this method cannot be used. And if the loading on the casters cannot be assumed to be reasonably even, then again, this method cannot be used. Despite these limitations, because roughly evenly loaded round turntables spinning about their centers are commonplace, this method will be useful most of the time.

Rotational Bearing Friction

Rotational bearings range between something as simple as a chunk of wood with a hole drilled through it supporting a spinning dowel on up to a high precision crane bearing capable of supporting one million pounds. All are designed to transfer loads between machine parts spinning relative to each other, while simultaneously minimizing the frictional resistance to rotation around one axis. (Chapter 17 details some of the many practical aspects of bearings. Here we are interested in and will discuss mainly their friction characteristics.) For such seemingly simple devices, their behavior is remarkably complex, being in part influenced by their materials, the speed of rotation, the presence or absence of a lubricant, wear, manufacturing tolerances, lubricant viscosity, the load being supported, temperature, and on and on.

Bearings are categorized into two broad types:

- plain bearings, where, at low speeds at least, sliding friction is involved between a shaft and the bearing that surrounds it. (In engineering books this is called boundary lubrication. At speeds much higher than moving scenery would typically involve, the shaft and bearing are separated by a film of pressurized lubricant, and the sliding friction effects vanish to be replaced with the behavior of viscous liquids. These are journal bearings, as you would find on the crankshaft in a car engine, but not on scenery.)

- rolling element bearings, which use rolling balls or rollers to eliminate sliding contact.

Not surprisingly, plain bearings are subject to the effects of static and kinetic sliding friction, and rolling element bearings to rolling friction.

The design of the bearing, whether plain or rolling element, determines its ability to support four categories of loads (illustrated at the right of Figure 9.4):

- Radial, or loads that act along a line formed by a radius of the shaft. The bearing on a rope sheave, for instance, is designed to support mainly radial loads.

- Axial, or a load that acts along the line formed by the axis or rotation. Thrust bearings are a common name given to a bearing designed mainly to carry axial compressive loads. The bearing at the bottom of a revolving door, for example, would need to withstand a large axial load from the weight of the door.

- A moment, or a load that tends to twist the bearing in its housing. Many bearings are not designed to resist moment loads, and these types must be used in

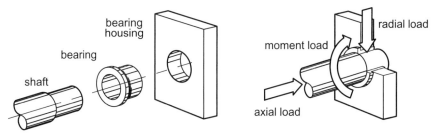

Figure 9.4   A simple flanged plain bearing, showing alignment of radial, axial and moment loads.

pairs spaced apart to turn the moment into a pair of oppositely directed radial loads, one on each bearing. Crane bearings, very large diameter (up to 30 feet!) ball or roller bearings, are however a type of bearing designed to accept moment loads because, as their name implies, they are designed to carry the large eccentric loads imposed on the swiveling boom of a crane.

- Combined, or a load that has any combination of radial, axial, and moment aspects to it. Many bearings have the capability to deal with combined loading to some extent, but as just one example, the bearings supporting the wheels of a car see both radial forces from weight, and significant axial forces during cornering.

The most basic formulas used to determine the torque needed to overcome bearing friction will depend on both the type of bearing involved: plain or rolling element, and the loading conditions: radial, axial, moment, or combined. In the very simplified coverage of the topic presented here, only plain bearings resisting radial and axial forces, and radially loaded rolling element bearings will be mentioned. As is always true, if you need more specific information about a particular bearing, consult a bearing manufacturer's web site, or their engineering staff.

Plain bearings—a bronze bushing holding a steel shaft, the pivot of a conventional hinge, or a bolt through a pair of holes drilled in two pieces of angle iron— have higher frictional losses than rolling element bearings, but they are simple to make and inexpensive. The torque needed to overcome the effects of friction on a radially loaded plain bearing is

$$T_{friction} = \mu F_L r$$

Where $T_{friction}$ = the torque required to overcome bearing friction (ft-lb, in-lb, Nm)

μ = the coefficient of static or kinetic friction (as appropriate) for the two materials involved (unitless)

F_L = the radial load supported by the bearing (lb, N). This would be the sum of any weight, any cable or roller chain tension, any gear induced force, forces due to acceleration, or, in other words, anything that loads the bearing perpendicular to the axis of rotation.

r = radius of the shaft (ft, in, m)

EXAMPLE: A drawbridge weighing 400 lb is 10 ft high by 5 ft wide when measured in its up position. It is pivoted at its base on a large steel piano hinge that has a 3/8 inch diameter hinge pin. Assuming that the hinge is new and well oiled ($\mu_s = 0.30$), and that all move accelerations are so gentle that T_{accel} is negligible, what worst case torque is needed to overcome bearing friction?

SOLUTION: Since both the coefficient of friction and shaft diameter are given, only the load on the hinge needs to be determined. This load arises from several sources: the weight of the unit, the static and dynamic effects of any actors that might cross it during a move, components of the lifting cable tension that must be opposed at the hinge, and the torques and forces needed for acceleration during a lift. In addition to these factors, the hinge load also changes throughout a move as the drawbridge to cable angle changes, and as the load shifts between a shared support by hinge and cable when the bridge is down to the full load being on the hinge when the bridge is up (because the raising cable is essentially horizontal here and can apply no lifting force). An equation could be derived that would take into account all these issues, but as the goal in all this is usually to get a reasonable estimate as easily as possible, only the two extremes of bridge up and down will be considered.

For this setup, the hinge load for the vertical bridge situation is easy to see, it is just the 400 lb weight of the unit (assuming both that the thickness of the bridge is negligible and that the raising cable provides no lift in this position).

When the drawbridge is down, its 400 lb weight, acting through the center of mass in the middle of its span, must be supported by equal 200 lb vertical reactions at both the hinge and the cable end. Since the cable pulls at an angle of 45° to the surface of the bridge, the cable tension needs to be

$$\sin 45° = \frac{200}{F_{cable}} \qquad or \qquad F_{cable} = \frac{200}{\sin 45°} = 283 \; lb$$

to create the 200 lb vertical component. This cable tension has, given the simple symmetry of the situation, an obvious horizontal component of

$$\sin 45° = \frac{F_{horizontal}}{283} \qquad or \qquad F_{horizontal} = \sin 45°(283) = 200 \; lb$$

The hinge must counter with an equal but oppositely directed force, and so the hinge too has a resultant load on it equal to the cable, or 283 lb.

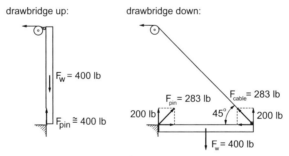

Of the two situations just considered, the force on the hinge is worst when the bridge is up. The torque to overcome friction in this position will be (including the conversion of shaft diameter in inches to a radius in feet):

$$T_{friction} = \mu F_L r = (0.3)(400)\left(\frac{0.375/12}{2}\right) = 1.88 \; ft\text{-}lb$$

This value could be inserted into the maximum power formula as $T_{friction}$, but given that the worst case lifting torque alone for this same drawbridge is 2000 ft-lb, $T_{friction}$ is of insignificant size relative to this and could be ignored.

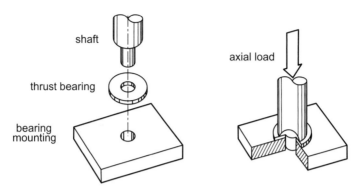

Figure 9.5 Plain thrust bearings generally only accept axial loads

Plain thrust bearings, which are generally either in the shape of a washer, or just a plate onto which a shaft will bear, are usually designed to support only axial loads (Figure 9.5). As usual, complexities abound, but a rough estimate of the torque needed to overcome friction can be obtained from:

$$T_{friction} = \mu F_L\left(\frac{d_1 + d_2}{4}\right)$$

Where $T_{friction}$ = the torque needed to overcome the friction (ft-lb, in-lb, Nm)
   $\mu =$ the coefficient of static or kinetic friction (as appropriate) for the two materials involved (unitless)
   F_L = the axial load supported by the bearing (lb, N)
   d_1, d_2 = the outer and inner diameters of the area of contact between the shaft and the bearing (ft, in, m). Since they add together in the formula, which is which is unimportant. If the bearing is just a surface (no center hole), then one of these diameters will be zero.

EXAMPLE: A pivoting panel weighing 85 lb rests all its weight through a steel shaft onto a bronze thrust washer. The bearing outer and inner diameters are 1.25″ and 0.5″ respectively, and the shaft from the panel is 1″ in diameter, with a 0.5″ diameter turned down stub on its end. The coefficient of kinetic friction between bronze and steel is 0.20. What torque is needed to overcome the friction from the thrust washer in this setup?

SOLUTION: The shaft and the bearing share an area of contact that is defined by the 1″ shaft diameter, and the 0.5″ inner dimensions of both. A ring shaped portion of the bronze bearing will lie outside the diameter of the shaft, but it cannot contribute to friction because the shaft does not touch it. The torque needed to pivot this panel is therefore:

$$T_{friction} = \mu F_L\left(\frac{d_1 + d_2}{4}\right) = 0.20(85)\left(\frac{1 + 0.5}{4}\right) = 6.38 \; in\text{-}lb \;\; or \;\; 0.531 \, ft\text{-}lb$$

Since a kinetic coefficient of friction was given, a starting torque of up to 50% more could be anticipated to break the panel away from the static situation.

Rolling element bearings—ball, and roller bearings—take advantage of the fact that rolling involves less frictional power loss than sliding. The material used in their construction is hardened steel, except for a very small percentage of plastic and ceramic bearings, so unlike the plain bearings, friction does not vary because of different materials, but rather because of other differences. Lubrication viscosity, bearing temperature, dirt shield or seal friction, ball surface finish and sphericity, wear, extra loading due to misalignment, and more all contribute to a bearing's performance. The friction that results from all of this is not easily calculated because of the numerous poorly quantifiable variables involved, and manufacturers do not often supply any information on friction. Despite this, the same formula as given in the plain bearing section above can be used, with appropriate coefficients. One company lists friction coefficients in the range from 0.0015 up to 0.006 for their pillow and flange block product line (see Chapter 17 for a definition of these bearing types).[2] Given this range, a very conservative value of 0.01 would be a useful rule of thumb value to use in the absence of a specific rating.

$$T_{friction} = \mu F_L r$$

Where $T_{friction}$ = the torque required to overcome bearing friction (ft-lb, in-lb, Nm)
           μ = the coefficient of friction for the bearing being used (unitless)
           F_L = the load supported by the bearing (lb, N)
           r = radius of a circle that passes through the center points of the bearing's rollers or balls (ft, in, m). This can usually be estimated from the manufacturers dimensions for a given bearing. An average of the bearing's inner and outer diameter, converted to a radius, is usually acceptable:

$$r = \frac{d_{id} + d_{od}}{4}$$

Given how low the coefficients of friction are on rolling element bearings, the friction involved is often insignificantly small in the context of typical scenery movements.

EXAMPLE: Given the exact same drawbridge problem solved in the plain bearing section above, but here, in place of the hinge, is a shaft supported by two mounted bearings. Assuming that the bearing radius is 0.75″ and that the coefficient of friction is 0.004, what is the worst case torque needed to overcome bearing friction?

---

2. INA Wälzlager Schaeffler oHG, *Ball Bearings, Housed Bearing Units, Catalogue 517*, Nürnberg, 1999. (INA is sold through McMaster-Carr, and therefore is quite common in this country.)

SOLUTION: The givens here are, including the worst case loading found in the earlier problem,

$$\mu = 0.004 \qquad F_L = 400 \; lb \qquad r = \frac{0.75}{12} = 0.0625 \; ft$$

So the torque needed to overcome bearing friction in this case is:

$$T_{friction} = \mu F_L r = (0.004)(400)(0.0625) = 0.10 \; ft\text{-}lb$$

This value is extremely small in comparison to the worst case lifting torque for this drawbridge, 2000 ft-lb. This should not be surprising given that the main function of these bearings is, after all, to minimize friction as much as possible.

While the friction effects of both plain and rolling element bearings can be calculated, they rarely end up being included in the final tally of all the torques due to friction, at least when analyzing typical moving scenery. Caster friction however is rarely negligible. The few pounds it may take to move one wheel is effectively multiplied once by a sizable radius, and then again by the considerable number of casters commonly used on a turntable.

Problems

1. A conventional round turntable, 22 ft in diameter and weighing 2850 lb, sits on a deck raked at 1/2" to the foot. It rolls on casters, with $\mu_r = 0.025$, that are essentially evenly distributed around the underside of the table. What torque would need to be supplied just to overcome the effects of friction, or what is $T_{friction}$?

2. A turntable made from a 5 m square platform, which weighs 1300 kg, pivots around one of its corners. Casters, with $\mu_r = 0.03$, will be distributed around evenly under this platform. Estimate the torque needed to overcome friction, $T_{friction}$.

3. A long narrow platform, weighing 435 lb, pivots about the midpoint of a narrow end. The platform is 4' wide by 20' long and has only six casters supporting it. They are positioned on a line that runs 4" in from each edge of the platform, as detailed in the plan below. If the wheels have a coefficient of rolling friction of 0.035, what is $T_{friction}$? Assume this unit runs on a level stage floor, and that the pivot point does not bear any weight.

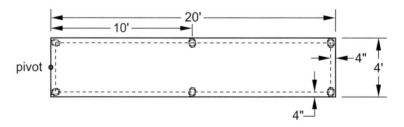

4. As an idea for a snow drop machine, a piece of 1′ diameter cardboard concrete form tube (Sonotube™) is to be supported by two plain bearings made of plywood sheets cut with holes just slightly oversized enough to allow them to slip onto either end of the tube. Assuming that the tube filled with stage snow weighs 22 lb, and that the coefficient of static friction between the tube and plywood is 0.35, what is the worst case torque due to friction for these makeshift bearings? Ignore the effect of the pile of snow shifting to one side of the tube as the tube spins (yet another difficult to model real world complexity).

10

The Lifting Torque, T_{lift}

Overview

In theatre, moving scenery against the pull of gravity is common—it occurs in fly systems, in wagons run up and down raked decks, and with lifts hauling loads up out of the trap room. But all these moves are linear. Lifting during rotation is much less common, in part because set designers rarely ask for anything beyond a turntable on a flat floor. Occasionally though, a turntable on a raked deck is needed, or a draw-bridge-like movement, or maybe even a Ferris wheel. These effects will usually involve lifting against gravity via a torque about an axis of rotation, and that situation is the topic to be detailed in this chapter.

Lifting torque is somewhat unusual in that it can be described quite clearly with a few simple words, and yet a precise mathematical definition seems convoluted by comparison. The most important of the words are "out of balance", as in "lifting torque will be needed if a rotating object is out of balance, *and* its axis of rotation is anything but perfectly vertical". Somewhat more specifically, lifting torque involves any component of weight that acts both perpendicular to and at some distance from an axis of rotation (see Figure 10.1). The perpendicular requirement implies that if the always straight down direction of weight is parallel to an object's

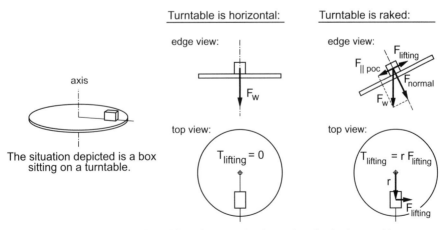

Figure 10.1   An example of the lifting force on horizontal and raked turntables.

axis of rotation, then there cannot be any component of weight that is perpendicular to that axis. Put simply, if a rotating object's axis of rotation is vertical, then the lifting torque will always be zero, or $T_{lifting} = 0$. The lifting torque that can result from a non-vertical axis of rotation will depend on three factors:

- the rake angle (which equals the axis of rotation's degree of tilt off of vertical),
- the weight of the objects involved, and
- the distance between the axis of rotation and the center of mass of the objects being analyzed.

The first two factors are defined exactly as they were in the linear motion chapters, but center of mass needs to be formally defined.

The Center of Mass

There are a number of qualitative definitions of the concept of the center of mass of an object. One is that the center of mass is that point where, if that object was suspended from a string, it would not tend to rotate or settle into any particular position. A mass suspended in this way would be in balance and hold any position it was placed in. Another description is that the center of mass is that point where a force can be applied to accelerate the object and only linear acceleration results—no rotation occurs. This can be simply demonstrated by pushing a book across a tabletop by tapping it with a finger. Tap it along a line not through the center of mass and it spins. Tap along a line through the center of mass and it moves in a straight line. (Strictly speaking this is only true if the friction between the book cover and the tabletop is homogeneous across the cover's area.) One final image is that if an object is thrown upward with a spin, the object will inherently rotate about its center of mass, and that center will follow the parabolic path that projectiles accelerated by gravity will always follow (assuming that air flow friction is negligible).

Mathematically, the process of determining the location of the center of mass is not all that different from that used to find the moment of inertia. An object is conceptually broken up into many small parts, each of which has a mass and a set of x and y coordinates describing its distance from some chosen reference point. For our purposes here, that point is the axis of rotation (a third coordinate in the z direction could be used to find the actual point in space that is the center of mass, but all that is needed here is the perpendicular distance between the center of mass and the axis of rotation). Two calculations are made:

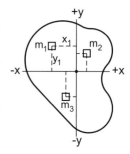

$$x_{c\,of\,m} = \frac{x_1 m_1 + x_2 m_2 + \dots}{m_{total}} \qquad y_{c\,of\,m} = \frac{y_1 m_1 + y_2 m_2 + \dots}{m_{total}}$$

Where $x_{c\,of\,m}$, $y_{c\,of\,m}$ = the distance to the center of mass in the x or y direction from the chosen reference axis (ft, m).

$x_1, x_2, \dots, y_1, y_2, \dots$ = the distance parallel to the x and y axes between the reference axis and the center of mass of some part or piece of the whole object (ft, m).

$m_1, m_2, \dots$ = the mass of the part or piece (slugs, kg). Weight can be used too since the units cancel out in the end. Just be sure that both numerator and denominator use the same units.

m_{total} = the total mass (or weight) of all the parts accounted for above (slugs, kg).

The centers of mass of many simple homogeneous shapes are obvious and do not need to be calculated. They are points in the center of spheres, disks, cubes, or cylinders for example. But to find the center of mass of a more complex shape or a collection of individual pieces may require the use of these calculations.

EXAMPLE: For the turntable illustrated, determine the distance between the axis of rotation and the center of mass of all the objects which will influence the lifting torque. (The details of weights and dimensions will be given as needed in the solution.)

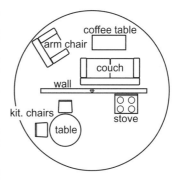

SOLUTION: If the center of mass of an object lies on the axis of rotation, that object is in balance around that axis, and it will never require any lifting torque. In this setup, the centers of mass of the turntable and the wall can be assumed to be on the axis of rotation, and for the purposes of lifting torque calculations, they can be ignored. The location of the center of mass of all the other pieces combined together is not obvious, and so that location needs to be calculated.

With the turntable and wall removed, a Cartesian x and y coordinate system is drawn onto the furniture plan. Its origin, the (0,0) point, must be at the turntable's axis of rotation. The alignment of the x and y coordinate axes to the collection of furniture shown here is totally arbitrary, any other choice will result in the same end result. Each piece of furniture has a given weight, and a set of x and y distances from the axis

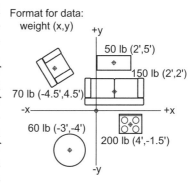

of rotation to each object's center of mass. Because the weight of the kitchen chairs is probably minor relative to the weight of the other pieces, and to simplify seven pieces down to five, the weight of those chairs has just been added into the weight of the table. Calculation of the $x_{c\,of\,m}$ and $y_{c\,of\,m}$ distances for the collection of furniture can now be done. The formulas here have been written in weight units instead of mass since the weight of the pieces is given. In the x direction:

$$x_{c\,of\,m} = \frac{x_1 F_{w1} + x_2 F_{w2} + \ldots}{F_{w\,total}}$$

$$x_{c\,of\,m} = \frac{-4.5(70) + 2(50) + 2(150) - 3(60) + 4(200)}{70 + 50 + 150 + 60 + 200} = \frac{705}{530} = 1.33\,ft$$

In the y direction:

$$y_{c\,of\,m} = \frac{y_1 F_{w1} + y_2 F_{w2} + \ldots}{F_{w\,total}}$$

$$x_{c\,of\,m} = \frac{4.5(70) + 5(50) + 2(150) - 4(60) - 1.5(200)}{70 + 50 + 150 + 60 + 200} = \frac{325}{530} = 0.613\,ft$$

Finally these x and y coordinates can be converted to a single radial distance between axis of rotation and center of mass by using the Pythagorean theorem

$$a = \sqrt{b^2 + c^2}$$

$$r_{c\,of\,m} = \sqrt{1.33^2 + 0.613^2} = 1.46\,ft$$

This result puts the center of mass roughly in the center of the back of the couch, and it is not a large distance, meaning the turntable, even with the furniture in place is not far out of balance. The role this dimension has is as the radius in the lifting torque formula, and that will be fully described just below.

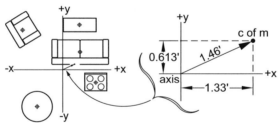

The Lifting Torque

One of the three torque components in the rotational version of the maximum power formula,

$$P_{max} = (T_{accel} + T_{friction} + T_{lifting})\,\omega_{max}$$

lifting torque is proportional to the distance between the axis of rotation and the center of mass of the objects being considered, and the lifting force

$$T_{lifting} = r_{c\,of\,m} F_{lifting}$$

$$T_{lifting} = r_{c\,of\,m} F_w \sin\theta_{rake}$$

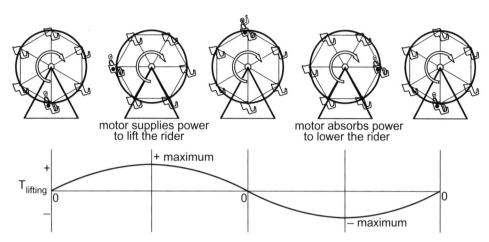

motor supplies power
to lift the rider

motor absorbs power
to lower the rider

Figure 10.2   Lifting torque varies sinusoidally over one full revolution.

Where $T_{lifting}$ = the lifting torque, calculated for the worst case situation (ft-lb, Nm)

$r_{c\,of\,m}$ = the radial distance between the axis of rotation and the imbalanced load's center of mass (ft, m)

$F_{lifting}$ = the lifting force, as defined in Chapter 5 (lb, N)

F_w = the weight of the imbalanced load (lb, N)

θ_{rake} = the rake angle (degrees). Defined such that a flat floor has a $\theta_{rake} = 0°$ and vertical movement has a $\theta_{rake} = 90°$. Put another way, θ_{rake} is the angle the axis of rotation forms with a perfectly vertical line.

The lifting torque will vary sinusoidally as rotation occurs, and over any one full revolution, there will be one positive and one negative maximum, and two places 90° from these where $T_{lifting} = 0$ (see Figure 10.2). The worst case value is what is needed for the maximum power formula, and it will occur when the direction of $\boldsymbol{F}_{lifting}$ is perpendicular to that of $\boldsymbol{r}_{c\,of\,m}$ and in an upward facing direction.

EXAMPLE: Given the turntable setup used in the example finished just one page back, what would be the worst case lifting torque if that table was set up on a stage raked at 1/2″ to the foot?

SOLUTION: The givens obtained from the earlier problem are:

$$F_{w\,total} = 530\ lb \qquad r_{c\,of\,m} = 1.46\,ft$$

The rake angle can be determined from the given rise and run values.

$$\tan\theta_{rake} = \frac{rise}{run} = \frac{0.5}{12} \qquad \theta_{rake} = 2.39°$$

With these values, the worst case lifting torque can now be determined.

$$T_{lifting} = r_{c\,of\,m}\,F_w\,\sin\theta_{rake}$$
$$T_{lifting} = (1.46)(530)\sin 2.39° = 32.3\,ftlb$$

This is the torque needed just to hold the turntable in position against its tendency to want to spin until the center of mass is at the lowest point in its travel. In this given situation the lifting torque is not a large number, even one actor standing out at the edge of the turntable could triple it. Although actors were not included as part of this simple example, do not ignore their effects.

EXAMPLE: A portal shaped as shown travels drawbridge-like 90° between vertical and horizontal playing positions. It is hinged along its lower edge and moved with cables attached to points 4 ft down from the outer corners. Its weight averages 5 psf, and it is 10″ thick. What is the worst case lifting torque, and what cable tension is needed to counter this?

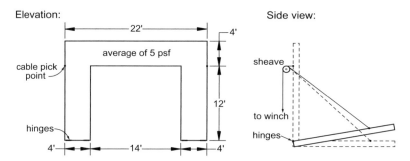

SOLUTION: Since lifting torque is defined as

$$T_{lifting} = r_{c\,of\,m}\,F_w\,\sin\theta_{rake}$$

the issue here is to determine the value of each of these three terms.

The radius between axis of rotation and center of mass, $r_{c\,of\,m}$, can be found using the center of mass formulas. The x and y coordinates of those formulas refer to distances off the axis of rotation, and so dimensions referenced to the side view of the portal must be used, not the elevation as might first come to mind. The placement of x and y onto the object is truly an arbitrary choice, and so here it will be assumed that the drawbridge is up, and that x is horizontal, and y vertical. Next the piece needs to be broken up into smaller units of mass, each with easily identifiable centers of mass. Given the relatively simple shape of this portal, two 4 ft by 12 ft legs and one 4 ft by 22 ft top piece seems a logical division, though other breakups are possible too. Individually, these pieces weigh

$$F_w = (area)(weight/ft^2)$$
$$F_{w\,leg} = (4 \times 12)(5) = 240\,lb$$
$$F_{w\,top} = (4 \times 22)(5) = 440\,lb$$

Now use the center of mass formulas. In the x direction the center of mass of each of the three pieces will be 5″ (half the given thickness of the portal) to the right of the hinge point, and so not surprisingly the center of mass of the group will be there also:

$$x_{c\,of\,m} = \frac{x_1 F_{w1} + x_2 F_{w2} + \ldots}{F_{w\,total}} = \frac{2(x_{leg} F_{w\,leg}) + x_{top} F_{w\,top}}{2(F_{w\,leg}) + F_{w\,top}}$$

$$x_{c\,of\,m} = \frac{2(5/12)(240) + (5/12)(440)}{2(240) + 440} = \frac{383}{920} = 0.416\,ft \;\; or \;\; 5''$$

In the y direction, the results are not so predictable, so the calculation is more necessary.

$$y_{c\,of\,m} = \frac{y_1 F_{w1} + y_2 F_{w2} + \ldots}{F_{w\,total}} = \frac{2(y_{leg} F_{w\,leg}) + y_{top} F_{w\,top}}{2(F_{w\,leg}) + F_{w\,top}}$$

$$y_{c\,of\,m} = \frac{2(6)(240) + (14)(440)}{2(240) + 440} = \frac{9040}{920} = 9.83\,ft$$

And now finally, the exact radius from axis of rotation to the unit's center of mass is the hypotenuse of a triangle with sides $x_{c\,of\,m}$ and $y_{c\,of\,m}$, or

$$r_{c\,of\,m} = \sqrt{x_{c\,of\,m}^2 + y_{c\,of\,m}^2}$$

$$r_{c\,of\,m} = \sqrt{0.416^2 + 9.83^2} = 9.84\,ft$$

The second term in the lifting torque equation is something already figured out above, the weight of the portal.

$$F_{w\,portal} = 920\,lb$$

The final term of the lifting torque equation uses the rake angle, but here there is no rake here in the conventional sense. Another way of defining the rake angle is the angle between the axis of rotation and a vertical line. In this example, the hinge line forming the axis of rotation is 90° to vertical, and so

$$\theta_{rake} = 90°$$

The worst case lifting torque will occur when the portal is tipped up off of horizontal enough to lift its center of mass to the same elevation as the hinge pins. In this position the full weight of the piece acting at $r_{c\,of\,m}$ needs to be opposed by the lifting torque. Mathematically:

$$T_{lifting} = r_{c\,of\,m} F_w \sin\theta_{rake}$$

$$T_{lifting} = (9.84)(920)\sin 90° = 9050\,ftlb$$

If the cables shown are to support the portal, they must provide sufficient tension at some distance to generate the lifting torque. The angle they make with the portal reduces their ability to efficiently generate this torque because the angle between radius and force is not 90°. From a quick sketch made in a CAD program, the actual angle between radius and force is found to be 134° (This angle could be determined mathematically, but using CAD as a calculation tool is nowadays often quicker and more intuitive than using trig and a calculator.).

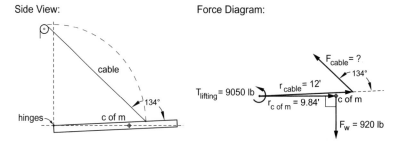

Side View: Force Diagram:

Given this angle then, and the value of lifting torque just found, the cable tension needs to be,

$$T = r\,F\sin\theta$$

$$T_{lifting} = r_{cable}\,F_{cable}\sin\theta$$

$$9050 = (12)\,F_{cable}\sin 134°$$

$$F_{cable} = 1050\ lb$$

This tension would be shared, theoretically 50/50, between the two cables on either edge of the portal, so each individual cable would have to withstand 525 lb, due to lifting torque alone. The actual worst case tension would be greater than this once the torques needed for acceleration and to overcome friction were taken into account.

Problems

1. For the turntable depicted (consider it Act 2 of the table shown in an earlier example), how far away is the center of mass from the axis of rotation?

2. An actor weighing 200 lb stands 10 ft away from a turntable's axis of rotation. If the turntable sits on a deck raked at 4°, what worst case lifting torque is created by this one actor alone?

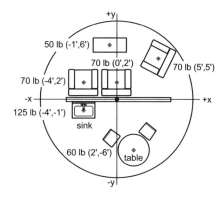

3. A drawbridge weighing 515 lb moves 90° between horizontal and vertical. Assuming it is 10 ft wide by 15 ft high and 1 ft thick (dimensions referring to it in its vertical position), and that it rotates conventionally around hinges located

along its lower edge, what worst case lifting torque would it impose on the machine running it?

4. A 4 m square turntable with a mass of 1100 kg sits on a deck raked at 8 cm/m. Its axis of rotation is located 1 m in from a corner, on the line running from that corner to the one diagonally opposite. What is the worst case lifting torque?

11

Maximum Power and Torque

Power

Power in rotational form is the product of both torque and angular speed, and so it follows that no power is required if either of these two terms is zero. Torque, for example, commonly exists without any power being required to sustain it. A weight hanging on a cable wound around a stationary winch drum will twist the drum's shaft, but as long as no movement occurs, no power is ever needed to hold that weight in place. Rotation too can exist without power if torque is zero, but since friction is always present to impede movement, we never experience constant unpowered rotation. It is only when both torque and angular speed act together that power exists.

The generalized definition of rotational power involves torque and angular velocity in their vector form, in a way that is analogous to the linear power dot product $P = \mathbf{F} \cdot \mathbf{v} = |F||v| \cos\theta$ that appears at the beginning of Chapter 6. But because the rotational power formula would involve infinitesimals (recall that angles cannot be true vectors unless they are infinitesimally small), the formula in its generalized form is potentially more cryptic than clarifying. Given this, we can skip immediately to a simplified version that works for the one-dimensional motion always assumed here.

$$P = T\omega$$

Where P = power (ft-lb/sec, w)

T = torque, assumed to be acting around the axis of rotation (ft-lb, Nm)

ω = angular speed (rad/sec)

The torque and angular velocity vectors cannot be totally ignored because their directions are important. They lie along the axis of rotation, with their directions following a right hand rule, as illustrated in Figure 11.1. If, as has been assumed from the start of these rotational motion chapters, motion is confined to one dimension, then these two vectors can only point in the same direction, or in opposite directions (see Figure 11.2). The $\cos\theta$ term that is part of the definition of the dot product will therefore resolve to $\cos 0° = +1$ when the torque and angular velocity are in the same direction, or to $\cos 180° = -1$ when they are opposite. The sign of the result from this cosine term sets the sign of the power resulting from the

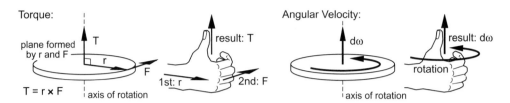

Figure 11.1   The directions of both torque and angular velocity follow a right hand rule.

interaction of torque and angular speed. A positive sign for power, when torque and angular speed are both in the same direction, means power is being supplied from a power source to a load, a situation sometimes called motoring. Conversely, a negative sign for power, when torque and angular speed are in opposite directions, means power is flowing from the load to something that can absorb it, such as a brake, the inefficiency of a gear reducer, or a motor acting as a generator.

The simplified non-vector approach used here comes to the same conclusion through a slightly different path. Instead of vectors, scalars with signs are used for torque and angular speed. An arbitrary choice is made at the beginning of every problem as to whether a given direction of rotation, either clockwise or counterclockwise, is the positive direction or negative. Regardless of the choice, if torque and angular speed are both in the same direction relative to each other, their signs will be the same, and the outcome of their multiplication will be positive power: $(+T) \times (+\omega) = +P$, or $(-T) \times (-\omega) = +P$. If they are in opposite directions from each other, one term will be positive and the other negative, and the outcome will always be negative power: $(+T) \times (-\omega) = -P$, or $(-T) \times (+\omega) = -P$. This behavior

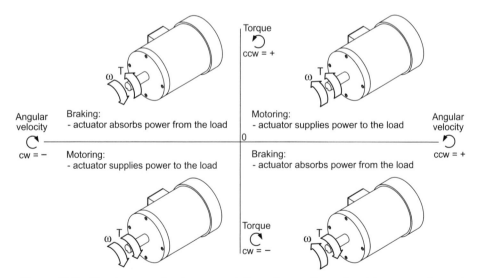

Figure 11.2   The four quadrant representation of one-dimensional torque and angular velocity. Each quadrant represents a unique pair of directions, clockwise or counterclockwise, for these two terms. (The directions are shown in intitutive rather than vector notation.)

is identical to the results that would be obtained using the cosine in the definition of the dot product, and so the power formula for one dimensional rotation using signed scalars for each of the torque terms and angular speed can be written as either

$$P_{max} = (T_{accel}\,\omega_{max}) + (T_{frict}\,\omega_{max}) + (T_{lift}\,\omega_{max})$$

or as it has been presented all along.

$$P_{max} = (T_{accel} + T_{friction} + T_{lifting})\,\omega_{max}$$

The first version of the power formula listed above is most useful conceptually. The total power needed by a system is the sum of a group of component powers. As written, it is the sum of the power to accelerate, the power needed to overcome friction, and the power required to lift against gravity, which is all very standard and nothing new. But if an effect was more complex than one object rotating, say two turntables connected together by roller chain such that one always spun at twice the speed of the other, then the power needed by each turntable could be calculated independently, and the results then just added together. This rarely needs to be done, but it is a technique worth remembering because it can quickly simplify the analysis of complex effects.

Maximum Power

In estimating the loads a particular effect will place on the machine that will run it, two worst case situations are the most important. One is the maximum power that needs to be delivered to the effect at the worst case combination of acceleration, friction, and lifting torques that can occur at the effect's top speed. The second, to be discussed in the next section, is the maximum torque that the effect, its actuator, and potentially the building structure it connects to will have to withstand. Both are of course related to the maximum power formula:

$$P_{max} = (T_{accel} + T_{friction} + T_{lifting})\,\omega_{max}$$

The effect the three torque components have on maximum power can be summarized as:

- T_{accel} will be zero both while the effect is at rest, or while it is moving at a constant angular velocity. It will be in the same direction as ω_{max} during acceleration, and opposite in direction during deceleration. Therefore, the power needed just for angular acceleration will always be at its positive maximum during the acceleration portion of a move.
- $T_{friction}$ is the torque that must be applied to overcome the effects of friction. It is always present during movement, and is always in the same direction as ω_{max}. The power needed to overcome friction is, given the simple models for friction used here, independent of speed, so it is at its maximum whenever movement is occurring, regardless of the move's direction.
- $T_{lifting}$ is always zero in two common situations, whenever an effect's axis of rotation is vertical, and in any orientation of the axis of rotation if the effect's center of mass lies on that axis. In all other situations, $T_{lifting}$ will vary sinusoi-

dally during rotation, hitting identical magnitude positive and negative maxima during each revolution.

Not surprisingly then, the worst case power use will occur during acceleration, when the lifting torque is at its positive maximum.

The top speed, ω_{max}, is related to the needs of the move, or in other words what speed is needed to travel the required distance in the desired amount of time. In terms of power, the direction of the angular speed is unimportant if an effect revolves one or more full turns, because the cyclical nature of rotation will bring the maximum lifting torque into play once each revolution. But if an effect rotates only some portion of a full turn, a drawbridge for instance, then the direction of rotation during maximum power use is the one that moves the center of mass up.

The following example will illustrate the interaction of the three torque components at different points in a typical move, and it will function as a review of some of the techniques covered in the previous chapters. It is also quite long as is typical of rotational problems.

EXAMPLE: A large turntable, depicted below, sits on a raked deck. Scenery for the show beyond the turntable will only be props, with the heaviest unit being a 200 lb throne that will sit in the center of the small circle. A cast of 15 may all appear in the throne scene, but rehearsals have not begun, so their blocking is unknown. The turntable is mounted on casters having a $\mu_r = 0.03$. A motion controller will set acceleration and decelerations times to as little as 2 seconds, and the turntable's top speed will be 3 rpm. Three questions need to be answered:
- What is the maximum power needed during acceleration?
- What are the maximum and minimum power needs during the constant velocity portion of a move?
- Does the turntable drive need to absorb power, or act as a brake, during a normal show move deceleration?

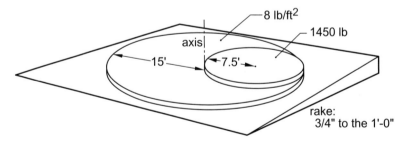

SOLUTION: This is a somewhat vaguely specified problem, exactly as would be expected at the beginning of the production process. Assumptions will have to be made about the weight and placement of the cast, as this will have a major impact on all three torque components. There are an infinite number of possible choices here, some clearly wrong, like piling everyone up in the center, and some that would seem to be a reasonable worst case given the setup involved. Here, assume that the 15 people

form an arc centered on the axis of rotation, at
a radius equal to the average caster radius,

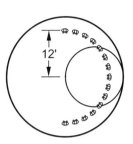

$$r_{avg\,c} = 0.8r_{turn} = 0.8(15) = 12\,ft$$

creating a half circle that runs over the raised
circular platform. Not great blocking, but this
layout was chosen both to force a larger lifting
torque, and to ease later friction calculations.
Other perfectly reasonable layouts exist, for
instance distributing the cast evenly around the small disk, so do not see
this as the one and only choice you too should have come up with, but
merely as a choice. As to the weight of the actors, the general rule of
thumb is to assume something around 175 lb per person if the cast is
roughly divided between male and female, and so that number will be
used here.

None of the questions asked can be answered until all the component
torques and the top speed have been determined, and so adopt a methodical approach, and jump in.

• *What torque is needed just to accelerate this turntable, or what is T_{accel}?*
The torque needed to angularly accelerate an object is:

$$T_{accel} = I\alpha$$

The moment of inertia for this turntable involves 4 main units: the large
disk, the small disk, the throne, and the actors. The 200 lb throne is a
small enough number that it could be just added into the small disk, but it
is also not difficult to calculate it separately.

The large disk spins around its center of mass, and so its moment of
inertia is found using one of the basic moment of inertia formulas

$$I_{ldisk} = \frac{mr^2}{2} = \frac{\left(\frac{F_w}{32.2}\right)r^2}{2} = \frac{\left(\frac{area \times lb/ft^2}{32.2}\right)r^2}{2} = \frac{\left(\frac{\pi 15^2 \times 8}{32.2}\right)15^2}{2} = 19800\,slug\text{-}ft^2$$

The small disk does not spin around its center of mass. so the
moment of inertia must be found using the transfer of axis formula.

$$I_{sdisk} = I_{c\,of\,m} + mr_{tr}^2 = \frac{mr^2}{2} + mr_{tr}^2 = \frac{\left(\frac{1450}{32.2}\right)7.5^2}{2} + \left(\frac{1450}{32.2}\right)7.5^2 = 1270 + 2530 = 3800\,slug\text{-}ft^2$$

The throne's contribution to the total moment of inertia will almost
certainly be trivial, but until the calculation is done, that cannot be
proven. No dimensions are known, so it is assumed that, in plan, it is 3′ by
3′.

$$I_{throne} = I_{c\,of\,m} + mr_{tr}^2 = \frac{m}{12}(a^2 + b^2) + mr_{tr}^2 = \frac{(200/32.2)}{12}(3^2 + 3^2) + \frac{200}{32.2}7.5^2 = 359\,slug\text{-}ft^2$$

The throne is less than 2% of the inertia of the large disk, and it could be
ignored, but since its inertia is now known, it will be added in to the total.

The moment of inertia of the cast will simply be 15 times the moment of inertia of one person. Since the 12′ axis translation distance is so much larger than the side-to-side or front-to-back dimensions of a person, getting an accurate $I_{c\,of\,m}$ is not critical. Assume in this case that the person is a disk with a radius of 0.75′.

$$I_{actor} = I_{c\,of\,m} + mr_{tr}^2 = \frac{mr^2}{2} + mr_{tr}^2 = \frac{\left(\frac{175}{32.2}\right)0.75^2}{2} + \left(\frac{175}{32.2}\right)12^2 = 1.53 + 783 = 784\ slug\text{-}ft^2$$

Notice two things, the choice of formula for the $I_{c\,of\,m}$ term had no bearing on the final answer as that term is mere tenths of a percent of the end result, and that the moment of inertia of one actor is more than twice that of the throne. Taking into account all the actors

$$I_{cast} = 15(784) = 11760\ slug\text{-}ft^2$$

The actors will not appear on the designer's ground plan, nor are they something built in the shop, but they do have a major impact on the requirements of the machines that automate scenery, so never forget them.

The total moment of inertia is the sum of the four elements

$$I_{total} = I_{ldisk} + I_{sdisk} + I_{throne} + I_{cast}$$

$$I_{total} = 19800 + 3800 + 359 + 11760 = 35719\ slug\text{-}ft^2$$

• To find the angular acceleration with an equation of constant acceleration, the given top speed will first have to be converted into the proper units.

$$rpm \times 0.105 = rad/sec$$

$$\omega_{max} = 3(0.105) = 0.315\ rad/sec$$

With this top speed, the given $\Delta t_{accel} = 2\ sec$, and the assumption that acceleration will start from a speed of zero, Equation 7.1 can be solved for angular acceleration.

$$\omega_2 = \omega_1 + \alpha\Delta t$$

$$0.315 = 0 + \alpha(2)$$

$$\alpha = 0.158\ rad/sec^2$$

And finally, the torque to accelerate this turntable can be calculated.

$$T_{accel} = I\alpha = 35719(0.158) = 5640\ ft\text{-}lb$$

• *What torque is needed just to overcome the effects of friction, or what is* $T_{friction}$? Whenever a conventional circular turntable is being analyzed, it is worth considering whether the simple friction calculation involving average caster radius can be used:

$$T_{friction} = r_{avg\,c}(\mu_r F_n) = 0.8r_{turn}(\mu_r F_n)$$

It's simple, it's fast, and it provides a value that is accurate enough for typical needs. It does require that all casters have identical coefficients of

friction, which is certainly possible here, that they are distributed relatively evenly under the turntable, also not a problem here, and that the
load on the wheels is roughly the same on each, which is definitely not
true here. This last point would seem to eliminate the possibility of using
this simple formula and force the use one of the lengthier techniques, but
two facts about this particular setup will allow its use.

First, when the actors were placed on the turntable in order to account
for their mass in the moment of inertia calculations, they were placed in
an arc with a radius equal to the conservative value of average caster
radius.

$$r_{avg\,c} = 0.8r_{turn} = 0.8(15) = 12\,ft$$

This means their weight will act, via the normal force, at exactly the same
radius as the large disk portion of the turntable, and so because of this
their weight can just be added to that of the large disk. This would not be
true if the cast was located elsewhere, but giving thought at the beginning
of the solution of a problem to what might be both a reasonable placement in artistic terms and a simplifying one in a technical sense allows this
easier outcome. Second, the small disk is a circle spinning around an axis
of rotation at its edge, which matches one of the average caster radius case
formulas (see Figure 9.2). The torque to overcome friction on just the
small disk can be computed separately and then added to the result
obtained from the large disk (plus cast) calculation. This is allowable
because the mathematical model for friction being used throughout this
text is linear (in the mathematical sense of one term being directly proportional to another, not in the straight line sense). It does not matter
whether the two disks ride on their own sets of casters with the resulting
frictional torques being summed, or the casters under the small disk carry
the sum of the load from both disks, the end results will be the same.

So the torque to overcome caster friction is the sum of two quantities,
the large disk and the cast, and the small disk with the throne added on to
its weight

$$T_{friction} = T_{frict\,ldisk\,\&\,cast} + T_{frict\,sdisk\,\&\,throne}$$

$$T_{friction} = 0.8r_{ldisk}(\mu_r F_n) + 0.7d_{sdisk}(\mu_r F_n)$$

$$T_{friction} = 0.8r_{ldisk}(\mu_r F_w \cos\theta_{rake}) + 0.7d_{sdisk}(\mu_r F_w \cos\theta_{rake})$$

The rake angle is calculated from the given rise and run

$$\tan\theta_{rake} = \frac{rise}{run} = \frac{0.75}{12} \qquad so: \qquad \theta_{rake} = 3.58°$$

and with this the torque to overcome friction can be determined.

$$T_{friction} = 0.8r_{ldisk}(\mu_r F_w \cos\theta_{rake}) + 0.7d_{sdisk}(\mu_r F_w \cos\theta_{rake})$$

$$T_{friction} = 0.8(15)(0.03)(8280)\cos 3.58° + 0.7(15)(0.03)(1650)\cos 3.58°$$

$$T_{friction} = 2975 + 519 = 3494\,ft\text{-}lb$$

• *What torque is needed to lift the imbalanced portion of this turntable up the rake, or what is $T_{lifting}$?* Since this turntable is both on a rake, and not balanced around its axis of rotation, it will definitely have a lifting torque. The lifting torque formula (in two forms),

$$T_{lifting} = r_{c\,of\,m}\,F_{lifting}$$

$$T_{lifting} = r_{c\,of\,m}\,F_w\,\sin\theta_{rake}$$

shows that aside from the rake angle and the weights involved, the distance between the axis of rotation and the center of mass, $r_{c\,of\,m}$, needs to be determined. To simplify this process slightly, the large disk can be ignored because its center of mass falls on the axis of rotation, and so it has no effect on lifting.

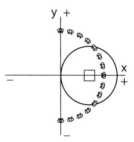

The process used to find the center of mass of a collection of objects involves placing an x and y coordinate system onto a plan of the objects, with its origin centered on the axis of rotation. If the objects have an obvious axis of symmetry, then the placement of the coordinates should align to that symmetry. In this problem, a choice for the axes is to align the x axis through the centers of the small disk and the throne. The benefit of this is that one of the center of mass calculations, the y axis one here, will not have to be done, because, by symmetry, the y coordinate of the location of the center of mass is zero.

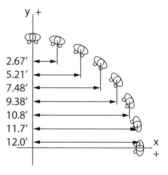

The x axis center of mass calculation requires the distances in the x direction between the axis of rotation and the centers of mass of all the objects involved. The small disk and the throne centered on it both have x distances of 7.5 ft. The x distance for each of the actors is not a given, and so it must be calculated using trig, dimensioned on a quick cad drafting, or scaled off a ground plan. The illustration shows the results of one of these techniques for the upper half of the arc, the lower half would have identical dimensions. The two actors standing on the y axis are not dimensioned because they balance each other out and do not contribute to the lifting torque.

$$x_{c\,of\,m} = \frac{x_1 F_{w1} + x_2 F_{w2} + \dots}{F_{w\,total}}$$

$$x_{c\,of\,m} = \frac{7.5(1450 + 200) + (2.67 + 5.21 + 7.48 + 9.38 + 10.8 + 11.7)350 + 12(175)}{1450 + 200 + (13 \times 175)} = 7.90\,ft$$

The total weight of the out of balance load is in the denominator in the expression above, so

$$F_w = 1450 + 200 + (13 \times 175) = 3925 \; lb$$

Putting these values into the lifting torque equation, using the rake angle found earlier, yields

$$T_{lifting} = r_{c \, of \, m} F_w \sin\theta_{rake}$$
$$T_{lifting} = 7.90(3925)\sin 3.58° = 1940 \; ft\text{-}lb$$

Now that all the terms in the maximum power have been determined, the original three questions can be answered.

• *What is the maximum power needed during acceleration?* The answer to this question is straightforward. All the terms in the maximum power formula are positive.

$$P_{max} = (T_{accel} + T_{friction} + T_{lifting}) \, \omega_{max}$$
$$P_{max} = (5640 + 3494 + 1940) \, 0.315$$
$$P_{max} = 3488 \; ft\text{-}lb/sec \qquad or \qquad 6.34 \; hp$$

This is the power that needs to be delivered to the turntable to accomplish the move as specified. It is possible that a 7.5 hp motor acting through an efficient speed reduction stage could be used to power this effect, but that would leave little or nothing as a power contingency to deal with differences between the problem as figured, and the unit as it is built and used. (The efficiency of specific types of speed reduction is discussed in later chapters) It may also be possible that this amount of horsepower is beyond what can be afforded for this production, in which case significant changes will have to be made. Making the turntable smaller and light would reduce all the torques. Eliminating the rake eliminates the need for lifting torque (but that change alone would not drop the power needed below 5 hp). Since the torque to accelerate is by far the largest term, lengthening acceleration time would also reduce the power needed. The top speed could also be reduced, if a longer move time is acceptable. Finally, the number of cast members on the turntable during a move could be reduced, though this is generally a poor option to choose because it potentially forces the director into awkward blocking. Any or all of these changes are possible, but which are acceptable is ultimately the choice of the production's artistic team, usually the director and set designer. It is the technical designer's job to use the information provided by the power formula to provide alternatives, knowing with confidence the exact implications that any changes agreed to will have.

• *What are the maximum and minimum power needs during the constant velocity portion of a move?* During constant velocity, acceleration is zero, setting the torque to accelerate term also to zero. The torque due to friction term remains constant, and always in the same direction as angular speed. The lifting torque will vary, oscillating between being in the same direction as speed, and in the opposite direction from speed. During the portion of the move where lifting requires the most power:

$$P_{max} = (T_{accel} + T_{friction} + T_{lifting})\, \omega_{max}$$
$$P_{max} = (0 + 3494 + 1940)\, 0.315$$
$$P_{max} = 1712 \; ft\text{-}lb/sec \qquad or \qquad 3.11 \; hp$$

During the portion of the move where the out of balance load acts to run down the rake, the power needed is

$$P_{max} = (T_{accel} + T_{friction} + T_{lifting})\, \omega_{max}$$
$$P_{max} = (0 + 3494 - 1940)\, 0.315$$
$$P_{max} = 490 \; ft\text{-}lb/sec \qquad or \qquad 0.890 \; hp$$

Though this is not a set of values often calculated, here it does show that the motor will have to supply power to the turntable throughout the whole revolution. This implies there will not be any visible surging motion that could potentially be caused by both backlash or slop in the power transmission system, or by changes in motor speed as it goes from supplying to absorbing power.

• *Does the turntable drive need to absorb power, or act as a brake, during a normal show move deceleration?* The ability of a motorized system to absorb power will depend on the specifications of the motor drive being used to control motor speed and on the efficiency of the speed reduction system running between the motor shaft and the effect. Both are beyond the topic at hand at the moment, but determining the magnitude of any power that will have to be absorbed is answerable here. The worst case will occur when a deceleration is begun just when the lifting torque is at its negative peak, or

$$P_{max} = (T_{accel} + T_{friction} + T_{lifting})\, \omega_{max}$$
$$P_{max} = (-5640 + 3494 - 1940)\, 0.315$$
$$P_{max} = -1287 \; ft\text{-}lb/sec \qquad or \qquad -2.34 \; hp$$

Since this answer is negative, the turntable's drive system will have to absorb power, roughly 1/3 of the maximum that it provides during acceleration.

These results can be presented graphically, but because of the varying nature of lifting torque, the presentation is not as simple as the linear problem presented in Chapter 6. The nine plan views of the turntable show its position as it goes through a cue of slightly more than 1.5 turns counterclockwise. The starting and ending positions were chosen to align with the maximum power needed by the turntable, at *b*, and the maximum braking power, at *h*. The first graph shows a trapezoidal angular speed motion profile, with its typical acceleration, constant speed, and deceleration periods. The individual torque graphs, shown below, include the sinusoidal variation of the lifting torque characteristic of rotation. Note the connection between lifting torque values and the plan views, with

$T_{lifting}$ being at its positive and negative maxima when the center of mass of the out of balance objects is straight across the rake from the axis of rotation, at positions b, d, f, and h, and that $T_{lifting}$ is zero when that center of mass is straight up or down the rake from the turntable's axis, at positions c, e and g. The next graph shows the sum of the three torques, with several key points labeled. Finally, in the bottom graph, power is the product of torque and speed. The power needed to rapidly accelerate the turntable is clearly evident as a peak in the graph, and therefore it is obvious—where it might not be quite so in the numbers—that a longer acceleration time could easily reduce the maximum power needed for this effect.

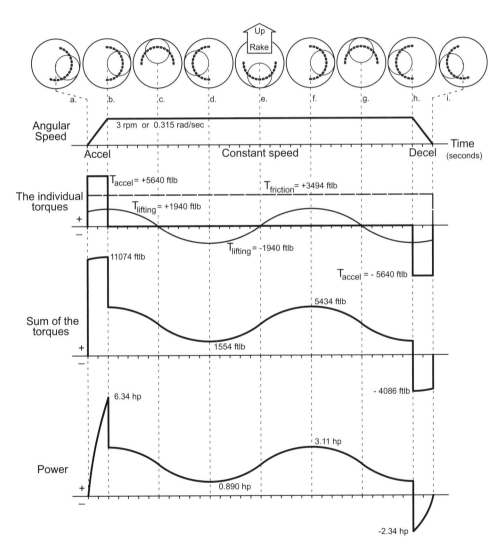

Figure 11.3   A graphic presentation of angular speed, torque and power

Maximum Torque

The three torque components in the maximum power formula will sum to different values over the time it takes to run a cue, but for the purposes of determining the maximum power needed to run an effect, the worst case invariably occurs when the end of the acceleration portion of a move coincides with the peak lifting torque. This sum of torques, in conjunction with the angular speed, works well to define the maximum power, but it rarely describes the maximum torque the drive system will have to withstand. This is because, during an emergency stop, decelerations from full speed to zero may happen in a fraction of a second, and this so radically increases the T_{accel} component that this situation defines the worst case for torque. Motor power is not an issue during this time, as friction throughout the system and brakes are used to absorb the power needed to force the scenery to a stop, but it is at this time that the drive system's components experience their greatest stress. So in other words, for any effect it is important to determine both the maximum power and the maximum torque, and to understand that these may occur at different times within a move.

During a worst case deceleration situation, the magnitude of the torque components will depend on the specifics of the problem being solved, but the signs of the torques relative to that of angular speed will always follow the same pattern:

$$P_{max} = (T_{accel} + T_{friction} + T_{lifting})\ \omega_{max}$$

signs will be either: $P_{max} = (\ [-]\ +\ [+]\ +\ [-]\ )\ [+]$

or: $P_{max} = (\ [+]\ +\ [-]\ +\ [+]\ )\ [-]$

Friction opposes motion, and power must always be sent from an actuator to the load to overcome it. Therefore $T_{friction}$ will always have the same sign as angular speed so that their product is positive power. The other two components will be opposite in sign from the angular speed. This is because both deceleration and lifting (at least in half its cycle) require a retarding or braking torque that represents negative power.

EXAMPLE: In the effect shown, a draw-bridge-like action converts a balcony into a dock. Two hydraulic rotary actuators, attached to the axis of rotation, turn the unit through 90° at a top speed of 12°/sec. The scenery weighs 230 lb, it has a calculated moment of inertia of 694 slug/ft², and has a center of mass located at a radius of 9.0 ft from the axis of rotation. If the valve controlling the rotary actuators is rated by the manufacturer to close in 0.25 sec, what is the maximum torque needed to decelerate this unit during an e-stop? Assume that friction is negligible. (The concept used in this example is based on an effect in the 2002 Broadway

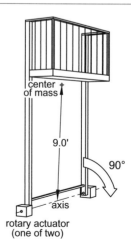

center of mass

9.0'

90°

axis

rotary actuator (one of two)

production of *Man of La Mancha* designed by Paul Brown, and technically designed and built by Hudson Scenic Studio.)

SOLUTION: Because friction is to be ignored, the maximum torque during deceleration will be the sum of the torque to decelerate the unit and the lifting torque. The torque to decelerate will equal:

$$T_{decel} = I\alpha$$

Since the moment of inertia is a given, only the angular deceleration needs to be determined. An emergency stop can occur at any time, so the worst case for deceleration would be a stop from the full speed of 12 deg/sec to a stop in the valve closing time of 0.25 sec. After converting the given top speed into rad/sec, using the conversion given in Chapter 7, an equation of constant acceleration can be solved for the e-stop's deceleration.

$$12 \; deg/sec \times 0.0175 = 0.21 \; rad/sec$$

$$\omega_2 = \omega_1 + \alpha\Delta t$$
$$0 = 0.21 + \alpha(0.25)$$
$$\alpha = -0.84 \; rad/sec^2$$

The value is negative because the initial speed, ω_1, was assumed as positive, and this is a deceleration. The torque to decelerate this scenery is:

$$T_{decel} = I\alpha = 694(-0.84) = -583 \; ft\text{-}lb$$

Since moment of inertia is always positive, the negative value for acceleration forces the torque to be negative, which only means that the torque to decelerate is applied opposite to the direction of speed. It is this opposition that is important (and fairly obvious—to slow down requires a twist back from direction of movement). Below, when this and the lifting torque are summed, the sign will be switched to positive because the magnitude of the worst case torque is all that is needed, not its sign.

The standard lifting torque formula,

$$T_{lifting} = r_{c\,of\,m} F_w \sin\theta_{rake}$$

includes the rake angle, θ_{rake}, one definition of which is the angle the axis of rotation forms with a perfectly vertical line. That means here, in the absence of any conventional rake, that the rake angle is 90° because the axis of rotation is horizontal. Since the $\sin 90° = 1$, the formula for this situation is simply:

$$T_{lifting} = r_{c\,of\,m} F_w$$

Inserting the givens yields a lifting torque of

$$T_{lifting} = r_{c\,of\,m} F_w = 9.0(230) = 2070 \; ft\text{-}lb$$

The worst case torque will occur when the unit is traveling down at full speed, approaching horizontal, and an emergency stop occurs. The value of that torque here is

$$T_{max} = T_{decel} + T_{lifting} = 583 + 2070 = 2653 \; ftlb$$

This is a huge torque considering it will be applied directly at the axis of rotation. Both the choice of the actuators and the design of the scenery's structure would be critical to withstanding this torque. An emergency stop system is an essential part of all scenery automation, and so the forces and torques that develop from its activation must be considered during technical design. It would be ridiculous if the safety system itself caused failures that would then make the whole setup a hazard.

One of the reasons there are two rotary actuators running this effect is to provide part of a single failure proof system. This concept is discussed in much greater detail in Chapter 13, but basically should one actuator fail, the other must be capable of safely stopping the scenery, but not be able to continue to operate it as if nothing were wrong. This is being mentioned here because ultimately each actuator alone must be able to withstand the worst case torque.

An Important Caveat—Mass and Spring Vibrations

Throughout the previous chapters it has been assumed that the materials being used are perfectly rigid, implying that they will have no deflections under load. This is of course not true in reality. All materials deform when placed under tension and compression, shafts twist; wire rope, roller chain and belts either stretch or go slack; and the steel structure of an effect will deflect. Provided that stresses are kept below the material specific levels that would cause permanent deformation, most materials behave as simple springs with a deflection proportional to the applied force (or torque). Combining this inherent springiness with the mass that every material has creates a system that will prefer to oscillate or vibrate at particular frequencies. This will occur only if the system is driven by some force that changes over time rapidly enough to excite those preferred resonant frequencies, but forces or torques that change relatively rapidly over time are common in stage automation—accels, decels, or e-stops for instance. If a scenic effect's actuator, be it a motor, cylinder, or stagehand, starts or stops quickly, the effect may start oscillating, only coming to rest after being damped out by friction. For instance, it is easy to envision that the drawbridge-like effect in the example above would bounce, oscillating up and down after a rapid stop.

This behavior cannot be predicted using the simple mathematical models presented here, but instead either differential equations would need to be created to account for the spring constant and mass of each component in a setup and then solved, or a CAD model would have to be developed and analyzed in appropriate finite-element-analysis software to get any accurate information on what might occur. Both of these techniques are well beyond the scope of this text. Despite this there are qualitative concepts worth keeping in mind that will help minimize issues with oscillation, two of which relate to material already covered, and others of which will be expanded on in later chapters.

- *Keep accelerations and decelerations as slow and smooth as possible.* Consider this analogy. Strike a bell with a hammer and it rings at its resonant frequencies. Now imagine using the same hammer to develop the same force as earlier, but with the hammer moving towards the bell very slowly, maybe at an inch/hour. No ring would result, the bell would simply be pushed. Impulses, the hammer strike, or in the context of scenery movement something like a very rapid acceleration caused by a hydraulic valve turning on a cylinder in 0.1 second, contain a wide range of frequencies. A goal in machinery design is to keep the lowest resonant frequency of a mechanism higher than that created by the drive system. This is why devices such as motor drives, and proportional valves are in common use. They allow speed control for smooth and gentle speed changes, and hence little impulse behavior.

- *Reduce friction, and choose materials with as little difference between their static and kinetic coefficients of friction as possible.* Higher forces or torques are generally needed to start something moving rather than to keep it moving. This static to kinetic difference means any compliant or springy member in the power transmission path will deflect more during the effort to overcome a static situation than it will need to during the kinetic. A surging motion can result as the extra deflection built up at the start releases once movement begins. This effect can appear in the movement of a tracked wagon pulled with a long length of too small a diameter cable, or in many pneumatically driven effects.

Vibration is not a major issue in typical scenic effects—wagons, turntables, and flying—simply because the designs of conventional machines have evolved, eliminating those that work poorly. Vibration should be considered whenever something unusual or untried is being developed.

Problems

1. Assume that the platform from Chapter 9 Problem 3 (page 100) is run by a drive system that could stop it in 0.3 second from a top speed of 4 rpm during an emergency stop. What torque would be required to do this? Assume the platform's weight is evenly distributed across its area.

2. The turntable shown on page sits on a deck raked at 1″ per foot. It spins one half a revolution in 10 seconds, with acceleration and deceleration times set by its controller to 3 seconds. What is the maximum power needed by this effect? Assume all its casters are identical, that they have coefficients of friction of 0.03, and that they are evenly distributed around underneath the turntable. Also assume that the total weight for the two end tables by the bed, the coffee table, and the console by the door is 100 lb, and that it can just be added into the turntable weight. The two walls are typical hard cover flats braced to each other with material that has no significant weight. The *x* and *y* coordinates for three major

pieces of furniture relate to the coordinates shown at the center of the plan view of the turntable. The cast for this show totals just 3 actors.

PLAN:

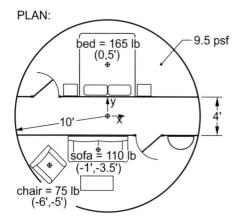

SIDE ELEVATION:

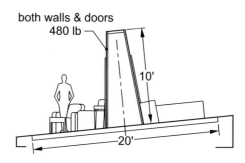

12

Combining Multiple Motions

Overview

In all the chapters prior to this, the movements analyzed involved just one piece of scenery moving in a one-dimensional linear or rotational manner. While this covers the majority of effects, it does not cover them all. Treadmills, roll drops, and scissor lifts for instance, combine both linear and rotary motion into one effect. In these, part of the effect moves linearly, the stretcher pipe at the bottom of a roll drop for instance, and some part rotates, the roll tube that stores and unfurls the drop. Beyond just the movement of scenery, the machines that power the effects sometimes need to be included into the loading conditions for a move. Electric motor rotors or armatures, for example, have relatively large moments of inertia that can have a significant impact the acceleration or deceleration of the systems they power (though that is quite rare in most stage machinery). The speed reduction ratios of gear reducers, roller chain, belts and of the systems that are combinations of these working together transform torque and speed, which greatly affects the relative torques needed to accelerate the masses mounted on their input and output shafts.

The techniques presented below cover the range of topics suggested above, offering several ways to analyze these somewhat more complex systems.

Combining Linear and Rotational Power

There are a few standard effects that are not solely linear or rotational—roll and oleo drops (top of drop attached to drum, which just rotates to unfurl the drop down, and bottom of drop attached to drum, which then travels down as the drop is revealed respectively), treadmills, and traveling cycloramas for example—so these effects cannot be analyzed by the techniques covered to this point. Two simple techniques, both closely related to all that has already been done, do allow determining the forces, torques, and powers needed to move these effects. One is based on adding separately calculated powers together, and the other converts forces to torques or torques to forces.

There is nothing different between the 2 hp used to move a wagon along a straight deck track, and the 2 hp that might be needed to spin a turntable—power is power. If both these effects are for some reason to be run off one machine, then that machine will have to supply 4 hp. The powers for the two different motions just add. For effects with both linear and rotary aspects to their motions, the maximum power formula can be applied twice, once in its linear version accounting for those parts moving in a straight line, and once in its rotational form to cover the rotating parts.

$$P_{max} = (F_{accel} + F_{friction} + F_{lifting})v_{max} + (T_{accel} + T_{friction} + T_{lifting})\omega_{max}$$

The difference between this approach and anything done earlier occurs in the splitting up of the effect into linear and rotational parts. The full weight of the effect, for instance, will never appear as one number anywhere in the formula. Instead, that portion of the full weight that is moving in a straight line will appear in the normal force and mass calculations in the linear section, and only the portion of the effect's weight that spins will be used when determining moment of inertia. An example will illustrate how this technique works.

EXAMPLE: A treadmill is to be built into a level stage deck. A commercial grade conveyor belt material 3.0 ft wide and weighing 0.87 psf will be used to create a moving surface 20 ft long. The drive and idler rollers are made from pipe 6.625″ in diameter, and they have calculated moments of inertia of $I_{roller} = 0.115\ slug\text{-}ft^2$ each. Beneath the walkable portion of the treadmill is a plywood support surface covered with UHMW polyethylene to reduce friction (with a kinetic coefficient of friction between belt and plastic being $\mu_k = 0.15$). The 5 mph top speed of the treadmill is reached in as little as 1.5 seconds, and 4 actors at most will be on it while it is running. Ignore any friction in the bearings supporting the rollers. What power does this effect need?

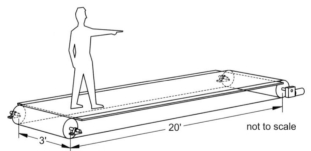

not to scale

20'

3'

SOLUTION: The load on a treadmill is a bit unusual. Typically a treadmill is used for the effect of actors walking or running, without them actually going anywhere. If it is assumed that the actors will always move on the belt to keep themselves stationary relative to the stage, then they are not accelerated by the treadmill's drive motor, and F_{accel} would not need to account for them. If the actors just stand on the belt, then their mass would be included into the F_{accel} calculations, and this is the safe assumption to make. They could also run in the direction of the belt movement, doubling, or even tripling their effect on F_{accel}, but since they would very quickly just run off the belt, this is an unlikely option. The force due to friction developed because of their weight, however, would be the same regardless of the acceleration situation assumed to apply.

Beyond the actors, the treadmill itself has sections that move linearly, the upper and lower runs of belt, and sections that rotate, the rollers and the two half wraps of belt around those rollers. In terms of power, it does not matter that the upper part of the belt is going the opposite direction from the lower, the same motor power will be needed to accelerate each of these pieces, so the direction is unimportant. Likewise it does not matter that, at the rollers, the belt is always transitioning from linear to rotary and then back to linear. The mass of the belt in linear and rotary motion always remains constant. Given this, the illustration below shows roughly the breakup of the treadmill into its linear and rotational parts.

The maximum power needed to drive this treadmill will be the sum of a linear power and a rotary power:

$$P_{max} = (F_{accel} + F_{friction} + F_{lifting})v_{max} + (T_{accel} + T_{friction} + T_{lifting})\omega_{max}$$

Given that the roller's bearing friction is to be ignored, and that there is no lifting force or torque, the equation simplifies quickly to:

$$P_{max} = (F_{accel} + F_{friction})v_{max} + (T_{accel})\omega_{max}$$

The given top speed of 5 mph needs to be converted to ft/sec and rad/sec for use in the formula. (As always, do not forget the conversion of diameter into a radius, and inches into feet as needed.)

$$v_{max} = \left(5\ \frac{miles}{hour} \times 5280\ \frac{ft}{mile}\right) \div 3600\ \frac{sec}{hour} = 7.33\ ft/sec$$

$$v_{max} = r\omega_{max} = 7.33 = \frac{6.625}{2(12)}\omega_{max} \qquad \omega_{max} = 26.6\ rad/sec$$

The accelerations in both forms are also needed. Either one can be determined by using an equation of constant acceleration, and the other converted as was just done for speed.

$$v_2 = v_1 + a\Delta t$$

$$7.33 = 0 + a(1.5)$$

$$a = 4.89\ ft/sec^2$$

$$a = r\alpha = 4.89 = \frac{6.625}{2(12)}\alpha \qquad \alpha = 17.7\ rad/sec^2$$

The weight moving linearly is that of the actors and the upper and lower runs of belt. Assume the actors weigh, on average 175 lb each.

$$F_{w\,actors} = 4(175) = 700\ lb \qquad F_{w\,belt} = 2(3)(20)(0.87) = 104\ lb$$

The force and torque terms can now be solved. First, the force to accelerate the mass moving linearly is

$$F_{accel} = ma = \frac{(700 + 104)}{32.2}4.89 = 122 \; lb$$

Next the force to overcome friction. Here a reasonable assumption is that only the upper run of belt slides across the plastic surface, the lower run just hangs free between the rollers.

$$F_{friction} = \mu_k F_n = \mu_k F_w \cos\theta_{rake}$$
$$F_{friction} = (0.15)(700 + 52)\cos 0° = 113 \; lb$$

The one remaining term, the torque needed to accelerate the two rollers and one wrap of belt material, equals

$$T_{accel} = (2I_{roller} + I_{belt})\alpha$$

The moment of inertia for the rollers are given, but that of the belt needs to be calculated. The area of the belt times the given weight per area will equal its weight.

$$area = circumference \times length = \pi dl = \pi\left(\frac{6.625}{12}\right)(3) = 5.20 \; ft^2$$

$$F_w = 5.20(0.87) = 4.52 \; lb$$

Assuming that the thickness of the belt is insignificant relative to the diameter of the rollers it wraps around allows the use of the simple "thin ring" moment of inertia formula.

$$I_{belt} = mr^2 = \left(\frac{4.52}{32.2}\right)\left(\frac{6.625}{2(12)}\right)^2 = 0.0107 \; slug\text{-}ft^2$$

With this now determined, the torque to accelerate can be calculated.

$$T_{accel} = (2I_{roller} + I_{belt})\alpha = (2(0.115) + 0.0107)17.7 = 4.26 \; ft\text{-}lb$$

Finally, the maximum power can be found.

$$P_{max} = (F_{accel} + F_{friction})v_{max} + (T_{accel})\omega_{max}$$
$$P_{max} = (122 + 113)7.33 + (4.26)26.6$$
$$P_{max} = 1720 + 113 = 1833 \; ft\text{-}lb/sec \qquad or \qquad 3.33 \; hp$$

It is always a good idea to write out everything in this last solution step to help clearly show the relative contribution each aspect of the effect gives to the whole. Here the power needed for rotation is a relatively small portion of the total, less than 10%. This is not surprising since the major masses and all the friction occur in conjunction with the actors. Also clear here is that if a smaller power motor was a goal, perhaps to allow it to fit within a show deck, there is no obvious single standout factor that might be changed, except to drop the top speed. Since that could radically change the look of this effect, it would be best to stay with these results, and look for a more compact motor.

Converting Terms within the Power Formula

Another technique that allows an accounting of both linear and rotational parts of a single effect is to convert torques to forces, or forces to torques. By using the definition of torque

$$T = rF$$

as a conversion formula, torques can be inserted into the linear power formula,

$$P_{max} = \left(F_{accel} + F_{friction} + F_{lifting} + \frac{(T_{accel} + T_{friction} + T_{lifting})}{r} \right) v_{max}$$

and forces into the rotational.

$$P_{max} = (T_{accel} + T_{friction} + T_{lifting} + r(F_{accel} + F_{friction} + F_{lifting})) \omega_{max}$$

Where The torque terms refer to the rotating part of the effect.
The force terms refer to linear movement parts of the effect.

These formulas are in truth only slight variations on the earlier technique of adding linear and rotational powers separately. They are simpler in only one trivial area, only one version of the effect's speed is needed, either in linear or rotational form.

EXAMPLE: A roll drop 25 ft square rolls onto a 6″ diameter 1/8″ wall thickness aluminum tube. The drop weighs 0.3 lb/ft^2 and it has a 3/4″ schedule 40 steel pipe as a stretcher running through a pocket sewn along its bottom edge. If it accelerates to a top speed of 4 ft/sec in a time of 2 seconds, what is the maximum power needed by this effect? Assume the roll tube is left covered with one full wrap of fabric when the drop is fully extended, and that both friction and the mass of the roll tube support shafts are negligible.

SOLUTION: A roll drop is somewhat complex in that both the weight lifted and moment of inertia spun is constantly changing as the drop rolls onto and off of its tube. Given that the desired answer is the maximum power needed to run this effect, there is no need to develop a mathematical model that gives an accurate second by second description of this behavior. Since the worst case *would appear to be* the power needed during the acceleration up of a fully extended drop, that situation alone will be evaluated. This is only an assumption, possibly made in error, but technical design is filled with such decisions. If sufficient doubt about this assumption exists after the numbers in this first case have been determined, an analysis of the other extreme of this move, where most of the drop is on the roll tube increasing its moment of inertia, could be done.

Both versions of the power formula will provide the same answer, but depending on what is already provided in the problem statement, one form or the other will be slightly easier to use. Here, because the top speed is given in linear terms, the formula using that speed will be used.

$$P_{max} = \left(F_{accel} + F_{friction} + F_{lifting} + \frac{(T_{accel} + T_{friction} + T_{lifting})}{r}\right) v_{max}$$

As a first step in solving this equation, simplify it by eliminating those terms known to be zero, and filling in values that are givens. Here, friction is considered negligible, so both friction terms are zero. Also the roll tube itself is in balance, so the lifting torque will be zero (the drop hanging off the tube will be accounted for by the lifting force).

$$P_{max} = \left(F_{accel} + 0 + F_{lifting} + \frac{(T_{accel} + 0 + 0)}{3/12}\right) 4$$

The remaining three unknown terms need to be determined.

The force needed just to accelerate the part of this effect that is moving linearly, here the drop and its bottom pipe, is

$$F_{accel} = ma$$

The mass is that of the drop and the pipe. (The fact that by the time the drop reaches full speed some of it will have wound onto the roll tube and would not be considered part of this mass will be ignored.)

$$m_{drop} = \frac{area \times weight/area}{32.2} = \frac{(25^2)(0.3)}{32.2} = 5.82 \; slugs$$

$$m_{pipe} = \frac{length \times weight/length}{32.2} = \frac{(25)(1.13)}{32.2} = 0.877 \; slugs$$

$$m_{total} = m_{drop} + m_{pipe} = 6.70 \; slugs$$

The acceleration can be found using an equation of constant acceleration:

$$v_2 = v_1 + a\Delta t$$

$$4 = 0 + a(2)$$

$$a = 2 \; ft/sec^2$$

The force needed to accelerate the linear movement portion of this effect is:

$$F_{accel} = ma = (6.70)(2) = 13.4 \; lb$$

Because this is a lift straight up, the lifting force simply equals the weight of the drop and pipe (again ignoring that some of the drop would have rolled onto the tube by the time top speed is reached).

$$F_{w \; total} = F_{w \; drop} + F_{w \; pipe} = (25^2)(0.3) + (25)(1.13) = 216 \; lb$$

The last unknown term in the power formula is the torque needed to angularly accelerate the roll tube.

$$T_{accel} = I\alpha$$

Determining the moment of inertia of the roll tube is relatively simple because only the aluminum tube and a wrap of fabric need to be considered. The tube's weight is unknown, but it can be found by multiplying the volume of metal in an 1/8″ wall, 6″ diameter, 25 foot long cylinder times the density of aluminum (0.098 lb/in^3, a number which can be looked up in reference books, or searched for on the web). As is always true, consistent units must be used, so convert as necessary.

$$F_{w\,tube} = volume \times density$$

$$F_{w\,tube} = area \times length \times density$$

$$F_{w\,tube} = \pi(r_{od}^2 - r_{id}^2) \times l \times density$$

$$F_{w\,tube} = \pi(3^2 - 2.875^2) \times (25 \times 12) \times 0.098 = 67.8\ lb$$

The fabric weight is given as 0.3 lb/ft^2, so one full wrap of fabric has a weight of (all units here are in feet):

$$F_{w\,fabric} = area \times weight/unit\ area$$

$$F_{w\,fabric} = circumference \times length \times weight/unit\ area$$

$$F_{w\,fabric} = \pi(0.5) \times 25 \times 0.3 = 11.8\ lb\ per\ wrap$$

Since fabric wraps onto the tube as the drop rises, the worst case weight of the fabric that has to be accelerated is not just the one wrap on the tube at the start of the move, but what is on it at the end of acceleration. (Yes this effect was ignored earlier, but it was conservative to ignore it then, and it is conservative to account for it here now.) During acceleration, the drop travels

$$\Delta x = \frac{v_1 + v_2}{2}\Delta t = \frac{0 + 4}{2}(2) = 4\ ft$$

Given that the circumference of the tube is $\pi d = \pi(0.5) = 1.57\ ft$, this 4 ft of travel represents roughly 2.5 more wraps, or a total of 3.5 wraps, on the tube. Given the weight of the fabric, this is a considerable number and is worth being included in the moment of inertia calculation.

$$I_{total} = \frac{m}{2}(r_{od}^2 + r_{id}^2) = \frac{\frac{(67.8 + (3.5)(11.8))}{32.2}}{2}\left(\left(\frac{3.1}{12}\right)^2 + \left(\frac{2.875}{12}\right)^2\right) = 0.210\ slug\text{-}ft^2$$

The angular acceleration is found by converting the already found linear acceleration to rotational form. The radius of the drum must be in feet to match the units used for linear acceleration, and it could have some small amount added to it to account for the thickness of the fabric wrapped on it, but that will be ignored here. (Again, a conservative choice.)

$$a = r\alpha$$

$$\alpha = \frac{a}{r} = \frac{2}{3/12} = 8\ rad/sec^2$$

The torque needed to angularly accelerate the roll tube can now be determined.

$$T_{accel} = I\alpha = 0.210(8) = 1.68 \ ft\text{-}lb$$

Finally, all the calculated values can be inserted into the power formula.

$$P_{max} = \left(F_{accel} + 0 + F_{lifting} + \frac{(T_{accel} + 0 + 0)}{3/12}\right)4$$

$$P_{max} = \left(13.4 + 0 + 216 + \frac{(1.68 + 0 + 0)}{3/12}\right)4$$

$$P_{max} = (13.4 + 0 + 216 + 6.72)\,4 = 944 \ ft\text{-}lb/sec \qquad or \ \ 1.72 \ hp$$

The lifting force dominates the component forces to such an extent that the assumption made at the start that accelerating the completely unfurled drop up would be the worst case for power seems justified. After all the effort to find the effect of angularly accelerating the roll tube, it requires less than 3% of the force involved.

Combining Multiple Speed Effects

When scenery is automated, more than just the scenery moves. Motors, fluid powered cylinders, gears, drums, roller chain, and shafts may all to some extent be involved in the machines that power the movement. Up to now the translation or rotation of one object alone has been analyzed, with it moving at only one speed at any given point in time. This analysis does predict the power and torque needed to move that piece, but it does not account for anything else. The total moving system in a mechanized effect is both the scenery and all the machinery used to run it. Most effects are driven by electric motors, with some form of speed reduction—using gears, roller chain, or toothed belt—between that motor and the scenery. Because of this, different parts of a mechanical system will be changing speeds at different rates as a move accelerates. A turntable may for instance accelerate from 0 to 4 rpm in the same time it takes the motor running it to go from 0 up to nearly 1800 rpm. The moment of inertia of the motor's rotor is nowhere near that of the scenery it spins, but its acceleration can be hundreds of times greater. Part of the goal of this section is to illustrate some of the instances where the full system should be investigated, and some where it is generally not necessary.

Accounting for the moment of inertia of a system of spinning parts when there are intervening speed reduction stages requires the use of a concept called the reflected moment of inertia. This allows the inertia of parts on one shaft to be effectively transferred to another. A quick derivation will show all the relevant aspects of this concept.

In a perfectly efficient speed reduction setup, the power flowing into a reduction stage equals the power flowing out of it, or

$$P_{in} = P_{out} = T_{in}\omega_{in} = T_{out}\omega_{out}$$

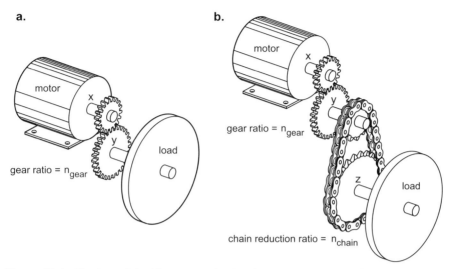

Figure 12.1   Single and double stage reduction between a motor and a load.

By rearranging the torque and speed portion of this formula to solve for output torque, a ratio of input to output speeds appears, and this is defined as the speed reduction ratio, n.

$$T_{out} = T_{in}\frac{\omega_{in}}{\omega_{out}} = T_{in}n$$

The simplified drawing of a motor, reducer and load in Figure 12.1a, shows two shafts, x and y, that spin at speeds related to each other by the gear reduction ratio, n_{gear}, such that $\omega_x = n_{gear}\omega_y$. So if, for example, the gear ratio is 3:1, this simply means the angular speed on shaft x is 3 times that on shaft y.

The torque needed to accelerate the load, from the point of view of the load shaft, y, comes from the standard acceleration torque formula—Newton's second law in rotational form—with subscripts indicating the shaft involved added in:

$$T_{accel\,y} = I_y\alpha_y$$

This torque can also be created by a torque on the motor shaft, at the high speed side of the gear reducer. Solving the earlier reducer input and output torque relationship for T_{in}, and then substituting in the acceleration torque for T_{out} yields:

$$T_{in} = \frac{T_{out}}{n} \qquad or \qquad T_{accel\,y\,from\,x} = \frac{I_y\alpha_y}{n_{gear}}$$

The long subscript used here borders on the ridiculous, being almost a sentence, but the goal here is clarity, not brevity. It denotes that this is the torque to accelerate the load on shaft y from a torque on shaft x.

One last step is required to complete this view of the torque needed to accelerate a load on one shaft from another, and that involves framing the angular acceleration in shaft x terms, not shaft y. The relationship between the accelerations of the two shafts follows a similar relationship to that of the speeds.

$$\alpha_x = n_{gear} \alpha_y$$

Solve this for α_y, substitute it in, and the result is:

$$T_{accel\ y\ from\ x} = \frac{I_y \alpha_y}{n_{gear}} = \frac{I_y \frac{\alpha_x}{n_{gear}}}{n_{gear}} = \left(\frac{I_y}{n_{gear}^2} \right) \alpha_x$$

The term in parentheses is called the reflected moment of inertia, and it represents the translation of the moment of a spinning mass back through a speed reduction stage onto another shaft.

$$I_{ref} = \frac{I_y}{n^2}$$

Where I_{ref} = the reflected, or effective, moment of inertia of an object on a low speed shaft, as seen at the high speed shaft (slug-ft^2, kgm^2)
  I_y = the moment of inertia on the slower spinning shaft (slug-ft^2, kgm^2)
  n = the reduction ratio between shaft a and b (unitless). If, for example, the reduction ratio is 10:1, then $n = 10$.

Notice that if the reduction ratio is 1:1, implying the two shafts spin at the same rate, the n^2 term is just 1, and the reflected moment of inertia simply equals the original inertia. Nothing surprising there. But if the ratio between a motor and a turntable is 400:1, a fairly typical value for that application, then the turntable's moment of inertia appears, from the motor's shaft point of view, to be $n^2 = 160000$ times smaller. This may put it on par with the inertia of the motor's armature, and that will mean the maximum power calculations will need to consider more parts of the system than just the turntable alone, as the following example will illustrate.

EXAMPLE: The specifications given below are for a fairly typical turntable setup by regional theatre standards.

$$F_{w\ turntable} = 5000\ lb \qquad\qquad r_{turntable} = 10\ ft$$

$$I_{turntable} = (mr^2)/2 = 7760\ slug\text{-}ft^2 \qquad T_{friction} = 1200\ ft\text{-}lb$$

$$\omega_{max} = 4\ rpm = 0.419\ rad/sec \qquad t_{accel} = 2\ sec$$

$$\alpha = 0.210\ rad/sec^2 \qquad T_{lifting} = 0$$

It is driven with a 3 hp motor through a speed reduction setup of 437.5:1, which means the table spins at the required 4 rpm when the motor is running at its top speed of 1750 rpm. The motor rotor, and the attached brake disk and gear reducer input shaft, have a moment of inertia of 0.004 slug-ft^2. What maximum power is needed by just the turntable, and by the combination of the turntable and motor rotor?

SOLUTION: Two answers are needed, and both will come out of the maximum power formula. First, calculate the power needed by just the turntable in the conventional way.

$$P_{max} = (T_{accel} + T_{friction} + T_{lifting})\omega_{max}$$

$$P_{max} = (I\alpha + T_{friction} + T_{lifting})\omega_{max}$$

$$P_{max} = ([7760(0.210)] + 1200 + 0)0.419 = 1190 \ ft\text{-}lb/sec \qquad or \ 2.16 \ hp$$

Now, using the concept of reflected moment of inertia, include into this system the effect of the motor's moment of inertia. Since the given formula for reflected moment converts the inertial effect of a slowly spinning mass into its equivalent on the high speed shaft, that will have to be inverted to give the high speed spinning rotor's effect at the much lower speed of the turntable. The original formula solved for the low speed equivalent of a known high speed shaft inertia is

$$I_y = I_{ref}n^2$$

or simply put, the moment of inertia of the high speed spinning object appears much larger (specifically n^2 times larger) when viewed from the low speed end of the system. This moment of inertia is just added to any others moving around the low speed axis, and the power formula can be refigured.

$$P_{max} = (T_{accel} + T_{friction} + T_{lifting})\omega_{max}$$

$$P_{max} = ((I_{turntable} + I_y)\alpha + T_{friction} + T_{lifting})\omega_{max}$$

$$P_{max} = ((I_{turntable} + I_{ref}n^2)\alpha + T_{friction} + T_{lifting})\omega_{max}$$

$$P_{max} = ([7760 + 0.004(437.5^2)](0.210) + 1200 + 0)0.419$$

$$P_{max} = ([7760 + 766](0.210) + 1200 + 0)0.419 = 1250 \ ft\text{-}lb/sec \qquad or \ 2.28 \ hp$$

It takes roughly 10% more power to accelerate the turntable and rotor than just the turntable. This is not a great amount more, and would normally fit within the power contingency automatically created when using a motor the next size up from what is needed by the scenery. In this problem, 2.16 hp is needed, and a 3 hp motor, which is the next available increment above that, offers enough power to easily accelerate both scenery and rotor (this ignores the very important issue of speed reduction inefficiency which could force the motor to even larger sizes, but that discussion will be deferred to later chapters). For the machines and control systems typically used to move scenery, this type of calculation is rarely essential to do, as long as you remain aware of the common need to provide an extra 10 or 20%.

The basic formula reflected moment of inertia formula can be expanded to take into account multiple stages of speed reduction, as found, for example, in a turntable drive system consisting of a motor, connected to a gear reduction stage, which in turn runs a roller chain stage that then runs an endless wire rope loop that spins the table. The formula for the reflected moment of inertia for multiple speed reduction stages is:

$$I_{total} = I_a + \frac{I_b}{n_1^2} + \frac{I_c}{(n_1 n_2)^2} + \frac{I_d}{(n_1 n_2 n_3)^2}$$

Where I_{total} = the total moment of inertia, as seen at the high speed shaft (slug-ft^2, kgm^2)

I_a = the moment of inertia of everything on the high speed shaft (slug-ft^2, kgm^2)

I_b = the moment of inertia of everything one speed reduction stage away from the high speed shaft. (slug-ft^2, kgm^2)

I_c, I_d = the moment of inertia of everything two speed reduction stages away from the high speed shaft, c, and three stages away, d. (slug-ft^2, kgm^2)

n_1 = the reduction ratio between shaft a and b (unitless). If, for example, the reduction ratio is 10:1, then n_1 = 10.

n_2, n_3 = the reduction ratio between shaft b and c, and c and d respectively (unitless).

This discussion only begins to touch on the performance of a system of parts connected together with speed reduction stages because it is a complex topic that overlaps with the characteristics of the control system being used. For instance, if extremely fine speed control and positioning ability are needed (rare in regional theatre automation, but becoming more common in Broadway and Las Vegas scale productions), high performance servo motors and control systems are used, and they come with recommendations for the ratio between the reflected moment of inertia of the load being run to that of the motor/brake/reducer input shaft. An inertia ratio of somewhere between 3 and 5 would usually be suggested for highest system performance. In the example above, the ratio of reflected load to rotor inertia is: (In the problem the rotor was reflected to the turntable shaft, here, by convention, the turntable is being reflected to the rotor. The same answer will be obtained either way.)

$$inertia\ ratio = \frac{I_{ref}}{I_{rotor}} = \frac{\frac{I_y}{n^2}}{I_{rotor}} = \frac{I_y}{n^2 I_{rotor}} = \frac{7760}{(437.5^2)0.004} = 10.1$$

The inertia ratio for this setup is poor relative to the high performance criteria, where a lower number is better. Any of the three terms in the formula could be changed to improve the situation: reduce the inertia of the turntable by making it smaller or lighter, increasing the reduction ratio between motor and turntable, or using a larger motor. The first two are not usually viable options, and so larger motors are often used. An analogy to cars is not too far off. A sports car has a much larger engine in it than is needed just to get around, it is there for rapid acceleration, and for maintaining a fixed speed under widely varying terrain. Those cars are also generally smaller and lighter to reduce their mass. If you want that level of performance, you will need to pay extra for it. So convince your managing director you need a Ferrari for your next project.

Problems

1. A roll drop 30 ft long and 15 ft high rolls on to a 10″ diameter 1/8″ wall thickness aluminum tube. The drop weighs 0.2 lb/ft^2 and it has a 1/2″ schedule 40 steel pipe (0.85 lb/ft) as a stretcher running through a pocket sewn along its bottom edge. If it accelerates to a top speed of 3 ft/sec in a time of 1.5 seconds, what is the maximum power needed by this effect? Assume the roll tube is left covered with one full wrap of fabric when the drop is fully extended, and that both friction and the mass of the roll tube support shafts are negligible.

Part II: Stage Machinery Components

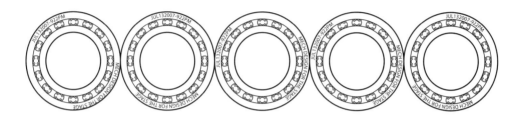

The machines we built in theatre are assembled, for the most part, from pre-manufactured component parts that are designed for use in general industry. Electric motors, gear reducers, bearings, wheels, shaft couplings, brakes and other parts are all made in huge quantities for markets much larger than theatre will ever provide. This saves us, and all the others who use these components, the time and effort and expertise involved in designing and making those parts ourselves. What we can buy off the shelf is well designed, has been proven in use, comes fully rated, and for all this is relatively inexpensive. No manufacturer would survive in the market place long if their products did not meet the needs of their customers.

Inspect any given theatre machine and all the parts used, aside from framing, cable drums, and shafts, are generally stock parts bought from some distributor. Given this, it is essential that a mechanical designer know intimately the characteristics, typical uses, and advantages and disadvantages of what is available.

In Part II of this book, encompassing Chapters 13 through 23, the more common components and techniques used in the design and construction of stage machinery will be covered. TENV versus TEFC? QD versus taper lock? Self-aligning versus rigid? The jargon involved here (and the acronyms), can be daunting, but it is essential information to know. Here, of necessity, there is much detail left uncovered. The minutia involved in every available variation of pillow block, chain sprocket, or gearmotor results in product catalogs of hundreds of pages long—and this would be for just one manufacturer. The information contained in these chapters is a good starting point, but it has been kept generic. You will have to look on the web to find, for instance, that a Browning VPS-220 pillow block has load ratings up to 1371 lb under certain conditions. Important information, but too specific to be included here.

Despite the fact that this Part covers machine components, its first chapter, beginning on the next page, is not about any component, but rather safety. Safety is a difficult topic to place within the material covered in a book intended, in part, to be used sequentially as a course text. Where might a discussion of safety topics prove most valuable? Safety must be a concern during every portion of a mechanical effect's life from its inception as an idea discussed between director and set designer, to its technical design, construction, load-in, tech, run, and strike, and so it infuses everything. Pulling it out as a topic to stand alone risks implying less importance elsewhere, and putting it here before any machines have been discussed risks an incomplete understanding of all its implications. That said, safety is an important topic to emphasize early on, and often. The best approach is to read, and then later on re-read the chapter to get the most from it.

13

Safety

General Concepts

Mechanical effects can present many inherent dangers, ranging from pinch points within the machine to multi-ton wagons traversing a dark stage. Safety considerations must be paramount from the very beginning of the design process, and before attempting any mechanical effect, careful consideration must be given to all possible hazards. While it is impossible to eliminate all risks from any design, there are many factors to consider which can greatly affect the safety of any given effect.

As the mechanical designer of an effect, you are both ethically responsible and legally liable for your designs. It is up to you to ensure that you recognize both your abilities and limitations, and work within them. No effect should ever be attempted which is beyond the abilities of the designer, the shop producing it or of the venue and its staff to consistently safely operate. While one of the things which makes technical design for theater interesting is the constant presence of new challenges, it is important to realize when an idea is simply beyond the means of the group to implement safely. Many factors can contribute to this decision, such as the time, money and labor available. Keep in mind that sometimes the safe solution is not to build the effect.

Most shows have an extremely tight production schedule. There can be tremendous pressure to solve each design problem quickly and move on to the next one. However, every effort must be made to resist the temptation to rush through the mechanical design process. Given that many mechanical effects are one-off designs, not refinements of traditional methods, they are unsuited to the typical rapid-paced design and construction methods which compressed production schedules often lead to.

Prior to beginning the design process, the mechanical designer must attempt to gain as full an understanding as possible of the desired effect. Unless all of the forces and loading conditions are understood, it is impossible to determine what is needed for any given effect. While many people may simply suggest oversizing all components to allow for errors or changes to the idea, the best approach is to fully analyze the effect and then make conservative choices which work with that analysis. Since the production concept often evolves throughout the rehearsal process, the mechanical designer must continue discussions with the rest of the creative team, especially the stage manager and the set designer, so that there are no surprises during the technical rehearsal period.

A hazard on stage, such as an open hole in the floor or a wagon moving at high speed, can potentially affect three groups: the audience, the cast, and the crew. Because the implied risk to these groups is not equal, the relative need to protect them is also not equal. Audience members assume no risk when attending a performance, and certainly will have received no training to help safeguard them, and so they must receive the highest level of protection. Any project involving the public with a mechanical effect should be evaluated and approved by a licensed engineer. Performers and crew can and should be trained to understand the hazards present and to avoid them, and therefore may not need as stringent a level of safeguarding. Equity rules allow the cast to refuse to perform on any set they deem unsafe, so it is always best to include an Equity representative in discussions as early as possible to address any concerns.

Risk Assessment

Theater is different from general industry in that the performers' assumption of risk is one of the things which can make a moment visually and viscerally exciting. Flying, drop traps and rapid full stage scene shifts are all examples of exciting but potentially dangerous moments. Risk assessment is the analysis of a machine or situation to determine the specifics of the risks involved. There are many different techniques which have been devised, all of which try to determine the level of hazard present. Knowing the level is important since the level of safeguarding required depends on the severity of injury possible from a given hazard. Most assessment methods involve identifying each possible hazard in a given system, and then determining:

1. The severity of potential injury from a given hazard
2. The frequency of exposure to the hazard
3. The probability of injury from the hazard

Once these three levels are known, their totals can give a sense of the relative risk for the given hazard and appropriate safeguarding can then be determined to deal with it. After each individual hazard has been studied and hopefully remedied, the system as a whole has been evaluated and made as safe as possible.

Hazard Abatement

After the Risk Assessment phase, each hazard which has been identified needs to be dealt with. One common method applies one of five solutions (listed in descending order of efficacy) to identified hazards:

1. Design the hazard out of the system.

   This is clearly the ideal solution, although there may be no way to achieve this within the design constraints of a given effect. The obvious way to design the hazard out of the system is to not do the effect. It is important to keep this option in mind since some hazards may be severe enough that this is the only safe solution. There are, however, many solutions which can remove the hazard from the system. Exposed roller chain drives within a stage winch, for example, have crush points wherever the chain meshed with a sprocket. If the chain can be eliminated from the design and the shaft directly driven by the gear reducer, then the hazard has been abated.

2. Guard against the hazard.

   If the hazard cannot be removed, guards can be added to keep people or objects out of the danger areas. Examples could include railings around holes in the floor, screens over moving parts or cages around high voltage equipment.

3. Post appropriate warning signs.

   Clearly visible signs which alert operators and bystanders to potential hazards can help in many situations where guarding is either impossible or incomplete.

4. Provide personal protective equipment.

   Depending upon the hazard, items such as safety glasses, gloves or steel toed boots may help to minimize risks, although this is rarely an option for performers.

5. Train personnel to work safely with all equipment.

   This can be the least effective solution, since it requires constant attention from all personnel involved with or in the vicinity of the effect. The tech rehearsal process can serve as a very effective training period. Effects must be thoroughly explained to those involved and run multiple times slowly in full light. The sequence should never be tried at full speed with lights and sound until the process is running smoothly and everyone involved is comfortable with the effect.

Single Failure Proof Design

A safety concept that relates directly to a machine's components is single failure proof design. Single failure proof "…means that the system must be designed and built so that a malfunction of any one structural, mechanical, or electrical component due to misuse, hidden defect, or long time wear would not create a damaging condition, but would rather stop the operation of the system and give notice that the fault has to be corrected."[1]. While this concept is a fairly simple one, it takes time to analyze the consequences of failure for each component. (A formal process called failure mode and effects analysis, or FMEA can be used. See Chapter 27.). In some cases, making equipment single failure proof can add complexity and cost very quickly, although there are many simple changes which can be implemented relatively easily. One fairly straightforward design change which can help to single failure proof a stage winch, for example, is the addition of a secondary brake which will hold the load if the primary brake on the motor fails. For this brake to be effective in all circumstances, it should mount to the drum shaft, not the motor, in case the failure is at the connection of motor to drum. Additionally, the brake should engage automatically when power is cut off, so that the system remains in a safe, locked state until power is restored. The drawings in Figure 13.1 show another idea, this one simple and inexpensive—the addition of keeper bolts to sheave assemblies to hold the sheave and cable even if the axle shears. In this case, the bolts must be rated for the load and spaced such that the sheave cannot fall out between them.

---

1. Olaf Sööt, *Single-Failure-Proof Design for Theatre Safety*, a Paper delivered at the USITT Convention, 1986, pg 1

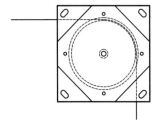

Muling Sheave supported by axle
Retaining bolts keep cable in groove

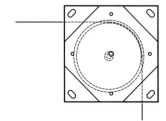

Muling Sheave after axle has sheared
Sheave and cable are supported by retainer bolts

Figure 13.1   Single Failure Prone and Single Failure Proof Sheave Plates

The more complicated aspect to single failure proof design is having the first failure stop operation of the system without causing further failures. It is fairly easy to design a system with sufficient redundancies to continue operation after one component fails, but if the operator cannot tell that a failure has occurred, then the effect may continue to operate post failure, and will no longer be single failure proof. An example of a properly designed single failure proof hydraulic lift utilizes two cylinders to provide lift. If the cylinders are appropriately sized and the pressure is set properly (see Chapter 14) the failure of one cylinder should prevent the remaining one from lifting the load, and the counterbalance valves will be sufficient to keep the load from falling. In this case, the failure of the lift to operate will alert the operator to the existence of a problem without a catastrophic failure. Similarly, in the example of a sheave with keeper bolts, the operator should (hopefully) feel the increased drag or hear the sheave dragging on the keepers and stop to investigate the problem, or torque limits on the motor drive should prevent the effect from running due to the excessive friction.

While machine control is not the subject here, it is worth mention that it is quickly becoming common that safety critical parts of a control system involve single failure proof design. For instance, the signals from two encoders, one perhaps on the motor shaft and one on the drum, are monitored to ensure that they both track together. If they ever do not, something is wrong, and the machine in emergency stopped. Safety relays and programmable logic controllers, PLCs, are constructed so that they monitor themselves for their own failures as well as failure in the components connected to them. The use of this equipment will only grow.

Design Factor and Factor of Safety

The terms design factor and factor of safety are often used interchangeably (if not specifically correctly) to refer to the ratio of the breaking strength of a material or component to the expected load. Both are used to compensate for inconsistencies in manufacturing, unanticipated loads, and other unknown factors which affect equipment after it has been put in service. The difference between the two terms is that design factor refers to the reductions taken during the design phase and the factor of safety is the ratio of the load to the strength of the equipment holding it.

EXAMPLE: What is the Safe Working Load (SWL) of 1/4″ aircraft cable with a breaking strength of 7000 lb which has been terminated with swage fittings? Use a design factor of 10:1.

SOLUTION: Swage fittings are 95% efficient, so

$$Breaking\ Strength \times 0.95 \times \frac{1}{10} = SWL = 7000\ lb \times 0.95 \times 0.10 = 665\ lb$$

If forged cable clips, which are 80% efficient, are substituted during construction, the safe working load becomes:

$$Breaking\ Strength \times 0.80 \times \frac{1}{10} = SWL = 7000\ lb \times 0.80 \times 0.10 = 560\ lb$$

If this latter setup was loaded with the 665 lb calculated for swaged terminations, the factor of safety would be 8.4:1 instead of the desired original design factor of 10:1.

As engineering has evolved from simple rules of thumb and trial and error practices into the more rigid, scientific approach used today, design factors have also continued to evolve lower as all aspects of particular situations have been better understood. Materials, such as steel, aluminum and wire rope, have become more uniform in their properties, both within an individual sample and from batch to batch. Formulas account for more variables than ever before, allowing industry to optimize designs to use materials more efficiently and decrease cost. The design factor used can vary widely, from the 1.5:1 of commercial aircraft to the 12:1 to 14:1 of some passenger elevators. Theater values speed of design development and robustness over optimizing weight and size, and therefore design factors at the conservative end of the spectrum are more appropriate for our needs.

For this text, a design factor of 10:1 is recommended for any potentially life threatening situation, such as overhead lifting or an elevator. For situations where a failure would be less catastrophic, a design factor of 5:1 is acceptable, although higher ratios may be more appropriate in certain situations. Note that some situations which are not obviously hazardous, such as a heavy wagon on a raked deck, may actually have great potential risks and should therefore utilize a higher design factor.

In order to use a design factor, it is necessary to know the breaking strength of the components used. Many manufacturers list their own Safe Working Loads instead of a breaking strength. If the manufacturer's design factor is known, it can be used to determine the breaking strength of the component, or compared to the design factor of the effect, and additional reductions can be taken if required to achieve the desired design factor. It is important to note that the rating supplied by the manufacturer applies only to new components. In any potentially hazardous situation, only parts with known histories and of reputable manufacture should be used. Applying a design factor to a ten year old, rusty shackle which has been dropped from the grid does not qualify as safe practice.

Emergency Stop

All automated scenic effects must have an Emergency Stop (E-Stop) designed into the system. In normal operation, to stop a cue before its limit, the operator uses a regular stop which decelerates the machine to a gradual, gentle stop. In an emergency situation, the E-Stop stops the machinery instantly, which may be necessary to prevent accident or injury. The National Fire Protection Association (NFPA) Article 79 includes many specifics on E-Stop operation.

While the specifics of E-Stop loop design are control issues which are beyond the scope of this text, there are certain basic principles which should be covered. For theatre use, generally the best solution is to have the E-Stop kill power to the system, thereby stopping all motion quickly and safely. NFPA 79 defines this as a Category 0 Stop "Stopping by immediate removal of power to the machine actuators." The NFPA also states that no electronics be used, and that the operation not rely on any software or communication networks. E-Stop buttons should be located in as many locations as are needed to ensure safe operation of all cues. Hitting the E-Stop should stop every axis, not just an individual effect, and the button which has been hit should require a physical reset before any cues may be restarted. The buttons should be red latching mushroom type and should be wired normally closed so that if a connection is broken, the E-Stop will engage, alerting the operator to the problem. All systems should be set up such that a power outage results in the same condition as engaging the E-Stop, and should be designed so that cues do not resume automatically when power is restored. It is important to always keep in mind that an emergency stop will usually cause a rapid deceleration with correspondingly high deceleration forces. All components in a machine (as well as any elements it mounts to or interacts with) must be designed to withstand these forces. For example, if a winch is used to fly a heavy scenic element, such as a wall, all the winch components (including the frame), its supports, the rigging connecting it to the wall and the wall itself must all be capable of resisting the shock loading of an emergency stop initiated when the unit is traveling at full speed.

Codes and Standards

Codes and standards have been developed to aid engineers and fabricators in producing safe, well designed products. In an ideal world, the rules and guidelines would be concise, clear and easy to read and understand. In this ideal world, mechanical designers would study the relevant documents prior to beginning any design and apply them throughout the process, from initial idea through completion of the project. Unfortunately, we live in the real world where written standards are numerous, overlapping, sometimes contradictory, lengthy and confusing. In the U.S. alone, there are literally thousands of pages of codes and standards in effect, some having the force of law, and others acting more as an indication of recommended practice. It is a fairly safe bet that no individual has ever read all of them. That being said, all mechanical designers are obligated to follow all applicable codes, regardless of how daunting this task might be. Finding and reading the relevant codes and standards is a necessary part of any mechanical designer's job. On some commercial projects, literally dozens of codes and standards may be listed for compliance in the technical specifications of the show. Although it is not stated in every section, virtually all of the information in the following chapters is based on standards as applied by product manufacturers.

Among the multitude of codes and standards, there are some which are referenced fairly regularly in theatrical mechanical design. These include the

- Code of Federal Regulations §1910.212 "General requirements for all machines" (Federal law, which defines OSHA),
- NFPA Article 79 "Electrical Standard for Industrial Machinery,"
- NFPA 70 "the National Electrical Code,"
- the Wire Rope User's Manual, and
- the American Welding Society Standards.

The Entertainment Services & Technology Association (ESTA) and other entertainment industry groups are working on standards for some specific applications, such as motorized rigging, but at the time of writing, these efforts were still in draft form. In a text of this size it would be impossible to summarize even just the OSHA and NFPA codes relevant to theater. Readers are directed to refer to the complete original documents before proceeding with the design process.

As an example of the types of issues addressed in codes, we will look at the OSHA regulations outlined in CFR §1910.212. Since this section covers machinery in general, it definitely applies to stage machinery. Unfortunately, given its broad scope, it has only two rules:

(a) "one or more methods of machine guarding shall be provided to protect [those] in the machine area from hazard" (29 CFR §1910.212.a.1), and

(b) "Machines designed for a fixed location shall be securely anchored to prevent walking or moving." (29 CFR §1910.212.b).

Section (a) covers guarding of operators and others near machinery from pinch points and other hazards inherent to equipment with moving parts. Most stage machinery is designed either to be as compact as possible to fit into the constraints of the set design or as open as possible to allow ease of adjustments and installation. Often winches and other machines are contained under the deck or otherwise physically separated from people, but that is not always the case so, by regulation, guards which "shall be so designed and constructed as to prevent the operator from having any part of his body in the danger zone during the operating cycle" (29 CFR §1910.212.a.3.ii) must be included in the design. Guards must be mounted sturdily, but should be designed such that if they need to be moved for maintenance or inspection, their reinstallation is simple enough that workers are likely to replace them when done. The code does not mention the use of electronic sensors as interlocks to disable the machine, but these solutions can greatly increase safety. Another option to consider if complete machine guarding is impossible or insufficient is to in a sense broaden the size of the guard to an area of restricted access, and only people qualified to evaluate the hazards present are allowed entry. Clearly visible signs to warn those in the area of the dangers present can be useful too, but they effective only to the extent that they are noticed, read, understood, and followed. The requirement that machines be anchored is less of an issue in theater since the demands of the design generally insure that this requirement will be met.

Some other points in the OSHA relevant to stage machines include:

- Shaft ends must be guarded, or not project more than half their diameter, with no keyway, and finished to a smooth surface (1910.219.c.4). This is to prevent the spinning shaft end from snagging clothing which might then wrap onto the shaft drawing a person into the machine.

- The point of contact in a friction drive must be guarded (1910.219.g). Entrapment points can catch fingers or clothing. Friction drives on the outside edge of a turntable would be a prime example where this applies.

- No projecting keys or setscrews should exist on moving parts (1910.219.h).

- Shaft collars must be round, and they cannot have any projecting setscrews or clamping bolts (1910.219.h.i).

- Floor openings (as for a lift or trap), when open, must be either attended by someone watching and warning about the opening, or by a removable standard guard rail (42″ high, with a mid rail, and 4″ toeboard) (1910.23.a.5).

Formalized Procedures

Safety concerns of course continue on after a machine is designed and built. Clearly establishing a set of procedures for the load-in, testing, rehearsal and show operation of a machine can provide a framework for safe operating procedures.

Load-In
- Have all written testing and operating procedures ready by load-in.
- Plan enough time for adjustments and changes.

Testing
- Have all video and audio monitors working before testing machinery.
- Always use a standardized verbal question and response dialog between operator and run crew. For example: "Lift 1 ready to run?,""Clear," "Running ...Complete." Never run an effect without communication, even if you are sure that no one is near it.
- Anyone with the responsibility to vouch for proper operation of the effect should be what the standards refer to as a "qualified person." This is someone who, whether by training or experience, knows how the effect should work, and is able to recognize when something is wrong.
- Include adequate time for training of all stage crew (not just individual operators, but everyone who may be in a position to monitor for safety, or who may be in potential danger).
- Test equipment unloaded and at slow speeds, under full work lights.
- Any flying effects should be tested at double the weight of the performer before flying any people.
- During the testing phase, try to determine potential operator errors and design them out of the system (ideally, the vast majority of these will have been eliminated during the design phase).

- Have a "paper tech" so all crew members are familiar with the cuing before attempting to operate the effect.
- Check for potential costume interactions (e.g., high heels and deck tracks, flowing costumes and the edges of lift platforms, etc.).
- Train all operators prior to the beginning of tech rehearsals.

Technical Rehearsals
- When first integrating mechanical effects into the rehearsal, the mechanical effect must be the only focus of the rehearsal. This means that full worklights must be up, no atmospheric effects (fog, etc.) in use, and no other cues being run (sound, projections, etc.).
- Here, too, as during the testing period, use a consistent dialog, probably now over headsets. If the stage manager has a good view of the stage, their "Go" instruction and the operator's "Running" may be all that is needed, but other crew members monitoring the stage and giving a verbal "Clear" are essential in some situations.
- Allow performers to see all equipment operate before they interact with or travel on it.
- Gradually increase speeds of effects up to performance speed to allow all performers to become comfortable with them.

Inspection and Maintenance

One vital and fairly simple way to minimize the risk of accidents due to mechanical failures is to institute a policy of regular inspection and maintenance of all mechanical effects. Before every rehearsal or performance, all equipment should be visually inspected and cues should be run which utilize the full travel of all machinery. While the automation operator is running the cues, additional personnel should be observing from a vantage point which allows a clear view of potential problems. For an especially complicated cue or one which involves potential danger to those on stage, more observers may be required either to keep the area clear or simply to see all parts of the cue. Stage management or the deck head should be informed of the time needed for this in advance so that it can be planned into the schedule to avoid a rushed or haphazard inspection. Depending on the complexity of the effects in a show the preshow inspection can range from a relatively quick visual check to a thorough and more time-consuming look at all components. Pre-show checks often include some of the following items:

- All video and audio monitors - check output at all screens, speakers, and headsets
- All control mechanisms - check E-Stop, all cabling, limit switches
- All rigging components - check all cables, sheaves, turnbuckles, shackles, etc.
- Electrical cords and connectors - check for loose connections, kinks, abrasions, arcing, strain relief
- Hydraulic components - check for leaks, nicks or abrasions in hoses, bent fittings
- Chain - check lubrication, look for signs of wear, proper tension
- Tracks and travel paths - check for foreign material or damage

- All components - check for chipping, metal shavings, other signs of damage
- Any custom built, modified or prototype equipment - fully inspect

Inspections are also critical to perform after any unforeseen event which might have affected the system, such as a shock load, power outage or water leak. After any such event, all components about which the designer is not 100% confident should be replaced before the equipment is put back in service.

For venues with longer performance runs, regular maintenance should be performed on all stage equipment. The actual procedures carried out and their scheduling will vary with the show, given differences in the frequency of equipment use and complexity of components, but certain tasks can be cited as examples.

Frequency	Task
Every week	Lubricate parts
Every 2 Months	Inspect aircraft cables
	Tighten all bolts
Every 6 Months	Replace HPU filter

Obviously, this short list is by no means complete nor universally appropriate. A show-specific list should be created during the design and testing process of any equipment.

Additional Information Sources

Numerous books have been written on safety issues in mechanical design, although none specifically relating to theater equipment. The Entertainment Services & Technology Association, ESTA, has been working for a number of years to develop technical standards for the theatre industry. To date, the document most closely related to a stage machinery topic is the draft version of BSR E1.6-1, Powered Winch Hoist Systems. A list of some of the other more commonly referenced codes and standards is included in the bibliography.

14

Actuators

Electric, Hydraulic or Pneumatic

Mechanical effects may be powered by one of several types of actuators. The vast majority of machines use either electric motors or fluid power cylinders (either hydraulic or pneumatic), and so these two basic types will be the primary focus of this chapter. The selection process involves first choosing whether a motor or cylinder is most appropriate for the given application and then determining the sizing and configuration of the individual actuator. The advantages of each will be covered in the sections which follow, as well as the process used to select the appropriate actuator.

Powering the Actuator

All actuators require an external power input. Electric motors require a motor starter to control them, or if variable speed is required, an appropriate motor drive is necessary to provide speed control and full torque throughout the speed range. Hydraulic actuators need a hydraulic power unit to provide the required pressure and flow, and valves to control the speed and direction of the oil. Pneumatic actuators require a compressor (generally already present in any shop likely to attempt to build stage machinery, but not necessarily available on stage) and valving to control the flow of air. Since discussions of these motor drives and hydraulic or pneumatic controls are beyond the scope of this text, suggested sources for more information are listed at the end of this chapter.

Section I: Electric Power

Electric Motors

Electric motors are the most commonly used power source in theatrical mechanical design, generally being the first choice for deck winches, turntable drives and motorized rigging systems. Their advantages include:

- Widespread availability
- They are well understood by many, making it relatively easy to get advice on proper use, troubleshooting, and maintenance

- The most commonly used motor types are relatively inexpensive, and speed control costs continue to drop
- They are a clean, efficient power source
- A wide variety of sizes and configurations are available

These advantages are offset by the fact that electric motors:
- Can present a shock hazard in certain circumstances
- Are mainly a high speed rotary motion power source
- Are primarily large and heavy
- Require the addition of a gear reducer in most applications

Common Motor Types

Electric motors are manufactured in countless configurations, sizes and styles, and covering all of the choices available to the mechanical designer is far beyond the scope of this text. This section will briefly touch on the three most common types of electric motors used in stage equipment: permanent magnet DC (direct current), three phase AC (alternating current), and servomotors, which are not actually a distinct type, but a performance classification. All are typically available in a variety of sizes, from fractions of a horsepower up to sizes larger than any conceivable theatrical effect could use. The most common nominal speed is 1800 rpm (typical full load speed is around 1750 rpm), although there is a wide range of available speeds. For the majority of theatrical uses at least one stage of gear reduction (covered in the next chapter) is added to slow the speed down to a range appropriate for typical stage machinery.

Permanent Magnet DC

For many years DC motors were the dominant type for stage machinery given that DC speed control is relatively simple and inexpensive, and it provides high torque even at low speeds. Since general industry has switched over to AC motors for their new installations, DC motors are no longer produced in mass quantities, and this, in conjunction with some other factors, has set the price of these motors quite high. The cost of a 3 hp PM DC motor will today be roughly 5 times that of its AC counterpart—certainly an incentive to go AC. Some theatres and commercial shops continue to use their stock of permanent magnet DC motors, both to avoid the cost of switching over, and because of their proven reliability. They are a brush-type motor, which means that a carbon brush makes and breaks electrical contact repeatedly with windings on the armature as the motor spins. The brushes on any permanent magnet motors that run for long periods of time will need to be replaced regularly, but for typical stage applications this is not an issue, given the short operation cycles of most effects.

Three Phase AC

Three phase AC induction motors have become the most common choice because they are relatively inexpensive, easily available, extremely reliable, and require little to no maintenance in typical stage use. Three phase motors, when combined with an appropriate electronic motor drive, can provide high torque throughout the speed range, smooth reversing and quiet performance. These advantages are the reason that many mechanical designers choose three phase AC motors for their designs. Stage equipment typically uses 208 volt 3-phase motors, although 240, 480, and 600 volt motors are also available and may be used for high power hydraulic pumps on Las Vegas or theme park work.

Servomotors

Servomotors are a special class of motor which are selected for tasks which require high positioning accuracy, exceptional performance, and quick reversing. Servomotors are commonly manufactured with a shaft mounted encoder (for positioning detail) and a specific motor drive to control them. Today, servomotors are usually AC or brushless DC, and they generally provide a higher power to size ratio than other motor types. Servomotors have one important difference from standard AC and DC motors, which is that they do not conform to the same mounting configuration standards as other motors, and so cannot share gear reducers and other equipment with standard motor frames. Their advantages are the extreme positioning accuracy they can provide and their relatively high power to size ratio. The main drawbacks are their increased cost over other choices and the greater complexity they entail.

Sizes and Configurations

There are two basic motor frame configurations, foot mount and face (flange) mount (see Figure 14.1). Foot mount motors have a base on the bottom of the motor frame which can be bolted to a mounting surface to secure the motor. This option is less common in theatrical mechanical design since it is generally only used if additional gear reduction is not needed or if a gear reducer which uses a shaft coupling or V-belt sheaves for connection will be used (Figure 14.2). Face mounted motors are supported by their flange, which is generally attached to a gear reducer, but could be mounted to any other device machined to match it. In the U.S., both foot and face mount electric motors are built to standardized dimensions for a particular frame size classified by the National Electrical Manufacturer's Association (NEMA). The dimensions cover such things as shaft diameter and length, key size, mounting bolt hole spacing in the foot mount, and the size of the face mount bolt pattern. These standard sizes allow motors which conform to them to be inter-

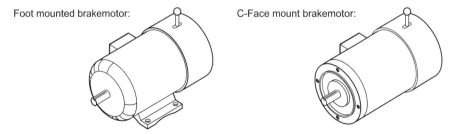

Foot mounted brakemotor: C-Face mount brakemotor:

Figure 14.1   Foot Mount and Face Mount Motors

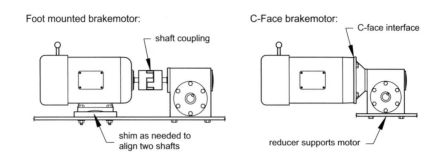

Figure 14.2   Brakemotors coupled to gear reducers

changeable, regardless of the motor's manufacturer. NEMA frames are designated by a two or three digit number sometimes followed by a letter or two, e.g., 56C or 184TC. While a larger number (and therefore frame size) generally means more power, there are no set rules for matching horsepower to a specific NEMA frame number, so any given frame size will be available with a range of motor powers. NEMA standards include several varieties of face mount motors, but by far the most common (and therefore the recommended choice) is the NEMA C Face, which comes in a variety of sizes for motors up to approximately 20 hp. One advantage of the NEMA specifications is that within a given frame size, any C-face motor will fit any C- face reducer, allowing a relatively small set of stock parts to provide a wide variety of output options.

The rest of the world generally uses an equivalent set of dimensional specifications published by the International Electrotechnical Commission, the IEC. They are naturally based on metric dimensions, so that none of the IEC motors are exact equivalents with NEMA sizes. They too are available in foot and flange or face mounting styles.

A chart of NEMA frame dimensions can be found in any Grainger catalog, or online at any major motor manufacturer. For instance, both NEMA and IEC dimensions are available at www.baldor.com/pdf/IEC_NEMA_Charts.pdf.

Brake Gearmotors
In recent years many technical designers have switched to AC brake gearmotors, which combine the motor, gear reducer and brake into one package (Figure 14.3). This option has several advantages over the traditional separate motor and reducer

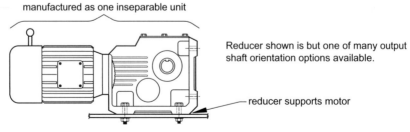

Figure 14.3   Brake Gearmotor

concept. The first is that the selection process is greatly simplified, since the manu-facturer's catalog lists the horsepower of the motor, its gear reduction ratio and type, efficiency, output RPM, output torque and total weight. Next, the three com-ponents are single sourced, so one order replaces the two or three orders to differ-ent vendors previously required. Next is that the motor arrives from the manufacturer ready to mount, saving the labor time to connect the motor to the gear reducer. Finally, the unit is designed to act as a whole, and all parts are sized to match each other efficiently, resulting in a relatively compact package well matched to the given set of specifications.

The Speed/Torque Curve

The speed and torque of an electric motor interact in a way best shown in a graph. The speed/torque curve for a motor shows how it behaves in several key areas. NEMA specifies different speed/torque curves (designated A, B, C, or D) for three phase AC motors. Figure 14.4 shows the Design B speed/torque curve, the most common.

Speed - how fast the shaft spins (rpm).

Torque - the twisting force provided at the motor shaft. As a rule of thumb, an 1800 rpm motor produces 3 ft-lb of torque per rated hp.

Torque at Rated HP - the torque provided at the power for which the manufacturer rates the motor. For three phase AC motors this is typically 1/3 to 1/2 the maximum available torque.

Full Load Speed - the speed of the motor at its rated power.

Nameplate Rated HP Point - this point corresponds to the horsepower listed on the nameplate which is continuously available. Up to three times this power is available for brief periods, but running the motor above rated HP for any length of time would cause it to overheat and burn out. Motor overload protection required by the National Electrical Code would also prevent operation in this overloaded state.

Locked Rotor Torque - the torque available at startup. Machines, such as dead-haul winches, require motors which provide high locked rotor torque to reliably and eas-ily start heavy loads. Both permanent magnet DC and three phase AC motors have high locked rotor torque.

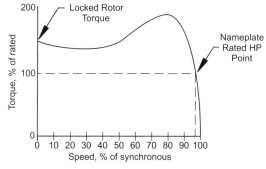

Figure 14.4   Generic Speed/Torque Curve

Enclosures

Motors are available in a variety of enclosures which can protect the motor from moisture, dirt or other outside contaminants. The enclosure also protects personnel from contact with moving or electrically charged parts. Motor enclosure types cover a wide range, listed here from least to most enclosed:

- Open - basically an unenclosed motor, used mainly within the enclosure of the case of some manufactured product, and so generally not useful in theater.
- Dripproof (DP) - the motor case has open holes or slots for ventilation, but dripping water would be kept out by their shape and placement. Acceptable for theater, but not the best choice as dirt and dust will be drawn into the motor. ODP (open dripproof) enclosures are also available.
- TE - the Totally Enclosed series
    - TEFC - Totally enclosed, fan cooled, which is a good choice for theater machinery. The motor case has no openings, so dust is excluded, and a fan blade is mounted to the motor shaft to cool the motor case.
    - TENV - Totally enclosed, non ventilated. For a given motor power, this type tends to be larger than the TEFC since the case must be designed to dissipate heat without the aid of a fan.
    - TEAO - Totally enclosed, air over enclosures are designed to be used as fan motors, where the fan provides they run also cools the motor itself. Not a good choice for theater.
- Washdown - Sealed against streams of water. Used in food processing machines.
- XP - Explosion Proof enclosures are designed to be used in explosive environments, such as around gas, flammable dusts, gasoline, etc. These enclosures are sometimes called TEXP, given that they meet the requirements of the totally TE series.

Service Factor

The service factor is the amount of overload a motor can continuously deliver without overheating. It is generally abbreviated SF on the motor nameplate before a numerical value for the service factor. For example, a 1.25 SF motor can continuously produce 125% of its rated load. While it may seem that a service factor of 1 will suffice if the motor is selected to match the expected loads, a higher service factor will allow the motor to deliver more than the nameplate rated power safely, or to have a power contingency to handle greater than anticipated loads if needed.

Choosing an Electric Motor

After deciding between AC and DC motors based upon the merits listed earlier or upon other considerations such as available power or control systems, selecting the correct motor is relatively simple. If a gear reducer is to be added, select a C Face motor which provides the output speed and torque required by that reducer to appropriately power the effect (see Chapter 15 for gear reducer selection and input needs). If no gear reducer is needed or a shaft mount one will be used, select either a face mount or foot mount depending on the configuration of the machine and specify the power and speed.

Section II: Fluid Power

Hydraulic Actuators

Hydraulic actuators come in three basic configurations: cylinders, motors and rotary actuators, all of which are available in a variety of sizes and mounting methods. These components share many similarities with their pneumatic equivalents, and so the basics of their operation will be discussed together later in this chapter. The advantages of hydraulic actuators include:

- Easy speed control, including graceful non-catastrophic stall
- Low inertia—jerky motion is easy to achieve—which can also be a disadvantage
- Immense force or torque is simply obtained
- Speed reduction is not often needed
- Actuators are generally quiet
- Linear motion is easy to achieve
- Very compact power sources (both cylinders and motors)
- Relatively safe, reliable, tried and proven technology

The disadvantages inherent to hydraulic actuators are:

- Expensive initial investment, more so for backups
- Messy during assembly and disassembly or if problems occur
- Potential for environmental hazard
- Pumps are noisy, and their noise can travel as pulsations through system plumbing
- Synchronization of multiple actuators is nearly impossible without mechanical or electronic means
- Parts are rarely off-the-shelf, lead times can be months for some components
- The potential for oil injection injuries from high pressure leaks

Pneumatic Actuators

Pneumatic actuators are available in the same basic configurations as hydraulic ones, as well as some unique ones, such as air bearings and gas springs. Since they are designed to operate at significantly lower pressures than hydraulic actuators (roughly 100 psi instead of 1000-1500 psi), pneumatic components are generally smaller and rated for lower loads, which can be both an asset and a liability, depending on the specifics of the show. The advantages of pneumatics include:

- Least expensive by far of the three actuator types (not including the compressor)
- Small, simple, relatively powerful (although not as powerful as hydraulic actuators due to the lower pressures typically used)
- High speed
- Includes some unique devices, such as air bearings, gas springs, and rubber bladder devices (such as the Firestone Airstroke® line)
- Compact power source
- Large availability of sizes and types

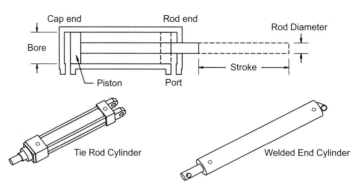

Figure 14.5   Cylinder Basics

• Environmentally benign. Spilling air does not require a cleanup.
Disadvantages:
  • Speed control is a bit touchy, difficult to predict accurately, and sensitive to friction in the system
  • Positioning to other than a hard stop is difficult
  • Compressibility can cause a surging motion
  • Exhaust from valves can present a noise problem
  • Synchronization of multiple actuators is near impossible without mechanical means

Cylinders

Cylinders, both pneumatic and hydraulic, are by far the most commonly used fluid power actuators. A cylinder is defined by the five major characteristics shown in Figure 14.5: its stroke length, bore size, rod size, construction style and whether it is pneumatic, hydraulic or both. Welded end cylinders (also called farm duty) are relatively inexpensive, which makes them a good choice for theater use, although they are not available in as great a variety of configurations. Tie rod cylinders are generally more robust, and are built to industrial standards set by the National Fluid Power Association (NFPA) so that all parts are replaceable and maintainable. They are available in a greater variety of styles and mounting options. The options will affect the cost, but, on average, a tie rod cylinder costs three to four times as much as a similarly sized welded end cylinder. As shown in Figure 14.6,

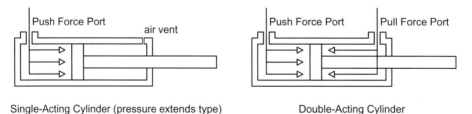

Single-Acting Cylinder (pressure extends type)   Double-Acting Cylinder

Figure 14.6   Single- and Double-Acting Cylinder Operation

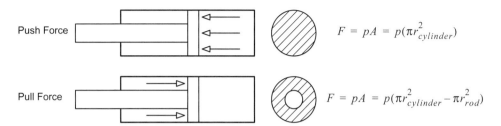

Figure 14.7   Push and Pull Force

the basic operation is extremely simple. Pressurized fluid (air or hydraulic oil) pushes against a piston to move the cylinder's rod. A single-acting cylinder (relatively rare in hydraulics) has one port and is designed to either pull or push, relying on gravity or some other force, such as a spring, to reset. A double-acting cylinder has two ports, one on either side of the piston, to control the rod's motion in either direction, depending on the flow. The force with which a rod pushes or pulls is determined by the pressure of the fluid and the area of the piston, expressed as:

$$F = pA$$

Where F = the force exerted by the cylinder (lb, N)
  p = the fluid pressure (psi, N/m^2)
  A = the area of the piston (for pull force, A = the area of the piston minus the rod area) (in^2, m^2)

In one direction, force is proportional to the bore size of the cylinder, and in the other it is proportional to the bore area less the rod area, so double-acting cylinders develop more force in one direction than in the other (see Figure 14.7). This can

Bore (in)	Push Area (in^2)	Rod Dia. (in)	Rod Area (in^2)	Pull Area (in^2)	Cylinder Ratio*
1-1/2	1.77	5/8	0.307	1.46	1.21
		1	0.78	0.99	1.79
2	3.14	1	0.78	2.36	1.33
		1-3/8	1.48	1.66	1.89
2-1/2	4.91	1	0.78	4.13	1.19
		1-3/8	1.48	1.66	1.89
		1-3/4	2.4	2.51	1.96
3-1/4	8.29	1-3/8	1.48	6.81	1.22
		1-3/4	2.4	5.89	1.41
		2	3.14	5.15	1.61
4	12.56	1-3/4	2.4	10.16	1.24
		2	3.14	9.42	1.33
		2-1/2	4.91	7.65	1.64
* The cylinder ratio equals push area divided by pull area					

Table 14.1   Pull and Push Areas of Common Cylinder Sizes

usually be compensated for by allowing gravity to assist the weaker pull force. To choose a minimum bore size for a cylinder, simply find the required area using the above formula and then select the closest cylinder bore size which exceeds that required area. Table 14.1 shows common bore and rod sizes and their push and pull areas.

Mounting Configurations and Rod Sizing
Cylinders are available in a variety of mounting configurations, of which the three most common for theater use are rigid, clevis and trunnion mount. While Figure 14.8 shows only one of each style, there is a wide variety of options within each category. Manufacturer's catalogues list all of the various configurations available and should be examined before determining the mounting choice. The rod can be plain, threaded internally or externally or drilled out for a pin connection. How the load run by the cylinder is guided often determines the type of mount to use. Cylinder rods are not generally designed to accept any side loads, which will at best cause seals to wear more quickly and at worst bend the rod or buckle the cylinder. The straight line of motion set by the rod as it extends must always be precisely parallel to the line of movement of the load. It is difficult in a typical theater shop, for instance, to achieve the exact tolerances necessary to have a rigid mount cylinder run a guided lift since the lines of movement of the rod and guide must be set parallel to within a few thousandths of an inch. Consequently clevis and trunnion mount cylinders, which can pivot to align themselves with the line of movement, are used for most machines.

When a cylinder is used in compression, which is the most common loading condition, it acts essentially as a structural column. The book *Structural Design for the Stage* covers the issues involved in column design in more detail than is possible here, and a review of the chapters on columns is recommended. The primary factor used in determining whether a column will buckle is its slenderness ratio, which is the ratio between its unbraced length and its width. In simple terms, the wider or shorter a column is, the greater a load it can support. The same is true of cylinders, with the additional factor that the mounting configuration dramatically impacts the effect that the rod length has its ability to support a given load.

Shorter unbraced cylinder lengths or connections which support the rod as it travels allow smaller rod sizes. Manufacturers use different methods to calculate

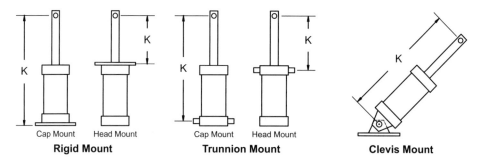

Figure 14.8 Cylinder Mounting Styles

Thrust Force (lbs)	Cylinder Rod Diameter								
	5/8"	1"	1-3/8"	1-3/4"	2"	2-1/2"	3"	3-1/2"	4"
400	35	84	134						
700	30	68	119						
1,000	26	60	105	156	190				
1,400	24	54	93	144	175	244	308		
1,800	23	48	84	127	160	230	294	366	
2,400	18	45	75	114	145	214	281	347	
3,200	16	40	68	103	131	196	262	329	398
4,000	12	38	63	93	119	174	240	310	373
5,000	9	36	60	87	112	163	225	289	359
6,000		30	56	82	102	152	209	274	342
8,000		25	51	76	93	136	186	244	310
10,000		21	45	70	89	125	172	221	279
12,000		17	41	64	85	117	155	210	270
16,000			35	57	75	110	141	188	233
20,000			28	52	66	103	136	173	218
K Distance, in inches									

Table 14.2 Cylinder Rod Diameter and K Distance (All K distances shown have a safety factor of 5:1 or better.)

the effective length of the cylinder. Some use a multiplier which is applied to the stroke length (stroke factor is one term used for this number) and others use terms such as K distance or simply L to refer to the result of the application of the stroke factor. This section will use K distance for all examples. Figure 14.8 shows how K distance is measured for the configurations shown, but check the manufacturer's catalog for specific information when sizing a cylinder. These K distance values are for a cylinder whose rod is guided as it travels. If the rod is not supported, for example, lifting an unguided load, the K distance increases dramatically. Once the K distance and load are known, the minimum required rod diameter can be looked up in the manufacturer's charts. Table 14.2 shows a typical rod sizing table.

To use Table 14.2, match the given load to the appropriate line in the "Thrust Force" column and read across until the K value shown exceeds the actual K. The minimum required rod diameter can then be read from the top of that column.

Specialty cylinder configurations are also available, such as double ended, which have a rod at each end; cable cylinders, which have a cable connected to the piston instead of a rod; and pancake cylinders, which have a large bore size and a short stroke, making them ideal for use in retractable casters.

Stop Tube

A stop tube is used to maintain a minimum overlap between the cylinder rod end and the top of the cylinder (see Figure 14.9). This distance helps the cylinder resist bending moments much better than a cylinder in which the piston can travel to the end of the bore. Stop tubes are required when the K distance is greater than 40″,

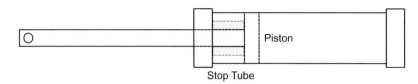

Figure 14.9   Stop Tube

and 1″ of stop tube should be specified for every 10″ (or fraction thereof) above 40″. Stop tubes will make a given stroke cylinder correspondingly longer, and this will affect the K distance of all but head mount styles.

Cylinder Selection

There are several steps to selecting an appropriately sized cylinder:

1. Determine stroke length based upon the specifications of the effect.
2. Determine push force and area required and, if applicable, pull force and area.
3. Decide on a mounting configuration.
4. Determine K distance.
5. Find rod size appropriate for the given load and K distance.
6. Determine if a stop tube is necessary and reconfirm K distance and rod size.
7. Specify bore and select cylinder.

EXAMPLE: A simple lift, using 2 cylinders aligned vertically to push a rigidly guided platform up, must travel 42 inches. The maximum load is 1200 lb, which takes into account all static and dynamic forces. An HPU with a maximum output pressure of 1400 psi is available, but leave aside 400 psi to account for pressure losses across valves, fittings, and plumbing. Determine cylinder bore, rod, and stop tube requirements and mounting configuration.

SOLUTION: Follow the seven steps, and assume that the HPU provides 1000 psi to the cylinders, and that the load is rigidly guided.

1. Determine stroke length.

   Since this lift is a simple, straight lift, the stroke length is equal to the travel, or 42 in.

2. Determine push force and area required and, if applicable, pull force and area.

   Since two cylinders are to be used, the load per cylinder, and therefore the required push force, is half of the total load, or 600 lb.

$$\frac{Total\ Load}{2} = Load\ per\ Cylinder \qquad \frac{1200\ lb}{2} = 600\ lb$$

Determine push area:

$$F = pA = 600\ lb = 1000\ psi\ (A)$$

$$Area = \frac{600\ lb}{1000\ psi} = 0.6\ in^2$$

Since gravity will assist the cylinders to retract, determining the pull force and area is not necessary.

3. Decide on a mounting configuration.

For a straight lift, a rigid mounting configuration would be extremely difficult to align perfectly to the guided lift platform, so a trunnion mount style should be selected. To limit K, a trunnion mount at the top of the cylinder, called a head trunnion mount, will be used. To connect the rod to the load an internally threaded rod will be specified so that a mounting plate can be bolted to the rod and the lift.

4. Determine K distance

Given the head trunnion mount configuration, K = Stroke + The distance from the base of the rod to the center of the trunnion = 42″ + 1″ = 43″. The 1″ value here is specific to the cylinder. The distance from the base of the rod to the center of the trunnion can only be determined by looking at the sizing charts of a specific model of cylinder, and so at this point the manufacturer and model become a fixed choice. If the model changes, all the steps after this one must be repeated.

5. Find rod size appropriate for the given load and K distance.

There are two cylinders, but for single failure proofing, each one should be able to hold the load without buckling, so use the full load when determining the correct rod diameter.

From Table 14.2, a 1″ rod is the minimum diameter appropriate for this application.

6. Determine if a stop tube is necessary and reconfirm "K" distance and rod size.

Since K = 43", a 1" stop tube is necessary. Since this is a head mount configuration, the addition of the stop tube does not affect the K distance and so does not affect rod size.

7. Specify bore and select cylinder.

From Table 2.1, a 1-1/2″ bore cylinder has a push area of 1.77 in^2 which is more than adequate for this loading condition.

The full specification for the cylinders used in this lift is two 1-1/2″ bore, 1″ internally threaded rod head trunnion mount double acting cylinders with 42″ stroke and 1″ stop tube.

Counterbalance Valves

While a discussion of all the valves and fittings necessary to operate hydraulic effects is beyond the scope of this text, it is important to mention that counterbalance valves are required on cylinders where a failure of the control valve or of the hoses could allow the load to move because of the force of gravity. A counterbalance valve prevents fluid flow out of the cylinder unless it is intentionally opened. In order to work most effectively as a safety feature, the counterbalance valve must be plumbed with steel fittings directly to the cylinder so that a failure between the valve and the cylinder is much less likely than if a hose connected the two. When designing a hydraulic effect, draw the counterbalance with the cylinder to make sure that there is sufficient clearance for it throughout the full range of motion of the cylinder.

Additional Information Sources

Some of the most useful sources of information on sizing and configuration are manufacturer's catalogs and websites, which generally list all of the information required to make a selection. Some electric motor manufacturers whose products are often used in theater include SEW-Eurodrive, Nordgear, Baldor, Leeson, and Dayton. Cylinders are made by many companies, including Tolomatic, Bimba, Parker, Hanna, and Miller.

An excellent source of information on electric motors can be found by searching the web for the *Cowern Papers*, offered via numerous sites that sell Baldor motors. A classic work is Bodine Electric's *Small Motor, Gearmotor and Control Handbook*, available for free download off their web site (www.bodine-electric.com/Tools/Handbook.asp). Both of these works give clear practical information on motor operation and use.

Additional information sources include publications from various trade groups, such as the *Power Transmission Handbook*. For information on HPUs and valves, see Parker's *Design Engineers Handbook*.

15

Speed Reduction

Speed Reduction

The rotary motion created by most motors occurs at speeds too high to be applied directly to moving scenery. The speed of a motor's shaft must be reduced to usable levels, generally by a gearbox, although V-belts and toothed belts are also occasionally used. Regardless of how speed is reduced:

$$P_{in} \times Efficiency = P_{out}$$

$$T_{in}\omega_{in} \times Efficiency = T_{out}\omega_{out}$$

Where P_{in}, P_{out} = power put into, and power received out of the speed reducer (ft-lb/sec, watts)

$Efficiency$ = the decimal value of the percentage of power passed through the speed reducer (if reducer is 72% efficient, use 0.72)

T_{in}, T_{out} = torque at input shaft, and torque at output shaft (ft-lb, Nm)

ω_{in}, ω_{out} = angular speed at input shaft, and output shaft (radians/sec)

Manufactured speed reducers rarely list efficiency directly, but instead they provide a sample set of input and output power values or input power and output speed and torque. Efficiency can be calculated in both cases using the formulas above if needed.[1]

EXAMPLE: A manufactured gear reducer has the following published specifications. Calculate its efficiency.

Ratio	Input RPM	Input HP	Output RPM	Output Torque	Overhung Load
20:1	1750	0.99	87.5	588 inlb	680 lb

---

1. Worm gear efficiencies vary with speed, but some manufacturers ignore this in their published specification charts. It is only if you calculate efficiency from several of their listed values would you ever find this out. There are few practical consequences of this, but it is curious.

SOLUTION: Convert the knowns to a consistent set of units:

$$P_{in} = 0.99 \ hp = 545 \ ft\text{-}lb/sec$$

$$T_{out} = 588 \ in\text{-}lb = 49 \ ft\text{-}lb$$

$$\omega_{out} = 87.5 \ rpm = 9.16 \ rad/sec$$

Calculate the efficiency

$$P_{in} \times Efficiency = P_{out} = T_{out} \, \omega_{out}$$

$$545 \ ft\text{-}lb/sec \times Efficiency = 49 \ ft\text{-}lb \times 9.16 \ rad/sec$$

$$Efficiency = 0.82 \quad or \ 82\%$$

The difference between a speed reducer's input and output shaft speed is usually expressed as the reduction ratio. Mathematically:

$$n = \frac{\omega_{in}}{\omega_{out}}$$

Where n = the reduction ratio (unitless). Usually written as n:1, and spoken as "n to 1," for example 20:1, or "twenty to one."
ω_{in} = input shaft speed (rad/sec, rpm)
ω_{out} = output shaft speed (rad/sec, rpm)

EXAMPLE: The gear reducer specs listed earlier state that ω_{in} = 1750 rpm and ω_{out} = 87.5 rpm. What is the reduction ratio?
SOLUTION:

$$n = \frac{\omega_{in}}{\omega_{out}} = \frac{1750 rpm}{87.5 rpm} = 20$$

The reduction ratio is 20, or 20:1. The output shaft turns at one twentieth the speed of the input shaft and, if the gears were 100% efficient, at twenty times the input torque.

The change in speed indicated by the reduction ratio (n) is set by the geometry of the gears or sprockets involved, and is always exact (except when using V-belts, where belt slip or creep can affect n). Efficiency has no effect on this ratio, but the change in torque does however depend on both efficiency and n, and so at times a speed reducer's output torque may be radically less than n times the input torque.

On occasion a speed increase is needed between driver and driven shafts. In these situations, the formulas above are still valid. Calculations will yield "reduction" ratios less than one, for instance 0.667:1, and output torques will be smaller than those input.

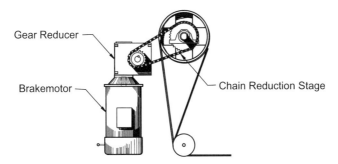

Figure 15.1   Typical Motor, Gear Reducer and Chain Stage Setup

The total reduction ratio in a machine can be increased by linking multiple reducers together. The total speed reduction ratio created by placing two reducers in series is simply:

$$n_{system} = (n_{reducer1})(n_{reducer2})$$

When this is done each separate reducer is called a stage. A three-stage gear reducer would have three pairs of gears in it. The ratios of each of the stages are multiplied together to obtain the ratio of the whole reducer.

For a typical deck winch system which consists of a motor, a gear reduction stage, a roller chain reduction stage, and a winch drum, the total reduction ratio between motor and drum is the product of the gear ratio times the chain ratio (see Figure 15.1). This total reduction ratio can be adjusted by altering either reduction stage, although usually the chain stage is altered, as replacing a chain sprocket is far less expensive than changing gear reducers.

Speed Reduction Methods

The three most common methods for slowing the rotation of a motor shaft down to a usable speed are gearing, using roller chain and sprockets, and using belts and sheaves. The sections below describe the performance characteristics of these three methods.

Gearing

All gears work on the principle of enmeshed teeth, where force is transmitted from a tooth on the driver gear to a tooth on the driven gear. The most common gear types are spur, helical, bevel and miter, worm, and rack and pinion (see Figure 15.2). The characteristics of these different types can be summarized briefly as:

Spur - Relatively inexpensive; single stage reduction ratios up to about 5:1 are commonly available; very efficient (95% to 98%); potentially noisy; generally only one tooth in contact at any given time, resulting in potentially high wear and small variations in torque and speed at the output shaft; rarely sold except for

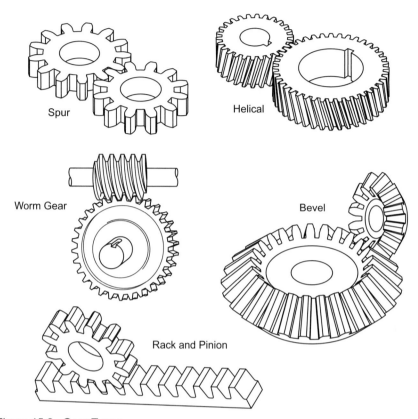

Figure 15.2   Gear Types

very small power applications, such as 1/10 hp or less, or for very low speed work as in a slewing ring or crane bearing (see Figure 17.6).

Helical - Relatively expensive; single stage reduction ratios up to about 6:1 are available; very efficient (95% to 98%); quieter than spur gears; tooth geometry is inherently strong so a given size helical gear will be able to transmit more torque than an equal size spur gear; good for all speeds and power levels.

Miter (always a 1:1 speed ratio) **and Bevel** (all other ratios) - Miters and bevels are used for special purposes, mainly to change the direction of a shaft (usually by 90 degrees and with no speed reduction); available with straight teeth or with spiral (helical) teeth; they therefore have characteristics similar to spur and helical gears respectively.

Worm - Relatively inexpensive; single stage reduction ratios up to 70:1 are available; smooth power transmission; quietest gear type; efficiency is low and dependent mainly on reduction ratio and lubrication. A subset of this type is the double-enveloping worm, manufactured primarily under the brand name Cone Drive, which uses a curved worm gear to increase the number of teeth in contact simultaneously.

Rack and Pinion - Used to convert rotary motion to linear, or vice versa.

Gear Reducers

While individual gears can be purchased and installed into stage machinery, it is far easier, more reliable, and in the long run less costly to purchase manufactured gear reducers. The reducer case will hold the gears in proper alignment; bathe the gears in lubricating oil; keep out dust, dirt, and straying fingers; absorb some of the gear noise; and provide various options for mounting the reducer to a frame and the motor to the reducer. Figure 15.3 shows a typical gear reducer.

Parallel shaft reducers, not surprisingly, have output shafts parallel to their inputs. They use helical or spur gears in pairs, or in multi-pair stages, to create speed reduction. They are extremely efficient, as much as 98%, although this efficiency comes with a high price tag. Multiple reduction stages are used even for low reduction ratios, and the cost of many pairs of gears adds up. For a given ratio and power handling capacity a parallel shaft reducer will usually cost 2 to 4 times the cost of a worm reducer. In industrial use, the power savings that result from high efficiency defray the cost of the reducer. For theatre, where mechanized effects usually run for only minutes or even seconds a night, the cost of power lost is not a concern. The high efficiency can even be, at times, a disadvantage since the reducer will create little braking or holding effect on a load at the output. Recently several brands of helical and helical-bevel reducers have appeared in gear-brakemotor combinations at significantly lower cost, which has led to an increase in their use in theatre.

Planetary gear reducers are a subset of parallel shaft reducers which use spur and internal gears. They are similar to parallel shaft reducers in terms of cost and efficiency, but tend to be smaller for a given torque rating. This is because multiple spur gears contact the internal gear simultaneously, sharing the load and providing a high strength to size ratio which makes them a popular choice for use with servomotors, which are also very compact.

Right angle gear reducers, predictably, have an output shaft perpendicular to the input. The two shafts are typically vertically offset from each other, and this offset amount is referred to as the center distance.

The most commonly used right angle reducer is the worm gear reducer, which utilizes a worm and a worm gear. The worm, which has the general appearance of a piece of threaded rod, is enmeshed with the worm such that the worm threads push

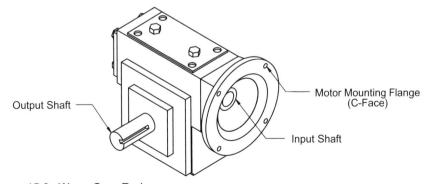

Figure 15.3 Worm Gear Reducer

the worm gear teeth. Worm gears are a very common type of gearing used for stage machinery because they

- are commonly available with reduction ratios up to 70:1 in a single stage (multiple stage reducers go up to at least 3600:1)
- are relatively small compared to equivalent parallel shaft reducers
- are inherently quiet
- are relatively inexpensive compared to equivalent capacity parallel shaft reducers

The one major quirk of worm gear reducers is generally low efficiency, which is a complex function of many factors including speed, lubrication, geometry of the gears, wear, vibration, etc. This inefficiency can in some applications be an advantage since it can help to brake or hold loads, but "help" is the key word here.

CAUTION: The holding force of inefficient gear reducers should never be relied upon as the sole way a load is held. In situations where a load will accelerate due to gravity, brakes—connected directly to the drum or other load-holding device—must be included in the drive system to prevent any motion.

Helical bevel gear reducers are right angle units which use helical and bevel gears to achieve much higher efficiency ratings than equivalent worm gears. Their efficiency (and also cost) are similar to those of parallel shaft reducers.

Terms Used in Gear Reducer Selection

The power handling capabilities, reduction ratio, size, and other information about a gear reducer will be provided by the manufacturer in its reducer ratings or specifications. Unfortunately, since there are no standards for the content or format of this information, both the information and its appearance vary widely from manufacturer to manufacturer. At least some of the terms defined below will be found in any given reducer specification.

Input Horsepower - The amount of power applied to the input shaft of the reducer. The input hp listed in the manufacturer's specs is the maximum power that the reducer can safely handle.

Output Horsepower - The amount of power available at the output shaft. Due to losses caused by inefficiency, it will always be less than the Input Horsepower.

Center Distance - This applies mainly to worm gear reducers, and is the perpendicular distance between the axes of the input and output shafts. This number is directly related to the size of the gears, and therefore usually to the reducer's output torque capacity as well as its cost.

Cost - The cost of a reducer is mainly a function of the cost of the gears. Large gears equate to large center distances, large torque capacity, and large cost. Cost in worm gear reducers is not a function of the reduction ratio until the ratio gets large enough to force a crossover from single stage reduction to dou-

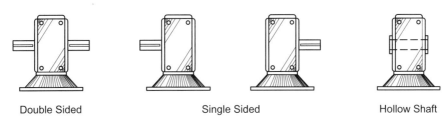

Double Sided   Single Sided   Hollow Shaft

Figure 15.4   Output Shaft Configurations

ble stage reduction. More gears add cost, so single stage reduction is usually less expensive than an equal capacity reducer with multiple stages.

Mounting, and Mounting Position - Never assume anything about the way a reducer might mount. Mounting feet may be stock on one reducer, and a bolt-on option on another. One reducer might have mounting holes that will accept a nut and bolt, while others have relatively shallow tapped holes in the housing that require particular length mounting bolts. These tapped holes may be in inch or metric sizes, so check before trying to force a bolt in. Some reducers that mount with a nut and bolt have so little wrench clearance that they are hard to mount—make sure that the framing they are to connect to accounts for this and provides ample access to the bolts.

Shaft seals may not be rated to hold in the lubricating oil in all possible mounting positions, or the vent plug may leak if the reducer is not oriented to keep the vent above the oil level. Variations in seal and vent plug design means that while one reducer may work just fine if mounted with the input shaft facing down, another may leak all its lubricating oil. The position may also affect the amount of oil needed by the reducer for proper lubrication. Always check the manufacturer's specifications to ensure the desired orientation is appropriate.

Shaft Configuration - Both the input and output shafts need to be specified. The input shaft will usually be either a standard size keyed shaft, or the hollow socket of a C-face type input. The output shaft will be one of the following: single ended, double ended, or hollow shaft. Figure 15.4 shows various shaft configurations. If there is sufficient room, a double sided output shaft provides more flexibility for re-use of a reducer into a different machine design.

Overhung Load - A force perpendicular to the axis of a reducer shaft will cause bending moments in that shaft and radial loads on the bearings. Overhanging loads are present when, for instance, V-belt sheaves or roller chain sprockets are mounted on a shaft. A typical specification: "Overhung load - low speed shaft = 225 lbs at center point of shaft extension" means that the reducer will operate normally with up to a 225 pound force acting perpendicular to the output shaft at a point along the shaft halfway between the case and the end of the shaft. Figure 15.5 includes examples of overhanging loads. Shaft bending and bearing loads are magnified when the load is placed at the end of the shaft, and minimized when the side loads are located as close to the shaft bearings as possible as shown on the right in Figure 15.5).

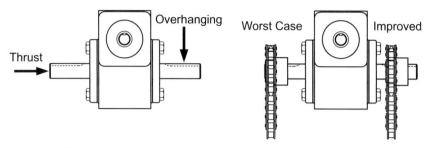

Figure 15.5   Examples of Overhanging and Thrust Loads

The overhung load created by a given setup can be estimated from:

$$OHL = \frac{T(K)}{r}$$

Where   OHL = the Overhanging Load (lb, kg)
T = torque (in-lb)
r = radius of the sprocket, sheave, etc. (in, m)
K = a coefficient that accounts for the amount of side loading caused by the power transmission components hooked onto a gear reducers shaft:
1.00 = Roller chain drives
1.25 = Gears
1.50 = V-belt drives

Thrust Load - A force acting parallel to the axis of a reducer shaft (see Figure 15.5). A thrust load might be created, for instance, if a gear reducer was used to support the entire weight of a small diameter turntable. The effects of thrust loads and overhanging loads are not independent, so if both might be present, the manufacturer should be consulted.

Input Mechanical Horsepower - The maximum power that can be put into a reducer based on limitations due to the strength of the reducer's parts.

Input Thermal Horsepower - The maximum power that can be put into a reducer based on limitations due to overheating the lubricating oil. Thermal ratings are not usually a problem for theatre uses because we typically run our machines in short bursts. One manufacturer states "Thermal ratings may be ignored when the continuous operating period does not exceed 2 hours and the shutdown period equals or exceeds the operating period."[2]

Efficiency - The efficiency of any power transmission system is expressed as:

$$Efficiency = \frac{P_{out}}{P_{in}}$$

2. Hub City, *Engineering Manual no. 4*, 1992

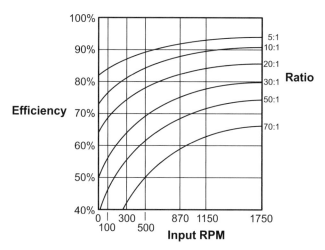

Figure 15.6   Efficiency Versus Input Speed for Generic Worm Gear Reducers

Where   Efficiency = the amount of power transmitted through a system, expressed
as a decimal (a 55% efficient reducer would have an efficiency
of 0.55)

P_{in} = the power put into the power transmission system (hp, watts)

P_{out} = the power at the output of the power transmission system (hp,
watts)

The efficiency of a worm gear reducer is a complex and non-calculable function of gear geometry, input shaft speed, and friction (which encompasses the
effects of lubrication, gear materials, vibration, and gear wear). Figure 15.6
graphs approximate efficiency versus input shaft speed for a range of reduction
ratios of properly lubricated and broken-in worm gear reducers. This generalized graph shows two characteristics common to worm reducers in general:
that efficiency differs between reducers of different reduction ratios, and that
efficiency varies with the speed of the input shaft. Manufacturer's specs unfortunately rarely provide the actual curve for a specific reducer.

Only a few manufacturers specifically list efficiencies in their reducer specs,
instead listing values of P_{in}, ω_{out}, and P_{out} or T_{out}. Since the power, torque,
and speed required to drive a device, such as a turntable or lift, are known, and
those quantities have to be supplied by the power coming out of the reducer,
these numbers are actually in a form that is more immediately useful than the
efficiency.

Self-Locking, Backdriving - When a motor supplies its power to a load through a
worm gear reducer, the flow of power is from motor to worm, to worm gear,
and from there to the load. Whenever the load attempts to drive the motor,
which might happen during a period of rapid deceleration or the lowering of
flown scenery, the flow of power is from load through reducer to the motor. If,
in this situation, the gears do turn and the load drives the motor, this is called

backdriving. If the gears do not turn, regardless of the torque applied to the worm gear shaft (the "output" shaft), then the reducer is called self-locking.

Self-locking will occur whenever any reducer's efficiency is less than 50%, and backdriving can occur if efficiency is greater than 50%. Spur and helical gear reducers have high efficiency, and so are never self-locking. In worm gear units, given that efficiency varies with input shaft speed and the reduction ratio, a given reducer might backdrive at one speed, and self-lock at another. No worm gear reducer manufacturer will say that self-locking can be relied on as a load holding device, so it bears repeating:

CAUTION: The holding force of inefficient gear reducers should never be relied upon to hold a load. In situations where a load will accelerate due to gravity, brakes—connected directly to the drum or other load-holding device—must be included in the drive system to prevent any motion. Never rely on gear reducer inefficiency to hold a load.

Service Factor - Essentially a design factor multiplier used in formulas to account for the duty cycle of the machine, the type of power source used to run it, the specific application, and the expected peak or shock loads that will occur. Values range from 0.8 for a fan run by an electric motor for less than 1/2 hour per day up to 3.5 for a steel mill duty crane in continuous use. Since theatrical applications are unlike any general industry tasks, the charts that list these factors for a range of different applications are of little value. For the relatively undemanding requirements of a typical deck winch, for example—no shock loads, a low duty cycle, and an electric motor power source—a service factor of 1.0 can be assumed.

Lubrication - Gear reducers vary widely in their lubrication requirements. Oil is by far the most common lubricant, but some reducers use grease. In general, the viscosity of oil used varies by gear type, for example a worm gear may use 400 weight oil and a spur or helical gear might use a 90 weight oil. Manufacturers will, of course, list the recommended lubricant for their products. Some gear reducers ship from the factory filled with oil, some do not, so always check. In general, gear cases get filled about half full, but check the specs. Many reducers include a threaded fitting called a breather to be installed by the user at a high point on the reducer. These devices let air out or in as the lubricating oil expands and contracts as the reducer heats up in use or cools during idle times. Since the duty cycle is so low in most theatre applications, and the reducers are used in the relatively constant temperatures present indoors, these breathers often are not installed.

Using the Reducer Ratings

EXAMPLE: A winch, consisting of a 1750 rpm motor and a worm gear reducer which directly drives a 12″ diameter drum (no chain stage), needs to move a load at 4 feet per second. The total force required to move the load, including all static and dynamic forces, is 300 lb. The effect will have a low duty cycle and is unlikely to be shock loaded, so use a service factor of 1. Select an appropriate gear reducer from Table 15.1 and specify motor horsepower and frame size.

SOLUTION: First, determine the output speed needed to select a reduction ratio. A 12" diameter drum wraps 3.14' of cable per revolution

$$Cable\ Travel = Circumference = \pi d = \pi(1ft) = 3.14ft$$

To determine the drum rotation speed necessary to move the load at 4 feet per second, divide the travel speed in feet per minute by the drum distance per revolution.

$$Drum\ speed = \frac{4fps \times 60}{3.14ft} = 76.4rpm$$

$$n = \frac{\omega_{in}}{\omega_{out}} = \frac{1750rpm}{76.4rpm} = 22.9\ or\ a\ 22.9{:}1\ ratio$$

Worm gear reducers are generally manufactured in only a few ratios: 5:1, 10:1, 15:1, 20:1, 30:1, 40:1, etc. Given this, the closest available ratio that will meet or exceed the needs of this winch is 20:1, providing an output speed of 87.5 rpm.

$$\frac{(1750rpm)}{20} = 85.5rpm$$

Using a 20:1 reducer will provide a higher top speed than requested, but this extra cushion may be useful if the needs of the effect change. If travel at faster than 4 feet per second is deemed to be unsafe, the control system must include provisions to limit the speed of the effect (generally achieved through programming the motor drive).

The output torque required is found by multiplying the load by the radius of the drum:

$$Output\ torque = 300lb \times 6in = 1800inlb$$

Now select an appropriate reducer from a catalog. The listings on this table are for a 20:1 reducer connected to a 1725 rpm motor, so the listed output speed is slightly different than the calculated one.

	Nom. Output RPM	Worm Center Dist. (in)	NEMA Frame	Continuous Duty Output Torque at Input Motor HP shown (in-lb)				Max. Torque (in-lb)
				1	1.5	2	3	
1	86	2.00	56C	619				615
2	86	2.37	56C	620	947			989
3	86	2.63	56C	623	953	1283		1312
4	86	2.63	140TC	623	953	1283		1312
5	86	3.00	56C		956	1287	1950	1959
6	86	3.00	140TC		956	1287	1950	1959
7	86	3.00	180TC		956	1287	1950	1959
8	86	3.50	180TC			1233	1950	2730

Table 15.1   Excerpt from a Worm Gear Reducer Selection Chart (values for Winsmith Maximizer reducers as listed in Grainger Catalog 394)

For this application, the last four reducers are the only options which will provide sufficient output torque since they all produce 1950 in-lb of torque when connected to three horsepower motors. The last reducer on the list, number 8, has a larger center distance, and so will cost more than the other three. Given the similarity of output characteristics of the other three, the decision should be based upon the availability of a matching brakemotor frame size. 3 hp brakemotors are fairly common in the 140TC size, so reducer number 6 would be a good choice.

Gear Motor Selection

As discussed in Chapter 14, and brake gearmotors are an increasingly popular choice for mechanical designers. The selection process for a gear motor is very similar to that used for separate gear reducers.

EXAMPLE: Specify an appropriate gearmotor for the deck winch above. For this example a small section from the 40 pages of gearmotor selection information for one style of reducer in the SEW Eurodrive catalog has been reproduced.

SOLUTION: From the earlier example, the requirements are as follows: an approximately 76.4 rpm output speed which can produce at least 1800 in-lb of torque. Select an appropriate gearmotor from Table 15.2.

	Motor Power (hp)	Output Speed (rpm)	Service Factor	Torque (in-lb)	Max. OHL (lb)	Ratio	Gear Stages	Model Gear	Model Motor
1	3	88	1.7	2150	1150	19.58	3	K47	DT100LS4
2	3	86	2.0	2200	1690	13.25	3	K57	DV112M6
3	3	79	1.5	2400	1160	21.81	3	K47	DT100LS4
4	3	76	2.1	2500	1730	22.71	3	K57	DT100LS4
5	3	75	1.9	2530	1730	15.22	3	K57	DV112M6
6	3	75	2.5	2520	2920	15.19	3	K67	DV112M6
7	3	72	2.0	2650	1740	24.05	3	K57	DT100LS4

Table 15.2   Sample Gearmotor Specification Chart (information drawn from SEW Eurodrive Constant Speed Gearmotors catalog 2000)

For this example, numbers 1, 2 and 3 are all fast enough and provide sufficient torque. Number 4 is close enough that it would probably be acceptable, and has a higher service factor and output torque. For this application, number 3 is a good compromise between size and output power and speed. The full specification for this gearmotor is K47DT100LS4BM(G)4. The BM(G)4 at the end of the specification denotes brake information.

Some aspects of the table worth noting are that the reduction ratios vary from what might be expected because the motors are not necessarily all 1750 rpm motors, and that the size range of the gearmotor can be inferred from the gear number, which increases with the size. In addition, the listed output torques are considerable higher than in the previous example despite both using 3 hp motors. This is both because the output speed is lower here than earlier, allowing torque to be greater, and because of the efficiency differences between the earlier example's worm gear reducers and this example's helical-bevel gear reducers.

Roller Chain and Sprockets

Roller Chain

ANSI standard roller chain consists of links designed to mesh precisely with toothed wheels (sprockets) in order to efficiently transmit power from one rotating shaft to another. The rollers which give roller chain its name rotate rather than slide onto and off of the sprocket teeth, reducing friction and wear. During manufacture chains are riveted together into continuous lengths from two types of links: roller links and pin links. When an endless loop of chain is needed around two sprockets, an appropriate length piece is separated from a long length using a chain breaker, and the two ends are connected together with a connecting link. If an odd number of links is needed to make up a loop of the correct length, the connection of chain end to chain end must be made with an offset link and a connecting link, or an offset section and two connecting links. Figure 15.7 shows examples of roller chain, connecting and offset links.

Roller chain and sprockets are often used to achieve speed reduction. In a typical chain speed reduction stage a sprocket mounted onto the output shaft of a gear reducer transfers power through a roller chain loop to another sprocket mounted to the input shaft of the effect, such as the drum shaft on a deck winch. To calculate the reduction ratio, divide the tooth count on the output shaft by the tooth count of the input shaft. Mathematically:

$$n = \frac{\textit{Number of Teeth on Output Shaft}}{\textit{Number of Teeth on Input Shaft}}$$

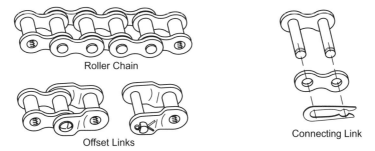

Roller Chain

Offset Links

Connecting Link

Figure 15.7 Roller Chain, Connecting and Offset Links

EXAMPLE: What is the reduction ratio of a roller chain stage with a 17 tooth sprocket on the input of the chain stage and a 48 tooth sprocket on its output?

SOLUTION:

$$n = \frac{Number\ of\ Teeth\ on\ Output\ Shaft}{Number\ of\ Teeth\ on\ Input\ Shaft} = \frac{48}{17} = 2.82$$

The reduction ratio is 2.82:1.

Roller chain stages can also be set up to increase the output speed (with an equivalent loss of torque) or they can be set up with matching sprockets to directly drive the effect without changing the speed.

The basic unit of chain size is pitch—the distance between the centers of two adjacent axles.

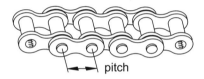

pitch

In ANSI standard roller chain, pitch appears in the two or three digit number that designates a particular size and type of roller chain. The number or numbers to the left of the rightmost digit represent the pitch of the chain, in eights of an inch. Number 40 chain, for example, has a pitch of 4/8″, or 0.5″. The right digit can take on one of only three values:

0 = standard style roller chain
1 = narrow, light weight style roller chain (currently only available in size 41)
5 = rollerless chain (usually in small sizes such as 25 and 35)

Roller Chain Strength

The minimum ultimate tensile strength (*muts*) of standard weight roller chain, which is the breaking strength that any sample of new chain is guaranteed to exceed, is given by the following formula:

$$F_{muts} = 12{,}500\ (Pitch^2)$$

Where F_{muts} = the minimum ultimate tensile strength of the roller chain (pounds)
Pitch = the distance between two adjacent roller axles (inches). Number 60 chain has, for instance, a pitch of 6/8″, or 0.75″. When calculating F_{muts} the unit (inches) is ignored.

EXAMPLE: What is the minimum breaking strength of ANSI #40 roller chain?

SOLUTION: #40 chain has a pitch of 4/8″, or 0.5″.

$$F_{muts} = 12{,}500\,(\text{Pitch}^2) = 12{,}500\,(0.5^2) = 3125 \text{ lbs}$$

A design factor is applied to this value so that a chain is never stressed to near its ultimate strength. For scenic effects involving little low speeds or low mass and sufficient friction to cause a rapid deceleration to stopped should a drive chain break, a design factor of 5 is usually considered sufficient. If forces due to gravity will cause an unrestrained load to move, then a design factor of 10 is often used. Chain used in a system that flies scenery, runs a lift, or moves a wagon up and down a rake would fall into this category. No manufacturer of roller chain states explicitly that their products are acceptable for overhead lifting, and many specifically state that they should not be used for these types of applications (these, of course, should not be used). Therefore, the following can be stated.

CAUTION: Make every effort to avoid using roller chain in lifting machines. If the decision is made to use it, use a conservative design factor (at least 10:1) and pay special attention to single failure proofing the setup. Redundant chains, each sized to hold the full load, and overspeed triggered brakes connected directly to the drum or other load-holding device are options to consider. Any potentially hazardous effect requires frequent inspection by qualified personnel.

In addition to F_{muts}, manufacturers list the average tensile strength of roller chain, which is the average tensile load at which samples will break. Table 15.3 lists the common sizes of roller chain used in theatre, minimum strength, calculated safe working loads, and sample values of average strength (this last number is supplied by a chain's manufacturer, and therefore will vary).

ANSI Chain Number	Pitch (in)	MUTS (lb)	SWL 5:1 Design Factor (lb)	SWL 10:1 Design Factor (lb)	Average Tensile Strength (lb)
25	1/4	781	156	78	1,050
35	3/8	1,758	352	176	2,400
40	1/2	3,125	625	313	4,300
50	5/8	4,882	976	488	7,200
60	3/4	7,032	1,406	703	10,000
80	1	12,500	2,500	1,250	17,700

Table 15.3   The Tensile Strength of ANSI Chain

Roller chain is fully rated to these values only when it is new. Used roller chain can only be evaluated if the prior use is known. If the chain is of unknown origin, it should be discarded. In any situation where the strength of the chain is critical, the cost savings of re-using chain are not worth the potential risk.

For applications which require a higher strength than standard roller chain of a given size can provide, multiple strand roller chain is available. It uses all the same components as single strand chain except for longer pins to connect across multiple strands. Sprockets for multi-strand chain have identical dimensions as their single strand counterparts, but instead of a single sprocket, there are two to four sprockets mounted on a single hub. Because the chain tension cannot be divided equally across the strands, the strength of multi-strand chain is as follows:

$$2\ strand\ =\ 1.7 \times Single\ Strand\ F_{muts}$$

$$3\ strand\ =\ 2.5 \times Single\ Strand\ F_{muts}$$

$$4\ strand\ =\ 3.3 \times Single\ Strand\ F_{muts}$$

Roller Chain Sprockets

Roller chain sprockets follow the same ANSI numbering system as chain. Sprocket specification includes: roller chain number, number of teeth, mounting style, and bore (the size of the shaft the sprocket will mount on). Stock sprocket sizes generally range from 7 to 112 teeth. As chain size increases, so does the diameter of a sprocket with the same number of teeth, so that a 17 tooth sprocket for #25 chain will be smaller than a 17 tooth sprocket for #40 chain.

Sprockets with very few teeth create torque and speed pulsations as they spin. This is due to the relatively large variations in the distance between the center line of the chain just leaving or entering the sprocket and the shaft axis that occur as the sprocket rotates, an effect called chordal action (see Figure 15.8). For smooth motion, manufacturers recommend that the smallest sprocket in a system have 17 or more teeth for low to moderate speed drives, and at least 21 teeth for high speed drives.

Sprockets that mount directly on a shaft are available in the following standardized styles:

Flat Plate - A sprocket type designed to be drilled out and welded onto a shaft. The least expensive and the most complicated to use sprocket type. Designated "A type."

Minimum Bore - The sprocket has a small hole drilled through a substantial center hub to mark center. The correct bore and keyway have to be machined by the user. This sprocket style is rarely a good choice for a typical theater shop.

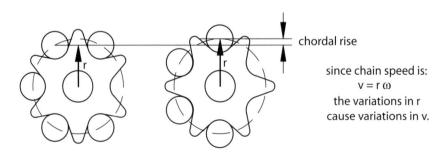

Figure 15.8 Chordal Action

Fixed Bore - The sprocket comes drilled out to a particular bore size, and has a keyway and a set screw to secure it to the shaft. Designated "B type." This is a good inexpensive choice, but is usually not stocked by local parts suppliers.

Tapered Bushing - The sprocket has a standard size tapered hole into which a bushing fits (see Chapter 16, Shafting, for a discussion of shaft mounting options). The tapered bushing, which comes bored out and keyed for a particular sized shaft, firmly grips the shaft as it is wedged into the sprocket by mounting bolts or setscrews. One of the advantages of tapered bushing sprockets is that a relatively small inventory of parts can cover a range of shaft and sprocket sizes that would require a much larger inventory if all the sprockets were of the fixed bore type. They are, however, significantly more expensive than the fixed bore type.

Idler sprockets are sprockets which include a bearing to allow them to spin freely and are used to redirect chain or to help tension it. Chain tension can also be maintained using spring loaded plastic guides against which the chain can slide relatively quietly and efficiently.

Roller Chain Guidelines[3]

- Provide guards to protect both people and the machine.
- When using two sprockets of different sizes, make sure that the chain wraps around at least one third of the smaller sprocket's teeth. This generally means that ratios beyond 7:1 should be avoided.
- The distance between the axes of a pair of sprockets should normally be 30 to 50 pitches, and never more than 80 pitches without chain guides.
- Chain is lubricated with oil, never grease. The oil penetrates to the sliding surfaces, (inner surfaces of the rollers and outer surfaces of the pins). For the low speed use common on stage machinery, lubricating the chain by hand every so often is sufficient. If possible, provide a dust free area since dust will cling to the oil, negating much of the oil's benefit.
- Provide proper tension. A properly tensioned chain drive should have a slight amount of sag or looseness. Tensioning a chain until it is completely taut stresses it excessively and causes it to wear out more quickly.
- Make sure sprockets are properly aligned to ensure quiet operation and to prevent the chain from jumping off its sprockets.

V-belts and Sheaves

A V-belt transmits power from one shaft to another due to the frictional force that develops between the sheave grooves and the surface of a tensioned belt. Belts work best in the high speed components of a machine, typically between a motor's shaft and a reducer's input (the C-face motor/reducer connection has eliminated

---

3. Drawn partially from Browning Manufacturing, *Catalog No. 11*, F-83.

the need for belts here, and so V-belts are rare in stage machinery). Because friction alone "connects" belt and sheave, all V-belt systems have the potential to slip. This fact alone rules them out for use on any machinery operating a life-threatening effect.

V-belts come in a variety of cross-sectional sizes and belt lengths:

L series - Also called fractional horsepower (FHP) belts. Belt length is denoted by the outside circumference of the belt in tenths of an inch. For example, a 4L belt with an outside circumference of 54 inches is a 4L540.

Letter series belts - An old but still common designation. Belt length is (roughly) denoted by the inside circumference of the belt in inches. For example, a B belt with an inside circumference of 54 inches is a B54. The easiest way to size an existing belt, provided you can't read the number off of the back of the belt, is to look up its outside circumference in a chart. The B54 belt has an outside circumference of 57.0 inches.

Narrow belt series - Belt length is denoted by the outside circumference of the belt in tenths of an inch. For example, a 5V belt with an outside circumference of 54 inches is a 5V540.

Unlike roller chain, V-belts are never rated for ultimate tensile strength. Nor can power transmitted by a V-belt be determined using a simple formula. Instead, manufacturer's charts which take into account the diameter of both the driver and driven sheaves, driver sheave shaft speed, and belt type must be used to select V-belt components. Manufacturer's catalogs can have as many as 200 pages of charts to cover all of the combinations and variables involved.

Toothed Belts

Toothed belts, also known as timing belts, offer the V-belt-like properties of light weight and flexibility combined with the no-slip advantage of roller chain. They are available in a variety of sizes and materials, and therefore strengths and in premade loops or in bulk lengths. This information as well as other technical data is listed in the manufacturer's catalogs. The most commonly available belts are not rated for strength, and therefore should only be used in situations where failure will not present a hazard. Toothed belts with reinforcing wires and load ratings are available from some manufacturers for use when loads are a concern. One fairly common theatrical application for toothed belts at the smaller end of their applications is to connect encoders or limit pots to motors for control system feedback.

Additional Information

For more information on the design and selection of speed reduction components see *The Speed Reducer Book, The Power Transmission Handbook, The Complete Guide to Chain*, and *Chains for Power Transmission and Material Handling*. Manufacturers of speed reduction products include Browning, Dodge, Hub City, Martin, SEW Eurodrive, and Tsubaki.

16

Shafting

Shaft Basics

Shafts are used to transmit rotational force, or torque, from one location to another. They are generally round, solid steel bars, although hollow round, solid square or other shapes may occasionally be used for a particular design benefit they offer. Unlike most components discussed in this book, shafts are designed based upon basic structural design factors, not selected from ratings given in a catalog. The two most important factors to keep in mind while selecting a shaft are that it must be strong enough to support all anticipated loads, and be fabricated to tolerances which will allow it to integrate with other components.

Shaft Strength

Shafts are used to transmit rotary power from one location to another. The power in any shaft is given by the product of the torque passing through it times the shaft's angular speed, expressed mathematically as $P = T\omega$. The shaft must be designed to withstand the maximum torque applied to it, any tension or compression it must withstand axially, and the bending forces placed on it by the side loads caused by chain sprockets, gears, or a drum, the action of gravity, and possibly even resonances within the shaft that occur at certain speeds. To keep a shaft safe from failure due to torque alone, torque must be limited to values appropriate to the material used (generally steel) and the shape and size of the shaft. For shafts affected by torque only:

$$T = S_{ts}Z_{polar}$$

Where T = the maximum allowable torque, or twisting moment, on the shaft being analyzed (in-lb, Nm)

S_{ts} = the allowable torsional shear of the shaft material (psi, Nm^2) (the values given for S$_{ts}$ include a design factor, so additional reductions are not required)

Z_{polar} = the polar section modulus of the shaft (in^3, m^3). See Figure 16.1.

The allowable torsional shear of the shaft material, S_{ts}, is rarely given in charts listing the properties of various materials, probably because materials other than

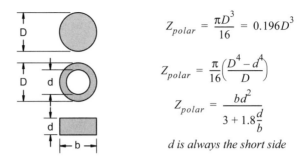

$$Z_{polar} = \frac{\pi D^3}{16} = 0.196 D^3$$

$$Z_{polar} = \frac{\pi}{16}\left(\frac{D^4 - d^4}{D}\right)$$

$$Z_{polar} = \frac{bd^2}{3 + 1.8\frac{d}{b}}$$

d is always the short side

Figure 16.1   Polar Section Modulus of Various Shapes

steel are rarely used as shafts. Even for steel the situation is somewhat casual: "The ASME (American Society of Mechanical Engineers) code of recommended practice for transmission shafting gives an allowable value in shear stress of 8000 psi for unspecified steel..."[1] In other words, 8000 psi is a conservative value for allowable torsional shear, and any steel choice you make will be equal to or stronger than that. In order to minimize shaft diameter the allowable torsional shear of many materials can be estimated from the following two equations (true only for unkeyed shafting):

$$S_{ts} = 0.3 \times Yield\ Strength$$

or

$$S_{ts} = 0.18 \times Ultimate\ Tensile\ Strength$$

The smaller of the two resulting values is the allowable torsional shear.

For the most common shaft material, C1018 steel (where C stands for cold rolled or drawn steel and 1018 specifies the alloy), the allowable torsional shear can be calculated to be:

yield strength = 50,000-70,000 psi $0.3 \times 50000\ psi = 15000\ psi$
tensile strength = 70,000-85,000 psi $0.18 \times 70000\ psi = 12000\ psi$

Since 12,600 psi is the smaller of the two values, the allowable torsional shear (S_{ts}) of C1018 cold rolled steel is 12,600 psi.

Whenever shafts are cut with standard size keyways, the allowable torsional shear value is derated by 25% to account for the loss of material and the stress concentrations created by the keyway. Therefore, for the most common shaft material (C1018 cold rolled steel) the allowable torsional shear for a keyed shaft is:

$$S_{tsKeyed} = 0.75 \times S_{ts} = 0.75 \times 12,600 psi = 9450 psi$$

For a keyed steel shaft whose properties are unknown, the same reduction can be applied to the conservative 8000 psi allowable shear stress estimate:

$$S_{tsKeyed} = 0.75 \times S_{ts} = 0.75 \times 8000\ psi = 6000\ psi$$

---

1. Popov, *Engineering Mechanics of Solids*, p. 185.

Thus, for any unknown alloy, keyed, solid, round steel shaft, a value of 6000 psi for allowable torsional shear should be used to give a conservative, and therefore safe, result.

Shaft Diameter and Torsional Stiffness Rule of Thumb

Choosing a shaft diameter based on the above considerations will result in a shaft strong enough to avoid failure by torsional shear, but it may not be rigid enough to avoid excessive springiness. A shaft will exhibit angular deflection, or twist, throughout its torque transmitting length proportional to the magnitude of the torque being transmitted. A rule of thumb developed in the days when power was distributed throughout factories by overhead lineshafts states that the angular deflection in a shaft should never exceed 0.08° per foot of shaft length. This criteria requires that solid round steel shaft diameters correspond to applied torques in the following way:

$$D = k \sqrt[4]{T}$$

Where D = the shaft diameter (in, mm)
k = 0.29 for U.S. customary units, 2.26 for SI units
T = torque on the shaft (in-lb, Nmm)

EXAMPLE: A turntable, requiring 1650 ft-lb of torque to spin, is to be directly driven by a long solid round keyed steel shaft coming up from a motor and gear reducer located on the floor of the trap room. What are the minimum shaft diameters for torsional shear and limited angular deflection? Using these numbers, select an appropriate shaft diameter from the commonly available sizes.

SOLUTION: Assume that there are no axial or radial forces acting on the shaft, and that it spins slowly enough that resonances can be ignored. The minimum shaft size for torsional shear is:

$$T = S_{tsKeyed}Z_{polar}$$

$$1650 \, ft\text{-}lb \times \frac{12 in}{ft} = (6000 \, psi)0.196D^3$$

$$D = 2.56 \, in$$

A 2-11/16″ shaft is the smallest commonly used increment above 2.56″. The shaft size to restrict angular deflection to 0.08° per foot is:

$$D = 0.29 \sqrt[4]{T}$$

$$D = 0.29 \sqrt[4]{1650 \, ft\text{-}lb\left(\frac{12 in}{ft}\right)}$$

$$D = 3.44 in$$

A 3-7/16″ shaft, at 3.438″, is close enough since angular deflection is not a failure mode.

The considerable size difference between the diameter needed to avoid failure and the diameter recommended to minimize the negative effects of springiness is typical of these two formulas.

The shaft diameter ultimately selected will often depend on a judgement call between the desirability of a smaller shaft diameter and the importance of reducing shaft twisting. As a rule of thumb, whenever the length of the torque transmitting portion of the shaft is greater than 10 times the shaft diameter, limiting angular deflection is advisable. The length of the torque transmitting portion is essentially the distance from the torque input device to the output device (see Figure 16.2).

The above example also demonstrates why turntables are rarely center shaft driven. The cost and weight of 3-7/1" or larger shafting, bearings, and especially the associated gear reducers would not be warranted for most turntable setups.

Other Shaft Stress Sources

Theoretically, a full analysis of any shaft could be performed to determine the maximum stresses involved due to a combination of:

- Torque being transmitted through the shaft
- Bending due to gravity acting on the shaft and the sprockets, drums or other equipment it supports, called hanging stress
- Bending stresses that arise due to oscillations in the shaft resulting from an interaction of the springiness of the shaft and its rotational speed
- Bending due to side loads caused by chain sprockets, cable drums, or V-belt sheaves
- Axial loads from supporting weight, or other thrust sources
- Stress concentrations due to keyways, shaft diameter step-downs, holes drilled for pins, or slots used to accommodate retaining rings.
- Any of a number of influences which are relatively rare in theater setups: high temperature, corrosion, or shaft surface finish, for instance.

During the process of shaft design, some of the difficulties of a full structural analysis can be avoided through the use of case formulas and rules of thumb that cover the most common shaft situations. Below is a presentation of some of these simplified procedures.

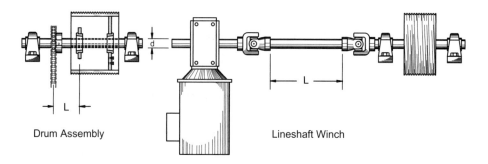

Drum Assembly   Lineshaft Winch

Figure 16.2   Torque Transmission in a Shaft

Combined Torque and Bending Shaft Analysis

The two formulas given above offer approaches to determining shaft size, but they are useful only when a shaft is loaded only in torsion. Side loads caused by sprockets, drums or belts put bending stresses on a shaft, and the combination of torsion and this bending must be resisted by the shaft. The bending loads on a shaft affect it differently than bending loads in a typical structural beam. This is because, as the shaft spins, each part of the shaft oscillates between tension and compression with each rotation. The following equation, which takes into account combined torsional and bending loading, is based on ASA B17c-1927 (American Standards Association Code for Transmission Shafting), circa 1927 and withdrawn in 1954, which, while old, still provides usable conservative results (this assumes no axial load, and no turned down sections).

$$D = B \sqrt[3]{\frac{5.1}{p_t} \sqrt{(K_m M)^2 + (K_t T)^2}}$$

Where D = shaft diameter (in, mm)
   B = hollow shaft factor (see below)
   p_t = allowable torsional shear under combined loading (psi, N/mm^2)
   K_m = combined shock and fatigue factor for bending (see below)
   M = maximum bending moment on the shaft (in-lb, Nmm)
   K_t = combined shock and fatigue factor for torsion (see below)
   T = maximum torque on the shaft (in-lb, Nmm)

The hollow shaft factor, B, allows the lower strength of a hollow shaft to be computed. The value of B for a solid shaft is 1. For hollow shafts:

$$B = \sqrt{\frac{1}{\sqrt[3]{1 - \left(\frac{ID}{OD}\right)^4}}}$$

Where B = the hollow shaft factor
   ID and OD = the inner and outer diameters of the shaft (in, mm)

K_m and K_t are multipliers to compensate for various types of loading. They are not formulaic, but rather determined off a chart (see Table 16.1) with the addition of some judgement. Most theatre machinery is quite gentle in its movements, and so the two lower cases will generally be appropriate. Heavy shocks occur in industrial machines such as rock crushers or log conveyors, but it is difficult to imagine a theatre application that would ever fit that category.

Type of Load	K_m	K_t
Gradually applied and steady	1.5	1.0
Suddenly applied, minor shocks only	1.5 - 2.0	1.0 - 1.5
Suddenly applied, heavy shocks	2.0 - 3.0	1.5 - 3.0

Table 16.1   Load Multipliers for Combined Loading for Shafting

EXAMPLE: A shaft mounted 8 inch diameter drum supports a 350 lb load (see Figure 16.3) The shaft is supported at either end by bearings spaced 1 ft apart. What size shaft is appropriate to resist the combined loading? The shaft is steel, but its properties are unknown.

SOLUTION: First, determine the maximum bending moment, M. Since the shaft is a simply supported beam, the following case formula applies.

$$M = \frac{Pl}{4} = \frac{350lb(12in)}{4} = 1050 \; in\text{-}lb$$

Where P = the load (lb)
l = the unsupported length (in)

Second, determine the maximum torque on the shaft, T. An 8 inch drum has a radius of 4 inches, so

$$T = rF = 4in(350lb) = 1400 \; in\text{-}lb$$

Where T = maximum torque on the shaft (in-lb)
r = the radius of the drum (in)
F = the magnitude of the force producing torque (lb)

Next, choose appropriate values for K_m and K_t. By industrial standards, typical stage machinery tends to have smooth and gentle motion, at least compared to rock crushers or punch presses, but since any stage machinery may need to be emergency stopped, it is conservative to assume that suddenly applied, but minor shocks may be experienced. Given this, both K_m and K_t can have a value of 1.5. Now plug these knowns in the equation.

$$d = B \sqrt[3]{\frac{5.1}{p_t} \sqrt{(K_m M)^2 + (K_t T)^2}}$$

$$d = 1 \sqrt[3]{\frac{5.1}{6000psi} \sqrt{(1.5(1050 \; in\text{-}lb))^2 + (1.5(1400 \; in\text{-}lb))^2}} = \sqrt[3]{0.00085 \sqrt{6890625}} = 1.3 \; in$$

A 1-7/16″ or 1-1/2″ shaft would be appropriate for this application.

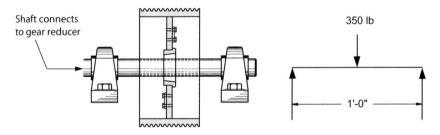

Figure 16.3 Combined Loading Example

Combined torque and bending loads on power transmission shafts are very common. Side loads from roller chain, belts, or cable drums all create bending moments, and since these often work in pairs (a typical deck winch for instance has a chain stage and a drum) the bending moment will be the result of multiple side loads. The weight of the shaft too will create a bending moment, and while for short shafts this effect is negligible, always consider it if shafts are horizontal and span significant distances between supporting bearings.

Resonant Speed

Whenever a shaft rotates, inevitable imbalances will cause the shaft to vibrate, or resonate, at certain frequencies. If these vibrations are severe, loads on bearings increase greatly, and stresses in the shaft could cause a repetitive stress fracture or yielding failure in the shaft material. The resonant frequencies of the shaft are dependent on its structural properties and its unsupported length. At a specific speed, the rate of rotation will exactly match a resonant frequency, and the shaft will be stressed to a maximum in its effort to resist deflection. To avoid the stresses due to vibration, a shaft of a given size should not spin any faster than 70% of its lowest resonant speed. Conversely, if the top speed of a shaft is known, a minimum diameter can be determined (this formula considers just a rotating shaft, as in the long runs of shaft between drums in a line-shaft winch):

$$L_{resonant\ speed} = 1580 \sqrt{\frac{D}{RPM}}$$

Where $L_{resonant\ speed}$ = unsupported shaft length (in)
D = shaft diameter (in)
RPM = shaft angular speed (rpm)

An analysis of a setup more complex than just a shaft between bearings can be done, but that is well beyond what can be covered here. Engineering software packages allow sophisticated analysis of the behavior moving machinery, but the use (and need) for that in theatre is still rare.

Stress Concentrations

Whenever there are changes in the shape of a shaft, the stresses that develop under loading will have local peak values that can far exceed the level of stress that would otherwise exist. Keyways and shafts turned to step down from one diameter to another are common examples of the shape changes that cause stress concentrations. Calculation of the higher stress value is usually performed using a multiplier obtained from graphs that describe specific situations.[2] Finite element analysis programs have reduced the need for these graphs, allowing engineers to calculate the worst case stress for any shape and loading condition.

---

2. See *Machinery's Handbook*, or for a very thorough discussion: Pilkey, Walter D.: *Peterson's Stress Concentration Factors*, John Wiley & Sons, 2nd ed. 1997.

For keyways, the 25% reduction in the allowable torsional shear takes into account stress concentration. If a stepped shaft is required for a non-critical application, radius the step as smoothly as possible to limit the stresses, and design the smaller diameter of the shaft conservatively for the torque it must carry. Even the venerable keyway has been redesigned with radiused corners to minimize stress concentration though the use of this new design is still rare in America (it is standard on British metric keyways).

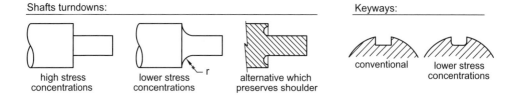

Shafts turndowns:

high stress concentrations   lower stress concentrations   alternative which preserves shoulder

Keyways:

conventional   lower stress concentrations

Keys and Keyways

Torque must be transmitted between shafts and sheaves, sprockets, and shaft couplings without any possibility of slipping. The most common way this is accomplished is through the use of square or, for shafts above 6″ in diameter, rectangular steel keys that fit into keyways machined into both the shaft and whatever it connects to. In the U.S., the key size for a given shaft size is standardized as shown in Table 16.2. Key material is generally sold slightly oversized and must be filed down to fit into the keyway.

Shaft Diameter (in)		Key Size (in)	Shaft Diameter (in)		Key Size (in)
Over	Through	Inches	Over	Through	Inches
7/16	9/16	1/8 x 1/8	1-3/4	2-1/4	1/2 x 1/2
9/16	7/8	3/16 x 3/16	2-1/4	2-3/4	5/8 x 5/8
7/8	1-1/4	1/4 x 1/4	2-3/4	3-1/4	3/4 x 3/4
1-1/4	1-3/8	5/16 x 5/16	3-1/4	3-3/4	7/8 x 7/8
1-3/8	1-3/4	3/8 x 3/8	3-3/4	4-1/2	1 x 1

Table 16.2   Key Sizing

The torque acting through the key causes both shear and compressive stresses on the key. The shear stress equals:

$$S_{shear} = \frac{2T}{DWL}$$

Where S_{shear} = the shear stress on the key (psi)
        T = torque transmitted through the key (in-lb)
        D = shaft diameter (in)
        W = key width (in)
        L = length of the key that is under stress (in)

The compressive stress on the key is:

$$S_{compressive} = \frac{2T}{Dh_1L}$$

Where $S_{compressive}$ = the compressive stress on the key (psi)
T = torque transmitted through the key (in-lb)
D = shaft diameter (in)
h_1 = one half the key height, or the depth of the key in the shaft's or hub's keyway, whichever is smaller (in)
L = length of the key that is under stress (in)

The allowable stresses for one typical key material (AISI C1018) is:

$S_{shear\ (allowable)}$ = 7500 psi $S_{compressive\ (allowable)}$ = 15,000 psi

---

EXAMPLE: Given a 2″ long standard key for a 1-7/16″ shaft, what torque can be transmitted? Assume that the keyway is cut to 1/2 the depth of the key.

SOLUTION: A 1-7/16″ shaft uses a 3/8″ × 3/8″ key.
Testing for shear:

$$S_{shear} = \frac{2T}{DWL}$$

$$7500\ psi = \frac{2T}{1.4375in(0.375in)2in}$$

$$T = 4043\ in\text{-}lb$$

Testing for compression:

$$S_{compressive} = \frac{2T}{Dh_1L}$$

$$15000\ psi = \frac{2T}{1.4375in(0.1875in)2in}$$

$$T = 4043\ in\text{-}lb$$

The exact match of the two answers shows that, whenever a square key is seated half its depth into the shaft, as is common, only one of these two formulas needs to be used since they will produce identical answers.

Practical Shaft Design Considerations

Over time certain sizes of shaft have become common, as have their associated bearings, couplings sheaves and other fittings. Many of the most common sizes are 1/16″ less than what might be expected. This is because early fabrication techniques were too crude to produce exact shaft sizes, and so each nominal size, such as 2″, had to be turned down on a lathe to an exact size, in this case 1-15/16″. Though this is no longer necessary, the many components for shafting are still produced to these specs. For shaft diameters below 2″, components now exist for more "logical" sizes like 1″, 1-1/4″ and 1-1/2″, although it is worth checking the availability of components before designing with a certain size in mind. Table 16.3 lists the shaft sizes which are readily available, and therefore recommended.

Recommended Shaft Diameters				
15/16"	1"	1-3/16"	1-1/4"	1-7/16"
1-1/2"	1-11/16"	1-15/16"	2-3/16"	2-7/16"
2-11/16"	2-15/16"	3-7/16"	3-15/16"	4-7/16"

Table 16.3   Commonly Available Shaft Sizes

Shaft Couplings

Shaft couplings allow the transmission of torque from one shaft to another. There are two broad classifications of shaft couplings, rigid and flexible. While both categories are designed to transmit torque, flexible couplings also allow a small amount of angular, parallel or axial misalignment between the two connected shafts (see Figure 16.4) This is crucial in theatrical applications where the precision necessary to use rigid couplings is often difficult to achieve. Additionally, flexible couplings can easily connect shafts of different diameters and reduce the transmission of vibrations from shaft to shaft. There are numerous flexible coupling types, which have differing torque transmission values, size ranges and tolerances for misalignment. The general characteristics of three of the more common types are described below, but only the manufacturer's catalogs contain the full specs of a given part. All shaft coupling specifications are unique to a given manufacturer's product line, and therefore no specific information can be inferred from just a coupling's type.

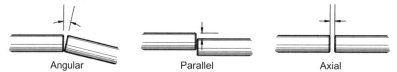

Figure 16.4   Types of Shaft Misalignment

Jaw Couplings

The jaw type coupling, often referred to by the brand name Lovejoy, is probably the most common flexible coupling because of its simplicity and low cost. Figure 16.5 shows a typical jaw type coupling which consists of three pieces, a "spider" of elastomeric material or bronze, and two coupling bodies which are bored and keyed to match standard shaft sizes. The jaws or teeth on the two bodies interlock, while the spider fits between to act as a cushion between the jaws, damping shock and allowing misalignment. Jaw couplings come in a variety of sizes, each of which is available in a range of bore sizes, so that different size shafts can be connected. The spider is available in several different materials with different properties such as torque transmission, misalignment tolerance, recommended speed

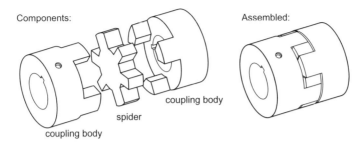

Figure 16.5 Jaw Type Coupling

range, springiness and temperature range (this last being generally unimportant in theater). Jaw couplings are generally best in high speed, relatively low torque applications, as in connecting a motor's shaft to the input shaft of a gear reducer.

Roller Chain Couplings

Roller chain couplings are representative of several all steel coupling types which are capable of transmitting high torque at low to moderate speed. They consist of two sprockets which are connected by a loop of double roller chain (see Figure 16.6). The chain transmits torque not by tension as in a typical chain drive stage, but by withstanding shear stresses on its pins. The sprockets' hubs are available either bored to match the shafts or with bushings to allow use with a variety of shafts. Roller chain couplings are loud at high speed, but at low speed and high torque they are silent. Covers are available to protect against snagging, keep lubrication inside and reduce noise somewhat.

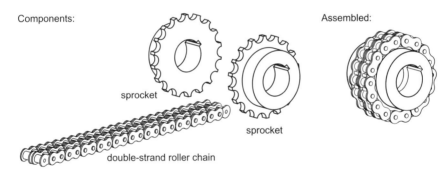

Figure 16.6 Roller Chain Coupling

Universal Joints

Universal joints, usually just called U-joints, allow much greater angular misalignment than other coupling types, as much as 30 to 40 degrees. They consist of two identical shaft mounted yokes that couple together 90 degrees apart with a part called the cross (Figure 16.8). A single U-joint can handle some angular misalignment, but because of the geometry of the yokes and cross, each revolution of the input shaft results in speed variations at the output that increase in magnitude as the angle between shafts increases. The graph shows that there are minor, and

Components: Assembled:

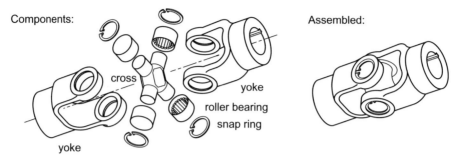

Figure 16.8   Universal Joint

probably unnoticeable, speed variations at 15° and below, but above that the variations grow rapidly to unacceptable levels with increases in the angles between shafts. The solution to this is to use universal joints in pairs. In a properly aligned

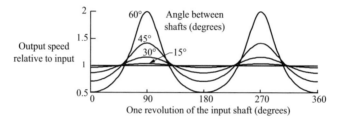

pair, one joint will remove the speed pulsations the other has created. Figure 16.9 shows proper, and improper, use of universal joints working in pairs.

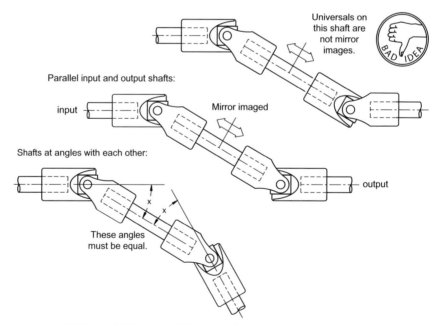

Figure 16.9   Universal Joints Working in Pairs

Bushings

Bushings are used to connect various components, such as sprockets, pulleys and drums, to shafts. Various standard bushing sizes, each available in a range of bores, allow one component to be used with several shaft sizes. The most basic way in which the various bushing types vary is in their method of torque transmission. Most bushings rely on a key to transmit torque between the shaft and a component, although some have done away with the key, allowing the component to be locked down at any point along or around the shaft.

Types of Bushings

There are three keyed types and numerous styles and brands of keyless bushings available. Some of the most commonly used in theater are pictured in Figure 16.10.

Taper Bushings, also known as taper bore or taper-lock depending on manufacturer, are a flush mount keyed style which uses set screws to compress the bushing, locking it to the shaft and the bore of the component. They are available in a variety of basic sizes, each of which may be ordered with one of several standard keyed bores. The key needs to fit snugly or be captured in a short section of keyway as there are no set screws used to hold the key in place. Though the names are not standardized, the dimensions and part numbering scheme are, so compatible bushings are available from several manufacturers.

QD Bushings are installed by tightening three cap screws, either through a flange into the component or through the component into the bushing, so they take slightly more room than taper-locks, but give the designer a choice for tool access when mounting. They are also available in a variety of basic sizes, each of which may be ordered with one of several standard keyed bores. QD bushings are manufactured to standardized dimensions, so they can be obtained from a number of manufacturers.

Split Taper Bushings are a proprietary Browning keyed bushing style. They have the same general appearance as QD bushings, but fit a different taper, so care must be taken to ensure that the bushing matches the bore in the component it will mate with. Unfortunately, the differences between the two types vary with size, so there is no single characteristic which indicates whether a bushing is a QD or split taper.

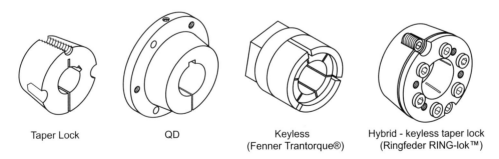

Taper Lock   QD   Keyless   Hybrid - keyless taper lock
                                   (Fenner Trantorque®)   (Ringfeder RING-lok™)

Figure 16.10 Bushings

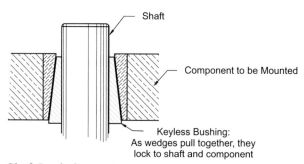

Figure 16.11   Keyless Shaft Lock Concept

Keyless Bushings usually work by expanding to tightly fill the space between a shaft and a hole bored straight through a hub. They are available to fit into taper lock, QD bushing bores, as well as a simple cylindrical through drilled bore. The advantages to keyless bushings are that they do not require a keyed shaft (allowing smaller shaft diameters because the 25% reduction in allowable torsional shear for keyways is not needed), and that when properly installed they can transmit higher torque than keyed bushings. Their disadvantages are higher cost, and that there is no visual indication of proper installation, which requires tightening either one large nut or a number of smaller screws to a specified torque.

Additional Information

The American Society of Mechanical Engineers standard "Design for Transmission Shafting" ANSI/ASME B106.1M 1985 (withdrawn 1994) is frequently cited in engineering texts. It takes into account many factors that the earlier 1927 ASA standard did not: surface finish, reliability, temperature, fatigue, stress concentrations, duty cycle, and others.

For more information on the design and selection of shafts and related components, see *Machinery's Handbook.* Manufacturers of shaft components include (among many others): Browning, Dodge, Fenner, Lovejoy, Martin, Ringfeder, and Tsubaki.

17

Bearings and Wheels

Bearings

Bearings are basic and essential components of all machinery. There are dozens of bearing types designed for optimum performance under different speeds, loads, environments, etc. Rotational bearings, the most common type, allow one component to rotate relative to another. These bearings must resist radial loads, which are forces perpendicular to the shaft's axis, and thrust loads, which are forces parallel to the shaft's axis. Thrust bearings are a subset of rotational bearings which are designed to take axial (thrust) loads only. Linear bearings, the other major class of bearings, are designed to optimize travel along the length of a shaft. All bearings must offer as little frictional resistance to movement as possible to minimize drive power loss.

Bearing nomenclature can be awkward and confusing. The term "bearing" can refer both to the device that allows the shaft to rotate with little friction, and to the whole assembly of that device in a mounting frame. For example, a pillow block can be referred to as a bearing, and it consists of a mounting frame that contains a bearing. In theatre machinery, it is unusual to need an unmounted bearing since most components we use have bearings already designed in—gear reducers, motors, and pillow blocks, for example. Nonetheless we still need an understanding of bearings to select an unmounted bearing when needed, or to select products with a bearing appropriate for the application.

The loads that a particular bearing can withstand can only be determined from manufacturer's ratings. Their catalogs usually have extensive engineering sections that present in great detail exactly what a particular bearing can and cannot do. The ratings usually list radial load capacity (in pounds, at a given RPM), appropriate ambient temperature, and hours of life. Thrust loads reduce radial capacity, but again only the manufacturer can state what capacity is allowed. Fortunately the low speeds, low temperatures, and short running times that generally occur in theater all lead towards high load capacity ratings, making it relatively easy to find an appropriate bearing. Since only a small subset of the whole range of bearing types is of practical use in stage machinery, this chapter will only cover those few types in any detail.

Rolling Element Bearings

Rolling element bearings have balls or rollers mounted between stationary and rotating parts that reduce friction to very low levels while still supporting substantial loads. There are several types of rolling elements available (see Figure 17.1):

Ball - Spherical steel balls roll between stationary outer and rotating inner races (the term race refers to the surface on which a bearing rolls). They are the most widely used bearing type, and provide inherently low friction, with moderately high radial and thrust load capacities.

Roller - Because roller bearings have more surface area in contact with inner and outer races, roller bearings generally provide higher load capacities than similarly sized ball bearings.

    Cylindrical Roller - Cylindrical rollers have the highest radial load and speed capacities of the roller types, but thrust load capacity is typical low.

    Needle Roller - Similar to roller bearings but with a greater length to diameter ratio (originally only applied to rollers whose length was at least six times the diameter). Needle bearings can carry significant radial loads in a relatively small amount of radial space since the inner race is usually the shaft itself, but they generally offer no thrust load resistance at all.

    Spherical Roller - Can support high radial or combined radial and thrust loads. Because the outer raceway is spherical, these bearings are self aligning and can usually accommodate 1-2° of shaft misalignment.

    Tapered Roller - Tapered cylinders are used whenever a bearing must resist high thrust or combined thrust and radial loads.

Selection of one bearing out of all those available is a daunting task which can concern load, load type (shock, or constant), loading direction (axial, thrust, or both), speed, mounting options, space concerns, friction, positioning precision, environ-

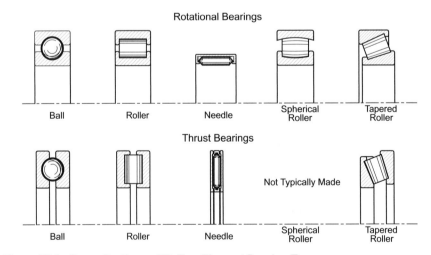

Figure 17.1   Cross Sections of Rolling Element Bearing Types

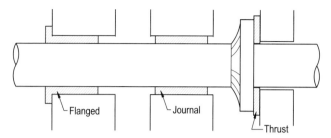

Figure 17.2   Typical Plain Bearing Configurations

ment, temperature, lubrication type, seals, etc. Even a short description of all the engineering needed to choose a particular style of rolling element bearing is beyond what a theatre mechanical designer will generally need to know, and this especially so because we rarely buy just a bearing, but rather components that have already been designed with bearings in them: reducers, motors, or pillow blocks for instance. Manufacturer's catalogs typically include lengthy sections on how to choose the best bearing for a particular application, and these can be used as needed.

Plain Bearings

Plain bearings, also referred to as bushings, journal bearings, or sliding bearings, rely on sliding contact between two surfaces. Their main advantages are low cost, simplicity and compact size. One surface, usually a shaft, is typically steel. The other surface, the bearing itself, can be made from many materials, such as brass, bronze, nylon or other plastics, ceramics, sandwiches of teflon and metal, or even wood. Regardless of the bearing material, the shaft should be hard and smooth, to minimize friction and wear. Physically, plain bearings are typically available in three shapes: flanged, sleeve or journal, and thrust (see Figure 17.2). The direction of load forces that these types can support are fairly evident from their shapes: sleeve bearings can withstand only radial forces, thrust bearings only compressive axial forces, and flanged bearings are primarily for radial, with some modest thrust support.

Plain Bearings and Lubrication

Most plain bearing applications can benefit from the addition of some lubrication between bearing and shaft, but the reduction in friction obtained from this varies, depending on shaft speed, load, and the viscosity of the lubricant. The practical aspects to the speed and load interaction can be summed up as follows:

- If speeds are low and/or loads are high, and a plain bearing is desired, then choose a bearing with inherently low sliding friction: bearings with teflon, graphite, or other inherently slippery materials. Or, better yet, select a rolling element bearing.
- If speeds are high, an oil lubricated plain bearing such as an oil-impregnated bronze bushing would be appropriate. An oil film will hydrodynamically support the shaft, and both wear and friction will be minimal.

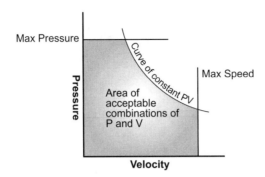

Figure 17.3 Typical Pressure Velocity Curve

Bearing Pressure, Speed, and PV

Plain bearing materials are usually rated to operate optimally under certain combinations of load and speed. They are rated with the following (see Figure 17.3):

- The maximum pressure a material can withstand. (psi)
- The maximum surface speed between shaft and bearing. (ft/min)
- The PV factor for the two materials in contact. (psi ft/min or lb ft/in^2 min)

There are a staggering number of materials from which plain bearings are made (an informal web survey yielded more than 60 without looking hard), so the values for these three ratings must be obtained from the manufacturer or distributor of the parts you are considering to insure that they apply.

Calculating Pressure and Velocity

The pressure and velocity involved in a given application can be easily calculated to see if they fall within the acceptable values for a bearing under consideration.

Pressure:

$$p_{max} = \frac{F_{radial}}{L_{bearing}D_{shaft}}$$

Where p_{max} = the maximum pressure caused by a shaft on a bearing (psi)
F_{radial} = the load on the bearing (lb)
$L_{bearing}$ = the supported length of the bearing (in)
D_{shaft} = the diameter of the shaft (in)

Velocity:

$$v_{max} = 0.262D_{shaft}\,rpm_{shaft}$$

Where v_{max} = the surface speed between shaft and bearing (fpm)
D_{shaft} = the diameter of the shaft (in)
rpm_{shaft} = revolutions per minute of the shaft (rpm)

EXAMPLE: A ½″ diameter shaft supports 65 pounds radially. It spins intermittently at a maximum rate of 40 rpm. There is no appreciable thrust loading. Is a pair of MDS filled Nylon bearings, installed into a 0.125″ thick panel, suitable for this application? Bearing information is reproduced below.

Material	p_{max}	Vmax	pVmax
MDS filled Nylon	2000 psi	400 fpm	3600 psi fpm

From McMaster-Carr, Catalog 113, pg. 1073.

SOLUTION: Assume each of the two bearings shares the load equally. Calculate P_{max} and V_{max}:

$$p_{max} = \frac{F_{radial}}{L_{bearing}D_{shaft}} = \frac{32.5lb}{(0.125in)(0.5in)} = 520psi$$

$$v_{max} = 0.262D_{shaft}rpm_{shaft} = 0.262(0.5in)(40rpm) = 5.24fpm$$

$$PV = (520psi)(5.24fpm) = 2725psi\,fpm$$

Each of these values is well below the allowable, and so these nylon bearings will work for this application.

Mounted Bearings

The term mounted bearings refers to bearings such as flange and pillow blocks that consist of both the bearing and its housing/mounting. The actual bearing may be a rolling element type or a plain bearing, although rolling elements are far more common. Mounted bearings can be broadly categorized by mounting type (see Figure 17.4):

- **Pillow Block** - Used when mounting surface is parallel to shaft.
- **Flange Block** - Used when mounting surface is perpendicular to shaft. They commonly are available in two and four bolt mounting styles.
- **Take-Up Bearings** - Made to be pulled along guides by a threaded rod. Used for belt and chain tension adjustment.

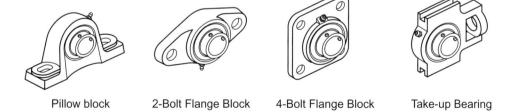

Pillow block   2-Bolt Flange Block   4-Bolt Flange Block   Take-up Bearing

Figure 17.4   Mounted Bearing Types

The bearing that holds the shaft can be mounted such that it is:

- **Self-aligning** - The shaft can force the bearing to shift in its frame to allow for shafts which are not perfectly aligned with the bearing's mounting surface. Generally the best choice for theatrical machinery. All self-aligning bearings must be used in pairs (one alone can be used if the bearings of some other component, such as a hollow shaft gear reducer, support the shaft). One bearing alone will just tip over sideways in response to any side load on the supported shaft. These bearings will often have a grease fitting, or Zerk (named after its inventor Oscar Zerk). The grease does not lubricate the bearing, those are often sealed and cannot be lubricated, but rather it lubes the spherical mount that enables the self-aligning feature. A maintenance greasing via this fitting is seldom needed for typical theatre applications.

- **Rigid mount** - The bearing is rigidly mounted into its supporting frame and cannot adjust to any misalignment of the shaft and the bearing mounting surface. This type is generally unsuitable for stage machinery because of the extreme precision required during construction of the frame to guarantee proper placement and alignment.

The bearing frame will typically be made from:

- **Stamped metal** - Light-duty and inexpensive. Only recommended for light loads.
- **Plastic -** An alternative choice for inexpensive, light- to medium-duty bearings.
- **Pot metal** - A casting of zinc alloy around a ball or roller bearing which is appropriate for medium-duty applications.
- **Cast iron** - Usually heavy duty. The most expensive, and also the most robust choice.

For the size bearings usually used on stage machinery, the shaft is held in place by:

- **Set Screws** - Usually two screws bite into the shaft. This deforms the shaft slightly, making bearing, sheave, or sprocket removal difficult. The set screw marks should be filed off of shafts being reused or installation of parts can be difficult.

- **Shaft Clamps** - A shaft collar on the bearing compresses part of the bearing's inner race onto the shaft. There is no deformation or marring of the shaft as with set screws. Sold under the name *Boa Concentric* by Browning, *D-Lok* by Dodge, and *Accu-Loc* from AMI Bearings, Inc.

- **Eccentric locking collar** - A collar jams against a specially machined part of the bearing to lock the shaft in place. Manufacturers usually do not recommend eccentric locking collars on shafts that reverse direction and for this reason they are not appropriate for most stage machinery.

EXAMPLE: The specification for a typical stage-use rotary bearing would include at least one term from each of the lists above. For example: a 1" bore, self-aligning, ball bearing cast iron pillow block with set screw mount. Once the selection has been narrowed this far, a specific choice can be made based on load ratings, cost, availability or other design considerations specific to the project.

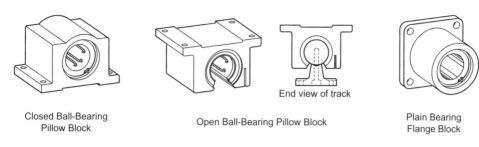

Closed Ball-Bearing Pillow Block

Open Ball-Bearing Pillow Block

End view of track

Plain Bearing Flange Block

Figure 17.5   Linear Bearings

Linear Bearings

Linear bearings allow one element to slide along another in a straight line. Like rotary bearings, linear bearings are available as plain bearings and as rolling element bearings, with the same general characteristics. Also like rotary bearings, the best way to select a linear bearing is through use of the manufacturer's published specifications. The most common uses of linear bearings in theatrical mechanical design are as tracks for scenery which needs extremely precise guiding, in guide rails for lifts and in zero fleet angle winches. There are numerous varieties of linear bearings available, which may travel on round shafts, specially extruded aluminum profiles, or hardened, ground steel tracks. Covering all of these types is beyond the scope of this work, so we will look at a few important aspects of linear bearings designed for round shafts, one of the more common types used in theater:

Closed Bearings - Fully surround the shaft and so can only be used in situations where a shaft held at both ends can support the load (See Figure 17.5).

Open Bearings - Used with continuously supported shaft (also called shaft and rail assemblies).

Double-Length - Contain two standard bearings in the pillow block. They can support twice the load of a regular bearing on the same shaft diameter.

Shaft Surface Finish, Hardness, and Dimensional Tolerance - These aspects of the track are critical for linear bearings since the bearings roll or slide against the shaft. Ball bearings, under any but very light loads, can quickly groove a plain cold rolled steel shaft because its surface is not hard enough to resist yielding under the ball bearing's contact pressure. Typical shafts are hardened, precisely round, and polished or chrome plated for a smooth surface finish. Costs are therefore quite high, with a 1″ shaft falling into the $1 per inch of length range.

Self-Aligning, Fixed-Alignment - Since linear bearings are often used in pairs mounted on two parallel shafts, use one self-aligning and one fixed-alignment bearing to prevent alignment issues which can lead to binding. Self-aligning linear bearings can typically withstand a few degrees of non-parallelism between shafts, but the misalignment distance that can be tolerated between shafts may be only a few thousandths of an inch.

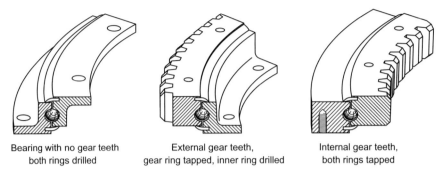

Bearing with no gear teeth   External gear teeth,   Internal gear teeth,
both rings drilled   gear ring tapped, inner ring drilled   both rings tapped

Figure 17.6   Sections of Three Variations of Slewing Rings

The load ratings for linear bearings may vary significantly depending on the direction of the load relative to the bearing's housing. Consult the manufacturer's specifications before using any open-type linear bearing for tensile loads, since they may not be rated for such use.

Slewing Rings, or Turntable Bearings

Slewing rings are extremely high load capacity, large diameter, rolling element bearings which are designed to take thrust, radial and moment loads. Also referred to as turntable bearings, "Roteks" after a major manufacturer, and as crane bearings, although this latter term is not used in the bearing industry. They are most commonly used in theater as a drivable center pivot for turntables, and in turtle units, which are wagons that both track and spin. Essentially large diameter ball or roller bearings, slewing rings are available as just a bearing, or with either internal or external gear teeth (Figure 17.6). By engaging a motor driven pinion with the slewing ring's gear teeth, the ring can be made to rotate (Figure 17.7). Diameters range from ten inches to more than twenty feet, and load capacities typically far exceed the needs of theatrical productions since 100,000 lb and up ratings are not unusual. They are correspondingly heavy too, with a 20″ bearing weighing on the order of 100 lb, and a 60″ bearing 550 lb. Prices vary with size and load capacity, but to give a frame of reference, a 30″ ID external tooth "light duty" slewing ring costs new $3000. There are distributors that sell refurbished and overstock bearings at a considerable reduction in cost.

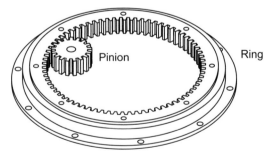

Figure 17.7   Slewing Ring and Pinion

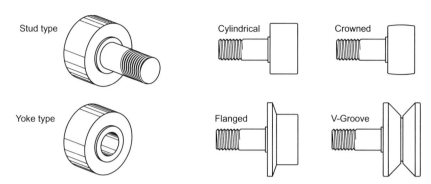

Figure 17.8 Cam Follower Types

Cam Followers

Cam followers, sometimes called track rollers, are essentially bearings with enlarged outer races sturdy enough for use as wheels. They offer load capacities far above typical casters (as high as 125 tons!) in relatively small packages (even a ½″ dia follower is usually rated to support more than 500 lb). Cam followers are good for small wheels, as guides, and, not surprisingly given their name, at following profiles or cams. The most common uses in theater are as the wheels in scissor lifts and as guides for lifts.

Cam followers are of the stud or yoke type, each of which is available with cylindrical, crowned, flanged, or V-groove wheels (see Figure 17.8). Manufacturers use different methods to allow the nut on stud type followers to be tightened. All types, of course, use a wrench on the nut, but they vary in the tool used to keep the stud from spinning. Some require a hex key, which works quite well, while others need a specialty tool similar to a very large flat head screwdriver with a curved end, which often works poorly (a hardened washer clamped in Vise-Grips creates a makeshift tool). Check this before you buy.

Since a stud type cam follower is supported only from one side, the structure that it attaches to must be sufficient to withstand the loads on the follower without significant deflection. The studs are therefore designed to attach to steel much thicker than is usually used in theatre. The threads on the stud of a relatively small 1-1/2″ follower, for instance, needs at least 3/4″ of material minimum or else the nut will run out of threads before it is tight. Stacks of washers under the nut may allow tightening, but the load capacity of the follower will be much reduced. Since the studs are not designed to be loaded in bending, do not use washer stacks between the follower wheel and the support.

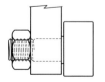

As manufacturer intended, with substantial support.

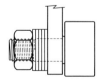

Tacky, but acceptable. Support arm is weak link.

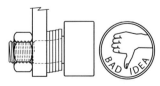

Awful. Shaft could fail from bending or shear.

Track Capacity

The load placed on a cam follower is transferred to the track on which it rides through the small area of contact between wheel and track. The force transferred equals the area of contact times the contact pressure, a variant of the $F = pA$ formula more often used in hydraulics. If both wheel and track are hard materials, then the area of contact remains small, and the contact pressure high. If contact pressure far exceeds the yield point of the material used for wheel or track, then a permanent deformation will occur in that material; tracks can become pitted or grooved, or wheels may deform out of round. (A small amount of yielding in steel surfaces will result in a beneficial surface work hardening.) Since cam follower wheels are usually manufactured from hardened steel alloys, the track is typically the main concern.

Calculating contact pressure is rarely done for theatre applications because typical theatrical loading is relatively light, but if especially heavy scenery is involved, the following equation can be used:

$$P_{contact} = 0.564 \sqrt{\frac{F\left(\dfrac{1}{r_1} + \dfrac{1}{r_2}\right)}{L\Delta}}$$

Where $P_{contact}$ = the contact pressure (psi, Pascals)
F = the force between wheel and track (lb, N)
r_1 = the radius of the wheel (in, m)
r_2 = the radius of the track (in, m). If a track is flat, its radius is ∞, and its $1/r_2$ term equals 0.
L = the width of the wheel (in, m)
Δ = a constant, based on the properties of the two material involved (for steel, $\Delta = 6.067 \times 10^{-8}$ in²/lb, or 8.79×10^{-12} m²/N)
For all materials:

$$\Delta = \frac{1 - v_1^2}{E_1} + \frac{1 - v_2^2}{E_2}$$

Where v_1, v_2 = Poisson's ratio for each material (0.30 for steel)
E_1, E_2 = Young's modulus of elasticity for each material (3×10^7 psi, 207×10^9 N/m² for steel)

EXAMPLE: A 2-1/2" dia, 1.5" wide cam follower supporting 1000 lb rides on a flat track. Both wheel and track are steel. What is the resulting contact pressure, and would A36 steel be an appropriate track material?

SOLUTION: Since both wheel and track are steel, $\Delta = 6.067 \times 10^{-8}$.

$$P_{contact} = 0.564 \sqrt{\frac{1000\left(\dfrac{1}{1.25} + 0\right)}{(1.5)(6.067 \times 10^{-8})}} = 52880 psi$$

The yield strength of A36 steel is 36 kpsi. This is far lower than the calculated contact pressure meaning A36 would be a poor choice for this track. To solve this situation, increase the diameter, width or number of wheels, lighten the load, or choose a harder steel track.

Bearing Selection Considerations

Speed - RPM of the shaft. High speeds, above several thousand rpm, can offer a design challenge, but this is rarely a problem for theatre machinery.

Loads - The load on a bearing will be one of three types: radial, which are loads along a shaft radius; thrust, which are loads along the axis of rotation; or a moment load acting to twist the two bearing races apart (see illustration below). Loads can also be characterized by where they fall on the continuum between the extremes of steady constant loading and heavy shock loading.

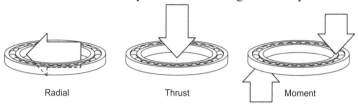

Radial   Thrust   Moment

Friction - Coefficients of friction can range from approximately 0.001 to about 0.2 depending on the bearing type. Some bearing types offer almost no difference between static (starting) and kinetic (running) situations, which can be useful if the starting torque is low.

Environment - Dirt is the most common environment hazard to bearings in theatre, but at times bearings might be subjected to water, paint, flame, welding splatter, confetti, sand or any number of contaminants. Because of this, sealed bearings are a necessity.

Mounting & Dismounting - What space is available for the bearing? How does it mount—press fit? retaining ring? bolts? etc. Does it need to be easily removed for reuse or maintenance?

Angular Misalignment Tolerance - How precisely will the shaft align to the bearing mounting? Will the shaft be perfectly perpendicular to the plane of the bearing outer surface? Will the shaft deflect significantly due to loading? Will the bearing allow frame warp without binding? Regardless of the amount of misalignment the bearing can tolerate, it is highly recommended that a maximum of two bearings per shaft section be used. This is because unless the bearings are aligned in a perfectly straight line (a task beyond the capabilities of most shops) the three or more bearings will define a curve, creating a bent shaft. Two bearings alone automatically define a straight line for the shaft to follow, preventing any alignment problems.

Shaft Material & Finish - The hardness and surface finish of a shaft are important for both plain and some roller bearings. The shaft material may also need to help carry heat due to friction away from the bearings.

Maintenance - Is the bearing lubricated for life or is periodic maintenance required? Anti-seize compound put on a shaft during assembly will help prevent corrosion from locking the bearing to the shaft over time.

Noise - How quiet does the machine need to be? Deep groove ball and sliding contact bearings are generally the quietest types. Regardless of bearing type, low speed rotation (below 100 rpm) is quiet.

Precision - Refers to tolerances such as amount of play in a bearing, the eccentricity of the center bore relative to the outer diameter, and the accuracy of dimensions from bearing to bearing. Generally the tolerances of manufactured bearings are more than adequate for theater machinery.

Life Cycles - How many hours of operation should the bearing provide? Most productions use machines for only minutes a day, but commercial shops have built scenery for stores and themed attractions that run continuously.

Temperature - Rarely an issue in theater, but outdoor productions or those with heavy pyro or flame effects located near the machinery may need to consider this.

Wheels and Casters

Wheels are used in numerous mechanical effects, but they are generally given much less thought than other components. Wheels are available in many materials and sizes, and in a large range of load capacities. As has been the case for most of this section, the best way to determine the right wheel for a given application is to check the manufacturer's specifications.

Wheel and Caster Terminology

Capacity - The load a wheel can support. Listed capacities are not strictly ratings, but are intended more as application loading guidelines, and should therefore be used conservatively. The capacity is usually just a single number, implied to be at roughly walking speed (± 3 m.p.h.). Continuous use at speeds above this can overheat the wheels, therefore load ratings should be reduced if extended high speed use is needed. Generally the load per wheel is determined by dividing the total load by the number of casters, but this only works if the load is perfectly evenly distributed. It is advisable to determine the actual loading on each wheel to prevent overloading, which can degrade performance or even destroy the wheel. Listed capacities do not allow for shock loads, abuse, obstructions or poor floors. If there is any doubt, the extra cost is well worth it for a higher capacity caster.

Wheel Diameter - Larger diameter wheels (within a given type of wheel construction) generally roll more easily and quietly because of slower rotational speed and less movement as they encounter dips or seams in the floor.

Tread Cross Section - The cross section of the tread can have important effects upon the performance of the wheel. A square or rectangular cross section increases the contact area, minimizing the point loading. Round cross sections reduce the contact area, which can give quieter operation and easier turning.

Durometer - A measure of material hardness which can indicate a wheels rolling properties. Softer wheels are quieter, offer cushioning and better traction. Harder wheels roll more easily, are more durable, and generally have higher capacities, but they can be noisy and may damage floors. For example, steel wheels are extremely hard, and typically have a very high capacity, but their noise levels generally relegate their use to utility dollies and similar tasks.

Bearings - Wheels can have rolling element or plain bearings or may come with a plain bore (no bearings). Always use wheels with bearings. The benefits in higher capacities and quieter operation far outweigh the cost increase.

Bore - The diameter of the wheel bore equals the outside diameter of the bearing or of the axle on wheels without bearings. The bore must be known to order replacement bearings or axles for wheels.

Caster - A complete assembly consisting of a wheel and its frame or mounting.

Swivel or Rigid Frame - Casters can be either swivel, which rotate to allow changes in direction, or rigid, which are limited to straight line travel. Many caster companies make frames and wheels which may be assembled in different configurations, so that various caster components may be assembled for a specific use. Locking swivel casters can be locked into a rigid position, usually in 90° increments.

Brakes - Casters are available with integrated brakes, usually foot operated, which prevent the wheel from spinning. For most stage machinery, it is advisable to use regular casters and provide external braking, but for uses such as carts to transport machinery, locking casters can be an excellent selection.

Solid Wheel - The same material is used throughout the entire wheel, eliminating the possibility of tread separation.

Tread and Core Wheel - A soft tread material is bonded to a hard core. The most common caster wheel type.

Pneumatic Wheel - An air-filled tire is mounted to a hub, giving excellent shock absorption and relatively quiet operation.

Flat-Free Wheels - Sometimes called semi-pneumatic wheels, these wheels provide a cushioned ride but are designed to prevent them from going flat.

Specialty Wheels

Drive Wheels - Instead of mounting bearings at their center, drive wheels are bored out and keyed to match standard shaft sizes, allowing them to directly transfer the torque of a shaft into motion. They are most frequently used as part of a friction drive to spin a turntable, although they can also be used with wagons or other machinery. Drive wheels are available in a variety of tread styles, including both solid and pneumatic.

Drive Rollers - Designed for feed mechanisms for everything from the paper in copy machines to plywood sheet moving along manufacturing production lines, drive rollers are generally small wheels (1/2″ to 6″ diameter) that set screw or, in the larger sizes, key to shafts. They generally are made with soft synthetic rubber treads to optimize friction for their driving function over load capacity. Good for small friction drives.

Zero-Throw Casters - Also called triple-swivel casters, these casters combine a pivoting mounting plate with three standard swivel castes to create a high capacity caster which can reverse its direction without the lurch typical of a single swivel caster. Figure 17.9 shows a typical configuration. Zero-throw casters can either be shop built or purchased in a variety of sizes from several theatrical suppliers.

Low Profile Rollers - Rollers like that shown in Figure 17.9 can be fabricated in a typical theatrical shop for use in minimal thickness pallets. Using sufficient numbers of rollers, tracked platforms as thin as 3/4" can be built to support fairly large loads.

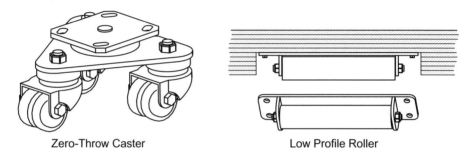

Zero-Throw Caster   Low Profile Roller

Figure 17.9   Low Profile Roller and Zero-Throw Caster

Additional Information

The quantity of information on bearings alone is vast, but the following companies offer products often used in theatre machines:

- Mounted Bearings, pillow and flange blocks: Browning, INA, Dodge
- Slewing Rings, or Turntable Bearings: Rotek, INA, Avon (they offer refurbished and overstock rings at lower costs than new)
- Cam Followers or Track Rollers: INA, McGill, Osborn
- Drive Wheels and Rollers: Fairlane Products, McMaster-Carr

18

Wire Rope and Sheaves

Wire Rope

Wire rope is frequently used in mechanical design in lifts, turntable drives, flying effects and deck tracks. It is unsurpassed as an inexpensive, flexible, high strength, light weight and compact tensile member, but there are many factors to consider when designing an effect using wire rope. These factors include recommended radius for bends, flexibility and terminations, many of which depend on size and construction.

Wire Rope Terminology

Breaking, Nominal, or Minimum Ultimate Strength - There are specific slightly different definitions for each of these terms, but despite this, they are often used in references and catalogs to refer to the same thing—the strength at which new wire rope will break under a static tensile load. This number must be reduced by the appropriate design factor to determine Safe Working Load. The manufacturer or vendor can provide the breaking strength of the wire rope.

Classification - Wire rope is classified according to the number of wires and strands (a strand is a series of wires twisted together). The first number always refers to the number of strands, the second to the number of wires per strand. For example, 7 × 19 wire rope consists of seven strands, each of which consists of 19 wires. The two most common classifications in use in theater are 7 × 19 aircraft cable and 19 × 7 rotation resistant rope (see Figure 18.1). There are dozens of

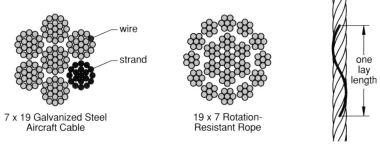

7 x 19 Galvanized Steel Aircraft Cable   19 x 7 Rotation-Resistant Rope

Figure 18.1   Wire Rope Construction Examples

varieties of wire rope constructions, from extremely stiff guy wires using 1×7 construction to very flexible tiller ropes using 6×42.

Core Construction - The outer strands of wire rope are wrapped around a core. There are two core types suitable for theatrical applications, Independent Wire Rope Core (IWRC) and Wire-Strand Core (WSC). Independent wire rope cores consist of an individual wire rope around which the outer strands are wrapped. Wire-strand cores use a strand identical to the outer strands. Other cores, such as natural or synthetic fiber cores, can flatten or crush under load and should not be used.

Galvanized Aircraft Cable (GAC or AC) - The most commonly selected wire rope in theatrical applications, GAC has a good balance between strength, flexibility, and abrasion resistance. Construction is most often 7×19, with a WSC below 3/8″ and IWRC above 3/8″. Aircraft cable is also available in stainless steel, which is both less strong and more expensive that GAC, and should only be selected if corrosion resistance is a primary concern.

Nominal Diameter - The listed sizes for wire rope are nominal, and the actual diameter of wire rope is usually larger than that listed. The amount of oversizing varies by diameter, and is listed in Table 18.1. This oversize impacts the diameter of sheave and drums grooves.

Cable Size	Oversizing Factor
Up to 1/8”	1.08 x Rope Diameter
Over 1/8”, up to 3/16”	1.07 x Rope Diameter
Over 3/16”, up to 1/4"	1.06 x Rope Diameter
Over 1/4”, up to 5/16”	1.05 x Rope Diameter

Table 18.1   Wire Rope Oversizing

Flexibility - Repeated bending and straightening around sheaves and drums is common for wire rope as used in stage machinery. These cycles of flexing fatigue the rope over time, damaging individual wires the same way that a paper clip is damaged by bending it back and forth until it snaps. The more flexible a wire rope is, the greater its resistance to this damage. The smaller each wire in a strand is, the greater its flexibility. For most applications, 7×19 GAC will be the right choice. If a small D/d ratio is necessary (see below) or if reverse bends are unavoidable, a more flexible construction, such as 6×25 or 6×37, may be a better choice. Regardless of what is selected, make sure that the breaking strength is known and apply the appropriate design factor.

Abrasion Resistance - Larger diameter wires resist abrasion better than smaller wires. Depending on the amount of abrasion expected in a system, which would be minimal in most theatre applications, abrasion resistance may or may not be a major factor in selecting a wire rope.

Service Life - A wire rope's service life is determined by regular inspections. Different standards exist for industry to determine when a rope should be retired.

The closest match to theatrical applications is the ANSI standards for personnel and material hoists, both of which allow up to 6 broken wires per lay. A lay is the distance along the rope in which one strand makes a helical convolution about the core. The codes also state that a rope must be retired if even one valley break (when the wire fractures between strands) is found.

D/d Ratio - The ratio between the tread diameter (the diameter of the bottom of the groove) of the sheave or drum and the nominal diameter of the wire rope is referred to as the D/d ratio. Repeatedly bending a wire rope around a tight radius damages it over time, and so low D/d ratios should be avoided when possible. The relationship between the service life of a cable and the D/d ratio is neither simple nor well documented. Sources often give both recommended and minimum ratios, but even these are based on an arbitrary choice of service life. For example, for 7×19 aircraft cable:

100% Service Life	Recommended	Minimum	Acceptable for short runs when lightly loaded
63^1	35^2	26^3	20^4
1. Interpolated from data on a graph in Macwhyte Catalog G-18, p.171			
2. Macwhyte p.170			
3. Macwhyte p. 170			
4. Based on experience over years of short-run productions (4 weeks) using Ralmark sheaves			

If other design considerations mandate a smaller than recommended sheave then the wire rope must be inspected more often for signs of wear and will likely need to be replaced more often. The effects of low D/d ratios are increased as tension in the line increases.

EXAMPLE: Does a 6″ sheave having a tread diameter of 5.375″ supply the recommended D/d ratio for 1/4″ 7×19 wire rope?

SOLUTION: To determine the D/d ratio, simply divide the tread diameter of the sheave by that of the wire rope.

$$\frac{D}{d} = \frac{5.375\ in}{0.25\ in} = 21.5$$

A 6″ sheave is smaller than both the recommended and the minimum, although, since the ratio is greater than 20, it would be acceptable for a run of less than a month if the loading is light. The minimum recommended size can be determined as follows:

$$Sheave\ Size = Cable\ Diameter \times 35 = 0.25\ in \times 35 = 8.75\ in$$

The recommended tread diameter for 1/4″ wire rope is 8-3/4″. It is worth noting that this is larger than the typical 8″ loft block used in most counterweight rigging systems, yet the wire rope running through those sheaves still has an acceptably long service life given the typical use of the system.

Reverse Bending   Improved Design   Out of Plane Bending
Original Design   Increased distance lessens damage

Figure 18.2   Reverse Bending

Reverse Bending - Reverse bending occurs when a wire rope is forced to bend one way and then back in the opposite direction. This can reduce the life of the wire rope by as much as 50% in extreme cases and so should be avoided when possible. Mule blocks are a common example of systems which can cause reverse bending. If reverse bending is necessary, its negative effects can be lessened by increasing the distance between the bends and increasing the D/d ratio. A variation on reverse bending which is often overlooked is out of plane bending, which has similar negative effects. Figure 18.2 shows examples of reverse and out of plane bending. Wire ropes subjected to reverse bends should be inspected frequently. Guidelines here are few and obscure at best. One source in the mining industry states that as a rule of thumb, reverse bend sheaves should be no closer together than the distance the cable will travel in one half a second at full speed.[1] Another source suggests 3 to 4 rope lay lengths between sheaves (albeit they are not here specifically discussing reverse bending).[2] Even if this guideline was doubled to 8 lay lengths, a 1/4″ 7 × 19 GAC, which has a lay length of approximately 1-5/8″, would set the minimum distance between sheaves at $8 \times 1.625 = 13 \; in$.

Construction Stretch - Whenever new wire rope is used, construction stretch will occur as the wires all compact into their working position. In applications which require tension to be maintained in the cable, this stretch must be dealt with by some tensioning mechanism.

EXAMPLE: How much will a 100 foot long loop of 7 × 19 GAC cable in a deck track elongate, just due to construction stretch? (7 × 19 GAC is listed as having a 0.25% construction stretch.)

SOLUTION:

$$100 \; ft \times 0.25\% = 0.25 \; ft \; or \; 3 \; in$$

The system must accommodate 3″ of cable stretch after the load is applied.

---

1. www.mcintoshengineering.com, *Handbook, Rules of Thumb*, Rule 14.16.

2. www.wwwrope.com, *Bethlehem Elevator Rope, Technical Bulletin, 10, Sheaves and Grooves.*

Lubrication - Most wire ropes are lubricated at the factory to increase their service life. In industrial applications, ropes are relubricated periodically, but this is nearly unheard of in theatre.

Rotation-Resistant Cable - In situations where the load is supported by a single line, the wrapping of the wire rope may cause the load to spin. In rotation resistant or anti-rotational wire rope the core is twisted in the opposite direction from the outer strands, which helps to resist rotation. Because of this special construction, in situations where one end is free to rotate, design factors applied to the breaking strength should be increased up to double those for standard wire ropes.

Finish - Wire rope is available in a variety of finishes, such as galvanized or stainless if corrosion is a problem, or black coated to minimize visibility. Spray painting wire rope black in the shop is not recommended since the paint's solvents can remove the lubrication in the wire rope, potentially weakening it.

Inspection

Regardless of the classification or the design details, wire rope should be inspected regularly. The frequency of inspections will vary from application to application, since factors like reduced D/d ratio, reverse bending, or a high number of cycles of use will necessitate more frequent inspection. If there are any signs of abrasion or broken wires, replace the wire rope. The terminations should also be scrutinized and any problems dealt with. If the thimble has been elongated, the cable has likely been shock loaded or overloaded. In this case, the loading conditions and operation of all equipment should be re-examined to ensure safety and, after determination of the cause of the damage, the wire rope should be replaced (possibly with one of larger diameter).

Sheaves

Sheaves are grooved wheels with bearings designed to redirect rope (wire or fiber) and to support the load connected to the rope. Sheaves for wire rope may be constructed of a variety of materials, although the most common by far are cast iron, turned steel, phenolic resin and plastics. Sheaves are available in numerous sizes and strengths and in different configurations. While larger sheaves generally can support higher loads, the manufacturer's specifications are the only source for load ratings.

Sheave Terminology

Block - A block, also called a sheave assembly, is a complete assembly consisting of sheave, axle, side plates, retainers and any necessary mounting hardware (see Figure 18.3). Keep in mind that the weakest part of the assembly will determine the load capacity of the block as a whole.

Fleet Angle - Fleet angle is the angle at which the wire rope leaves the sheave. It is important that the wire rope leave the sheave as close to parallel to the body of

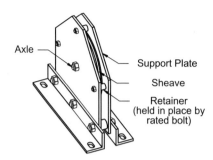

Figure 18.3   Block (Also Called a Sheave Assembly)

the sheave as possible to avoid abrasion of the sides of the sheave or the wire rope. The maximum recommended fleet angle is usually on the order of 1.5°.

Tread Diameter - The diameter of the sheave at the bottom of the groove. (See Figure 18.4.)

Pitch Diameter - The diameter of the sheave measured at the centerline of the wire rope.

Outside Diameter - The overall diameter of the sheave. Useful for determining the spacing of retainers.

Groove Diameter - The diameter of the groove in the sheave should be sized to match the wire rope. If it is too small, the wire rope and the sheave will both suffer abrasion, and if it is too large the wire rope will flatten out, weakening it. The groove should support at least 1/3 of the circumference of the cable and then flare out to minimize abrasion.

Multi-Groove Sheave - Multi-groove sheaves have more than one groove to hold multiple cables. If the cables are of different diameters, such as in a head block which has wire ropes and a fiber rope hand line, it is important to match the pitch diameter of the grooves for equal travel distances per revolution.

Idler - A sheave placed in the middle of a cable run to prevent excessive cable sag.

Mule Block - Mule blocks are sheave assemblies used to change the direction in which cables run. They are often used to prevent excessive fleet angles or to avoid obstructions in the cable's path.

Friction - Running a cable over a sheave will produce friction, which increases the force required to move a load. The effects of multiple sheaves are exponential;

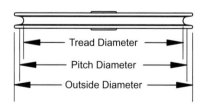

Figure 18.4   Tread, Pitch and Outside Diameters of a Sheave

for example, in a system using 5 sheaves, each of which has a 2% inefficiency, then the force required to move the load becomes:

$$F_{total} = (1 + Efficiency)^n F_{load} = (1.02)^5 F_{load}$$

Where F_{total} = The total force required to operate the system (lb, N)
            $Efficiency$ = the eficiency of a sheave expressed as a decimal (2% = 0.02)
            n = the number of sheaves the cable runs over (unitless)
            F_{load} = The force required to move the load (including all forces due to gravity, acceleration, friction etc.) (lb, N)

The sheave bearings, the friction within the wire rope as it bends over the sheave, and friction between rope and sheave groove flanges at any fleet angle other than zero will affect the inefficiency of a sheave. As a rule of thumb, inefficiencies in the range of 2% to 4% have proven useful for rolling element bearing sheaves, and 6% to 8% for sheaves with plain bearings.

Resultant Force - The two ends of the cable passing over a sheave produce a resultant force that must be resisted by the sheave's support shaft, the frame holding the sheave and the supports to which the assembly mounts (see Figure 18.5). The line of action of this force bisects the angle formed by the cable as it passes over the sheave. If the cables exit the sheave 90° apart, the resultant force (not including the effects of friction) can be found using the Pythagorean formula:

$$F_{resultant} = \sqrt{2(F_{load}^2)}$$

For non-90° situations, the resultant force can be calculated using the following equation:

$$F_{resultant} = 2 \times F_{load} \left(\cos\left(\frac{\theta}{2}\right) \right)$$

Where $F_{resultant}$ = the resultant force (lb, N)
            F_{load} = the tension in the wire rope (lb, N)
            θ = The angle between the two ends of the wire rope (deg.)

Both of the above equations ignore the effects of the sheave's friction on the tension in the cable, but the small percentage friction adds to the overall tension is usually negligible for this calculation.

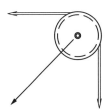 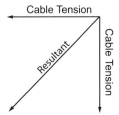

Figure 18.5   Resultant Force

EXAMPLE: The two ends of a cable form a 115° angle where the cable passes over a sheave. The total load (including all forces) is 200 lb. What is the resultant force?

SOLUTION: Assume the sheave to be perfectly efficient. Half of 115° is 57.5°, so the line of force of the resultant will act at 57.5°.

$$F_{resultant} = 2 \times F_{load}\left(\cos\left(\frac{\theta}{2}\right)\right) = 2 \times 200\ lb\left(\cos\left(\frac{115°}{2}\right)\right) = 2 \times 200\ lb(0.537) = 215\ lb$$

The resultant force is 215 lb.

Bore - Sheaves are available in different bores to allow the axle to be sized to match the load. Remember that a larger axle will not increase the strength of the sheave itself, so it may not actually increase the load bearing capacity of the block.

Support Plate - The support plate of a sheave assembly must be sized to support all the loads that the sheave will see and should be designed to allow the sheave assembly to be securely mounted. If multiple sheaves are included in one assembly, then a support plate should be included between each sheave. This not only helps keep the cable in place, but shortens the spans of the axle and retainer mounting bolts.

Retainer - Retainers are small sections of metal or plastic tubing which are placed tight to the circumference of the sheave to prevent the cable from jumping the sheave. If rated hardware is used to hold the retainers in place, they can also help to single failure proof the sheave by holding the load in case of an axle failure.

Many rigging suppliers sell assemblies for use in standard rigging configurations, such as loft and head blocks. For individual sheaves for use in mechanical effects the designer must turn to general industry suppliers. A popular choice for mechanical designs are aircraft sheaves and industrial cable pulleys like those made by Ralmark, Arvan, and Fenner. These sheaves are available in a range of diameters and bores and for different wire rope diameters. The sheave body is generally phenolic resin or glass reinforced nylon, although aluminum bodies are also available.

Additional Information Sources

Three excellent sources for information on wire rope and sheaves are the *Wire Rope Users Manual*, the *Macwhyte Wire Rope Catalog* (this company was bought out in 1999, but their classic reference/catalog can be found at times on Ebay or via abe.com), and Jay O. Glerum's *Stage Rigging Handbook*. Manufacturers of wire rope and sheaves include Efsin, Fenner Drives, H&H Specialties, J.R. Clancy, and Ralmark.

19

Cable Drums

Grooved Cable Drums

Grooved cable drums are extremely common on stage because they are an essential component of all winches, the most common piece of stage machinery. In essence, a grooved cable drum is a section of thick-walled pipe whose outer surface has been cut with a continuous spiral groove into which a wire rope will wrap. The groove supports and protects the wire rope, keeps its speed relative to drum rotation predictable and repeatable, and works against the snags and snarls a cable overwrapping itself can cause. Ungrooved drums, which are much easier to make, offer none of these advantages and are therefore inappropriate for use on stage. The following information describes the design of a grooved cable drum for typical show specific applications.

Drum Types

Spoked - Used in one type of drum construction, a spoke is an internal support which connects the drum to the shaft (see Figure 19.1). Narrow drums, those roughly 3″ wide or less, may have only one spoke, but two spokes, typically offset from each other by 90°, are more common. If a drum has only one spoke it must be kept narrow to avoid putting a large bending moment on the shaft and bushing.

Flanged - Flanged drums have side plates which have a larger diameter than the drum itself. These flanges help keep the cable on the drum if tension is lost. A

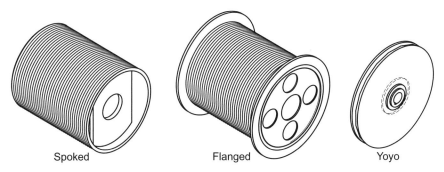

Spoked   Flanged   Yoyo

Figure 19.1 Drum Types

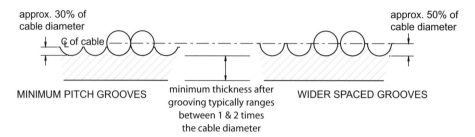

Figure 19.2   Section Views of Different Pitch Drum Grooves

potential added benefit is that one of the flanges can be used as the disk for a caliper brake, which keeps the braking torque off of the shaft.

Yo-Yo Drum - A very narrow flanged drum design in which the cable wraps onto itself in one large spiral. Speed and torque vary with the diameter changes that occur as the cable wraps on, but the fleet angle never changes. The drum sides need to be thick enough to withstand the force of the wire rope spiral wanting to collapse. This force could be minimized by, amongst other factors, lower cable tension, tight clearances between the cable and side walls of the drum, and keeping the diameter of the drum as small as possible. The two drum plate edges should be rounded to allow the cable to enter and exit smoothly. Since the wire rope is piling onto itself, it is not properly supported and so must be derated.

Drum Sections

Grooved drums are usually made by turning a single helical groove into thick walled pipe or tube on a lathe. Figure 19.2 shows section views of two different pitch drums, displaying the basic proportions of groove depth, spacing, and drum wall thickness. The minimum thickness of the drum after grooving relates to the torque the drum transmits, the bending it must withstand, and the crushing or buckling forces that arise from cable under tension wrapping over the whole drum. Because of the relatively large diameters of typical drums, drums work efficiently as hollow shafts resisting both bending and torsional stresses with modest wall thicknesses. It is the potential for buckling due to tensioned cable wrapped around the drum that is the limiting factor for drum wall thickness. *Roark's Formulas for*

A cable drum must withstand:

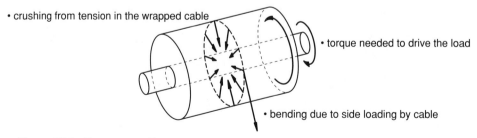

Figure 19.3   Forces on a Drum

Stress and Strain, a classic engineering reference book, lists an equation for the bulkling of cylinders, supported at their ends, due to an external pressure. Include into this formula that the pressure arises from the tread pressure of the cable, a design factor to allow a margin of safety between failure and working stresses, and solving all this for drum length yields:

$$l = \sqrt[4]{\left(\frac{1}{1-v^2}\right)^3 \frac{t^2}{r_{drum}^2}} \times \frac{0.807 E\, t^2}{k_{DF} F_{cable}\, r_{drum}} \times \frac{(2r_{drum} + 2t)d_{cable}}{2}$$

Where l = the maximum length of the drum (inches)
   v = Poisson's ratio, 0.29 for steel (unitless)
   t = drum thickness, or the distance from the bottom of a groove to the inside surface of the drum (inches)
   r_{drum} = the inside radius of the drum (inches)
   E = Young's modulus of elasticity, which for steel is 29,000,000 psi
   k_{DF} = the design factor to be used for this application, typically 8 (unitless)
   F_{cable} = the maximum working tension in the wire rope, usually its breaking strength divided by 8 or 10 (lb)
   d_{cable} = diameter of the wire rope (inches)

EXAMPLE: What is the maximum width of a drum turned for 3/16″ aircraft cable (4200 lb breaking strength) if a 10″ Sch. 40 pipe is used? Assume a design factor of 8 for both drum and wire rope.

SOLUTION: Two dimensions of the pipe appear in the formula, the inner radius, which for this size pipe equals 5.01″, and drum wall thickness, which will be dependent on the pipe's initial wall thickness and the depth of the grooves as machined. That thickness equals:

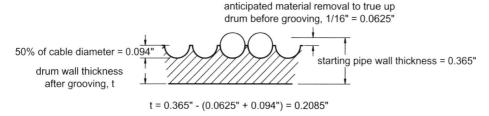

anticipated material removal to true up drum before grooving, 1/16″ = 0.0625″

50% of cable diameter = 0.094″

starting pipe wall thickness = 0.365″

drum wall thickness after grooving, t

t = 0.365″ - (0.0625″ + 0.094″) = 0.2085″

With these few dimensions and the given rope dimensions and design factors the result is:

$$l = \sqrt[4]{\left(\frac{1}{1-0.29^2}\right)^3 \frac{0.2085^2}{5.01^2}} \times \frac{0.807(29000000)\,0.2085^2}{8(525)5.01} \times \frac{(2(5.01) + 2(0.2085))0.1875}{2}$$

$$l = 10.3 \; inches$$

Any width drum up to this value would maintain the design factor of 8, or if a wider drum is needed with this size pipe, support disks inside the drum spaced no further than this dimension apart should be used.

As a rule-of-thumb, for the relatively narrow drum widths typically used, the minimum wall thickness of the tube after turning on the lathe usually falls between 1 to 2 times the nominal diameter of the rope to be used on the drum.

Drum Materials

The vast majority of drums are made of steel, with aluminum in a distant second place. In the past some drums were constructed of cast iron, but the brittleness of this material, which renders it capable of failing catastrophically without warning, makes it unsuitable for use as a cable drum. Plastic drums are used both for manufactured batten-flying systems, and on winches designed for performer flying in some of the large Las Vegas shows (to minimize abration on the synthetic fiber ropes used), but otherwise its use is rare.

Any steel or aluminum pipe or tube of sufficient thickness could be used, but the most common material choices are:

Drawn Over Mandrel (DOM) Steel Tubing - DOM has smooth, precisely round inner and outer diameters. It is formed from cold bent plate electrically resistance welded (ERW) together and then pulled through round internal and external dies to size and form both surfaces. DOM tubing is not usually a stocked product so it can be expensive and hard to find unless a supplier has surplus left over from an earlier order.

Schedule 80 or 160 Carbon Steel Pipe - Lower in quality than DOM steel tube, carbon steel pipe's inner diameter is uneven and marred by a weld seam. Scale on the outer surface from the hot rolling process makes machining somewhat harder than DOM steel tube.

Extruded Aluminum Tube - Extruded aluminum tube is available up to at least 12″ OD with acceptably thick walls. Aluminum is easy to machine, but harder to attach to steel shaft attachment components. Some keyless bushings mount into an untapered bore which can easily be turned, allowing an entirely aluminum drum to be built.

Groove Dimensions

The grooves on a cable drum need to be slightly over nominal cable size to accommodate the allowable oversize of wire rope. The allowable oversize varies with rope diameter (see Table 19.1).

Cable Size	Oversizing Factor
Up to 1/8"	1.08 x Rope Diameter
Over 1/8", up to 3/16"	1.07 x Rope Diameter
Over 3/16, up to 1/4"	1.06 x Rope Diameter
Over 1/4", up to 5/16"	1.05 x Rope Diameter

Table 19.1   Cable oversizing

To machine the drum grooves to these somewhat odd diameters, lathe tools are usually ground by hand to size, for example 0.265″ for 1/4″ cable (0.25″ × 1.06 = 0.265″ groove). The grooves do not need a 0.001″ accuracy, just sufficient oversizing to accommodate the cable.

Drum Diameter

To prevent excess bending of the cable, the diameters of drums should follow the same D/d ratio as sheaves. From the cable point of view, larger diameter drums are better, but the practical issues involved in making and using large drums are such that drums will rarely exceed 16″ in diameter, with 1 foot nominal drums being the most common. The amount of cable travel per revolution of the drum is equal to the circumference of the drum.

EXAMPLE: What is the travel distance per revolution of a 14″ diameter drum?

SOLUTION:

$$Travel\ Distance\ =\ 2\pi r\ =\ 2(\pi)7\ in\ =\ 43.9\ in$$

The travel distance is 43.9 in, or 3.67 ft per revolution.

Drum Width

The drum must be wide enough to hold the traveling portion of the cable, the dead wraps at the cable ends, and a few empty grooves at the extreme sides of the drum and between cables in the center. Mathematically:

$$Total\ number\ of\ grooves = dead\ wraps + empty\ grooves + travelling\ cable\ wraps$$

The first two terms are simply:

$$dead\ wraps\ =\ 3\ times\ the\ number\ of\ cables\ anchored\ at\ the\ drum$$

$$empty\ grooves\ =\ (2\ for\ the\ ends\ +\ 1\ per\ cable\ anchored)\ minimum$$

The number of grooves needed by the traveling cable depends on the number of cables coming off one side of the drum. For example, in a single-loop-of-cable system, used typically to drive a wagon in a deck track, one cable comes off the top of the drum while the other feeds onto the bottom. This system uses the same drum width for a given travel as a single cable because the drum grooves are being shared, with one cable winding onto the drum as the other winds off. The formula for calculating traveling cable wraps therefore becomes:

$$traveling\ cable\ wraps = largest\ number\ of\ cables\ off\ one\ side\ of\ the\ drum \times \frac{travel\ distance}{drum\ circumference}$$

Typically the "largest number of cables coming off one side of a drum" is one or two, but some flying systems use cable drums where 5 or more lifting lines all feed off of one side.

Drum Groove Threads per Inch Values

Old style lathes can only cut certain values of threads per inch, or TPI (in the case of cable drums, grooves per inch), due to the finite number of gear combinations possible between headstock and lead screw. Newer lathes have servo controlled feeds, and are therefore programmable to any TPI wanted – inch, metric, or anything else. Typical TPI values for a given cable size can be determined from the following information.

Minimum Drum Pitch
For a drum that allows the cable to wrap as tightly as possible without touching, turn the grooves using the TPI values determined from the equation below. Drum groove depth cannot be any greater than approximately 1/3 the cable diameter, which limits fleet angles to less than 1.5°.

$$TPI_{minimum} = \frac{1}{(n_{oversize}D_{nominal})}$$

Where $TPI_{minimum}$ = minimum threads per inch on drum
$n_{oversize}$ = oversizing factor from Table 19.1
$D_{nominal}$ = nominal diameter of the wire rope (in)

Comfortable Drum Pitch
The pitch determined using the following equation adds some space between cables at each wrap, allowing grooves to be cut deeper and fleet angles of up to 2°.

$$TPI_{comfortable} = \frac{1}{(n_{oversize}D_{nominal}) + n_{spacing}}$$

Where $TPI_{comfortable}$ = the comfortable TPI for a drum
$n_{oversize}$ and $D_{nominal}$ as defined above
$n_{spacing}$ = groove to groove spacing addition:
For ropes up to 1/4″   n = 1/32″
For ropes over 1/4″   n = 1/16″

Table 19.2 shows possible TPI values for various common cable sizes based on typical lathe TPI capabilities and the recommended pitch information

Cable Size (in)	Exact Minimum TPI	Closest Minimum Lathe TPI	Comfortable Exact TPI	Comfortable Lathe TPI
1/8	7.41	7	6.01	6
3/16	4.98	4-1/2	4.31	4
1/4	3.77	3-3/4	3.38	3-1/4
5/16	3.02	3	2.54	2-1/2
3/8	2.54	2-1/2	2.19	2
1/2	1.9	1-7/8	1.7	1-5/8

Table 19.2   Drum Pitches for Different Wire Rope Sizes

Cable Anchors

Cable ends must be anchored to the drum. If the drum has been designed to allow access to its inside surface, the anchoring takes place there. The cable passes through an oversized hole drilled into the drum groove at the required location and at an angle which allows the cable to bend as gently as possible from the groove to down inside the drum. Common anchor types include:

Pressed Stop Sleeves – Very strong, but not adjustable once installed.

Cable Clips - Adjustable, but awkward to tighten in the cramped confines of the drum. To work properly the clips need two pieces of cable, so the cable end is often wrapped once around the drum shaft and then back up to under the cable clip.

Clamp Plate - A small plate (approximately 1-½″ × ½″) which clamps down on the cable when the bolts holding it are tightened into tapped holes in the drum sides.

Set Screws - Set screws clamp down on the cable as it passes through a hole in the drum wall. Generally two or more screws are needed per cable to provide adequate grip. Use flat or oval point set screws of a diameter roughly equal to the cable diameter. Smaller screws just puncture the cable rather than clamp it. The limitations of this method are that it usually requires a thicker than normal drum wall, and is only possible at the drum's edge.

Specially Machined Clips - Custom machined clips that clamp the cable into the groove are connected to the drum by bolts threaded into tapped holes. A minimum of two clips should be used, with three being common. These are most useful for larger sized cables that cannot be bent easily into any of the other anchors.

The anchors do not have to withstand the full tension on the cable. If three wraps is the minimum cable left on the drum, the tension on the anchors will generally not exceed roughly 5% of the tension out on the working end of the line.

Drum Construction

Most theatre shops are not equipped to machine a drum in-house. Generally only the larger commercial shops have a metal lathe of sufficient size to groove a typical 10″ or 12″ drum. Most non-commercial shops wanting to produce their own winch will purchase drums from a commercial shop and then build their own frame. An alternative is to job out the production to a machine shop, although, since most of these shops will be unfamiliar with exactly what we would want, a much more detailed and specific set of drawings is required from the mechanical designer. Care should be taken when specifying tolerances and surface finishes, since machine shops work to tight tolerances unless specifically told otherwise in a specification or drawing. Drum width, for us, can usually have a tolerance of ±1/8″, and machining time would be wasted if a drum was built to any tighter tolerance. Quoted drum costs can vary by a factor of 10 depending on the level of precision, surface finish and materials assumed.

  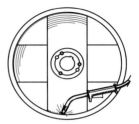

- Cut 5" x 1/2" stock to rough length
- Bore hole for weld-on-hub
- ough cut corners to slightly over the ID of the drum (one shown cut)

- Weld on weld-on-hub (if drum is two spoke design, weld hubs offset by 90°
- Mount onto a keyed shaft
- Mount onto lathe and turn the outer edge concentric with shaft and to the ID of the drum

- Cut drum stock to rough length, slide onto spokes and weld in place
- Mount onto lathe and turn outer surface concentric to shaft
- Face edges of drum to finished size
- Turn grooves onto drum
- Drill cable mounting holes

Figure 19.4 Traditional Spoke Drum Construction

Whether or not drum production is feasible, it can be useful to know the major points of the construction process. Figure 19.4 shows the basic steps for creating a cable drum in the traditional way. Today, drum spokes would often be water-jet or laser cut, eliminating much of their machining.

Drum Reeving

The wrapping of one or more cables around a drum is referred to as reeving. Figure 19.5 shows three common cable drum setups: endless loop, batten flying rig, and friction drive. The grooves have been omitted from this drawing for clarity, and each of these setups should utilize a grooved drum.

Endless Loop - In a typical endless loop setup one end of a length of wire rope anchors to the drum, wraps around it, runs out to and back from a turnaround sheave and anchors again at the drum. In a deck track situation, the most common use of endless loops, one of the lines running from the drum connects to the load so that movement of the cable will move the load. The space between the cable wrapping off the drum and the one wrapping on can be as little as 1/2 wrap since they can share grooves, but it is more typical to leave about two

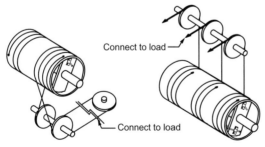

| Typical Endless Loop | Typical Batten Flying Rig | Capstan Winch Style Friction Drive |

Figure 19.5 Drum Reeving

grooves empty between the cables. To reduce the stress on the anchors, a minimum of three dead wraps of cable must stay on the drum at each end.

Multi-Line Dead Haul - In a typical batten flying rig a number of cables are individually anchored to the drum, wrapping the same way around and then together to connect to a batten or other flown unit. Each cable must leave a minimum of three dead wraps on the drum.

Friction Drive - In the capstan-winch style setup, the cable simply wraps around the drum four to six times instead of anchoring to it. This system relies on maintaining sufficient tension throughout the whole cable loop to create enough friction to hold the load. Although this setup can be made to work, it is not as reliable as anchoring the cables and should never be used in a situation where the load may move due to the effect of gravity.

Any of these reeving setups could benefit from the addition of a pinch roller, which is a roller that presses up against the cables on the drum to prevent them from jumping grooves and to keep them on the drum if tension is lost. The mounting of the roller should be adjustable to ease the cable reeving process.

Additional Information Sources

Detailed grooved drum information is rare, but some information on drums can be found in the *Wire Rope Users Manual*, the Macwhyte Catalog, and the *Stage Rigging Handbook*.

20

Screw Mechanisms

Screw Mechanism Basics

Screw mechanisms consist of two main parts, a rod formed or cut with one or more helical threads, and a nut that engages those threads. Screw mechanisms can translate rotary motion into linear motion or, more rarely, linear into rotary. The four different setups shown in Figure 20.1 result from driving either the screw or the nut, and whether the drive is rotational or linear. In addition to the screw and nut, mounting blocks which are designed to support the screw and allow it to spin freely are available. Screw mechanisms are available either as individual parts or as full assemblies which usually consist of one screw, one nut and two mounting blocks. There are two main categories of screw mechanisms, distinguished by the type of movement between nut and screw: sliding and rolling. There are some common terms which apply to both categories:

Efficiency - The ratio of power applied to the screw mechanism to power actually transmitted. Sliding contact screws have efficiencies ranging from 10% to 80%, while ball screw efficiency is generally 90% or greater. Any screw less than 50% efficient will self-lock, meaning no amount of force axially along the threaded rod will spin the nut, nor will any force on the nut, aligned in the direction of the long axis of the rod, spin the rod. Conversely, if efficiency is 50% or higher, forces on the nut will spin the rod, and vice-versa. A self-locking lift would use a screw with an efficiency well below 50%, while the classic Yankee screwdriver uses a high efficiency screw to convert linear motion into rotation.

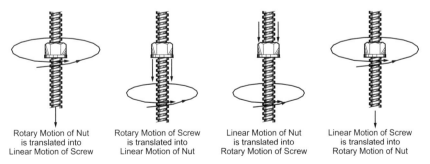

Rotary Motion of Nut is translated into Linear Motion of Screw

Rotary Motion of Screw is translated into Linear Motion of Nut

Linear Motion of Nut is translated into Rotary Motion of Screw

Linear Motion of Screw is translated into Rotary Motion of Nut

Figure 20.1   The Four Screw Mechanisms Motions

Pitch - The distance from thread to adjacent thread, along an axis parallel to the length of the threaded rod.

Start - The number of independent threads on a screw. In a typical bolt, the threading has one start. Power screw threaded rods and nuts are commonly available with 1 to 5 starts and can be purchased with as many as 10. Higher numbers of starts equate to greater travel of the nut per rotation. Many single start screws are self-locking (they cannot be backdriven), and most multiple start screws are not.

Lead - The distance a nut will travel per rotation.

$$Lead = Pitch \times Starts$$

Turns per Inch - Some manufacturers and vendors list turns per inch instead of lead to indicate travel speeds.

Major Diameter - The outer diameter of the threaded rod, measured at the highest point of the threads.

Sliding Contact Screws: Acme Screws

The profile of a thread affects its strength, efficiency, and resistance to abuse. The Unified and Metric M profile thread series used for bolts, for instance, are not well suited for power transmission, and so other thread profiles have been designed. By far the most common of these other profiles is the acme thread profile, developed in the late 19th century. Figure 20.2 shows a typical acme screw. Advantages of acme screws can include:

- High reductions in speed between the rotating input and translating output.
- Development of extremely high pull or push forces (commercially made screw jacks are available with capacities as high as 250 tons).
- Self-locking behavior, which occurs when no amount of force pushing the nut along the screw will cause the screw to rotate. This behavior can hold a load in place should the driving motor fail. This is only true of screws with efficiencies below 50%, generally those with a small lead, such as single start screws.
- Precise positioning of linear movement, such as can be done to the workpiece on a milling machine.
- Simplicity, ruggedness, and very predictable behavior. Screws and nuts are essentially specially machined pieces of metal or plastic—there are no electronics, wires, small parts, or fluids to leak.
- Relatively low cost.

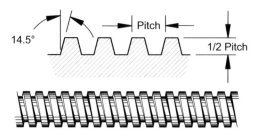

Figure 20.2 Typical Acme Screw

Disadvantages can include:

- Relatively low movement speed.
- Inefficiency. The self-locking behavior is a result of efficiencies less than 50%.
- All screw mechanisms are susceptible to dust and dirt entrapment, which increases both wear, and friction.
- Lubrication affects the efficiency of sliding contact screws, and requires periodic application. Dust and dirt will adhere to the lubricant, requiring either frequent cleaning or dust boots or shields. Sliding contact screws typically use grease, not oil, but check the manufacturer's specifications to determine the correct lubricant.
- Low duty factor. The power lost due to inefficiency is converted into heat which can destroy the lubricating grease. The heat generated is proportional to the power used, or load times speed. Heavy loads moving quickly can run for less time before a cooling period is needed than light loads moving slowly. Specific information and design guidelines are available from manufacturers.

Acme screws are available in a variety of steel alloys whose choice depends upon the load to be supported and the relative importance of factors such as rust resistance. Acme nuts are available in a wider variety of materials, including steels, plastics and bronze. Steel nuts may be easier to attach to machinery since they are weldable and are more robust, but plastic and bronze versions offer lower friction and quieter operation.

Rolling Contact Screws: Ball Screws

Ball screw components are similar to sliding contact screws in that they utilize the same nut and threaded rod concept, but the nut construction is far more complex. All sliding contact between the nut and rod is eliminated by a closed loop track filled with ball bearings, drastically lessening the friction. As the nut (or rod) spins, the balls roll along the thread helix. At one end of the nut, balls are "scooped" out of the helix into a tube that guides them to the other end, circulating them through the nut over and over (see Figure 20.3). Because of this design, the nut tends to be much larger than an acme nut, and will often have a threaded end or flange for mounting to the rest of the machine since it cannot simply be welded in place. The threading of the rod is different than either acme or other bolt threads, since it is designed not to mesh with other threads, but with ball bearings, resulting in a semi-

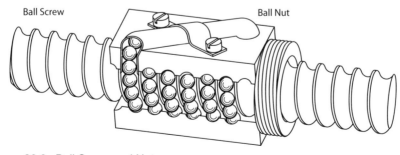

Figure 20.3   Ball Screw and Nut

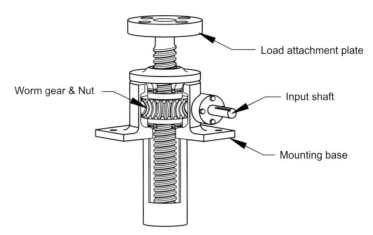

Figure 20.4   Cutaway of a Worm Gear Drive Screw Jack

circular groove. Because the bearings are simply held between the nut and the screw, removal of the nut from the screw may result in the ball bearings falling out. Ball screws are commonly available with one to four starts, with leads from 1/8″ to 1″. The high efficiencies of ball screws (90% and above) mean that they can be backdriven relatively easily, and so some form of braking mechanism is required to hold the load when the motor is off or in case of motor failure. One major disadvantage of ball screws is that their complex design results in both more noise and a much higher cost when compared to acme screws.

Common Screw Mechanism Uses

Screw Jacks

Screw jacks are most commonly used in theater in permanent installations such as orchestra pit lifts. They are sometimes used in show-specific, temporary applications, but their relatively slow travel speeds (one manufacturer lists a maximum speed of 2 feet per minute, for example) often lead designers to select other options, such as hydraulic or winch driven lifts. Screw jacks are prepackaged combinations of nut, rod, lubricant, and usually additional speed reduction. In a typical application, a brake-motor is connected to the screw jack input shaft with a flexible coupling. This input shaft turns a nut by way of a worm and a worm gear speed reducer (see Figure 20.4).

There are three commonly used configurations of nut and screw in screw jack systems (see Figure 20.5). In each of these systems, the setup is identical from the motor through the gear reducer to the bevel gears. In one, the screw is attached to the load and the motor/reducer/nut assembly is mounted to a stationary floor or framing member. Running the motor spins the nut, raising or lowering the screw and the load. One limitation which this setup faces is that when the load is down, the rod extends the full travel distance below the motor, which requires a clear space equal to the travel distance below. One solution to this problem is to mount the nuts onto the outside of the load platform and spin the screws. Alternately, the motor, reducers and nuts can be mounted on the load and travel the nut up and

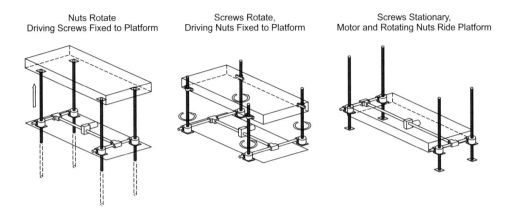

Figure 20.5   Screw Jack Configurations

down stationary screws. For either of the latter options to be possible, the screws must be mounted outside the footprint of the load, and so these configurations will not work in certain applications, such as on multiple lifts which butt into each other.

Regardless of the configuration, a typical screw jack lift uses multiple screw jacks coupled to a single motor, ensuring that all parts are synchronized and that the load remains level. Most screw jacks will operate in either tension or compression. Possible buckling of the rod due to compressive loads limits the maximum rated lift distance for a given load, and manufacturers usually supply a chart listing this information. The load is usually externally guided to avoid side loading the jack components. Combined screw jack and telescoping column systems are available which can support greater loads since the screw jack supports the vertical load and the column resists any side loads.

One advantage or disadvantage, depending on your point of view, is that worm gear driven, acme thread screw jacks are very inefficient in their use of motor power. On the positive side, any screw mechanism less than 50% efficient will not allow the load to backdrive the motor. These jacks will not fall on a motor failure, but in fact need to be driven down (motors will still have brakes as a redundant holding device). Unfortunately, these jacks require motors twice the power, or more, needed just to move the load upwards. The extra power is turned into heat due to friction, and this limits the duty cycle of a given screw jack—they must be given time to cool. As always, manufacturer's catalogs will provide design information, so seek it out.

Traveling Drum Winches
Certain applications may require that the cable exiting a winch have no fleet angle. To achieve this, some winch designs use screw mechanisms to move a sheave, the drum or the entire winch frame. In Chapter 30 three versions of zero fleet angle winches are shown. Designs like these are commonly used for low profile winches, such as truss mounted winches, where the drum must have a fairly small diameter

Plan: Side view: End view:

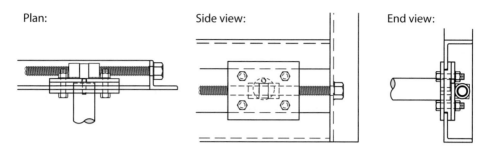

Figure 20.6   Typical Deck Winch Cable Tensioner Plan, Front and Side Views

due to space considerations. In order to gain sufficient cable travel, these designs often use a relatively long drum, which would result in high fleet angle changes as the cable wraps and unwraps if the drum and sheave both remained stationary.

Tensioning Devices

Probably the most common use of acme rods in mechanical design applications is for tensioning of cables and roller chain. Figure 20.6 shows a typical cable tensioner for a deck winch. In this design, acme rods on either side of the winch frame can be turned to slide a shaft back and forth, moving the tensioning sheaves mounted on it to tension the cable. The advantages of an acme rod here over a conventional threaded rod include its ability to withstand bumps and knocks that would deform conventional threads, and it will have a longer life because the design allows more wear to occur before replacement is needed.

Additional Information Sources

Manufacturer's literature, rather than any books, provides the best information beyond the introduction provided here.

- Acme and ball screws are made by, amongst others, Ball Screws & Actuators Co., Nook Industries, Inc., and Roton Products, Inc.
- Screw jack manufacturers include Duff-Norton (they manufacture the Spiracon® roller screw, a nut and screw using rollers in place of conventional threads or balls), Joyce/Dayton Corp., Nook Industries, Inc., and Power Jacks, Ltd. (UK).

21

Brakes

By far the major use of brakes on theatre machinery is to hold loads in place rather than to slow or stop moving loads. These holding brakes keep wagons in position and flown scenery up in the air when their winch motors are off. Two completely independent brakes are often used as part of a single failure proofing scheme in machines designed to run lifts or flying effects.

Spring-Set Brakes

For stage use, spring-set power-release brakes are by far the most useful. Whenever power is removed from the brake, force from a compressed spring or springs acts to press friction pads against a rotating disk or drum. The friction developed creates the braking torque. The value of this torque is the main rating given to a brake, and is the rating used to determine the suitability of a particular unit to a given task. Since the spring engages the brake, loss of power anywhere in the system will cause movement to stop, and the brake will hold the load, an essential safety feature.

The power to release the brake can be electric, hydraulic, pneumatic, or mechanical, and the application of this power will release the brake, allowing the braked shaft to spin freely. Electrically released spring-set brakes are usually either completely engaged or disengaged only, so partial braking to slow the load is not available. This is generally not a concern since the power source can be sized to handle slowing the load, leaving holding the load and emergency stopping as the only brake requirements. Fluid power released spring-set brakes can usually be partially engaged if this behavior is needed.

Spring-Set Brake Construction

There are three main types of brake construction: two which use disks, and one which uses a drum. Caliper disk brakes are similar to the disk brakes commonly used on cars. A caliper unit is fixed to a machine's framing and a disk is attached to the rotating shaft (see Figure 21.3). Friction pads on the caliper pinch the disk, providing a braking force which acts at some radius on the disk. Determining braking torque is relatively straightforward: $T_{braking} = rF_{braking}$. To increase braking torque, additional calipers may be mounted to the same disk, effectively increasing $F_{braking}$, or a larger diameter disk may be used with the caliper, thereby increasing the radius, r.

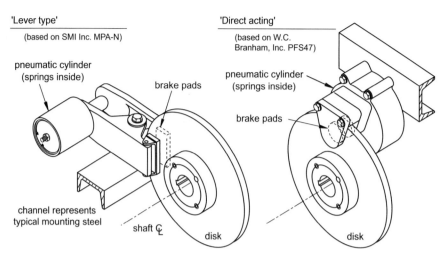

Figure 21.1   Two Styles of Caliper Disk Brakes

The other disk brake type, which has never been given a generic name, could be called an enclosed disk type as the disk is usually completely surrounded by the release magnet assembly. In this style, the friction pad is also a disk, so when the brake is engaged, the entire disk surface provides holding force, allowing smaller disk diameters than are available with caliper brakes (see Figures 21.2 and 3).

Drum brakes use friction pad(s) pressing against a rotating cylinder—the drum—to absorb the power of a spinning shaft (see Figure 21.4). These are available mainly in large sizes, and are not used often on stage machinery.

In general, enclosed disks are found on low torque, high speed applications—such as the brake on a brake-motor. Caliper brakes, generally hydraulically or pneumatically released, are good at low speed, high torque applications such as the brake on a drum shaft. Drum types are usually also designed for low speed, high torque applications, but are less common, and do not offer the same flexibility in use as caliper types.

Brake Noise

The exact construction of a brake determines to a large extent how noisy its operation will be, which can be a primary concern in theatre applications. Unfortunately

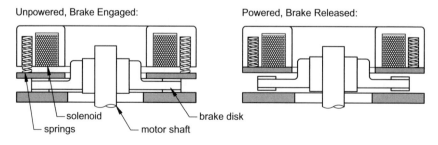

Figure 21.2   Cross section of brake, engaged and released

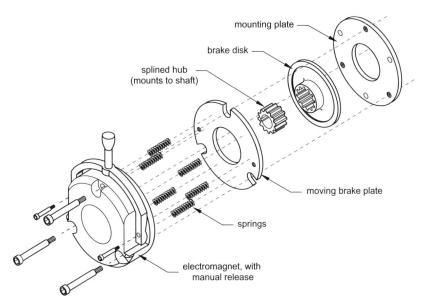

Figure 21.3 Exploded View of Spring Set Brake (simplified from KEB & INTORQ models)

manufacturers don't list noise ratings, and rarely provide cross section drawings to allow evaluation of the design type. Fluid power types can generally provide quiet operation because pressure and flow can be adjusted to limit noise. Electrically operated types fall into one of two major categories which are unfortunately not distinguished by any given name for their type, but only by their construction. In general, brakes in which a large toroidal electromagnet coil directly retracts the spring-loaded friction plate are relatively quiet. Types in which a small solenoid pulls linkages or levers tend to produce a louder click when power comes on, and will hum loudly if the solenoid parts don't seat properly. If noise is critical, testing a sample brake is often the only way to find out if its noise level is acceptable.

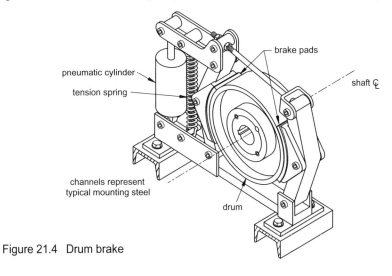

Figure 21.4 Drum brake

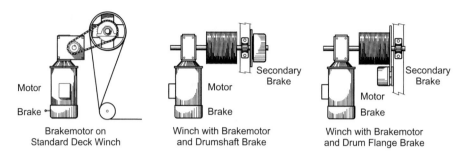

Figure 21.5　Common Brake Locations

Brake Placement

A brake can be installed in different places on a machine, and the location selected affects the torque it will have to resist, as well as its ability to single failure proof a system. On typical deck, lift, or fly winches, brakes will be found in two places: as part of a brakemotor, or on a drum's shaft (see Figure 21.5).

Brakes Placed on a Motor

Brakes on brakemotors generally have torque ratings in the range of 1 to 3 times the motor's torque at rated horsepower. A motor's torque at rated HP is:

$$T = \frac{k\,P}{RPM}$$

Where　T = torque a motor provides (ft-lb, Nm)
　　　　k = a constant (5252 for U.S. customary, 9.549 for SI)
　　　　P = nameplate rated motor power (hp, W)
　　　　RPM = nameplate rated full load speed of the motor (rpm)

Rather than using this formula, it is often simpler to remember that a 1750 RPM full load speed motor (the most commonly used) will have 3 ft-lb of torque per horsepower. For example, the brake on a 5 HP brakemotor would typically be supplied as a unit with rated torque somewhere between

$$5HP \times \frac{3\,ft\text{-}lb}{HP} = 15\,ft\text{-}lb \quad and \quad 15\,ft\text{-}lb(3) = 45\,ft\text{-}lb$$

Brakemotors are commonly used in stage machinery, but given their position in the power transmission path, they cannot hold the load if a chain or gearbox fails. Therefore, if the only brake on a winch is on the motor, that winch should only be used to run effects with a lifting force of zero, such as with a deckwinch running a wagon on a flat floor.

For situations when a standard C-face motor needs to be converted into a brake motor, double C-face brakes are available. Double C-face brakes have both male and female C-face surfaces, allowing them to be mounted between the motor and the gear reducer. They are generally small, sized only for motors up to 2HP, and, unfortunately, many of the commonly available units are quite noisy, and therefore inappropriate for stage use unless they can be located far enough away from the audience or contained in a soundproofing enclosure.

Brakes Located on the Drum Shaft

In situations where gravity would run scenery if a gearbox were to fail, a brake is usually mounted on the drum shaft where such a failure will not prevent it from holding the load. The torque ratings of these brakes need to be much larger than those of brakes placed on the motor shaft, as the drum shaft brake does not have the advantage of working at the high speed, low torque end of the power transmission path. The torque rating of the brake must be at least:

$$T = r_{drum}(F_{decel} + F_{lifting})$$

Where T = torque which brake must resist (ft-lb)
  r_{drum} = the radius of the winch drum (ft)
  F_{decel} = the force needed to decelerate the scenery at an E-Stop rate (lb)
  $F_{lifting}$ = the lifting force (lb)

$F_{friction}$ would help stop the load, but ignoring it here gives a conservative, worst case result for T. A term to account for the inertia of the drum could also be added in, $T = I_{drum}\alpha_{drum}$, but usually its effect is negligible.

Brakes with torque ratings from several hundred to several thousand foot-pounds are not unusual in these applications. As an example, the drum shaft brake on *The Phantom of the Opera* chandelier in New York is rated at 750 ft-lb. Brakes of this size are generally released by fluid power, which can add considerable cost and complexity.

Manual Release

It is often desirable to be able to release the brake manually to enable movement of the load without using the normal control circuits. This ability can be useful during load-in, or as part of a manual backup system for a winch. Some manufacturers provide a manual brake release on their products, either as a stock part or as an option, although large torque rated brakes generally cannot be manually operated. Brake releases may be either deadman, meaning the brake is released only as long as its handle is held open, or they may have what amounts to an on/off switch. When deciding if manual release is needed, and what release type is desirable, consider the consequences of brake release relative to the application. Will gravity cause the load to run if the brake is released? Can one person keep this load under control if it does? What problems could arise if someone releases the brake manually and forgets to re-engage it? One alternative to a brake release which has been used for decades on Broadway deck winches is to use a chain sprocket that can be released by pulling out pins, although if the load were to start to move, there is no way to restore the pins. A major advantage of release pins is that they can allow a drum to be turned by a crank handle without having to turn the motor and gear reducer.

Orientation

Certain orientations will cause binding, noise, or excessive wear in some brakes. In a brake mounted onto a vertical shaft, for example, gravity might pull the disk against the fixed brake pads, causing noise and wear. Manufacturers therefore do not recommend that their product be used in such an orientation. Before buying any brake, always find out if it is designed to be used in the orientation under consideration. Since this information is rarely in product literature, the manufacturer may need to be contacted directly.

Fluid Power Brake Circuits

Pneumatically released brakes are relatively rare. The forces generated by reasonably sized cylinders at typical air pressures of 100 to 125 psi are often not enough to overcome the tremendous clamping forces developed by the springs that set the brakes. Their operation, though, is fairly simple. The control system provides a brake release signal to a solenoid-operated 3-way pneumatic valve. The valve connects the brake cylinder to exhaust when solenoid power is off, and to approximately 100 psi of air pressure when the solenoid is powered on.

Hydraulically released brakes take advantage of the high power to size ratio typical of hydraulic systems since a fairly small cylinder can provide the force needed to release the brake when fed oil at 1000 to 1500 psi. The oil pressure can be provided by a conventional hydraulic power unit, although this is overkill since the volume of oil needed is generally on the order of one cubic inch. Pneumatic/ hydraulic boosters or intensifiers are often used instead. A booster is basically a large diameter pneumatically operated cylinder coupled to a small diameter hydraulic cylinder. If the ratio of pneumatic piston area to hydraulic piston area is, for example, 10:1, then 100 psi of air can create 1000 psi of oil. A 3-way pneumatic valve controls the booster, which is directly plumbed to the brake. Figure 21.6 shows a schematic view of a pneumatic/hydraulic booster operating a caliper brake. The valve and booster should be mounted close together to minimize the length of valve controlled pneumatic hose, and therefore help minimize response

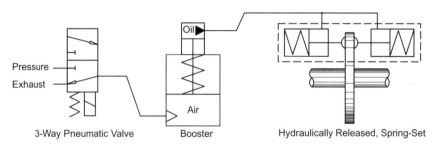

3-Way Pneumatic Valve   Booster   Hydraulically Released, Spring-Set

Figure 21.6   Schematic of Booster Released Hydraulic Caliper Brake

time. At the hydraulic end of the plumbing, steel tubing helps in this regard too. When designing a machine which will utilize a booster, keep in mind the space required to mount the booster and associated valving. While this design works, the system borders on a Rube Goldberg machine with electrical, pneumatic, hydraulic, and mechanical power all being involved, plus the boosters themselves are quite expensive.

Overspeed Braking

In a winch, the top speed set by a specific motor drive, motor, reduction ratio, and drum diameter is easily calculable and any speed higher than this top speed must be the result of some fault. In such a situation all load travel must be stopped. Many designs use an overspeed switch to trigger brake engagement whenever movement speed exceeds some preset trip point. Since the overspeed fault could be caused by a failure of one of several components, the brake should be mounted directly to the drum shaft or drum flange to single failure proof the winch.

Speed switches sense the rotational speed of the shaft they are monitoring in one of several ways. Centrifugal switches couple directly to the shaft or are connected to it by chain or belts. Inside the rotating switch, the centrifugal force of spinning weights works against a calibrated spring. When the switch spins too fast the weights move out far enough to trip a switch. These switches work, and are often used in permanent installations, but they have lots of moving parts that wear, trap dirt, corrode, etc. For a brief time, analog speed switches were used. Small DC generators created voltages proportional to speed which would trip the switch at a specific voltage, and its corresponding shaft speed. Digital switches are currently the most common choice. They generally consist of a shaft mounted collar or disk containing magnets and a magnetic sensor which detects the magnetic field changes that occur when the shaft rotates as individual pulses. A digital tachometer circuit calculates speed from the rate at which the pulses occur and triggers the brake at a user-adjustable speed.

The control logic should use the overspeed switch to reset a latched circuit that was set by pressing an enable button on the controller. In most cases, the overspeed signal should also be part of the E-Stop circuit for that axis. A setup to avoid is to have the speed switch just cut power to the control of the brake while the winch is in overspeed, for then a horrendous oscillation would occur as the brake turned on and off as the winch ran to overspeed and then was braked to just under overspeed, releasing the brake to restart the cycle. If the overspeed circuit is latched, the operator must release the brake to restart motion after determining the cause of the overspeed fault and remedying any problems.

Brake Engage and Release Speed

Larger electromagnetically operated brakes can take a considerable time to operate, sometimes as much as several seconds. In that amount of time during a startup, a motor could easily be on but stalled against the unreleased brake. When finally released, the motor and its load might surge forward. Worse yet, at the end of a move, the motor might shut down, but the delay could let the load fall until the brake engages. Manufacturers will list both engage and release timing information and suggest techniques to minimize lag. In general, electric brakes operate on DC (created from a rectifier circuit running off of AC). A brief over-voltage of the release signal will speed un-locking, and putting the control switch contacts on the DC side of the rectifier will speed engagement. In pneumatic, and pneumatically run hydraulic systems, hoses should be as short and large in diameter as possible, and regulators and valves should be located near the brakes they're running. Some manufacturers of enclosed disk brakes make stacked brakes, where two smaller brake units provide the braking torque of one larger unit. Engage and release times for these smaller paired brakes are significantly faster than those of one larger unit.

Additional Information

The best sources for design application information are manufacturer's catalogs and websites, which include rated torque, disk sizes, mounting orientation and other useful data.

- Manufacturer's of electrically released, spring-set brakes appropriate for stage use include INTORQ (formerly Lenze), Mayr, Matrix Engineering Ltd., SEW-Euro-drive, and Hilliard Corp.
- Fluid power released brakes are made by Tolomatic, the Airflex Division of Eaton Corp, Nexen Group, SMI Inc, and W.C. Branham Inc.

22

Control Components

Stage machines are at the end of a system of devices that starts with the operator who runs the effect. Control panels, position controllers, motor drives and pneumatic or hydraulic valves are some of the components which may be found between the operator and the machine. Few of these parts have a direct bearing on the design of the machine itself. This chapter will discuss the control components which directly interface with stage machines: sensors, limit and disconnect boxes, and connectors. Discussion of control consoles and networks, motor drives and fluid power control valves is beyond the scope of this work. An important decision for the technical designer of a mechanical effect to make is which components will mount within the frame and which will be separate. For example, the motor drive may be built into the control console, mounted into a separate rack with all the drives for the show, or be built into the frame as part of the winch package. There is no simple rule of thumb to aid in the decision between integrated or external components, so the decision must be made after evaluating the specific needs of a project.

External Sensors

There is a wide variety of sensors and switches available to the mechanical designer which can provide control systems with positioning information or which may form part of essential safety interlocks. In this text, the term sensor refers to an electronically actuated switch, while switch refers to purely mechanical systems. Both types can be wired either to break or close a circuit depending on the needs of the specific application. Some of the most commonly used include:

Limit Switch - A mechanical switch which is actuated by physical contact with a machine part. There are a wide variety of designs available from numerous manufacturers. One type commonly used in winch frames is the rotary limit switch, in which an input shaft turns adjustable cams which trigger switches. By adjusting the cams, the limits can be set to trigger when the load is in specific locations.

Photoelectric Sensor - Also referred to as photo eyes, these sensors transmit an infrared beam of light to a receiver or to a mirror which bounces the beam back to a receiver mounted in the same case as the transmitter. Blocking the light path triggers the sensor. One relatively common use for photoelectric sensors is around lifts to engage the E-Stop if a hand, foot or other obstruction is in danger of being injured by the moving lift bed. In this use, the sensor must be located far enough from the pinch point that the lift will come to a complete stop before injury occurs.

Bumper Switches - Also known as tape or mat switches, these sensors are triggered by contact. Smaller versions are used as safety interlocks for devices which require an actor to stand in a particular location before the effect will operate, and continuous tape versions are often used around lifts to stop travel in the same manner as a photo eye does. In this use, the lift must stop instantly or the tape must include sufficient cushioning to allow the lift to stop before injury can occur.

Slack Cable Detector - Some winch designs integrate a slack cable sensor to stop the motor if the cables go slack, preventing the cable from unspooling, and limiting potential shock loads if a flown unit is snagged and then releases after several feet of cable have been released.

Overwrap Sensor - A switch activated by a bar located close to the surface of a cable drum which will be triggered if the cable overwraps

Chain or Belt Sensor - A roller end limit switch can ride along the span of a chain or belt loop between sprockets or sheaves to detect whether the loop is tight and functioning correctly, or it has gone slack due to some failure.

Overspeed Switch - A switch which is triggered when the component it is monitoring (generally a shaft or cable drum) rotates faster than a preset limit. They are often used on flying winches to trigger an emergency stop in case some failure allows the system to move too quickly. Overspeed switches are commonly available in two types, centrifugal and digital. When centrifugal switches spin too quickly, weights within them overcome the holding force of calibrated springs and trigger a mechanical switch. Digital switches generally consist of a disk or collar containing magnets and a magnetic sensor which detects the magnetic field changes that occur when the shaft rotates as individual pulses. A digital tachometer circuit calculates the rotational speed based upon the pulse rate and triggers the switch at a user-adjustable speed.

Position Sensing

All positioning control systems have limitations which prevent the loads they control from moving exactly to any of an infinite number of spots. A positioning system using just two limit switches, for instance, can get a load stopped at either end of its travel, but the exact stopping points usually depend on friction, the load on the system, the speed of the load, deceleration rates, etc. In some situations all of these variables are consistent enough to make this inexpensive control system practical, although generally it is far too inexact to be useful. Additional switches will increase the number of positions available, but this option will quickly reach the point of diminishing returns.

Analog positioning systems, which use the information feedback of a potentiometer, or "pot," hooked to the scenery to determine position, have higher resolution, allowing greater accuracy in scenery moves. Pots output an absolute DC voltage proportional to the position of an input shaft. This output voltage is always the same level for a given position of the shaft, so the output voltage can be read as positional information. The input shaft of a pot has a limited travel which it can accept, commonly ten turns, although other configurations are available. If the limit box shaft can be turned beyond its usual travel distance, a slip clutch should be in place to prevent damage to the pot, but any additional travel of the machinery will not register accurately. The pots and the analog systems they connect to can generally indicate 1000 positions. While this sounds like a tremendously high resolution level, the actual precision of the system depends on the travel distance of the load.

EXAMPLE: How accurately can a lift which travels 9 feet be positioned using a 1000 point resolution control system?

SOLUTION:

$$\frac{9\,ft}{1000} = 0.009\,ft \cong \frac{1}{8}\,in$$

The lift can be positioned within approximately 1/8″, which is fine for most applications.

EXAMPLE: What if the same potentiometer is used to measure two revolutions of a 30 foot diameter turntable?

SOLUTION:

$$\frac{360° \times 2}{1000} = 0.72°$$

At first glance, this also seems like the system will provide more than ample accuracy, but the situation changes when the circumferencer of the turntable is included in the calculations.

$$Circumference = \pi d = \pi(30\,ft) = 94.2\,ft$$

$$\frac{94.2\,ft \times 2}{1000} = 0.188\,ft = 2.26\,in$$

For a 30 foot diameter turntable, the potentiometer will only provide accuracy within approximately 2-1/4″, which might be acceptable, but could prevent scenic elements like walls or floor seams from lining up. If the design calls for more rotations, the resolution will decrease proportionately. 3 revolutions of the 30 foot turntable, for example, would yield a resolution of approximately 3-3/8″.

Potentiometers are also available in configurations other than the common input drive shaft. One type which is often used with lifts or to read the position of cylinders is the string pot, which reads the position of the effect from a spring loaded drum which is turned as a small diameter wire rope is reeled off it.

Digital positioning systems, which routinely can provide 32 bit resolutions are relatively common (2^{32} = 4,294,967,296 or roughly 1 part in 4 billion), although the control panels which can interface with them are significantly more complicated and therefore more expensive than their analog equivalents. Instead of a potentiometer, these systems receive positioning information from digital encoders, which are essentially enclosed disks which alternately interrupt and pass a light beam as they spin and transmit those interruptions as signal pulses. The number of pulses can be translated into distance traveled and speed. There are two types of encoders, absolute and relative. Absolute encoders always know their exact location, whereas relative encoders only generate individual pulses without any reference to a zero point.

Regardless of whether an analog potentiometer or a digital encoder is selected, the mechanical designer must determine mounting position on the machine. One common choice is to mount the pot or encoder in an enclosure along with a rotary limit switch, both of which are driven by an input shaft. Combining position information with end-of-travel limit switches makes set-up easier, since only one unit needs to be connected to the machine. Limit boxes are commonly driven off of a chain or toothed belt drive connected to the drum shaft. Alternately, some designs will connect an encoder to the motor shaft and use limit switches located on the scenery, not the winch frame. For any controls mounted on the frame, adequate room must be left for adjustments (and for enclosure doors to be fully opened) in any orientation in which the machine is likely to be used.

Limit Box Ratios

In any motorized stage machinery system, the reduction ratio between motor and scenery must be set correctly for the system to run at the right speed. In machinery systems controlled with rotary limit switches, potentiometers or encoders, a reduction ratio must also be determined between the limit box and the scenery. Failure to find the correct limit box ratio is unlikely to crash the system, but the wrong ratio makes poor use of the available resolution and will make positioning less accurate. Whenever a winch is set up for a show, both the motor and limit box reduction ratios must be calculated.

EXAMPLE: A winch must move a wagon a distance of 20′ at a top speed of 4 ft/sec. A 1750 rpm motor drives a 10:1 gear reducer, which in turn drives a 10″ drum via a chain reduction stage. The drum shaft drives a limit box through another chain stage. The limit box includes a 1.5:1 gear reduction between the input shaft and the potentiometer which means that the input shaft turns 15 times for the full rotation of the ten turn pot. Determine both chain reduction ratios.

SOLUTION:
Motor to Drum Ratio:

$$Drum\ Circumference = \pi d = \pi \frac{10 in}{12} = 2.62 ft$$

Drum top speed, given the designed top speed of 4 ft/sec, will be:

$$\frac{4}{2.62} = 1.53 \ rev/sec$$

The top motor speed, in rev/sec is:

$$\frac{1750}{60} = 29.17 \ rev/sec$$

The total reduction ratio between motor and drum is therefore:

$$\frac{29.17}{1.53} = 19.1 \quad or \ a \ 19.1{:}1 \ reduction \ ratio$$

Since there is already a 10:1 gear reducer between motor and drum, the chain reduction ratio should be:

$$\frac{19.1}{10} = 1.91 \quad or \ a \ 1.91{:}1 \ chain \ stage \ reduction \ ratio$$

The chain stage reduction ratio is 1.91:1 (for example, a 21 tooth to 40 tooth combination).

Limit Box Ratio:
The limit box shaft turns 15 times for the full travel of the pot. In order to leave some room for changes in the extreme stop positions, 10% to 20% of the pot travel (in this case 2 turns on a ten turn pot) should not be included as part of the normal operating range. So, for this 15 turn limit box, 13 turns is a good range of rotation to match to the 20′ drum travel. The drum, during a move of 20′, turns:

$$\frac{20ft}{2.62ft \ per \ rev} = 7.63 revs$$

The limit box shaft, during this same 20′ move, should turn 13 times, so the chain reduction ratio should be:

$$\frac{13}{7.63} = 1.7 \quad or \ a \ 1{:}1.7 \ ratio \ (a \ speed \ increase, \ not \ reduction)$$

The limit box chain ratio is 1:1.7 (for example, 34 teeth on the drum shaft and 20 teeth on the limit box).

Disconnects

The National Fire Protection Agency (NFPA) Article 79 – Electrical Standard for Industrial Machinery, since it is written to apply to all machines, includes stage machinery, such as winches or lifts, any motor drives and also the control systems connected to them. Section 7 covers disconnects in detail and states:

- All machines must have an individual disconnect located on or near the device. Typically the disconnect is part of a commercially manufactured enclosure which is bolted to the machine frame.
- The disconnect ampere rating must be at least 115% of the full load of all equipment downstream of the disconnect.
- All hots must be switched, but no neutral or ground wires.

- The disconnect shall be interlocked such that the doors of the disconnect enclosure may not open if the power is connected.
- An attachment plug and receptacle (rated for 115% of the full load) may be substituted for a physical switch only on an AC motor of less than 2HP using less than 150 volts to ground. In addition, the plug must be located in sight of the operator and the ground pin must make contact before any other (standard for NEMA connectors).

The standard also includes specifications for wire type, size and color per application which should be reviewed before wiring an enclosure for any equipment. When designing stage machinery, it is important to consider the room necessary for the disconnect enclosure and to make sure that it is accessible (and that the door can be fully opened) in any orientation in which the machine may be operated.

Disconnects are also addressed in CFR §1910.147 "The Control of Hazardous Energy (Lockout/Tagout)." This portion of the law covers the maintenance of machines where the energization of the equipment could injure the worker. In essence, the code states that the worker must be able to lock the machinery power disconnect switch in the off position (lockout) or that there be an established labelling system so that it is clear to all employees that the switch must not be re-energized (tagout).

Connectors

Electrical connections occur between most machinery and the devices that control them. Motor and brake power, position signals, slack line sensors or overspeed sensors will all need connectors. There are numerous electrical connectors available for the machine designer to select from. While specific choices may vary from shop to shop, and there is no single right choice, there are a few general rules which can aid in the selection process:

- Create a standard for the shop so that each purpose, such as motor power, has its own connector type. Whenever possible, avoid connectors which other departments frequently use, such as stage pin plugs and XLR connectors. This will help ensure that all equipment can only be plugged in correctly and that there will be no confusion between departments over which cables or outlets are run for which purpose.
- Select connectors which match an industrial standard, such as NEMA connectors, so that replacements will be available in the future.
- Use connectors which have a locking mechanism, such as twist locks, to prevent problems with loose connections.
- Connectors where the wires connect to screw terminals are easier to field-repair than soldered connections.
- For equipment power connections, use connectors in which the ground pin makes first.
- Use connectors which have a good strain relief.

Additional Information Sources

The most in-depth source for information on all aspects of theatre specific automation control is John Huntington's *Control Systems for Live Entertainment*. The Goddard Design Company's *Analog Winch Unit Controller User's Manual* includes fairly detailed discussion of positioning feedback and control. NFPA's Article 79 – Electrical Standard for Industrial Machinery, and Article 70 – The National Electrical Code both include large quantities of information applicable to stage machinery.

23

Frames and Framing

General Concepts

While the frame surrounding and supporting stage machinery components seems to be simple, just a box or plate to hold the working elements in their proper alignment, it should be given the same careful consideration as the rest of the machine. The design of the frame can easily determine whether the whole machine is effective and elegant, or awkward and nearly unusable. The frame affects the machine's ease of assembly, how it is handled and transported from shop to stage, how quickly it loads in as part of the effect it runs, how well it accommodates the adjustments and maintenance needed during tech and run, and the safety of technicians and performers who work around it.

Open vs. Enclosed Frames

One of the first decisions to make is how extensive a frame is desired. The frame can fully enclose all components, to protect them in transport or to prevent injury to those nearby during operation, or the frame can be as simple as a mounting plate which connects the machine to the deck or grid and is open on all other sides. In general, the more enclosed concept is recommended, since it gives greater protection to both the machine and personnel, and, if designed well, can allow multiple lifting points and different mounting configurations. When designing an enclosed frame, the designer must envision the assembly of both the frame itself and the components to be mounted within it. Some questions to keep in mind when designing for fabrication and assembly are:

- Do welds need to be kept away from certain joints to keep surfaces flush for later component mounting?
- Will any welds warp the frame enough to affect the assembly or alignment of the machine? If so is a bolted up frame a viable option?
- Should any framing members be removable, and therefore bolted instead of welded?
- Is there sufficient room to drop in an assembly, for instance one consisting of a drum, shaft, sprocket, and blocks, or do these parts need to be assembled one by one within the frame (usually the worst choice)?

- Is there room for the tools necessary to assemble, adjust, and maintain all components?
- Can enclosures, such as limit boxes, open fully once the frame is installed on site?
- Is there good sightlines and hand access to all bolts, adjustment points, and controls?
- Do the mounting holes for one device, such as a gear reducer, rely on the precise positioning and welding of several pieces, or are the holes all drilled in their correct alignment on one plate that then gets welded in place?

While a compact frame design may seem like a very elegant solution, one which allows ample room to work is often far superior. The only common application for the totally open frame design is for permanent grid-mounted winches, which will only be transported for the initial installation and which generally do not operate with people around who will need barriers or guards for protection. The advantages to this open design include the ease of access to all components for maintenance and adjustment, lower weight and simpler fabrication.

Stock Shapes vs. CNC Plates

Traditionally, stage machinery framing involved stock shapes like angle and channel, but in recent years the decrease in cost of CNC (Computer Numerically Controlled) laser and water jet cutting has led to greater use of custom cut plates to create winch frames and other parts. CNC work allows extremely precise plate components to be fabricated directly from CAD drawings. Figure 23.1 shows two versions of a stock deck winch, one using angle iron and the other using CNC cut side plates. The advantages to stock shapes are generally lower costs, easy and quick modifications to the design and the ability to fabricate all parts in any reasonably equipped metal shop. In general, solid shapes, such as angle or channel are preferable to hollow tube choices, since they are easier to slot for adjustments and cannot be crushed when tightening down components. However, the use of such

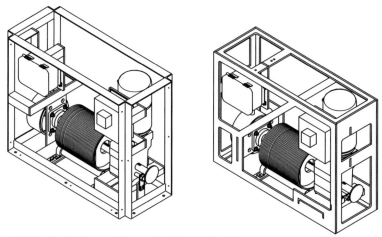

Figure 23.1   Angle Iron vs. Laser Cut Plate Framing

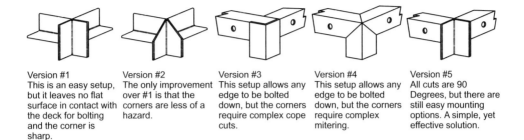

Version #1
This is an easy setup, but it leaves no flat surface in contact with the deck for bolting and the corner is sharp.

Version #2
The only improvement over #1 is that the corners are less of a hazard.

Version #3
This setup allows any edge to be bolted down, but the corners require complex cope cuts.

Version #4
This setup allows any edge to be bolted down, but the corners require complex mitering.

Version #5
All cuts are 90 Degrees, but there are still easy mounting options. A simple, yet effective solution.

Figure 23.2   Angle Iron Connection Options

shapes does require consideration of their orientation at joints, since the irregular shapes of channel and angle can lead to complex and time consuming miter or cope cuts if not carefully though out (see Figure 23.2).

CNC production allows identical, extremely precise machines to be produced using outsourced plates. These plates can practically be assembled like a three dimensional jigsaw puzzle (see Figure 23.3), speeding the assembly process and producing extremely consistent frames. The major drawbacks to this method are the cost (which can possibly be offset or even negated by the labor savings), the turn around time for the parts, and the difficulty of modifying the design during the assembly process which usually would entail waiting for new parts to be fabricated. The advantages to this method include the ability to remove any unneeded material from the design to save weight, the fact that it is easy to mass produce identical parts, stock parts can be pulled off the shelf and quickly fabricated, potentially large time savings (which increase as the number of holes or complicated cuts increases). When minimizing weight by removing material, careful thought must be given to ensuring that what remains is sufficient for the loads. As a guide to plate sizing for machinery, 2-5 HP winches generally use 3/8″ or thicker side plates since thinner material could be subject to buckling. To resist buckling forces, gussets should be designed in and the plates should be aligned so that their width resists the load, not the thickness. Commercial shops frequently use CNC parts for stock machines where the cost of outside machining is offset by the volume of parts and by the ability to produce multiple machines in an almost factory line style. Complex machinery components which require such high levels of preci-

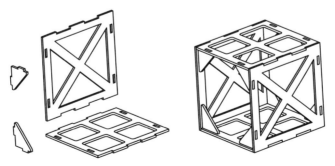

Figure 23.3   CNC Cut Plate Component Assembly

sion that they may be too time consuming to machine using traditional techniques are also often produced using CNC parts. As the cost of the machines drops, more shops may purchase CNC equipment, which should increase the use of plate designs over those using the more traditional stock shapes.

Steel vs. Aluminum

The vast majority of machine frames are produced in steel, although some shops choose aluminum for its potential weight savings, easy machinability, or for aesthetic reasons. Aluminum is approximately one third the weight of steel, three time the cost, and one third as stiff. This means that an aluminum frame equally strong as a steel one will cost approximately twice as much in material to end up with an aluminum frame weighing roughly one third less than the steel version. Aluminum has the advantages of its weight, machineability and availability in a tremendous variety of extrusions, offset by the disadvantages of cost (both in material and welding equipment), welding difficulty, and strength decreases when welded. Some designs now use CNC cut aluminum plates which bolt to cross members to produce lightweight designs which avoid the problems inherent to welding. The advantages of steel include its general availability, relatively low cost, easy weldability and predictable strength. Its disadvantages include weight and rusting. Regardless of material choice, it is a good idea to apply a finish to the framing. In addition to protecting the frame from corrosion (if it is steel), the paint will make the product look more finished and professional, which can help to garner respect from cast and crew. As to color, that is a personal choice, but Henry Ford wisely once said "You can have any color you want, as long as it's black."

Mounting and Handling Options

As part of the design of the frame, consideration should be given to how the frame will be transported and mounted. For a permanent installation, only one mounting configuration is required and the frame will likely only be handled once, so these issues are relatively minor. Stock equipment which may be used in multiple pro-

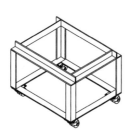

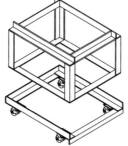

Castered Frame

Permanently installed wheels allow easy transportation. Frame can be tipped onto its side to secure it.

Custom Dolly

Cart built to match frame size eases transportation. Upside-down angle allows frame to be slid on instead of lifted up.

Figure 23.4   Two Castering Options for Frames

ductions should be designed for easy transportability and with multiple mounting options. For example, a stock winch with mounting holes on all sides of the frame can be oriented in a variety of ways to allow cables to run in any direction. While determining the framing layout, the designer should keep in mind lifting points for transport, either manually or using a hoist. Not only is it important to include the option for comfortable hand carry, but thought should be given to where slings or lifting eyes will go. While a framing member may be strong enough for the machine's operation, it may need to be larger to support lifting the unit, or may want to be shifted slightly to allow the frame to hang level. For units which will be transported often, provisions for casters or custom dollies can save a lot of effort, especially if thought is given to easy ways to move onto and off of the wheels (see Figure 23.4). One last handling consideration is to limit any protrusions which could snag or even be damaged and to try to round down all corners and sharp edges to make handling easier and more comfortable.

Structural Design Considerations

While a full analysis of all the loads and reactions within a frame would likely involve computer modeling, individual elements can be analyzed for their specific loading conditions. Most of the framing members can be viewed as either a simple beam or a column, or at worst as a relatively straightforward combined loading problem. The techniques required are covered in *Structural Design for the Stage* by Alys Holden and Ben Sammler. An important aspect to calculations for angle iron beams is the requirement for adequate lateral bracing since angle iron can buckle if it is not adequately braced. Great care must be given to ensuring that angle iron beams are short enough or well braced enough to prevent this type of failure. When determining the loading on frame members, it is important to remember that the load should be the worst case scenario (generally the forces involved in an emergency stop) and not simply the weight of the piece which the machine will move. Some members may need to be oversized from the requirements of the operating loads in order to support the combined weight of the machine and the load if they are used as attachment points for lifting equipment into position.

EXAMPLE: The maximum load which the drum shaft in a dead haul winch will experience has been calculated as 900 lbs. This includes the load due to gravity, the weight of the drum and shaft, all deceleration forces in an emergency stop from full speed, and the resulting combination of tensions from the wire rope and drive chain. The bearings at either end of the 16″ long drum shaft are at the center of 24″ angle iron frame members. Will 1-1/2 × 1-1/2 × 1/4 angle iron be an appropriate choice for the drum supports? (See Figure 23.5.) The requirement for adequate bracing is met in this case since the drum shaft will laterally brace the two angle iron beams.

SOLUTION: First, determine the load on each angle iron beam:

$$Load\,per\,side = \frac{Total\,Load}{2} = \frac{900\,lb}{2} = 450\,lb$$

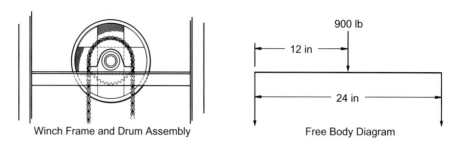

Figure 23.5   Winch Side View and Free Body Diagram

Next, look up the design variables for the angle iron:

$F_b = 23.76\ ksi$ $\qquad\qquad$ $S = 0.134\ in^3$ $\qquad\qquad$ $V_{allowable} = 3{,}740\ lb$

Next, determine M_{Max} for the load and span and then determine the allowable M_{Max}. To be conservative, a simply supported beam case formula will be used, though the actual connection details are closer to a rigid support situation.

$$M_{Max} = \frac{Pl}{4} = \frac{450\ lb\ (24\ in)}{4} = 2700\ in\text{-}lb$$

$$M_{Max(allowable)} = F_b(S) = 23760\ psi\ (0.134 in^3) = 3184\ in\text{-}lb$$

$$2700\ in\text{-}lb < 3184\ in\text{-}lb$$

Since the actual M_{max} is less than the allowable, the 1-1/2 × 1-1/2 × 1/4 angle iron passes for bending.

Next, check for shear:

$$V_{max} = \frac{P}{2} = \frac{450lb}{2} = 225lb$$

$$225\ lb < 3750\ lb$$

Since the allowable shear far exceeds the actual shear the angle iron passes. This result is typical for steel members, but since framing members can see high loads over short spans, it is important to check shear even though it is so rarely the ruling condition. Since deflection is not a failure mode and the span is so short, checking for deflection is unnecessary in this case. If the spans were longer and chain or cable tension issues were of concern, then it would be advisable to check the deflection.

The 1-1/2 × 1-1/2 × 1/4 angle is an appropriate choice.

With a few relatively simple calculations like this, the designer can have greater confidence that the frame will properly support the loads imposed on it and can avoid either over or under designing the frame.

While analyzing the loads on the framing, it is important to also consider the structure to which the machine framing will mount. Mounting an incredibly sturdy frame to a lightly framed deck or using only four lag bolts to secure a winch pulling 1000 lbs can lead to just as many problems as an underdesigned machine. The framing design process should include the surrounding area whenever possible, or a thorough site survey to determine what structure there is available to connect to. Alternately, it can be useful to fully contain all the forces within the framing of the whole effect, avoiding any reliance on building connections for anything but weight and minor hold-in-place forces. Figure 23.6 shows two versions of a winch and a muling assembly, one relying on the surrounding deck, the other incorporating everything into one frame.

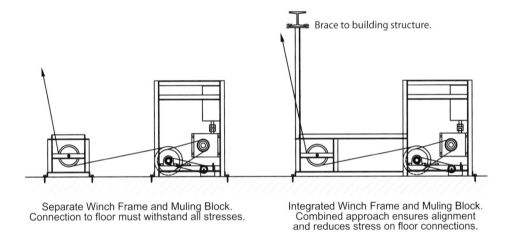

Brace to building structure.

Separate Winch Frame and Muling Block.
Connection to floor must withstand all stresses.

Integrated Winch Frame and Muling Block.
Combined approach ensures alignment
and reduces stress on floor connections.

Figure 23.6   Two Winch and Muling Sheaves Designs

Part III: A Mechanical Design Process

The calculations and components covered up to this point in the book are what the average person might consider representing the majority of mechanical design work. This may be because it was not all that long ago that engineering schools taught only this sort of information. Today however, it is clear that engineering involves much more than just calculations, part selection, and drafting. There are, for example, significant steps that occur prior to all of this involved in identifying and clarifying the problem that needs to be solved, as well as then generating concepts or ideas for a device that may solve that problem. No calculations can be done nor any components selected until first you know what needs to be done and then how that might be accomplished.

To aid in the development new products, engineers in general industry use a design process or procedure to guide their work along as efficiently as possible. A mechanical design process for our production-specific stage machinery can be somewhat simplified over that used in general industry (the issues of brand recognition, competition, and advertising are non-existent for such machinery for example), and this fortunately makes it easier to understand and apply. Four distinct steps are part of the process presented here: specification, concept design, detail design, and manufacture, and each is the topic of its own chapter. An additional introductory chapter will serve as an overview of that process.

The chapters in Part III are quite different from the rest of this book. What is covered here is not mathematical, it is open-ended (asking more questions than are answered), and it brings into play intangibles such as creativity and willpower. An inherent weakness of this section of the book is that you will not automatically become a good mechanical designer just from reading these chapters any more than you can become an expert skier from reading a book on skiing technique. You have to practice design and experience the reality of the process to see how well you can navigate through it. Paper projects, certainly the most common type of class work, can offer good experience to a point, but it is only when you follow the process through the shop, into load-in, tech, and performance that you will see the full impact of your design. The ideas presented in these chapters are often most clear just after you complete some project, while what worked well and what did not is fresh in your mind. Browse these chapters often, the value of this information grows with your experience.

All that said, please understand that what is written here is in no way the only process. Over the last 50 years, work on engineering design has progressed greatly, and a number of different design processes have been proposed. One of these, an elegantly simple process defined in Stuart Pugh's book *Total Design*, forms the framework for much of what is presented here, but it has been adapted and augmented to conform better to typical technical theatre practice. But, of course, we do that to nearly everything we use in theatre.

24

Mechanical Design in Theatre

> The writer, painter, or film maker is not constrained by the realities of the physical world, as the engineer is. Thus, engineering design is the most difficult of all the creative arts.
>
> Thomas Hanson, *Engineering Creativity*, 1987

Overview

Mechanical design is the act of developing a machine that will best meet some identified need: a more fuel efficient truck engine, a silent electric shaver, or, for us perhaps, a thin compact winch capable of fitting within a 6″ high platform. This design effort entails work in dozens of areas that range from the easily quantifiable ones of cost, weight, and size to the subjective issues of aesthetics or impressing an important client. A mechanical design process attempts to provide a structure within which this design effort is gently guided to a successful conclusion.

General industry has been forced by the competitive marketplace to adopt a rapid pace of development for their products, and in this environment, every effort is made to optimize the efficiency of product design and manufacturing so that a company can maintain a profitable place in that market. One aspect of the search to optimize was directed at research towards understanding exactly how engineers design new products. What triggers invention? How can creativity be fostered? What allows engineering design to proceed most efficiently? It was quickly realized that there was no one easy answer here, but that at least there was an order of events to follow—a design process—and that there were techniques to aid the creative and evaluative aspects of this process.

The concept of a product, at least in the mass market sense of cell phones or toasters, is far from what we do in technical theatre, but improving design and production speed, reducing costs, and making an overall better piece of scenery or winch to move it are all worthwhile goals. What will be discussed here is a process to follow during mechanical design, basically a suggested plan of attack for solving machine design problems.

Technical theatre has always involved problem solving, and everyone has developed their own techniques for it, but as the problems posed by the set designers and their solutions grow in complexity, a more structured process can help insure focus remains where it should be as the technical design progresses, and that critical issues are not inadvertently overlooked. This is not a rigid checklist type of process because the creative aspects of design are not yet well enough understood to allow design to be codified into one definitive step-by-step procedure. This process is only meant to be a loose framework for your own knowledge and creativity, one where simply having a knowledge of the steps and goals can be a helpful guide. Since, as far as I am aware, there has been nothing written on this topic for technical theatre, this is merely a starting point, or a first entry into uncharted territory.

Five Key Points

There are five key points about design that must be emphasized here at the beginning. The phrases highlighted below should always be kept in mind, while you read these chapters, and more importantly, while you are designing.

Design Is a Dynamic Process

Always expect that some portions of the design process will occur at a rapid pace. Concept generation and development often occur with mere seconds spent on an idea before it is changed, rejected, or replaced by something better. One of the great benefits of working out ideas as pencil sketches, for instance, is their speed, much faster than anything that can be done in CAD. They enable a rapid flow of ideas at a time in the process when that is especially critical.

Design is also dynamic in the topics covered during work on even seemingly simple things. Suppose a bolted connection between two pieces of angle iron is being considered. Is a bolt here better than a welded joint? What size bolt? What type nut? Is there enough wrench clearance to allow the bolt to be installed? Will the bolt snag a flowing costume passing by? Will it corrode over the life span of the machine due to the environment it experiences onstage, during transport, or in storage? Is its color important? How much does it cost? Can you get enough of them in the time available? Does it need to be installed with a torque wrench? Are the carpenters trained to use a torque wrench? What will happen to the machine if this one bolt fails? What might cause it to fail? The questions could go on and on, and this is just for one bolt. Typically most of these sorts of questions have easy answers, but they are questions that still should be asked, for each bolt, and for each and every other part of a machine. A wide range of topics from safety, to aesthetics, to training, to budget, and to a dozen other areas will arise over and over in a rapid progression during design.

Design Is an Iterative Process

Design does not flow in a single path that can be followed rigidly step-by-step from beginning to end. No checklist or program exists to guide you flawlessly through a design problem. Instead much of design involves the repetition of three basic tasks:

- 1st Conceptualize – Develop a possible concept or idea for a machine, or a sub-component of that machine, that might solve a given problem. Sketch it out in enough detail that the idea is clear.

- 2nd Analyze – Run some formulas, do some drafting, or perhaps build a mock-up model to determine the idea's size, cost, weight, or any other quantifiable measure that is of interest at this moment.

- 3rd Evaluate – Will this design satisfy the need? Will it function as needed? Is it too expensive, too hard to build, too big, or too delicate? Is it better than other ideas you have had, or worse?

After this, and with the knowledge gained, repeat the process, refining the design or starting anew.

Conceptualize- Analyze- Evaluate . . . repeat

Conceptualize- Analyze- Evaluate . . . repeat

Conceptualize- Analyze- Evaluate . . . repeat

Design Must Be a Flexible Process

In mathematics, most problems have only one correct answer, but in design, problems often have many acceptable solutions. Given this, never hold unwavering allegiance to any one idea, just let it go if it is not working as a solution for the problem at hand. If it was your idea, you may have to work hard against your own ego, but let it go. If it is your only idea, then you are in trouble. Reconsider the problem and start over. Pushing a bad idea through into a realized machine will not make that idea any better.

Question everything. If you always do something the same way, stop and ask yourself why. Asking the question may not ultimately change what you do, but at least the question opened up the possibility of discovering something new.

Assume nothing. The effect as defined by the set designer is not sacred and infallible, there may be a completely different way that better accomplishes the same basic goal. Sketch out your alternative ideas and ask. I have seen treadmills turn into turntables, lifts into wagons, and a wagon into an actor carrying on a chair.

Design Is Divergent. Design Is Convergent[1]

Starting with the singular depiction of an effect on the set designer's drawings, a mechanical designer must envision many possible solutions to the problem posed by that effect. This is a time of divergence—one effect leading to many ideas on how it might be accomplished. Creativity techniques can assist in the generation of numerous solutions from one problem. The more ideas there are, the more likely

---

1. Adapted from Whitfield, P.R., *Creativity in Industry*, 1975, as shown in Heywood, *Engineering Education*, 2005, 126.

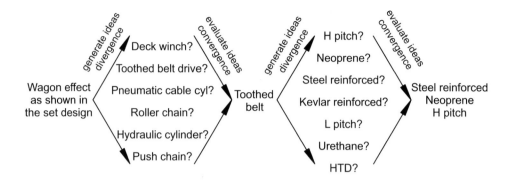

Figure 24.1   Two cycles of divergence and convergence out of the dozens typical in any given project.

that at least one of them is a good solution to the problem. To find the best, these ideas must then be reduced to the one worth pursuing by an evaluation of the relative strengths and weaknesses of each idea. This is convergence—many ideas being distilled down to what seems the best solution for the problem at hand (Figure 24.1). Often this sequence of growth and reduction occurs over and over during design, first perhaps with broadly stated concepts, then within the chosen concept on variations, and finally on the details until a final design is complete. Even just being aware of whether you are in a period of divergence or convergence can set your mind to the proper task for the moment.

Mechanical Design Must Be Rigorous

Stage machinery is used to move wagons, spin turntables, run lifts, and fly scenery, all of which may weigh hundreds if not thousands of pounds and travel at relatively high speeds. We ask the actors to work in amongst all of this movement, often in a complete blackout. Needless to say, but yet it must be said, this activity requires every possible effort to ensure safety. During design, every component must be verified as appropriate to the use. Depending on the application, an analysis of the failure modes of each component and the resulting effect on the system might be needed. In general industry, the majority of a design engineer's work on the problem might end with the passing of drawings on out to manufacturing, but in the smaller world of theatre, a machine designer must follow the progress of a machine through its construction, its installation during load-in, and its use during tech. No one else will know exactly what it was designed to do, and more importantly what it should not be asked to do. All this takes time, drive, and an unflagging attention to detail. You should not take on any mechanization project if you are not prepared to accept the full responsibility of all the work that it entails.

Automation control systems, which should be the topic of a whole other book, are at the very least equally critical to the safe operation of a stage effect as the machines they control, and they must too be designed with a rigorous analysis of all safety and failure modes.

Machine safety is your responsibility. You are ethically and legally liable for what you design, and so every effort should be made to insure that the machine operates safely, and that no credible failure will result in additional hazards.

Mechanical Design in Industry and Theatre

The engineering design process used to develop new products ranging from toothpicks to commercial aircraft has been the focus of intense research since the 1950s. This is because there is a huge economic incentive to making the product development process as efficient at creating innovative new products as possible—if you are the first to market with the latest must-have widget, you will become rich. There is much written on this topic, but unfortunately little of it relates directly to technical theatre due to some significant differences between how industry and theatre operate. Highlighting these differences though will prove useful to illustrate exactly where we are relative to industry, where there might be room for improvement in the production process, and in the expectations we traditionally place on a theatre technician.

Under each of the four topic headings below, a rough comparison will be given between general industry and theatre.[2] From the onset here I admit that this is an apples versus oranges comparison, there is truly very little in common with a company manufacturing to sell in quantities of 100,000 units per year and a theatre shop. Plus even within theatre there is a great diversity of goals between shops. At one end of the spectrum is the educational theatre scene shop whose mission is to provide scenery for the school's productions while giving students some modest experience in set construction. At the opposite end are the commercial scenic shops that must clear a profit on the sale of scenery and automation to stay in business. Despite all these major caveats, the comparison will still be instructive.

Time Line of Projects

Design takes time. Every iteration of concept, analysis, and evaluation takes some amount of time to perform, and the rigor of mechanical design demands that every step is followed through without cutting corners. Given this, in industry, 1 year is considered a minimum product development time, and many projects are given 3 to 5 years.[3]

In theatre, even the minimum would be considered an unimaginable luxury. Usually several weeks are all that can pass between the presentation of a complete set design, and construction draftings for that set, consisting of scenery and machinery, going into the shop. Exceptional rush jobs may require that a complete machine be designed and built in one week. A few rare Broadway shows with

2. The industry information is from Ulrich and Eppinger, *Product Design and Development*.

3. Ibid, 5.

unique complex effects will be given 6 to 8 months between the awarding of a contract to build the show and the first preview, but even this is a fraction of industry's 1 year minimum development time.

This pace of theatre production often forces the use of proven conventional machines over something new that might be better suited to the application, or if a new machine must be developed, the design process is greatly compressed relative to industry, and the risks inherent in the design increase rapidly. This puts considerable pressure on all parts of the design process, but most especially on the evaluation of design concepts, because there is little time to correct things should a new idea not work out. The more unusual the scenic effect's movement, the less predictable the time needed to find a conceptual solution for that move, and so these effects should be started first.

Design Teams

Industrial design projects usually involve teams of a company's engineers that are augmented with specialists hired on as needed. So, for example, a relatively simple product, the Stanley Tools Jobmaster screwdriver, which consists of three parts: metal blade, plastic handle, and rubber outer grip, was developed by an in-house team of 3, with the input of 3 others from outside the company.[4]

These teams are assembled with individuals having differing areas of expertise. If, for instance, a hydraulically operated machine was being developed, a design team might involve a team of a mechanical engineer to design the machine components, a manufacturing engineer to optimize the device so it can be fabricated and assembled as efficiently as possible, a specialist in hydraulics might be hired to advise and double check all work on the hydraulic system components, and an electrical engineer would design its control system (with the possible assistance of a software engineer if the control involved any sort of PLC or computer). Overseeing this team might be one of the team members, or an engineering manager, a relatively new but growing area of employment.

In theatre, it would not be unusual for a machine of this type to be designed by one person. This is not to say that there is no input from others. An ATD assigned to a project would consult frequently with the TD. Distributors and manufacturers of machine components often offer field support for their equipment. Large commercial shops will sometimes hire on engineering firms to design machine components that are beyond the expertise of in-house staff. This also occurs in the areas of software development or hydraulics. Despite all this, the expectations and responsibility placed on one person are, quite often, extremely high.

Training

The educational backgrounds of the theatre technicians that work as mechanical designers, and the people employed for roughly equivalent work in a general industry setting are, in general, vastly different. Why this is so is partly the result of some distant history. With the emergence of the scientific method and mathematical

---

4. Ibid, 5.

models of reality starting in the late renaissance, a divergence slowly occurred between the craftsmen with practical hands-on construction skills, and those educated in the sciences and mathematics that allowed them to design new devices solely on paper. By the early 20th century a formal education in engineering became an established path to design jobs in industry.

Because the construction of the majority of theatre scenery has changed so little from the cloth covered wooden flats used over the last 400 years, there was until relatively recently no need for workers with more than these craft skills. That began to change roughly 50 years ago with the inclusion of engineering based coursework into a few educational programs, but the rapid pace of technological progress and the slow adoption of science into drama programs means most college technicians are still unprepared for advanced technical design work relative to their engineering counterparts.[5,6] Even a cursory glance at the courses taken by undergraduate engineering majors versus those taken by the typical drama major specializing in technical theatre would point this out.

Technicians with career goals as technical directors in larger regional theatres, or as mechanical designers in commercial theatre will often not find the traditional path of moving up through the shop to be a practical one. All the design work that occurs prior to the arrival of construction drawings in the shop simply cannot be learned from building a machine on the shop floor. Technicians that are Drama majors in college, and are interested in pursuing these technical design jobs should take some mathematics and engineering classes, and then pursue graduate education in programs offering an emphasis on technical management and engineering based topics (structural and mechanical design, pneumatics and hydraulics, networking and show control, and motion control, for example).

Lest this sound too negative, practical experience in the shop and as stage crew during the run of a show is of tremendous value to any future technical design work. It provides an idea of what can be done in a theatre shop, what works well on stage, and perhaps just as important, what cannot be done or does not work. Indicative of this value, some engineering schools have only relatively recently added practical hands-on coursework back into their programs to give their students a grounding in the realities of materials, fabrication, and assembly.

Specialization

There are numerous divisions in the field of engineering: mechanical, civil, chemical, electrical, materials, and aeronautical to name some of the major ones, and within each of these there are other fields of study that serve as the focus for an individual's entire career. These fields are geared towards the needs of industry for engineers qualified to design machine subsystems at the highest level of expertise:

- a mechanical engineer designing the brakes for a car,

5. Edward C. Cole, Backstage Isn't Backstage Anymore, AIA Journal, Nov. 1960, 108. Mr Cole describes the need for theatre technicians trained in math, physics, statics, and electronics.

6. John Huntington, Rethinking Entertainment Technology Education, TD&T, Vol. 38 No. 4 (Fall, 2002).

- a software engineer writing the program that operates an ATM machine, or
- an electrical engineer designing the wiring for an elevator,

all critical components within their machines. Long established canons of professional ethics are sufficient to insure that people would never cross discipline boundaries, as both they and their employers would see them as not qualified for work outside their fields.

Many theatre technicians love the varied aspects of their work—it is for them a primary reason to choose theatre as a career. A mechanical designer's work day can easily encompass mechanical, structural, fluid power, electrical, and software issues. With this variety though comes the risk of being underqualified in an area critical for safety. Since there are no established procedures in the world of technical theatre to prove competence, only an individual's personal judgment and sense of ethical behavior guides what they will and will not do.

Summary

Though this discussion has only considered the differences between industry and theatre practice in four areas, the contrasts are great. If stage automation continues to include as many new technologies in the next 20 years as it has in the last 20, something will have to change. It does appear we are on the cusp of that change with companies that make only stage machinery and controls being able to sell to a big enough market to allow them to survive for more than a few years, but only time will tell.

Influences on an Individual's Design Abilities

Many things affect how efficiently a given individual will be able to perform on a mechanical design project, but they can all be broadly categorized into five main areas: knowledge, information, imagination, experience, and environment. All these areas need to be optimized for the most efficient design work to occur. If any one of these is below par, it will hold back the entire design capability in proportion to the severity of whatever is lacking. Just for illustration, examples of this can be imagined by taking any one of these areas to an extreme. Could anyone be effective at the design of stage machinery if they had no knowledge of math or drafting, no information on available gear reducers, no ability to imagine anything new, no experience in theatre at all, or had to work in the midst of an office party? Absurd extremes of course, but the point is that a mechanical designer needs to constantly work towards a balance in all these areas to be most efficient.

Knowledge

> Knowledge makes everything simpler.
> John Maeda, *The Laws of Simplicity*, 2006

To know something is to understand it, to be able to use it correctly, or to instantly see its application when a problem is posed. The wastefulness of 'reinventing the wheel' is an issue of knowledge. If you know about the wheel, or grommet drives, or shear stress on a key, you can apply that knowledge directly to a problem's solu-

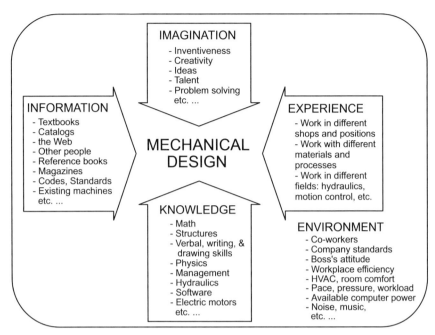

Figure 24.2   Influences on an individual's mechanical design ability

tion without having to spend the enormous amount of effort needed to come up with your own solution.

Formal training in a subject, usually by taking classes, is one traditional way to gain knowledge. But so too is reading a text book, an engineering magazine (*Machine Design*, *Power in Motion*, or *Hydraulics and Pneumatics* for example. All appear online for free.), or studying a manufacturer's catalog. Education should be pursued throughout your career, since learning never ends.

Information

No machine can be designed without the vast amount of information about materials properties, manufactured component ratings, dimensions, descriptions of part numbers, names of manufacturers, and more. It was only a few years back that catalogs, the kind actually printed on paper, were carefully collected and guarded, for without these it was nearly impossible to design anything technical. Today the Internet puts information from around the world at your disposal in an instant. Part specifications, 2D and 3D CAD drawings of components, product application guides, and illustrations of machines, are available to all, 24 hours a day.

People are, of course, a great source of information. Manufacturer's reps will help you find of choose the best of their products for a particular application. TDs that have experience in mechanized effects are usually glad to share their knowledge of what they have found to work well, or not. A licensed engineer can be hired to check, advise on, or perform the design of an effect.

Mechanical designers need a library of information sources at their fingertips, and this may take the form of a list of favorite web site links on their browser, a shelf of books and catalogs, a list of phone numbers, or probably a combination of all three.

Imagination

This is the least tangible of the five areas being discussed here, and the hardest to define. Imagination, creativity, and inventiveness all relate to the ability to generate something new, or something not seen before—at least to the individual involved. This is another "reinventing the wheel" issue. The result of imagination does not have to be earth shattering or profound to be useful. Even small improvements are still improvements.

Imagination can be improved with practice, and many techniques have been developed to help it along. That is the good news. Unfortunately there is never a guarantee of success when searching for the unknown. Given this, imagination is the weakest link in these five areas, and while it is wonderful when it provides a useful result, knowledge and experience are often more reliable providers.

Experience

Since the final product of a mechanical design effort is a real object destined for use in a real production, it is essential that the designer have experience with all that it takes to construct, load-in, use, and strike a machine in those circumstances. The imperfections, complexities, and unpredictably of reality is a great teacher of what works, and what does not. Directors and designers change their minds, shop tolerances are typically ±1/16″ at best, parts deliveries will be late, the trap room floor is not perfectly flat, and opening night will not be postponed. Designing with these sorts of real issues in mind is essential, and they are best picked up by working in a variety of different shops.

Environment

The value of a proper environment for design cannot be overemphasized. Most people work best when their surroundings are relatively quiet, clean, well lit, with a comfortable temperature, and uninterrupted by other activity going on around them, in short a standard office environment. Is that essential tool of modern mechanical design, a computer, loaded with the software needed and connected to the Internet?

Beyond this, and no less important, are interpersonal issues between you and your co-workers, and you and your boss. You will have a limited ability to affect change here if there are problems, but you can work to make it better, or decide to leave and work elsewhere.

A Brief Overview of the Mechanical Design Process

The next four chapters will each cover one component of the four that makes up the mechanical design process being described here. This overview will quickly introduce these components and give an overview of the entire process.

The mechanical design process fits within a much larger sequence of events that occurs between the decision by an artistic director or producer to mount a given production, and its opening night. A large and diverse team of people, from the director, the actors, all the designers, house management, accounting, technical personnel, and many others will all work towards the goal of a successful run.

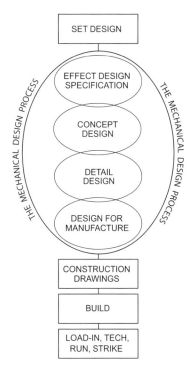

The set designer, collaborating primarily with the director, will develop the basic visual components of the set, and within that, every desired scenic effect—what scenery, actors, and major props move where and when. This information forms the heart of the problem that the mechanical design process will aim to solve. The diagram to the right shows the set design at the top, or the beginning, of the mechanical design process, as it is with this that the process starts. Occasionally a set design is not required, a shop may be designing a stock or rental machine to have on hand for many different uses, but even here some generic scenic move must be envisioned else there are no bounds to the design problem.

A budgeting period or bid process is the usual starting point for mechanical design involvement with the show's effects. Estimates of material and labor costs, and the time needed to realize the effect are made. This involves preliminary passes through the steps of the design process, each to be described in detail below and in the following chapters, but in short each effect is studied for what exactly it must do, ideas on how that might be accomplished are given, and the time needed and costs involved are estimated. Budgeting identifies effects that are technologically difficult (or in rare instances impossible), too expensive or time consuming to attempt, or even if the effects are straightforward, there may simply be too many of them to be feasible. The set design may change in response to the budgeting effort, and new effects may need to be estimated.

The budgeting or bidding process varies considerably from organization to organization. In commercial theatre shops, a mechanical designer might not even know of a show until after the shop has won the contract off bids developed by someone else. The exact technical design choices made by the person preparing the bid might not be those of the mechanical designer, but the estimated cost of equipment is usually generous enough to accommodate the differences between what was bid and what was eventually built. In regional theatre the TD and ATDs (who will technically design the whole show, including any machinery) are intimately involved from first budgets to the strike of the show so that such discrepancies should not occur.

In the descriptions of the mechanical design process that follow, the budgeting effort that would have to occur before beginning design work is implied but never specifically mentioned.

Effect Design Specification

No work on the design of a machine can begin unless a clear complete statement of what that machine needs to do is known. This statement is called the effect design specification, and it should ideally contain every possible detail about the problem that needs to be solved. Certainly the set design defines the basic move criteria— what moves and how far—but it alone is rarely specific enough to design from without the addition of other requirements and assumptions. The lighting, sound, and costume designers may be considering things in their designs that will impact the scenic move—set mounted lighting instruments or speakers, or long flowing costumes for instance—and so their work should be consulted too. Beyond this, there are numerous other details designers are not required to include on their drawings. The effect's speed, the live load on the effect, the load-in time available, the maximum size it can be and still fit on a truck or through a door, and many others. Stuart Pugh identifies 32 "elements" in his description of a complete specification.[7] They run from the inherently unquantifiable, such as aesthetics or politics, to those more easily defined: weight, size, and materials. The ideal effect design specification would detail all 32 of these for a particular effect.

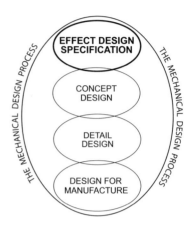

Specifications in theatre vary widely in their completeness. Written specs are common in commercial theatre, albeit rarely absolutely thorough ones. They form part of the contract documents between a producing organization and a scene shop hired on to design and build the effects. In regional and educational theatre, budget paperwork may contain brief spec statements, but often many of the details are kept in the mind of the technician, or are assumed as part of a shop's standard operating procedure.

Concept Design

A concept in the context of the mechanical design process is simply an idea of how a problem could be solved. This definition is intentionally vague because concepts can be expressed in words, such as "This lift could be run with hydraulics," in rough sketches drawn on scrap paper, or in the precise specificity of a CAD drawing of a complete machine.

---

7. Pugh, *Total Design*, 44.

Concept design is the twofold act of generating concepts that have the potential to solve the problem stated in the specification, and then evaluating them to identify the one concept to pursue further. This is the divergent and convergent aspect design mentioned earlier.

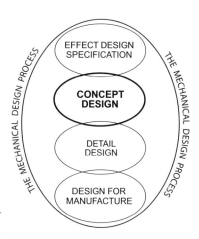

What an effect may need in terms of a concept varies from simply using an existing machine in a standard way to inventing something completely new. Given the limited time for design in a typical production calendar, the former occurs frequently and the latter is generally done only when necessary. There are, of course, many gradations between these two extremes. A new design might be just a scaled up version of an already proven machine, or it involves the re-arrangement and re-selection of machine components to fit into a different size or shaped frame. A variety of concept generation techniques can be used to create a number of options on how a design might proceed.

These concepts will need to be evaluated as to their suitability for solving the problem, and since in theatre there is rarely the time to thoroughly develop several promising concepts, any evaluation technique must be able to help identify the best idea to continue to pursue.

Detail Design

When most people think of an engineering textbook, they generally think of a tome filled with equations, charts, tables, and cryptic schematics. This information is the language of engineering and the essence of detail design.

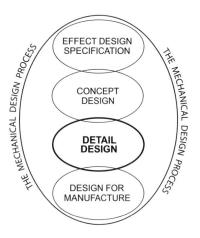

The relationship between concept and detail design is intimate. Detail design cannot be done without a concept to analyze, and a concept without detail cannot be built. Both are needed for the design process to succeed. Likewise, even when both are present, great detail design will not save a flawed concept, and the perfect concept can be brought down by bad details. Think of a relay race, both runners must show up and both must perform well for a winning outcome.

Detail design requires painstaking attention to avoid errors. Mathematics of course has to be done correctly else the answer is garbage. Mounting holes in steel are not forgiving of errors even if in the hundreths of an inch. And part numbers, a huge aspect of detail design for theatre machinery, must be correct or time will be wasted ordering and reordering.

Despite its reputation, detail design is the easy part of the design process. There is the seemingly endless minutiae of part numbers, and numerous calculations to be performed, but the parts need patience more than brainpower, and every mathematical problem is like a classic textbook problem with a list of givens and one correct answer. A computer cannot be programmed to design the machine, but it can do the math.

Design for Manufacture

Manufacturing is a foreign word in the context of technical theatre most likely because the act of constructing a one-off built-by-hand device is very distant from the production line work done in many factories. Semantics aside though, there are some tools and fabrication processes in common between scene shops and manufacturing in other industries, and so there is the opportunity to study what they have found to be efficient or beneficial to their production process and apply to ours.

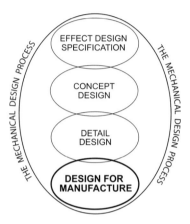

Design for manufacture is often broken down into two subcategories, design for fabrication and design for assembly. Fabrication involves machining of material by sawing, drilling, punching, or milling, for example. Assembly deals with the concerns of putting purchased and fabricated parts together into a finished machine, such as insuring that designs have good wrench access for mounting bolts, that drums and gearmotors can be installed easily into their support frames, and that the proper orientation of machined plates is obvious. Being aware of these issues during design helps machine construction become faster, with fewer errors, and results in an easily maintained device.

This is one area theatre technicians generally relate to very well, since most have shop experience in metal work fabrication and assembly. This is an invaluable asset for a theatre mechanical designer, helping them envision the practicality of making what they are designing.

Summary

Though described and illustrated as four separate steps, the process is never a rigid sequence of specify, conceptualize, detail, and design for build. There is a continual jumping around as needed to develop and refine the design, and it is only if you were to graph in which step you spent the majority of your time on any given day would you see the sequence. To reiterate, the design process is a loose framework, or a guide to help direct your design efforts.

The end result of all this design work is a complete CAD drafting of the machine, a parts list exactly detailing everything needed to construct this machine, and a machine specification now showing not a list of goals, but instead what the machine is rated to do. With these the design is complete.

25

Developing a Design Specification

Overview

It is impossible to design a machine for a task without knowing what that task is. This simple statement is so central to the whole design effort that it bears repeating. It is impossible to design a machine for a task without knowing what that task is. This means that it is essential to start off every mechanical design project with a clear definition of the goal of that project. What, exactly, is the effect that needs to happen? Walls shifting? Doors opening? A lift? A fly effect? The designer's drawings will be the first source of this information of course, but there will be numerous questions those drawings will never answer. What bounds or limitations beyond what is shown in the set design are placed on possible solutions to the problem an effect poses? These bounds can be those set by the obvious issues of budget, shop labor skills, shop space, or available time, for instance. They may also be defined by less often considered and even obscure issues such as local codes requiring biodegradable hydraulic oil, ambient temperature effects on nylon lock nut holding ability, or altitude based derating of air compressors. It is the goal of an effect design specification to clearly state every relevant requirement and limitation that is placed upon an effect so that the mechanical design process can proceed with full knowledge of exactly what needs to be done.

This is a lofty goal, and not one easily achieved. In reality, there is a wide variation in the level of detail found in theatre specifications. The size of the project, its cost, the hazards involved, the number of people in the design team, and other factors will drive what might be in a spec, and whether it appears only as a list of penciled-in notes on the edge of a set design plate, or as dozens of pages of text that form part of a legally binding contract between two entities.

In industrial situations, a design specification will either be supplied by a client who has hired a company to design a device, or it will be developed by individuals within the company for a product they wish to design and sell. Often this is a lengthy, formal document that has taken teams of people weeks or even months to create. Those in charge of new product development at a company, say Boeing, Apple, or Ford, need to have in hand a clearly presented, rigorously researched document detailing all the goals of some future product before fully committing the sometimes vast human and financial resources necessary to develop it. Considering the risks a company undertakes with any new product, this is merely prudent.

In commercial theatre, technical specifications, or "tech specs," are handed out with a set of designer draftings to scene shops considering bidding for the contract to build some or all of a new show. This document comes from the show's technical supervisor, an individual hired on by the show's producer to act as their agent and in their interests for all the technical aspects of the production. Often about half of a typical tech spec will be boilerplate, or text that is reused unchanged for every show, and that text covers general requirements that would apply to any show. For instance, there are often a number of statements such as:

- All materials used to fabricate this production must be new and of reputable manufacture.[1]
- All work will be to the highest professional standards.
- All work will comply with the applicable laws and codes for the City of New York.

These specifications can be quite vague, for what exactly is "reputable," or "highest professional standards"? To some extent these statements are there for lawyers to argue over should any litigation occur between the producers and the shop. This is a very rare occurrence, but the producing organization needs to protect their investment with contract language that could be used if needed.

Past this stock text is production specific information detailing the requirements of each major unit in the production, such as materials that must be used for construction, spare or replacement parts that must be supplied, or the maximum allowable weight a piece can be. If a show is new, the loads on and speeds of an automated piece will usually be unknown, so default rule-of-thumb values might appear in the specs, or even no values at all. Established shows that are being remounted as a tour will often use speed and load numbers from the original show, as these are much more representative of what is needed than any rule of thumb estimates could ever be.

A scene shop uses both the designer's drawings of the set and the technical specifications to develop cost estimates for each element, submits these as bids to the production's technical supervisor, and then, if the shop wins a contract based on their bid, the same combination of drawings and tech specs is used by a mechanical designer as the starting point for the mechanical design process.

The situation is much different in most regional and educational theatres. The contractual agreement between a producer and a scene shop that drives the creation of technical specifications in the commercial theatre world is not needed for most regional and educational productions because the producing entity and the shop are both parts of one single organization. So, for this reason at least, there is no need for a written technical specification. Written specs are rare in these theatres for other reasons as well. A technical director in one of these organizations oversees the design, construction, and use of all the scenery and machinery placed on stage, for a whole season, if not for years worth of shows. They and their staff carry in their heads the traditions and details of how things are done, and so there is

---

1. Aurora Productions, Technical Specifications, 7/25/94.

often little perceived need to write down what is already an established standard operating procedure. Finally, in many of these organizations, it would be unlikely that any of the people qualified to write a spec would have enough free time to do so. These reasons do not mean that there is no benefit to developing a spec, but just that there is generally no tradition of doing so.

When a Written Specification Is Useful

None of this is meant to imply any sort of formal spec is always needed. Quite often effects repeat in show after show—turntables, lifts, and wagons in deck tracks for instance—and they can often be implemented in more or less the same way each time they are needed. Provided that there are no significant changes from use to use, then the repetition of a design that has worked well in the past is a far more efficient use of time than to always start a design process from the beginning.

There are however a number of situations where a written spec becomes useful. These vary in their goals, but define the bounds or extents of a problem.

- Large projects involving multiple mechanical designers, and possibly multiple shops would benefit from a clear statement of the requirements and performance of the effect. This situation is common in commercial theatre, but might also appear during a regional theatre co-production.

- A person newly hired or assigned into a mechanical design position will benefit greatly from a written in-house design specification, or design manual, that details common techniques, systems, and procedures used by their organization. For example, this is one statement from a Yale Rep spec given to a graduate student TD or ATD that is about to embark on the design of a lift:

  > Lifts should be as much as possible self-contained modular units, capable of being loaded-in with little more than setting them on the trap room floor, and with all their lifting forces resolved through the lift's framing (and not through building structure). Under no circumstances should welding to building steel be considered as part of a load-in plan, and welding anything in the theatre should be avoided by planning bolted connections.
  >
  > This requirement reduces both the number of connections needed to the building structure, shortening the time needed for lift load-in, and it keeps the machine's forces running through structure specifically designed for the purpose. This technique also enables a trial setup of the lift to occur, which allows problems to be resolved in the shop, and before load-in.

  None of the information in a spec written for this reason would likely be new information to anyone who has worked at the theatre for awhile, but the goal here is to document and communicate shop standards for training and review.

- Effects that are very different than anything the individuals involved have ever done before. Set designers are remarkably inventive, and come up with new effects all the time. The act of writing a spec will help clarify and define the problem, always the essential first set in the design process.

- Mechanical design work sub-contracted out to others unfamiliar with the conventions of technical theatre. Engineering firms may, for instance, be contracted to design a machine. If they have not worked for a theatre before, they may be unfamiliar with things we take for granted. For instance, the capabilities and capacities of a theatre's shop to handle and fabricate steel, so that their designs do not exceed what can be built.

- Work that involves effects with significant safety issues—over audience mechanized effects, flying actors, unusually high speed moves, etc. Putting these specifications down on paper is a way to detail each measure needed to insure the effect is safe. (The safest thing to do here is, of course, not do the effect, and this must always be an option up for discussion.)

- Projects that present a significant business risk. If the failure of a project could bankrupt a company, and yet even with this knowledge that project still appears worth seeking, then every effort must be taken to ensure a successful end result.

No work on one of the major steps in the mechanical design process—specification, concept design, detail design, and manufacture—is ever done in total isolation from the others. A design specification should, for example, not waste time requiring things which cannot be built in the time available, or which involve construction techniques you know cannot be done. The specification should be a realistic practical statement of performance and characteristics, not a representation of the ideal or the ultimate. The specification is also intentionally vague about how the machine works—that is the job of concept design.

Elements of a Complete Specification

Stuart Pugh, in his book *Total Design*, gives a list of 32 "elements" that can have an impact on a product's design. The illustration he used to introduce these terms reminded others of many plates spinning on poles (a classic act of theatrical entertainers in the vaudeville days), and so "Pugh's plates" refer to these elements, and hints at the skill needed by a mechanical designer to keep them all actively spinning, and not forgotten and left to crash to the floor spoiling the whole act. I have reinterpreted the performer for the visual representation of these elements in Figure 25.1, because you do need to keep all these topics actively under consideration, though you may be handling only one or two at a given instant.

The names of each of these elements is from Pugh, but their description has been reinterpreted and augmented for the theatre context. Each description also includes some sample questions of the type you could ask yourself, with the answers forming part of the specification. In no particular order, the 32 elements are:

Performance - Quantifying how a machine should perform at the task it is being designed to do is fundamental to any specification. Performance, in the context of this list, refers mainly to the terms found in the maximum power formula: top speed, acceleration, the mass to be moved (which may be widely variable from scene to scene), and the presence of lifting in the effect. For example, if a deck winch is being designed for use in pulling wagons on a flat stage deck, then a performance spec might simply be a cable speed and pull force. Beyond these, performance may include how quiet it must be, its power source, travel distance, or maximum deflection acceptable under a given load.

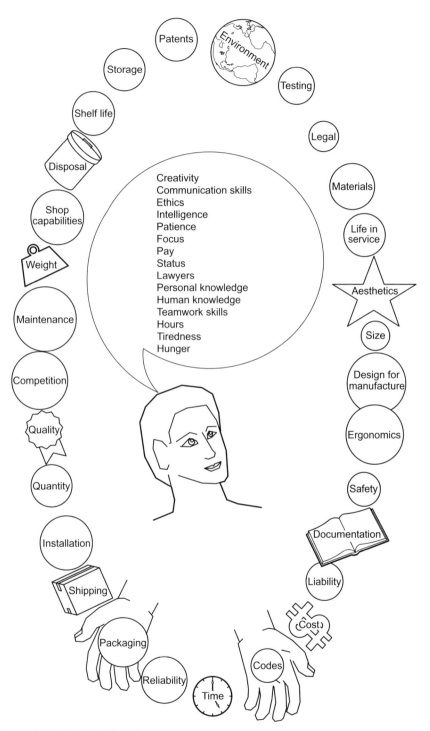

Figure 25.1   A difficult juggling act

- What cushion or contingency above the minimum performance requirements should this device have?
- What performance do you suspect will be asked for during tech that has not been asked for yet?
- Should any additional performance be added for versatility, accuracy, load handling, easy reuse, etc.

Aside: Rules of Thumb for the Top Speed of Scenery

In the quite common absence of any specifically stated speed or time requirement for a given move, the following values can be considered as a starting point, and then adjusted up or down as a specific situation might indicate.

Our perception of speed seems to be related to the size of the piece being moved. A very small piece, say a 1 foot cube, might need to track across stage at 8 ft/sec to look "fast," while a full stage box set on a wagon looks "fast" going at 2 ft/sec. Also upstage/downstage motion looks slower than does cross-stage.

Major commercial theatre productions would often assume values 50% higher than the maximums shown here.

Linear Movement:
- Lifts generally have top speeds of 1 to 2 ft/sec (0.3 to 0.6 m/sec)
- Deck winch top speed typically = 3 ft/sec (1 m/sec)
- Flying scenery generally travels faster = 4 to 6 ft/sec (1.2 to 1.8 m/sec)
- If motor control is just on/off, then set the speed somewhere around 1 ft/sec. This avoids excessive loads during start/stop.

Rotational Movement:
- Max edge speed of a turntable = 3 to 5 ft/sec (1 to 1.6 m/sec)

For reference, a typical walking speed of: 2.5 mph = 3.7 ft/sec
                                             4.0 kph = 1.1 m/sec

---

Effect Cost - In general industry, a product cost given in the design specification would relate to a cost-versus-features analysis of competitor's similar products. No new device is worth making if it cannot be sold competitively out in the open market. This concept is not foreign to commercial scene shops because they must submit bids for work both low enough to win the job over their competitors, and high enough that the shop makes a profit. (The dynamics of the business decisions involved in this process are more complex than implied here, but that topic is unfortunately beyond the scope of this book.) For regional and educational theatre, competition of this type is non-existent and there are usually no machines available for price comparisons. For them, an accurate design spec cost estimate will involve working out some plausible concepts and the corresponding component details to get a good sense of what the effect will cost.

Regardless of the organization developing the design spec, many factors can alter a straightforward estimate of cost, and some of these are brought up in the questions below.

- Is this a long term capital investment, or just for use in one short-run show?
- Is it worth spending more to decrease the effect load-in time?
- Is this a tried and true effect, or something quite new and different? The answer to this question should influence the cushion or contingency applied to the estimated cost.
- Will the shop be very busy during the build of this effect? If so, overtime may be needed to get the work done. This could be true in slower times too if the staff with the skills to do the build are booked, even if the rest of the shop is available.
- Is an outside contractor involved in design or construction? For example, commercial shops will often hire an engineering firm to design a complex safety-critical structure. Some Broadway production contracts require drawings to be stamped as approved by state-licensed engineers. Also, a shop may pay a specialist to advise them on improvements on a system in a hydraulic system. All of these choices involve significant costs for these services.

Time - It is obvious that it takes time to build, and load-in stage effects, and that time can be estimated, but a mechanical designer's time becomes harder to pin down the more unusual the effect. The spec should list critical dates: construction start dates, load-in, first tech, and opening are all important deadlines.

- Machines with components larger than one person can easily lift will require time for repositioning. Good design seeks to minimize frame movement during assembly. Should this be explicitly stated?
- How many people can be assigned to a job? If one person would take 100 hours to build a machine, could 100 people do it in an hour? Highly doubtful, but where are the breakpoints between these extremes, and what are the limiting factors: a small device might be too crowded to work on with more than one or two people. Limited tool availability can present a bottleneck.
- There is an economy to quantity and to repetition. The time it takes to build one of something times 10 is not the time it will take to build 10 of those things if they are all built simultaneously. Likewise, the time it takes to build something relatively complex the first time, is greater than the time it will take to build it again—provided the same people are involved.

Occasionally it may be worth considering esoteric factors such as:

- People's minds drift elsewhere around the Christmas and New Years holiday period, and in the day or two before a long vacation break. It is not realistic to expect 100% work output during these days.

- It is impossible to predict this beyond a few days, but widespread colds and flu can create major disruptions in a project, with absenteeism and lowered work efficiency.

Customer - The word customer has never been adopted into the world of technical theatre, even though, for instance, commercial theatre scene shops sell their products to customers. The concept of a customer is even more foreign to educational and regional theatre, where the customer could be considered the specific production being worked on, the theatre organization itself, or perhaps even the audience who pay to see a show. An exact definition of the customer is not as necessary as simply being aware of the numerous people beyond those that design and construct stage effects that interact with it. Stage hands will run the machinery, and actors will perform on, over, beside or under the loads it moves. The set designer and director have expectations for the effect that need to be met. And the audience has paid for the experience that stage automation in some part augments.

- Does a special client or event deserve an extra effort in an attempt to win their favor for supplying additional work?
- What statement do you wish your products and services to make to a client?
- Does the customer wield power you should be wary of (perhaps in the form of lengthy detailed contracts backed by many lawyers)?
- Are there penalties written into a contract should an effect not work when needed (this is not unusual for effects used during on-location movie shoots).

Processes - The machinery components we fabricate in our scene shops are primarily made out of steel, with little else beyond aluminum and various plastics being used at times. The processes used for this fabrication have traditionally been limited to methods that are both relatively inexpensive, and ones that can easily accommodate very small production runs of unique parts. Therefore sawing, drilling, welding, milling, punching and the like are common. Industrial processes, such as casting, forging, extrusion, or sintering use specialized tooling more appropriate to runs of thousands of identical parts and so are of little use. In the 1990s, CNC machining (computer numerical control) began to enter commercial scene shops with their purchase of automated routers and plasma cutters, and most recently water jet and laser cutters. The capabilities of these machines are creating a minor revolution in stage machinery design, fabrication, and assembly that is still evolving rapidly. Some of the issues within the context of process here can be expressed as questions such as:

- What processes are involved in the construction of this device? Does construction use just standard shop tools, or something new that will require a capital investment and shop staff training?
- Is there sufficient reason to send a job out for water jet cutting, or should the part be re-designed and fabricated in-house with conventional tools?

- If aluminum is being welded, should you specify TIG or MIG? Some contracts for touring Broadway shows require TIG welded aluminum deck framing, and since this is not a widespread technique in theatre, welding machines may need to be purchased, and shop staff trained in its use.
- Bolted joints avoid the possibility of heat warping that is common in welded connections. Does the shape of an assembly dictate one technique over another?

Assembly - The mechanical designer must always take into account how the machine will be put together, both initial assembly in the shop, and during load-in on stage. Do you need just one person with only a single wrench and a screwdriver, or several people with a full compliment of tools.

- Specify that access to all nuts, bolt heads, screws, chain links, etc. have a high priority, forcing the designer to think about wrench clearances, hand space, line of sight to hardware, etc.
- How are machines assembled during load-in? A crucial consideration for tours. For example, if deck effect winches can be built into the deck platforms, then loading in the deck simultaneously loads in the winches.
- Reduce different sizes of hardware as much as possible.
- Use the same grade of bolts throughout, eliminating the possibility of using a lower grade bolt where a higher grade is needed.

Size - Space backstage is usually at a premium, so compact machines are good, but if they are too tight, assembly and maintainability usually suffer.

- What are the dimensional limitations of all the load-in doors, hallway corners, or other restricted areas the machine will have to be moved through? This is an especially involved issue for tours with their variety of theatre venues.
- If transport via truck is needed, what are the limiting dimensions?
- If the machine is to be a stock piece, are easily remembered dimensions warranted? A conventional deck winch easily fits within a frame 20″ by 30″ by 40″.
- Should a device break apart into smaller pieces for easier handling?

Shipping - A few theatres are blessed with the shop adjacent to their stage, and for them shipping issues are moot. At the opposite extreme are the commercial scene shops, where everything produced rides a truck across town, across the country, or occasionally across an ocean. Designing a machine for easy handling and transport concerns its size, weight, robustness, and shape all in relation to the truck, trailer, sea container, plane that will carry it. Shipping, the project calender, and budget interact if air freight is needed instead of much less expensive ground of sea transportation.

    This is a big issue for touring shows because efficient truck packs can reduce the number of truck needed. Compact rectangular stackable box-like machine frames, or several machines in one frame are typical goals.

- If shafts, motors, muling sheaves or whatever protrude outside the machine's framing, they could be damaged during loading or by loads shifting as the truck travels. Conversely, the protruding components could puncture scenery, forcing repairs to it before it can be used. Should no protrusions be specified?
- Is a desiccant needed to reduce corrosion during transport? This is common if machines travel by ship overseas.
- Should everything heavier than 70 lb be given a castered dolly, hamper, or hand truck?
- Should machinery be protected within road boxes? This is an expensive and therefore rare choice for machines, but routine for the more delicate automation control equipment.
- What happens to oil in reducers and HPUs if unit is tipped upside down?
- What effect will temperature extremes have on the shipped equipment? For extremes consider a trailer parked in the mid-day summer sun in Las Vegas, or in Minneapolis overnight in winter.
- The pressurized nitrogen in hydraulic accumulators may be governed by transportation laws forbidding travel through tunnels.

Company Constraints - It is common for a shop to settle on one brand of component for everything they build. This choice then becomes one type of company constraint, a requirement based solely on a choice made by the company. Another form of constraint commonly occurs when someone in authority at a theatre or scene shop—the TD, a shop owner, or perhaps a faculty member at a school—may choose not to do some aspect of scenery automation for any number of reasons: lack of expertise on staff, too much risk involved (this commonly occurs in the area of performer flying), a technology is considered too expensive to use, etc.
- Is there a list of preferred component brands and vendors?
- Are there effects that this organization should not even attempt?

Disposal - The strike of a show traditionally creates a significant amount of trash. Machinery components, however, are generally reusable in show after show for many years. The frames built for unique machines that are unlikely to be reused can be recycled rather than just thrown out. Hazardous chemicals or materials are absent from stage machinery with the exception of gear and hydraulic oils, which can contaminate drinking water supplies if spilled. Waste oil, a common by-product of installing and striking a hydraulic setup, should be recycled through appropriate channels.
- The transportation of waste oil in quantities less than 55 gallons does not need an EPA supplied tracking number, but state and local laws may be more restrictive.[2] What are the regulations in your state?

---

2. http://www.epa.gov/epaoswer/hazwaste/usedoil/usedoil.htm#standards

- Is equipment that is no longer needed suitable for donation to a theatre school rather than just being thrown out?

Manufacturing Facility - A shop's space limits the size of the materials that can enter the shop, and what can be built in it. The presence of a forklift or bridge crane enables larger component pieces to be handled.

- Is there space for a trial set up of the effect, both in terms of floor space and vertical height? Is the power there sufficient to run the set up?

Politics - While a theatre's productions might touch off protests, theatre machinery is not itself socially controversial—we don't make bombs or mink coats. The theatre industry is just too small for its practices to fall on any concerned group's radar screen just yet.

Market Constraints - The concept of a market applies mainly to commercial theatre where a shop sells its products and services to a client. Therefore market constraints would relate to those things where the client, not the company, is making decisions that impact what the shop can do. For example, some Broadway technical specs have simply forbidden hydraulics from use on a show, eliminating that as a potential solution to actuate any effects. Also, tech specs have at times required TIG welded aluminum framing for a touring show, and that all deck winches be built within the deck to speed up the load-in process.

Beyond these specific technical constraints, theatre is not immune from the most basic market economy issue, value for the dollar. A scene shop will quickly go out of business if it never wins a contract because of high prices, no matter what the quality of the product. Regional and educational do not face the same sort of market, but none the less there are very real limits to what can be done with the funds available.

- Servo motors and their controls offer remarkable performance, but can their cost be justified in the market?

Weight - Lighter weight machines are of course easier to move and load-in, but heavier machine might stay in place without bracing, and they provide a mass that will dampen some vibrations and noise. Some commercial shops, operating in buildings formerly used by heavy industry, have bridge cranes capable of lifting 10 tons. For them weight of machine subassemblies is of little concern.

- Is only human power available for lifting, or a forklift, or a chain hoist?
- Is this device to be used on a tour, or loaded-in once for a long run?
- Should the requirement for lifting points on the machine be placed in the spec?
- Is a machine heavy enough to best be moved from shop to theatre by machinery movers? These companies, that mainly move large heavy machines into and out of factories, have the personnel and equipment needed to do what a theatre shop may not be capable of doing.
- Should wheeled dollies be included in the spec?

Maintenance - All components wear, need adjustment or lubrication, and may break. Maintenance is mainly an issue of easy access to parts, easy replacement of parts, and having replacement parts available quickly. Always think of what you would have to do if a part needed to be replaced.

- Should written documentation of maintenance procedures be required in the spec?
- Is a disposable machine a better concept for this effect than a maintainable one?
- What spare parts should be specifically listed in the spec?
- What skills and knowledge of the system will the person performing the maintenance have?

Competition - Business competition is unheard of in educational or regional theatre, but it is an occasional concern in commercial shops. Both the market and the supply of stage machinery products is yet too small to have any sort of brand name recognition equivalent to something like what Ferrari means to the world of automobiles, but that day may not be far off.

- What features of your competitor's machines would be valuable to include in yours?
- Can you produce your machines for less than your competitor?

Packaging - Machines tend to have frames that are their own packaging, and they are not generally delicate enough to deserve separate boxes. The electronic controls for the machines however are usually protected from shock and breakage during transport with road boxes.

- Is a case needed for noise reduction?
- Should multiple effects be assembled into one frame for faster load-in?
- Should the machine and its drive and control electronics be packaged together?
- Should channels for forklift forks be included into the machine's framing?

Quality, Reliability - One phrase defines the goal for reliability—"The show must go on!" Since it is nearly unthinkable to cancel or cut short any scheduled performance, the use of quality components, oversized for robustness, with some plan for backup in case of failure is considered standard operating procedure.

- How many levels of backup are needed? In a typical deck winch, there would be a computerized control system, itself with various forms of backup, and then at the winch a hand crank allows the piece to be moved manually, and as a last resort stagehands can walk out onstage, pull the knives off the wagon and push it offstage by hand.
- Will the failure of this effect force the cancellation of this show? Shows have been known to go into a "concert version" upon the failure of a major piece of machinery.

- Is a manual or mechanical backup even possible? Hydraulically operated scissor lifts, for instance, are nearly impossible to move by any means but by their cylinders.
- Quality craftsmanship is at issue here too. Ground off burrs and rounded edges on framing to ease handling, painted or plated steel surfaces to reduce the likelihood of rust, or good welds are all signs of attention to detail.

Shelf Life, Storage - Any machine built for stock will sit idle between uses. Are there any requirements appropriate to include in the specification to deal with, for instance, corrosion? Sometimes steel winch drums are plated to reduce rusting over time. Machine components, unlike the electronics that control them, generally tolerate wide storage temperature swings, and do not have parts that deteriorate rapidly over time.

- If a dolly is used under a machine to move it around, can it store on or in the machine when not in use? This is quite common for trusses on touring shows, the dollies store on top of the flown truss so they are not cluttering the stage, and it is less likely they will be lost.
- Bundles of parts can be shrink wrapped to keep them together during storage. This can minimize the temptation to cannibalize parts off one machine to use them in another.

Patents - Concern over violating a patent is very rare in theatre, and this is probably because most machines we design are simple variations on common designs that are in the public domain. Then too, there are very few theatre machinery specific patents. Four perhaps worth looking at are: Peter Foy's "Theatrical transportation apparatus" detailing one of his flying rigs (pat. 4,392,648), Gala's "Push actuator" marketed as their Spiralift (pat. 4,875,660), Show Motion's "Theatrical scenery carriage and movement mechanism" which is basically a form of traveller track (pat. 5,970,578), and a "Stage element movement assembly" invented by Jim Kempf of Scenic Technologies which allows cable driven deck tracks to cross (pat. 6,547,670). The typical process of patenting an invention is both expensive, with estimates highly variable but averaging in the several thousands of dollars, and lengthy, typically taking years.

Environment - The majority of theatre machinery operates in a relatively benign indoor environment. Occasionally though effects will require machines to work underwater, near flame effects or pyro, outdoors, or near or within public areas. A touring show's equipment will have to withstand the environment of a truck trailer (possibly very cold and/or very hot depending on the time of year and geography), and the physical abuses of travel and handling. Containers shipped overseas may expose the machinery to months of salt laden air. Finally, building codes in certain parts of the country may require that all equipment be designed for a given seismic loading condition, and that equipment used outdoors be capable of withstanding given wind and even snow loads.

- Is there any anticipated unusual environment the machinery will have to tolerate? Outdoors in rain, snow, or ice? Outdoors in the sun in Las Vegas? High altitude in Colorado?

- Are there any materials used in the production that may affect machine components? A set design may include sand, water, dirt, dried leaves, or any of a number of potentially corroding, clogging, or abrasive substances. In one Yale Rep production, a ring of coarse salt was laid down each night by an actor around a circular lift. Even after only a three week run, the corrosion of the lift's steel components was extensive.

Testing - A test of a machine will confirm that it can do what the specification requires it to do. This is especially important when an automated effect involves a completely new, and hence untested, machine. Time and labor should be assigned during the build period for a trial setup and tests to prove it is working within specs. It is generally easier to identify and correct any problems discovered in the shop, given that it is a well lit open space filled with the tools you may need, than in what is all too often a dark cramped corner of the theatre. All effects, and this is regardless of whether they involve new machines or the reuse of a stock ones, will need some time during load-in for a test and adjust period.

- If a custom machine is being bought from an outside contractor, which is quite common for scissor lifts for instance, what specifications must be met during the tests? Run at full load plus 20%? Test to prove that the required travel distance can be attained?

- Some theme park contracts require that an independent testing laboratory, such as UL or ETL, be hired to certify the equipment as meeting certain standards.

- Many commercial contracts require a demonstration test in the shop for the show's technical supervisor before a piece is allowed to leave for the theatre.

Safety - Since all machinery must be built to operate safely, the spec mainly needs to address special situations: perhaps requiring single failure proof design, the inclusion of light curtain devices to sense excursions into hazardous areas, a full failure modes and effects analysis (FMEA), or a purely mechanical overspeed brake.

- Is the general public involved physically with this effect in any way? Does it occur over their heads? Do they ride on it? If the answer is yes to any of these questions, hire a licensed engineer.

- What training procedures should operators and performers receive?

- What design factors are appropriate for this effect?

- Should there be slack line sensors on all wire ropes? chains? toothed belts?

- OSHA issues automatically apply, but do any of its provisions need to be specifically mentioned?

- Should the use of safety warning labels be required?

- Are there provisions made for an OSHA lock-out, tag-out procedure?

Legal - Rarely would there be a need to specifically cite a point of law as a requirement within a specification. So instead here legal could be seen as referring to the fact that there are legal liability issues with everything in, or not in, a specification. Should the worst happen and an injury occur that triggers a lawsuit, the specification would be looked at by both sides for what it says a given machine needs, or what it does not say. In today's world this is not a trivial issue. For more information on this complex topic, search for books on product liability law, or consult your company's legal advisor.

- Should all tech design staff have "errors and omissions" liability insurance?
- If you are an independent contractor, research the benefits of incorporation.
- What project documentation should be preserved to prove contract compliance?

Documentation - The documentation of show specific stage machinery is mainly in the form of CAD drawings, spreadsheets or hand written pages of concepts, notes, and calculations, and the records of purchases made obtaining parts. Notebooks or file folders should be required for each major project. CAD files need to be kept in some rational arrangement for easy retrieval when a similar project comes up. Company insurers may ask you to have instruction manuals for any product you make to help reduce liability.

- What drawing file name standards should be followed?
- Are as-built drawings required? These would be useful for stock machines.
- Is an operator's manual, or maintenance procedures paperwork needed?

Quantity - By any industrial standard, stage machinery would be considered as made in small quantities. Despite this though, making 6 identical things is more efficient than making 6 similar things with just slight differences between them. Standardize as much as possible. High quantities of any part may justify special tooling, or manufacturing by an outside source. Always check price breaks when ordering parts in quantity.

- Is this a unique machine, or one that is likely to be needed more in the future?
- When ordering in quantity, how many extras should be purchased?

Product Life Span - This can mean both how long should a given machine be expected to operate before it fails, and, for stock designs, how many years do you expect to produce this model? The issue of technological obsolescence, which occurs quite rapidly for electronic equipment, is rare for mechanical components, but it does occur. Shunt wound DC motors of 5 hp and larger, once common on stage machinery, are now so expensive as to be not worth even considering their purchase.

- Some products are rated with MTBF, or mean time between failure. This is the average length of time one of these devices will operate, or put another way, it is the time it takes for 50% of a large sample of these devices to fail. Any given single sample of that product will work longer or shorter than the MTBF.

- Is the machine being designed for a regional theatre show running 30 seconds a night for 3 weeks, or a store display running 24 hours a day for ten years?

Materials - Low alloy carbon steel and aluminum are typical in machines, but plastics for low friction slides or electrical insulation, stainless steel for corrosion resistance, hardened steel for cam-follower tracks, or baked-on powder coatings for a rugged attractive finish might all find their use in some application. The specification should state clearly what should be used, and if important, what distributor to purchase it from.

- Shaft materials: Cold drawn? Turned, ground, and polished, or TGP?
- UHMW versus Nylatron?
- Aluminum or stainless steel required for outdoor use?

Ergonomics - People need to interact efficiently, effectively, and safely with machines, and this interaction is the province of the study of ergonomics. A manual backup hand crank, for instance, will need to operate within the bounds of handle forces and speeds that a stage hand can be expected to produce. Anything designed to be lifted by hand could include handles located at a convenient height. Standard actions resulting from movements of adjustments or controls should be used. Turning something clockwise tightens, makes louder, or faster, or brighter. Valve handles should have logical correlations between their motion and the movement of what they control – handle up, scenery moves up.

- Is there a manual backup to the effect? If so, is it convenient for an operator to activate and use?
- What labels or color codes could aid in assembly, use, or maintenance?
- Are controls or adjustment points clearly and safely accessible?
- Can activities, such as tightening a roller chain, be easily and quickly performed by one person?

Standards - A lifetime could be spent reading and interpreting all the laws, codes, and standards that apply to machinery and machinery controls. There are federal, state, and local standards enforced by law that machinery designers must comply with in their designs. OSHA machine guarding, and the need for motor disconnects as stated in the National Electrical Code (NEC), are two examples. Beyond governmental standards there are industry standards covering recommended practices for welding, from the American Welding Society (AWS), for steel structure, from the American Institute for Steel Construction (AISC), and for gear ratings from the American Gear Manufacturers Association (AGMA), to mention just three. Within our industry, there is a growing list of standards coming out of ESTA. There are of course equivalents to all these across the world too, and so if international tours are planned, requirements for compliance with these standards will need to be investigated.

New York commercial theatre technical specifications can take the inclusion of standards into a contract to an extreme. It is not unusual that they state something to the effect of "all work on a production must comply with the requirements contained within the following standards." This is then followed by a list of a dozen or so standards organizations, such as NFPA or ANSI. All the NFPA standards alone occupy several thousand pages of text. One tech spec for a show touring to Europe listed the names of several German and Japanese standards organizations too. I can assure you that no one person on the planet has read all these standards, let alone understood them.

Despite this blanket coverage overuse of standards, specific references are appropriate. Perhaps to require the use of AWS A2.4 welding symbols on all shop drawings, or perhaps specifying an AGMA service factor for any gear reducers used.

Aesthetics - The aesthetics of a stage machine design has historically been a very low priority over all other issues. The look of machines is utilitarian at best. High quality components used in an elegant design fabricated with high craftsmanship will create an aesthetically pleasing machine.

- Is there a standard color all machines should be painted? A personal choice here, but shiny black is both attractive and does not distract if it is within audience sightlines.
- Is there a theatre or shop logo that could be included on any CNC cut parts?
- The TD or shop foreman could work to instill in all shop staff an expectation that all work will be to a high level of quality.

Installation - Theatre machinery is rarely built in place, but rather it is built in a shop, ideally set up there and tested, disassembled, shipped to a theatre, and loaded-in. An effect is therefore usually set up and struck twice at a minimum, and if the effect is part of a tour, many more of these cycles will occur. The specification should identify what aspects of the machine relating to its installation are most important. The size of the machine's parts, the weight of those parts, the speed of assembly, or an independence from a need to connect into building structure other than to sit on the floor may be seen as critical to the success of this effect.

- Connectors for wiring, and quick connects for hydraulic hoses are expensive, but they speed up interconnections during load-in and so may be justified.
- Who will be installing the machinery? Shop staff? Or does the unit get sent to a theatre and the staff there install it?
- If the production is a tour, what accommodations need to be made for the differences between venues?
- Should various connection points be color coded to speed identification of what part goes where?

Summary

Overall this is a daunting list of topics, though each one taken individually is not too involved. In most theatre situations a number of these would not even need to be considered: politics, aesthetics, competition, patents, shelf life, market constraints, and perhaps others. Also, in a typical regional theatre situation, the organization itself, and the shop and theatre spaces are unchanging givens. The elements covering manufacturing facility, shipping, installation, environment, legal issues, customer, company and market constraints, and probably disposal, life span, shelf life, documentation, quality, and reliability would not change. This leaves a more manageable list of half the size of the original:

- Performance
- Size
- Weight
- Standards

- Product cost
- Packaging
- Materials
- Ergonomics

- Testing
- Maintenance
- Processes
- Life in service

- Safety
- Cost
- Quantity
- Time

Often the mechanical designer will just use generic specs and common assumptions about materials, construction processes, and the machine's environment and try to keep all this information in their head. While it is surprising how often this works, this is not a good approach. Something critical could be forgotten, and the machine that results would be flawed and may fail catastrophically. Instead, let the shortened list above, or even the descriptions given earlier, act as a trigger to generate a list of requirements that become the effect design specification.

26

Concept Design

Overview

A concept is an idea, a scheme, or a plan that has been thought of as a potential solution to some problem. Concept design, in the context of the mechanical design process, concerns the development and evaluation of concepts to solve the problems posed in the specification, or put more simply, how are you going to perform the move the designer has requested.

Valid stage machinery concepts will evolve in specificity from the beginning to the end of a project. Very early on in the process, a perfectly acceptable concept for a machine actuator might simply be the phrase "…use pneumatics!", which would imply an air compressor, control valves, cylinders and associated hardware. Soon enough words alone will fail in easily expressing the concept, and so hand sketches may be made, as in the example on the left in Figure 26.1. Later on, if the pneumatic concept has been considered worth pursuing to greater depth, a scaled drawing investigating cylinder stroke might be done using only approximate dimensions just to test the concept. Eventually, as the design becomes exactingly specific about the parts being used, concept design and detail design become intertwined in an interplay of ideas worked out into drawings representing every part of a buildable machine, as shown on the right in Figure 26.1. (As an aside, note the relative clarity of the crude sketch below over the CAD drawing of the same device. CAD is pre-

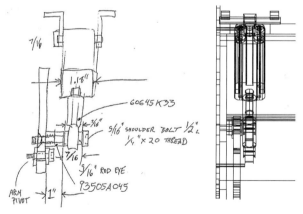

Figure 26.1   A hand and CAD concept sketch for a pneumatic cylinder pivoting an arm

cise and complete, but by no means necessarily clear except to those who are already intimately familiar with the machine being depicted.)

In each of these progressive stages of the development of a design—initial ideas, sketches, rough and then finally completed draftings—concepts will have to be constantly generated, and those concepts will just as constantly need to be evaluated for their suitability for solving the problem. The answer to "How can I do that?" will always be followed by "But will it work?" Since in theatre there is rarely the time to thoroughly develop each of several promising concepts to prove which best solves the problem at hand, it is necessary to choose the concept with the highest probability of success and work from there. Concept evaluation, often with incomplete information, is always the mate of concept generation.

Concepts do not have to be new or innovative to be useful. If a set design shows a wagon moving across stage, one acceptable concept for a machine to perform this move would be to use a deck winch you already have in stock. This type of concept hardly seems worthy of the name, but just because an idea is obvious does not invalidate that it is an idea. The obvious concepts are invaluable as they come to mind quickly and use time tested proven techniques.

The generation of concepts that will potentially solve a problem is essential to mechanical design, for if there are no concepts, there will be no solution, and the mechanical design process abruptly stops. Given this dire prospect, a mechanical designer should know a variety of concept generation techniques, and that is the subject of the first half of this chapter. Concept evaluation, or how the best of several concepts is determined forms the latter half.

Concept Generation Techniques

Concept design is the creative aspect of the mechanical design process. It can involve wild new inventions, or the mundane repetition of a tried and true device. It feeds on knowledge, information, and experience, but can be blocked in an instant by distraction, hunger, or fatigue. It can involve groups of people inspiring and being inspired by a team effort towards the same goal, or it can be done by one person alone in a quiet room.

Despite decades of research, how the human brain actually conceives something new is still not well understood, and so in place of the one way to come up with ideas, there are dozens of techniques that have proven of some use for some people in some situations. Concept generation techniques vary from the straightforward to the bizarre, but none of them guarantee a successful end result.

The requirements stated in the effect design specification provide the givens for a problem to be solved, and there are an infinite number of possible solutions. The ideas generated during concept design do not have to be new, in fact in the usually time pressed production process, using existing machine designs or minor variations on these is often a wise choice.

Just as no work can be done on a problem until the problem has been defined by some form of specification, no detail design work can begin until a general concept for a solution to the problem has been found, and so generating concepts, preferably many concepts, is essential to the progress of the design effort.

> A single idea is better than none,
> but many are superior to one.

If you seek concept generation inspiration, the Internet is invaluable. One web site, for instance, lists more than 180 creativity techniques (http://www.mycoted.com/ Category:Creativity_Techniques). A small selection of those are described below, listed roughly in order of from the most straightforward to the least, but if any one is not working for you, try something else.

Research Existing Machines and Copy One

This may not seem like a concept generation technique at all, but that is only because it is so simple and obvious. Research can come from the web, from machines you already have, ones you have seen, or ones in the compendium section of this book. The more different types of theatre machinery you know about, the more likely it is that you will have at least one good concept the instant a problem is posed.

The issue of copying a patented idea comes up here of course, and the law is very clear:

35 U.S.C. 271 Infringement of patent.

(a) Except as otherwise provided in this title, whoever without authority *makes, uses, offers to sell, or sells* any patented invention, within the United States, or imports into the United States any patented invention during the term of the patent therefor, infringes the patent.[1] [my emphasis]

There apparently is no equivalent of the fair use concept that applies to copyrights that would apply to patents, so the decision to copy or not is an ethical one you get to make. There are very few patented theatre machines, so this eases this issue considerably.

Scale an Existing Design Up or Down

Take a design for an existing machine that has the functions you need, and adapt it to a larger or smaller device as needed. This technique is nearly trivial if the scale change is minor, as would be the case, for instance, when developing a 3 HP deck winch from an existing 2 HP design, but it grows harder when the scale changes radically. If the goal is to start with a 2 HP deck winch design and make it 10 times smaller, scaled design may not be possible. Certain components—a stock limit box, for example—are not easily scaled down so far without a radical redesign. The human hand, used to load cable onto the drum, will not scale down with the design, and so the original design's ample hand room would become too small if the new design did not account for this.

---

1. 35 United States Code 271—Appendix L(a), which can be found at http://www.uspto.gov/ web/offices/pac/mpep/documents/appxl_35_U_S_C_271.htm

Evolve from an Existing Design

There are many scenic movements that occur again and again. A wagon running across a deck for instance. The winches built to pull wagons guided in tracks have evolved in small increments over time rather than being re-thought or re-conceptualized for each new use. Evolution in mechanical design denotes the gradual change, and hopefully gradual improvement, of the winch's various functions. An excellent example of this type of design from outside the world of theatre can be seen in the automobile. The similarities between a Ford Model T and the cars of today are obvious, and yet between then and now thousands of individual incremental improvements have made automobiles much more comfortable, longer running, and faster. Suggestions for evolutionary improvements on some existing device can probably be found by talking with shop staff that build these machines, or the stagehands who install or run them.

Concept by Selection

As concept design proceeds from initial broad stroke ideas to the final decisions on every minute detail of a machine, there is a time somewhere in the middle of this process when vague concepts must turn into more specific ideas. A hand sketch may have a motor and gear reduction stage blocked out as little more than rectangles. In some industrial settings, that motor and gear stage might be fabricated from scratch using basic raw materials, but in theatre we will instead design those parts by selecting a motor and gear reducer from a catalog. Most of the parts we use are designed by selection: bearings, cylinders, bolts, wire rope, roller chain, belts, and many others. Selecting components from a catalog is in fact a rapid combination of concept generation and evaluation. If a bolt is needed:

Concept:	Result of evaluation:
Hex head, Flat head, Socket head	Hex.
Metric, American Standard	Metric.
M10, M12, M14	M12.
Fully threaded, Partially threaded.	Partially . . . etc.

Many choices are offered, evaluation reduces those many to one.

Inversion

Can the problem you're attempting to solve be approached from the opposite direction, by flipping something around, or by exchanging what moves with what does not? For instance, instead of pushing a lift up with a cylinder, can it be pulled up? A typical winch is stationary and the cable and wagon it powers moves, but could the winch be on the wagon and cable be stationary relative to the stage? Can the problem change to conform to the machine's capabilities, rather that always thinking the machine must be made to conform to the problem.

Configuration Concepts

The arrangement of components within a machine can be as important to some of the functions of a machine as the choice of those components themselves. For instance, clear access to mounting hardware is essential for ease of assembly and

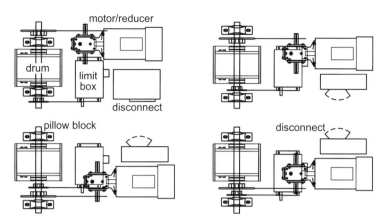

Figure 26.2   Configuration concepts examples. Four different layouts of the same parts.

maintenance. A given limit box may have a hinged door that will need to be swung open 100° or more for access to limit switches inside, and sightlines into these switches should be unimpeded. A configuration concept is one idea of the arrangement of a set of parts. Figure 26.2 shows four configuration concepts for a winch. The same parts occur in each concept, but they have been rearranged in an attempt to optimize limit box access, the overall size of the machine, ease of changing the chain stage reduction ratios, and other things. These configurations would be evaluated in light of requirements stated in the effect design specification.

A large part of mechanical design in theatre is the rearranging of components into a variety of configurations, often just to make them fit into a given space. Two dimensional sketches on paper or in CAD often make it difficult to visualize the third dimension—the one into and out of the paper or screen. Using 3-D CAD, or even simply laying out the actual parts on the floor will allow you to see how they interact in space, and how they might be most effectively arranged.

Analogy

What other machines from outside the world of theatre have you seen that perform a task similar to what is needed now? Industrial machines or components that you can find illustrated on the web, working at construction sites, or maybe even in your driveway may already have functions that are analogous to those needed in your problem: work platform scissor lifts, the telescoping action of fork lift masts, elevator guides and guide track, the hydraulic cylinder mounts on earth moving equipment, the sunroof of a car, etc. Study these similar machines to see if any of their mechanisms inspire a solution to your problem.

Other's Viewpoints

A piece of stage machinery will undergo scrutiny from many different people. Imagine how the operator will see or interact with your machine, or an actor walking by it on her way to an entrance. What do their viewpoints tell you about the design? Theatre mechanical designers, who almost universally have shop and show running experience, should be especially adept at imagining the perceptions of a carpenter building the machine, the load-in crew with their interests in size and ease of handling, and all on the run crew who will need to work around, on, and sometimes in this effect.

If possible, talk to these people about their prior experience with machines you both know about (whether you designed them or not). They may have a totally different opinion than you about one feature or another, and these comments are bound to provide a new perspective on your designs. Of course not everyone's opinion is valid, but even a complete misperception is useful information. It may indicate the need for different training, better parts layout, or perhaps the addition of a label in some key location.

Envision any number of people: an insurance agent, an industrial safety consultant, a patron on a backstage tour, or a licensed engineer. We're in theatre—play a role.

Osborn's Checklist[2]

Seven words that force you to think through a full range of options you could pursue to solve your problem. This is named after Alex Osborn who pioneered the brainstorming technique in the 1950s.[3]

- Adapt - Can something you already have, even though perhaps not ideal, be used as it is? Double purchase a winch cable to increase its force. Can the problem change to match a machine?
- Modify - What can be changed to make this idea work better?
- Magnify - Will something being thicker, stronger, bigger, higher, larger, longer, etc. make it better?
- Minimize - Remove something, make parts thinner, lighter, simpler, smaller.
- Substitute - Switch a part to something else. Pillow block to flange? 1800 rpm motor to 1200? Hydraulic cylinder to electric linear actuator? Change a material—a nylon gear for a steel one in an attempt to reduce gear noise.
- Rearrange - Move parts around from where they are now. Flip them sideways, upside down, mirror image, stack them up vertically, nest one inside the other.
- Combine - Add together functions or parts into one package.

Brainstorming

This is a technique where any and all ideas are encouraged, no matter how far out they may be, and absolutely no criticism of them takes place until after a large number have been stated. Traditionally this is a group design activity, but with practice one person can do this too. Speed, spontaneity, and free thought are the goals, with evaluation and criticism put off until later. The ideas would usually be expressed in very quickly done concept sketches, or in words if appropriate. A nearly frenzied speed is important here, as it forces you to simply free associate or

---

2. Fogler & LeBlanc, *Strategies for Creative Problem Solving,* 69.

3. Osborn, Alex F., *Applied Imagination: Principles and Procedures of Creative Problem-Solving.* 1957, New York: Scribner.

react rather than think. Fifty ideas in ten minutes might be a goal. Yes, fifty ideas at a pace of 12 seconds per idea. Fast, extemporaneous, improvisational.

This technique works best when concepts can be stated or sketched quickly. Detailed concepts may take too long to draw or state, killing the flow of the session. Even if you don't intentionally attempt brainstorming, keep a notebook handy at all times so you can write down things as they come to mind.

Negative Brainstorming[4]

Instead of the brainstorming technique of generating many ideas without any criticism, take a few existing ideas, and mercilessly tear them down by thoroughly answering the question "What could go wrong with this idea?" After this analysis has occurred, you essentially have a list of ways each of the ideas could be improved.

Do Something Else

One of the least understood capabilities of the brain is its ability to solve a problem that seems baffling one day, and clear the next. It is as if a part of our brain outside of our consciousness keeps working and serves up the answer when it is done. As with all of these techniques, nothing here guarantees a successful outcome, but it is an easy technique to try. Basically you must first spend some time on the problem. Consider the specification, try some concept sketches, discuss the problem with someone. When you feel you have progressed as far as you can, just stop and do something else, something completely different if possible. In a few hours, or preferably a day or two later, pick up the problem again and see what happens. It might appear easier, you might have thought of a solution, or at the very least the time spent away allows you to start with a clear head.

Random Triggers

This technique is one that could easily be considered in the bizarre category, but if you are in a deep rut and going nowhere it is worth a try. Flip open a book and point to a word—consider only nouns, verbs, and adjectives as valid. Free associate other words or ideas off that word. Use these to generate new words or ideas, and repeat this until you've redirected your thoughts from the random word to your problem. What is as important as anything here is the forced and jarring redirection of your thought process.

Random pictures have also been suggested as triggers to initiate new ideas, though one picture is so much more rich and complex than a single word that there is the risk of being overloaded rather than freed. Perhaps use a classic inkblot (available on numerous web sites), or pictures of individual items, as you would find on any randomly chosen page in a Grainger's or McMaster-Carr catalog.

> When in doubt, make it stout,
> out of things, you know about.
>
> Ullman, *The Mechanical Design Process*, 119

---

4. J. G. Rawlinson, *Creative Thinking and Brainstorming*, 1981.

Concept Evaluation

After a number of new concepts have been created, or a number of concepts drawn from existing designs have been extracted, they must be evaluated relative to the effect design specification and each other to determine which is the best one to continue to develop. How do you evaluate which design is the best? Guess? Gut feeling? These two are used, but they are far from the best techniques.

Since these concepts might range anywhere from existing machine designs that are very well known to potentially completely new ideas not yet fully fleshed out in detail nor tested to prove their abilities, the evaluation process is mainly about risk management. (Pugh calls it "minimizing conceptual vulnerability"[5]) The risk involved here is not a safety issue, but rather the risk of failure to get a working machine completed by the time it is needed. There must be a potential reward to a risky design, else it is not worth considering. The reward could be better performance, smaller size, a lower cost to produce, or anything that is perceived as better than other designs. Choosing to follow a new idea just because it is new should be avoided.

Here the very different amounts of time and money in the design process between industry and theatre cause big differences. General industry minimizes this risk by using long development times, large design groups composed of members with diverse areas of expertise, and by prototyping, market research, and testing. By putting various versions of the future product into the hands of as many people as they can, the strengths and weaknesses of each version becomes apparent. In theatre, we cannot do this. Short design and build times, and limited funds, preclude the construction of prototypes. Technical theatre often minimizes risk through the use of tried and proven technology, but when something new is attempted the risk of the project failing increases. Always ask:

- What exactly is the risk? The machine will not be powerful enough? Not easily controlled? Is the risk simply that this technique's behavior is unknown? Do you suspect that it may not be reliable?

- Do the potential benefits outweigh the risk? Less expensive? Better performance? More compact? This is the only identified way to do this effect?

- What are the consequences of this technique not working? Opening of the show delayed? That effect is just cut from the show? Failure to fulfill the contract, and a financial penalty?

- What resources can be brought to bear to reduce the risk? Make a sample and test it? Schedule a trial setup of the full system well in advance of load-in? Hire experts to make it work? Change to a different company's version of some critical component?

- What is the backup plan if this were to fail? Use existing equipment in a less than ideal way? There is no backup plan (if true, reconsider your options to confirm that this is an acceptable choice)?

---

5. Pugh, *Total Design*, 76.

Anything new involves some risk, but by carefully considering all the aspects and consequences of it, a plan can be formed to deal with it.

An Evaluation Matrix

Once several designs with the potential to solve a given problem have been created, an evaluation technique can be used to try to identify which design is the best solution to that problem. Evaluation is easy if the problem is not difficult and the choice of solutions are few, but most mechanical design problems involve multiple conflicting requirements—low cost with many features, or high power in a small size—and there are often many potential solutions with none being ideal. A simple technique that can help indicate the best solution for a given set of problem needs is an evaluation matrix. The matrix set up and evaluation process follows six steps:

1. One concept, an existing machine, or, lacking this, one of the concepts that seems at first glance to be the best, is listed at the head of the first column of a spreadsheet-like chart. It is considered the reference idea, or the idea to which all the other concepts will be compared.

2. Each of the other design concepts being tested are listed horizontally across at the top of their individual column.

3. A list of evaluation criteria or effect requirements is developed from the effect design specification. They are listed vertically, at the left of rows that run across the page.

4. For each criteria, each design concept is evaluated relative to the reference. The columns are marked with symbols indicating:

    + = better, cheaper, faster. The design superior relative to the reference.
    - = worse, slow, heavier. The design is inferior relative to the reference.
    s = The design and reference are the same.

5. After all the evaluations are done, sum all the positives, all the negatives, and all the sames, and record these numbers on the chart (see Figure 26.3).

6. Choose the best design based on the scores. Positives are great, but even one negative may condemn a design depending on what it refers to. If all the scores are more negative than positive, the reference concept is the best.

7. Refine the questions, change the reference and rerun. Does the same design win?

Criteria:	Design A	Design B	Design C	Design D	Design E	
small size	reference	s	–	s	s	
light weight		+	+	+	+	
low cost		–	–	+	–	
fast to build		s	s	s	–	
load capacity		s	s	+	s	
Sum of +		1	1	3	1	the best
Sum of –		1	2	0	2	
Sum of s		3	2	2	2	

Figure 26.3   Example of a concept evaluation matrix

As needed, the criteria or the comparisons can be weighted to take into account an exceptionally good or bad point relative to the reference (by adding extra pluses or minuses as seems appropriate: +++ or - - for instance). A question mark could be added to the list of symbols used during evaluation to represent an unknown. Any of these in a concepts column would be a red flag that that design is unclear and has added risks. This is not a rigid technique that should limit you in any way, add notes, use smiley faces, cross out some of the ideas if it becomes apparent they will never work. This is a tool for your use, not a technique that forces you to conform to it.

In the same way that a specification may be anything from a formal document to penciled notes and napkin sketches, the evaluation matrix can be an Excel spreadsheet with dozens of carefully stated criteria extracted from the spec, or a quick mental checklist run through once and forgotten. How important to you is being sure about the best way to proceed?

Freedom and Constraint

The subject of freedom and constraint, in the context of machine design, concerns how to design machine parts that can move in intended ways, that disallow unwanted movements, and that yet accommodate the inevitable differences between the ideal and real worlds. A lift, for example, must be allowed to travel vertically, and prevented from tipping or turning in any other way. Guides of various types can be used to allow the vertical travel and disallow the others, but these guides must still work and not jam or allow too much slop even if they are somewhat imperfect: warped, out of parallel, or deflected. It is a difficult subject, little written on, that is often only intuitively dealt with by good machine designers.

This is also a subject that has defied my ability to place it seamlessly into this text, so it fits awkwardly here, but little better anywhere else. Were it not for its great importance to the field of machine design, it would have been easier to just leave it out.

Degrees of Freedom

An object in space, free to move or rotate in any way, has the maximum possible six degrees of freedom, or 6 DOF. Three of these are translational, usually denoted x, y, and z, and three are rotational, rotate about x, rotate about y, and rotate about z. Other names can be more descriptive: the three degrees of translation being up/down, left/right, and forward/reverse, with the three rotational freedoms being roll, pitch, and yaw. True free bodies in space are of little use within

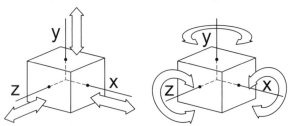

machines, instead constraints are placed on parts to limit their movements to what is needed: 1 DOF rotational for a motor shaft, 1 DOF translational for a wagon, or 2 DOF both translational for a platform on air bearings, for instance.

As a good, though basic, example of proper constraint, consider a shaft mounted in two self-aligning pillow blocks which are in turn mounted to a rigid frame. One block by itself, if its set screws are tightened down, will prevent all translation of the shaft, but allow all rotations. (The bearing allows 1 DOF rotational, and the spherical self-aligning bearing mount allows, within limits, the other two DOF rotational) Add in the second pillow block and the shaft is constrained in all but 1 DOF—it can rotate as desired, but not move any other way. Even with minor imperfections in the pillow block mounting surfaces, this 1 DOF will be preserved.

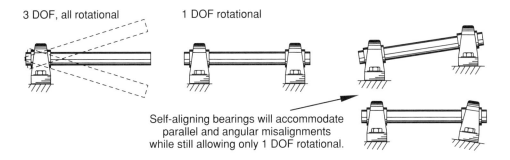

3 DOF, all rotational   1 DOF rotational

Self-aligning bearings will accommodate parallel and angular misalignments while still allowing only 1 DOF rotational.

Take this example one step further, and add a third pillow block onto the shaft. Since the first two blocks defined points of support to which the line of the shaft aligns, for a third pillow block to work in this setup, it would have to be aligned *exactly* to the line defined by the first two. Theoretically this is possible, but in practice it is difficult enough that it is best avoided if possible.

The third block, when not in perfect alignment, is an example of overconstraint. The symptoms of overconstraint in stage machinery are unfortunately common: binding, jamming, locking up, excessive wear or friction, and bent components.

Overconstraint Ordains Overloading!

Alexander H. Slocum, *MIT course 2.007 Web site*

There are three fixes to overconstraint, with the last better than the other two.
- Make your machine parts compliant. If, in the above example, the frame or shaft bent easily, the loading created by misaligned parts would be minimized. Not often a viable choice, but spring-loaded constraint is sometimes used.
- Increase the slop in all overconstrained parts. If the blocks above were 1", and the shaft was 7/8", then the three blocks could easily be made to line up close enough. Yes this is an absurd suggestion, but how often do we put a 3/8" bolt in a 7/16" hole, or use 1/4" knives in 1/2" wide deck tracks?

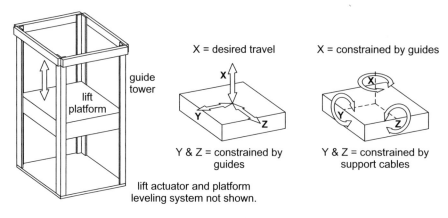

Figure 26.4   Simple lift guided by four lift columns

• Design the system properly in the first place to avoid overconstraint, buy machine assemblies manufactured to work despite overconstraint, or use in your designs those mechanisms that work well even though overconstrained.

There are ways to mathematically analyze a system for freedom, but it is a bit esoteric for us. Of more practical use is the simple technique of thinking about how each component in a machine needs to be free or constrained. Often this amounts to thinking about how reality differs from the world of perfection that can exist in CAD. For an example, think of four parallel vertical columns used as part of a lift guiding scheme (see Figure 26.4). In CAD, they can all be perfectly straight and parallel to each other. Guide wheels rolling along these perfect towers will never jam or bind. A lovely fantasy, but in reality each tower will warp a little differently during welding, and perfect parallelism isn't possible when a tape measure is your only reference. The guide wheels could jam, or just as likely could knock around loosely between the towers.

Knowing that the guide wheels could be a problem is perhaps the most important outcome of this mental process. The fixes are usually easy, it is being aware of where the problems are that is sometimes difficult. Possible fixes are:

• Construct the towers as parallel as possible in the shop rather than trying to set up four separate parts in the theatre. (It is almost always better to build something as a complete stand alone functioning unit than as parts that rely on their connection to the building before they can work.)

• Accept a certain amount of slop in the guides. If the shop can build the lift towers to within 1/8″ of perfectly parallel, is the resulting worst case 1/8″ sway of the lift platform acceptable?

• Rigid mount one set of guide wheels, and spring mount all the others. The spring-loaded guide will accommodate the non-parallelism, and the lift will follow one tower. In other situations the question to consider is hard constraint versus soft constraint. The rigidity of bolted or welding, versus sloppy pins or intentional flexure.

- Adopt a different guiding technique. The sides of one piece of steel are manufactured accurately parallel to thousandths of an inch. Guide off of one tower (or two to pick up a better DOC in rotation, as shown below).

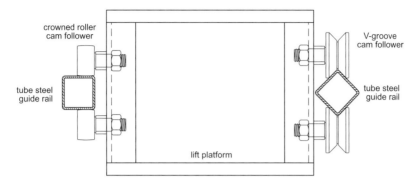

Never assume that the real world will be at all ideal.

- Parallel shafts or tracks will not be so in reality. The error will depend mainly on construction methods, materials, tolerances and quality control. Always consider the consequences of non-parallelism, and how the machine you are designing will deal with it. What slop in the system can be accepted? 0.001″? ½″? Hydraulic cylinders, for instance, need to be allowed to move the way they want to move, free from any side forces. Never rigidly mount a cylinder into a frame with a rigidly guided piece. Which one wins? Which breaks first? "Overconstraint ordains overloading!"

- Do not assume that walls are vertical or floors horizontal. Building surfaces are notoriously off from what they appear. Consider how this might affect the operation of guides.

- Perfectly straight lines and perfectly flat surfaces don't exist. Beware of designing a machine frame that by itself will work great, but that when bolted into place in the theatre stops working because of the deformation caused by bolting it to odd shaped surface. This happens all too often in theatre. Stage and trap room floors are not perfectly flat planes, battens bend and rotate, etc. Self-aligning pillow blocks (and spherical mounts of all types), shaft couplings, universal joints, and splined shafts are all designed to accept or allow some misalignment. Use them for this purpose.

Some Diverse Constraint Issues

Always look at existing machines to see how this issue has been dealt with in the past. The ways of a metal lathe, that allow the linear movement of the tailstock that supports one end of the work, have changed little over the last 100 plus years because the design is simple and works well. An upward facing V-shaped guide runs parallel with but several inches away from a flat guide track. The V does most of the constraint, but it needs the support of the flat track to firmly resist rotation.

This scheme can be easily adapted to a guide system using cam followers, and this forms one half of the lift guides shown earlier.

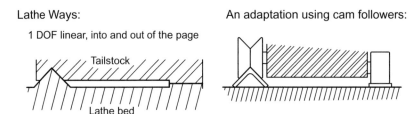

Lathe Ways:

1 DOF linear, into and out of the page

An adaptation using cam followers:

Underconstraint can cause as many problems as overconstraint. Loose, poorly held moving parts, vibration, noise, and drive chains that fall off are all possible outcomes of underconstraint. Bearings, for instance, are designed to support shafts, but to do this well they have to be used correctly. One self-aligning bearing by itself will not hold anything in place, the spherical mount that allows misalignment also means the shaft will just tip over in response to a side force. Two bearings will support a shaft well, but to insure rock solid support, keep the bearings spaced apart by at least 3 to 5 times the diameter of the shaft they support:

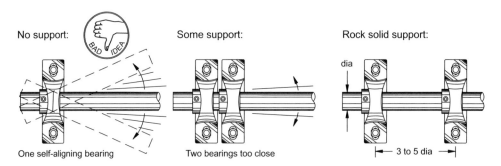

No support: Some support: Rock solid support:

One self-aligning bearing   Two bearings too close   3 to 5 dia

A good solid clean one DOF in rotation is easier to get than one DOF translation. Pillow and flange blocks are readily available and easy to use in our designs. Linear bearings and guides are available too, but they are usually quite expensive, and they are far more susceptible to dirt than bearings. So, can a move be done using a pivoting arm rather than a tracked action?

27

Detail Design

Overview

During concept design, the goal is to identify the machine's components in broad strokes, but the details of exactly what these parts are has not been set. It is detail design that involves the translation of concepts into specific parts. This translation involves work in three main areas:

- the mathematical analysis of parts to determine their size, reduction ratio, shear strength, cable capacity, output torque, service factor, material, etc.,
- the generation of a parts and materials list detailing every part number or type of raw material needed to build the machine, and
- the completion of a drafting showing a fully detailed model of the machine to be built, ready to be converted into shop construction drawings.

This chapter will be short because the first 23 chapters of this book are all about detail design. What is here are brief discussions of some detail design techniques, and suggestions.

Analysis

Analysis is what most people think of when they think of engineering, and it is what most mechanical design textbooks are filled with. Formulas that model the behavior of some aspect of reality give us the ability to predict how a real device will work before it is actually built. For example $F = pA$, or force equals pressure times area, shows unambiguously the relationship between the three terms, and this simple equation frees us from a trial and error, or build something and see if it works approach to design with fluid power cylinders.

The mathematics involved in routine analysis is usually only algebra or trigonometry, both easily done with just an inexpensive calculator. With proper care to enter numbers and functions correctly, and then writing the answers down in an orderly fashion in a notebook set up just for this purpose gives you a record of what you have done. This can be revisited a week later when you have forgotten the answer you obtained, or a year later when a similar effect comes along that can be driven with the same design machine.

In some ways this process is analogous to hand sketching or drafting. It works well, but there are flaws. The notebook page is worthless for double checking work

Torque due to load (conservative):

7.1 ft	x	2129 lb x cosθ	7 =	Torque	15003.24 ftlb
7.1 ft	x	2129 lb x cosθ	12 =	Torque	14785.63 ftlb
7.1 ft	x	2129 lb x cosθ	17 =	Torque	14455.5 ftlb
7.1 ft	x	2129 lb x cosθ	22 =	Torque	14015.38 ftlb
7.1 ft	x	2129 lb x cosθ	27 =	Torque	13468.6 ftlb
7.1 ft	x	2129 lb x cosθ	32 =	Torque	12819.34 ftlb
7.1 ft	x	2129 lb x cosθ	37 =	Torque	12072.53 ftlb
7.1 ft	x	2129 lb x cosθ	42 =	Torque	11233.85 ftlb
7.1 ft	x	2129 lb x cosθ	47 =	Torque	10309.69 ftlb
7.1 ft	x	2129 lb x cosθ	52 =	Torque	9307.074 ftlb

Must be countered by cylinder pushing at 1.75' from arm pivot:

r arm	T load	θ	F cyl	Height of lift:		
1.75	15003.24	-45	12123.75	7.1 x 2 x sinθ	7	1.730418
1.75	14785.63	-35	10313.92	7.1 x 2 x sinθ	12	2.952132
1.75	14455.5	-25	9114.083	7.1 x 2 x sinθ	17	4.151381
1.75	14015.38	-15	8291.264	7.1 x 2 x sinθ	22	5.319041
1.75	13468.6	-5	7725.739	7.1 x 2 x sinθ	27	6.446226
1.75	12819.34	5	7353.314	7.1 x 2 x sinθ	32	7.524358
1.75	12072.53	15	7141.906	7.1 x 2 x sinθ	37	8.545234
1.75	11233.85	25	7082.854	7.1 x 2 x sinθ	42	9.501085
1.75	10309.69	35	7191.661	7.1 x 2 x sinθ	47	10.38464
1.75	9307.074	45	7520.816	7.1 x 2 x sinθ	52	11.18917

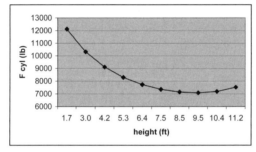

Figure 27.1   Excel spreadsheet calculating hydraulic cylinder force on a scissor lift

or for reviewing later if you have not written enough comments to make what you did intelligible, it is not a very fast process to run through calculations if there are many to do, and errors can enter the work in many locations.

Spreadsheet software is one possible solution to some of these issues. Spreadsheet programs are everywhere, and nearly everyone knows how to use them. A spreadsheet can be written to perform frequently done calculations, to determine winch reduction ratios and drum shaft torques for instance, or repetitive tasks such as graphing the force needed from a cylinder as a load is lifted on a scissor lift (Figure 27.1). The lift example, the specifics of which are unimportant to the context of the discussion here, shows a perfectly intelligible graph of cylinder force versus lift height, but the calculations, despite being annotated to some extent, are confusing at best (I assume they seemed clear when first done). This points out the major spreadsheet disadvantage. The formulas which set what a cell displays are hidden, and so the mathematics involved is simply not shown. When you do look at the formulas (provided you are looking at the spreadsheet on a computer, if you have a paper printout you are out of luck), they are not in standard mathematical form, but rather in a cryptic notation that obscures rather than clarifies. No one can glance at something like this and instantly know what it is doing:

=SQRT(B9^2+B10^2-2*B9*B10*COS(RADIANS(180-D19-B12)))

Variables are represented by cell numbers rather than variable names, and the coverage of functions delimited by parenthesis, such as the SQRT, is less clear than that of standard mathematical notation. The formula above is in fact just the law of cosines:

$$c = \sqrt{a^2 + b^2 - 2ab\cos\theta}$$

but it is hard to see that easily. Because of this, formula errors are difficult to notice, and at least one of the spreadsheet's results should be checked by hand to confirm that it is correct.

There are other mathematical software programs that eliminate some of these disadvantages, but of course they bring along their own issues. For instance Mathcad, a product of Parametric Technology Corp., allows formulas to be typed in standard notation with variable names of your choice, and the formulas are active, providing instant results on the screen (see Figure 27.2). The disadvantages though are exactly the opposite of spreadsheet advantages: the program is not common, relatively few know how to use it, and it is not inexpensive.

CIRCLE, axis at its center

$n := 500$ number of rings

$r := 1, 2 .. 1000$

$d(r) := (2 \cdot r) - 1$ number of areas per ring, 1,3,5,7,9...

$p := \sum_{r=1}^{n} [(r - .5) \cdot d(r)]$ sum of the lengths of all the radii

$q := \sum_{r=1}^{n} d(r)$ sum of the number of radii

$q = 2.5 \times 10^5$

$\dfrac{\left(\dfrac{p}{q}\right)}{(n - .5)} = 0.667$ average length of radii / o.d. = average radii in %
(a web search said average is 2/3, so this agrees)

Figure 27.2   Screenshot example of Mathcad (calculating the average radius of a circle, used for the average caster distance in torque due to friction calculations.)

Failure Modes and Effects Analysis, FMEA

Any component in a machine can fail, and the consequences of those potential failures should always be carefully considered. This is all the more true when the application is inherently more hazardous. The part failures of interest here are mainly those that would prevent an effect from stopping during a normal or emergency situation, or that would release a load, letting it freely run or fall. A motor that fails to run will ruin a cue, but a wagon that fails to stop could create a serious injury.

One standard technique used to search for possible failures of this type is called failure modes and effects analysis, or FMEA. In concept it is quite simple. For each individual part in the machine consider four things:

- how it might fail,
- what could have caused that failure,
- what effect that failure would have on safety, and finally, if necessary,
- how that failure mode could be eliminated, rendered sufficiently improbable, or mitigated.

What results, whether hand written or done in a spreadsheet format, would be something similar to the excerpt shown below:

FMEA	Portal Winch			12/2/2006
Part:	**Failure Mode:**	**Cause of Failure:**	**Effect of Failure:**	**How should this be dealt with?:**
Drum shaft pillow block	PB frame cracks	impact overload, shock overload	one side of drum free to move around, drive chain falls off	conservative design factor, replace after any significant overload event. Use flange block instead and use mounting plate to capture shaft
		manufacturer defect	"	choose reputable manufacturer
		uneven mounting surface	"	note on shop drawings to check for flatness
		hold down bolts too tight	"	training, torque spec?
	set screws loosen or fall out	did not check tightening torque	If only on one side none, if both screws loosen, drum shifts, drive chain falls off	training, periodic maintenance check, shaft locking collars either side of one block for redundancy
		vibration	"	check for and remove source of vibration, Loctite on setscrew?
	bearing fails	long term wear	noise, increased friction, in worst case same as set screw loss	maintenance, training of operators to bring nosie to attention
		manufacturer defect	"	choose reputable manufacturer
		shock overload	"	conservative design factor, replace after any significant overload event.
		lubrication failure	"	maintenance

The benefit of FMEA is that it places a rigorous and methodical structure on the analysis of failure and its consequences, since it forces you to consider these four issues for each and every part in a system. Since many potential improvements in a machine's design are often identified by this process, FMEA in general industry is often done several times throughout the design process. Unfortunately, a thorough FMEA process takes considerable time, which is at odds with typically rapid pace of theatre production, and so it is generally done only when required as part of the contracts commercial scene shops sign for theme park attraction work.

Finally, please indulge a brief editorial comment. This is one of those instances where it is ethically difficult to justify why we in theatre do not do something, just for the lack of time. If we do not have the time to do something right, then perhaps we should not do it at all. I anticipate FMEA in some form will become more common in theatre in the future.

Parts and Materials List

Since the majority of the machine components we use are manufactured by others, a large portion of mechanical design is selecting a specific part from a wide array of choices, and specifying it with the correct part number. Ordering the correct parts in the correct quantities in time for delivery when they are needed in the shop is not anything new to any theatre technician, but machines often involve many parts, some of which will probably have 15 or 20 character part numbers, and this makes a seemingly straightforward task surprisingly time consuming and difficult.

- Part numbers are not like words or sentences. Spelling or grammatical errors are not obvious. A KA47BDT90L4BM(G) is a SEW Eurodrive gearmotor with a completely different mounting style than a KA47DT90L4BM(G), but the difference between these two numbers are not obvious at a glance. Careful double checking of part numbers is critical.

- Salespeople can be great, or not. Early in my career I believed a saleman when he said that there was no difference that would affect us between a NEMA 184C and 184TC frame motor. He was wrong, the shafts are different sizes, and so the ordered motor would not fit the mating reducer. The moral here is that you need to be sure of your facts as others might not be.

- Hydraulic fittings, in my opinion, win the award for most confusing parts to select. Given the variations of size, different styles of threading, different types of adapters available (and maddeningly, those not available), there are literally thousands of fittings available, with just about all but one of those choices wrong for a given location in a system. It may take 4 hours to determine what fittings are needed just to connect 4 of 5 hydraulic components together. It has taken 40 hours of work just to select the fittings needed to assemble a dozen components together. Therefore leave open plenty of time for this process.

Drafting

Drafting machine parts and assemblies by hand is long dead. Using a pencil to sketch concepts on paper is still very useful for its speed and looseness, but beyond that all drawing should be done on the computer. The long standing conventions of drafting, or how information about three-dimensional parts is communicated via lines on a two-dimensional piece of paper, are still very much in play.

Two-dimensional versus Three-dimensional Drafting

Every time drawings for a machine are started, a question should arise about whether all the drafting should be done in conventional two-dimensional ortho-graphic views, or in a single three-dimensional model. Certainly one's abilities to draft one way or the other, and personal opinion will sway any given individual on this issue. I will only offer here some of my opinions.

- Mistakes or omissions can too easily occur in the three separate views—front, top, side—of a conventional 2D orthographic projection. In a 3D model, you cannot do the different views wrong, as there is only one model, so every view of it is true.

- The visualization of the machine obtained from a 3D model is generally superior to that from orthographic projections. The CAD software may allow hidden line removal, solids shading, or a dynamic view (the AutoCAD® orbit command), that enables a sense of real depth, or an ability to glance around an obstruction.
- Both of the above become all the more convincing as the complexity or compactness of the device being drawn increases. A single simple winch can be drawn easily and quickly in 2D, three winches fit within the confines of a custom piece of aluminum truss would best be done in 3D.
- If curved or non-rectangular components are involved, 3D is probably the better choice. Machine framing components themselves are rarely curved, but the machine may have to fit within and run round lifts, or a curved wall. At the extreme, a completely asymmetrical scenery and machinery combination, such as Pride Rock in *The Lion King* on Broadway, simply makes no sense in an orthographic projection. Pieces like that must be drawn in 3D.

It is possible that the 2D versus 3D debate is nearly moot as software evolves to make 3D drafting easier, and as more users learn 3D.

Dimensions and Tolerances

Construction drawings for scenery usually list dimensions in fractions to the 1/8″ or 1/16″. (The metric system would be so much easier to work with, but that battle is lost here in the U.S. for the time being.) These dimensions will generally work when detailing machine framing, but they are too coarse where machining is involved. Drums and their shafts are the two most common machine parts that are fabricated in a machine shop, but deck track sheave assemblies and dogs, and leaf chain end fittings are other possibilities. If this capability is in-house, then the machinist will be familiar with the typical tolerances and allowable surface finishes for their work. Outside machine shops cannot be expected to know what is acceptable for theatre, and so will often assume an unnecessarily expensive level of precision unless told otherwise. Somewhere on each drawing sent to an outside shop could be a key to a variety of tolerances.

Unless otherwise noted, tolerances are denoted by the format of the dimension, as shown below:	
Typical dimension:	Tolerance:
1.0″	±0.05″
1.00″	±0.02″
1.000″	±0.005″
1 1/2″	±1/16″

28

Design for Manufacture

Overview

Machine design cannot be done without a knowledge of manufacturing processes and assembly techniques because much of the design itself is driven by the realities of construction. This would include consideration of the properties of the materials involved, their method of fabrication into basic components, and the assembly of those components into the finished machine. While on the surface this seems obvious, and certainly something everyone must be doing already, there are many less well known details of construction that if considered during design will improve resulting machine.

In general industry, the field of design for manufacture, or DFM, is vast. Every manufacturing process and material has very specific techniques used to optimize some aspect of production, with the goal being to produce the highest quality device a given cost will allow. Unfortunately most of these techniques refer to processes not generally used in theatre, molding cast iron or forging steel for instance, and to economizing mass production quantities, an idea rarely considered for the one-off type of stage equipment being discussed here. Despite this, there are still a number of very useful techniques and tricks that have been developed in industry that do have a place in the repertoire of useful knowledge for a theatre mechanical designer.

Design for manufacturing appears as the last step in the mechanical design process mainly because it deals with the practicalities of how the parts chosen in detail design will be made, and how those parts can be efficiently assembled into the finished machine. In broad strokes, concept design could conclude that a shaft in a flange block mounted to a plate is needed as part of a machine. In detail design those parts might become a 1-1/2″ C1018 shaft in a Browning VF4S-224 bearing bolted to a 1/4″ steel plate. DFM might add that the bolt holes for the bearing should be 1/32″ oversized for easy hardware assembly, the bolts are 1-1/2″ × 1/2″-13 grade 5 because they are already used elsewhere on the machine, that the keyways on the shaft would be more easily milled with 12L14 alloy cold drawn shafting, and that Bob the shop machinist is not booked with other work and can easily do this. To reinforce an earlier statement, the steps of the design process are not rigidly separated and often occur in quick succession. It is possible that all the choices

317

just described, from concept to DFM, would take no more than a few minutes. Design is a dynamic process.

The field of DFM is often broken up into two areas—design for fabrication and design for assembly—even though these areas do often overlap, and despite the differences between industry and theatre, these categories will still serve us well here also.

Design for Fabrication

Optimizing the process of making each component part of a machine from some form of raw material is the concern of design for fabrication. We in theatre use a very small range of materials and fabrication techniques compared to industry, and so it is not surprising that much of the information concerning what constitutes design for fabrication for them is of no value to us. Just consider molded plastic parts, ubiquitous in everyday products, but nearly unseen in stage machinery (such parts do appear in the few mass produced machine products there are for the theatre market, such as in the Vortek® winch systems). Even if these irrelevant topics are omitted from discussion though, there are still many things worth considering during the design of a new machine.

There are no grand overarching themes here, but instead numerous individual bits of useful information. The text that follows therefore reflects this, and takes the form of individually themed paragraphs with little interconnection from one to the next.

Design for Fabrication Issues

Available tools – Possibly more than any other factor, the tools that are available affect what a shop can fabricate. If you have a milling machine, for example, keyways can be cut into shafts, slots cut into plates, and holes placed accurately to the thousandths of an inch. So too do other tools have unique capabilities. A TIG machine will allow aluminum to be welded, a metal lathe can turn down a shaft or groove a drum, and a hydraulic punch/shear (ironworker) punches holes or cuts bar stock much faster than a drill or saw. The current ultimate scene shop metalworking tool is a water jet machine, capable of cutting steel plate (or almost any plate-like material) into any two-dimensional shape desired.

There is no profound idea here since all construction is affected by the tools that are available. During the design of each and every part, a choice will need to be made to make the part in-house, job it out to a shop that can make it, buy the tool that allows it to be made in-house, or, if none of these are acceptable, redesign the part. The skills of shop staff, and their availability to work on this are important determining factors.

Materials – From a fabrication point of view, each type of material has effective methods for cutting, drilling, welding, etc. Take steel and aluminum, for instance. The machines needed to weld these materials are different, weight differences make the ease of handling a given size machine different, considerations about whether to paint or not differ, the recommended tooth pitch for saw blades is different, etc. The softness of aluminum allows it to be cut or machined at higher speeds than steel, potentially resulting in faster part production. If joints between dissimilar materials are needed, this will require the use of fasteners or adhesives, instead of the much faster welding.

- Labor – Shop staff knowledge of particular fabrication process may impact the choice of training, skills, numbers needed, labor cost . . .

Shape of parts – a roughly square flat plate is easily produced with standard tools, and framing members cut at 90° angles are easy. Odd or compound angle cuts slow fabrication. Accurately curved parts are very time consuming to make given the tools available in a typical theatre shop.

- Make or buy decisions – this we do all the time for motors, reducers, cylinders, pillow blocks, etc. We could also buy less familiar things like linear guides, screw jacks, crane bearings, keyed shafts, telespar . . .

The specific machining choice – A punched hole is fast, a drilled hole slower, and a milled slot is painfully slow. Avoid large numbers of hand tapped holes whenever possible, because they are time consuming, and tap breakage can render a part useless, forcing you to start over.

Materials size, weight, and materials handling equipment – During fabrication, the available space will set the size of the largest piece of raw material you can maneuver around in the shop. Check access doors, corners in hallways, ducts, sprinkler pipes, etc. to determine the limiting dimensions. Of course the limits of an assembled part extends from the shop to the theatre where it will be installed, including the truck that may carry it.

- Can the part be handled easily by one person, or will it take several to move it, or a chain hoist, or a forklift? or a bridge crane?
- Does material flow logically from raw stock arriving, stock storage, fabrication, assembly, and load-out?

Quantity of similar parts – Making one of something is much different than making 1000 of the same thing, but at what point between 1 and 1000 fabrication might change from one technique to another is not a simple question. Any part made in quantity should be simplified as much as possible. In books discussing the optimization of DFM, the time it takes for a given manufacturing task is often measured to the fraction of a second. Their point is that if the total time to produce one part is shortened by a few seconds, over a production run of 100,000 that amounts to a week or two less time spent. The small production quantities done in theatre do not deserve this level of time efficiency, but any operation or part that does not absolutely need to be included should be eliminated.

Part size - All tools have capacity limitations, and as a designer you must know what those limitations are. If you have a cold saw, how big an I-beam can it cut? If you need a 1-1/2″ hole drilled in the middle of a 3 foot square 1/4″ steel plate, how are you going to do that? A drill press or milling machine's throat depth will impose limitations, and hand drilling is generally impractical at that size. Can that part be redesigned to eliminate the need for that hole? At the opposite extreme, is a part too small to be easily machined with the tools available? Also consider the relationship of parts that will be assembled together. Two parts of radically different thickness, thin sheet metal and 1/4″ steel plate for instance, would be nearly impossible to weld together.

- Part weight - Capabilities of outside contractors - Flame, plasma, water jet, and laser cutting shops can easily cut out parts in shapes nearly impossible any other way. Steel shapes can be bent into rings or arcs in roll bending shops. Cable drums can be jobbed out to a machine shop. Custom aluminum extrusions or castings can be ordered. A cost versus benefit for the parts arising out of these procedures will determine whether their use is realistic for a specific project.

Tolerances – Any machine could be made with all dimensions accurate to the thousandth of the inch, but why? High accuracy is time consuming and therefore expensive. Carefully specify tolerances to outside contractors so that they know exactly what you expect. As an example, a drawing for a winch drum not carefully listing tolerances was sent out for bids to a number of local machine shops. The resulting bids varied between $450 and $2000. The low bid came from a shop that had done some projects for theatre clients before and assumed fairly wide tolerances, whereas the highest bid was because the shop assumed tight tolerances in the absence of anything stated on the drawings.

Simplicity – In comparing two designs that perform the same function, the design with fewer parts is often the better one. A design that requires highly accurate hole or part placement is worse than one that does not.

Frame corners are points where construction can be simplified. The frame at *A* has two angled cuts on each of the three frame pieces, an attractive corner, but hard to measure and cut accurately, and time consuming to clamp and weld. At *B*, there are two easily done 90° cuts, and one coped cut. The cope could be done with a metal cutting band saw, or with a cope shear option on a hydraulic ironworker, both unusual tools for the typical regional theatre shop. Three 90° cuts and a cap plate could be specified, as at *C*, but this too would take extra time to construct due to the extra part. During design determine if all the angle irons have to be mounted corners out, or is the design at *D*, with just three simple 90° cuts, acceptable? View *E* another simple cuts alternative, but the exposed sharp corners pose a potential hazard, and so those corners could be relieved, as at *F*, by cuts or grinding.

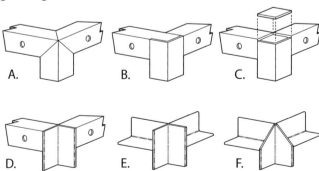

Tapped Holes - There are two major advantages of tapped holes in framing. One is that tightening a mating bolt can now be done from only one side—you do not need to have wrench access to both a nut and the bolt. This is very useful for cover plates, on any framing that will be installed against the floor or a wall, or anywhere that access to both sides of a joint will be difficult. Second, installing a nut, bolt, and possibly lock or plain washers is a two hand operation, not necessarily fast if many need to be installed and removed repeatedly, as might be common on a tour load-in and strike.

Tapping can be performed either manually with a tap wrench, which can be too slow if more than a few holes need to be tapped, or taps can be driven by hand held or stationary power tools.

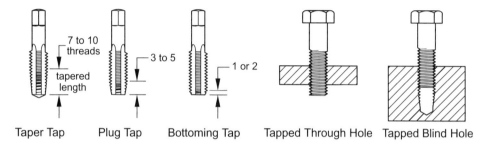

Taper Tap   Plug Tap   Bottoming Tap   Tapped Through Hole   Tapped Blind Hole

- A rule of thumb guide for the thickness of material needed for a tapped hole in a non-safety critical application is to make it the same dimension as the size of the bolt. In other words, a plate to be tapped for a 1/4″ bolt should be 1/4″ thick. Because both the tapped material and the screw fitted into the hole will deform under load, the transfer of force from tapped threads to bolts threads is not even across all the engaged threads, the first three threads carry most of the load.[1] Therefore, beyond a point, adding more threads does not make the joint significantly stronger. If the tapped plate and bolt are different materials, say a steel bolt turned into a tapped nylon block, then the radically different deformation characteristics of these two materials adds into this already difficult to analyze mix. When any joint loaded in tension is critical to safety, using a reputably manufactured graded nut and bolt is a better choice than a shop tapped hole.

- From an ease of fabrication point of view, through drilled holes are a better choice for tapping than holes drilled only part way into the material, both because a through drilled hole is easier to do than drilling to a given depth, and the chips generated during tapping clear out of a through drilled hole better.

- Taps come in three different styles: taper, plug, and bottoming. They differ in the number of starting threads that help to begin the tapping operation. Taper taps start easily, but if used in a blind hole, they leave many threads uncut, and screws will fit only part way into the hole. A bottoming tap is at the other extreme. They are difficult to start, but thread nearly to the bottom of a hole.

1. Bickford, *An Introduction to the Design and Behavior of Bolted Joints*, 24.

Plug taps are a compromise between these two. Tapping to the full depth of a blind hole is therefore a two-step process—use a taper or plug tap first, then use the bottom tap to fully cut the last few threads.

- Tapping holes is time consuming and, if a tap breaks, it may mean the part must be discarded and a new one started over. If you must tap, do that operation as early on as practical, before time is invested in other operations on that part. This is especially true for small taps, 4-40 through 8-32 for instance, that tend to break easily in hand tapping applications.

Rivet nuts and weld nuts - If a material is too thin to tap but the functions of a tapped hole are desired, then rivet or weld nuts are a possibility. A rivet nut works identically to the more familiar pop-rivet, in that it has a nut fixed into a metal sleeve that can be crimped in place with a tool specifically made for the purpose. Weld nuts come in fixed and floating styles. Since the welding process is never precise, the floating nut will accept some misalignment between the bolt and welded-on frame that holds the nut.

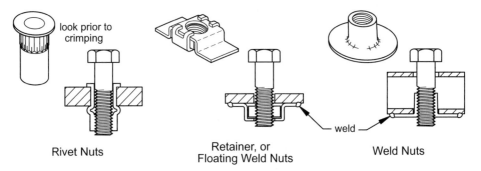

Rivet Nuts   Retainer, or   Weld Nuts
               Floating Weld Nuts

Outside Part Fabrication

The wide variety of fabrication techniques required to create stage machinery, especially for the large Las Vegas, Broadway, and theme park type shows, will eventually exceed the capabilities of even the best equipped theatre shops. In unusual cases machine components have required:

- Welded pipe fittings, liquid-tight to 3000 psi,
- The machining of one side of a 4′ square by 2″ thick steel plate to flat, ±0.01″,
- Furnace hardening of cam follower tracks,
- Rotary casting of a winch drum 4′ in diameter.

These unusual machine parts, and sometimes even more common ones, are better bid out to contract machine shops that have the tools and expertise for the job required.

CNC Cutting – Computer numerical control, or CNC, is the generic name given to a process that is run by a computer. A CNC milling machine, for instance, can either be programmed to manually run a sequence of operations—mill a slot, drill two holes, then square off an edge—or a CAD drawing can be interpreted by the mill's software to do the same thing. The latter possibility allows us to design a complete machine in CAD, and then send the drawings for the CNC parts via e-mail to a machine shop that will make them.

CAD drawings can be turned into precisely cut parts using five different processes. Cutting plate material is by far the most common and least expensive operation performed, but 5-axis machines will allow cuts in 3D (i.e. allowing something like a square hole cut into a pipe). From oldest technology to the newest:

- Flame: Using a cutting torch usually fed an oxacetylene mix, X and Y axis motors drive the torch over the plate-stock being cut. Usable on steel and some other metals in thicknesses far beyond what we would ever use in theatre (one company cuts up to 30″ thick steel stock). This technology has the coarsest cut tolerance of those listed here: roughly ±1/8″. Water jet and laser cutting have made this process obsolete in the thickness materials we would usually use.

- CNC Routers or Milling Machines: Except for the tool speed versus torque differences between routers (high speed at low torque) and mills (low speed at a high torque) both these processes are the same. Traditional cutting bits are accurately moved through aluminum, plywood, plastics, and steel by computer controlled servo motors. The finish of the cut edge will be identical to that of a manually run router or mill. This is the only technique listed here capable of creating a chamfered or shaped edge (by using shaped router bits or mills), and of accurately cutting only part way through a material, as for making letters on both sides of a sign for instance. Accuracy to the ten thousandths is possible on some machines, and with 3-, 4-, and 5-axis machines this technology can go far beyond simple cutting to allow complex three dimensional machining.

- Plasma: A plasma arc of up to 30,000° C cuts only electrically conductive metals up to 2-1/2″ thick. The technique is more accurate than flame cutting. Relatively inexpensive machines are manufactured for the home hobbyist to light industrial markets.

- Water Jet: This is THE hot new technology for stage machinery part fabrication. A stream of water and abrasives is pushed through a small nozzle at very high pressures—40,000 to 60,000 psi are typical. A water jet can cut just about anything: metal, plastics, stone, bulletproof glass, paper, fabric, etc. with no heat distortion, up to 15″ thick for easily cut material, and to accuracies of 0.001″ on thinner material. Wow! Machines are both expensive to purchase (initial costs for the smallest machines ballpark around $80,000), and to run (2/3 of the running costs are for the abrasive, which can be put through the jet nozzle only once, and is then thrown out). The most accurate cut requires a slow cutting speed, and therefore more time on the machine per piece, increasing part cost. Be sure to specify a dimensional tolerance as coarse as is acceptable for the part.

- Laser: An infrared laser beam vaporizes the materials it strikes. An extremely small kerf, on the order of 0.01, wastes little material. Cuts steel to 1″ thick, aluminum to 1/4″, plus wood, glass, rubber, etc. Very accurate, up to the ten thousandths of an inch in some cases.

Commercial shops are using these techniques more and more. Plates cut with lightening holes, equipment mounting holes, and interlocking slots and tabs for self-aligning assembly before welding are used for all sorts of framing. In the illustration of a pillow block mounting platform shown below, the parts form their own jig, with the pieces holding themselves in correct alignment for welding. The carpenters using these parts do not have to measure, cut, or drill anything, they instead just stack the pre-made parts, clamp them in place, and weld. Where shop labor rates are high, the part fabrication time saved in-house may more than pay for the cost of the outside CNC part cutting.

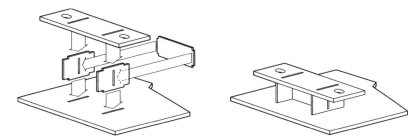

There are several key advantages this technology provides. It is very freeing during design to not have to decide which size flat bar to use for a particular part, or whether that is in stock or not. Just draw the part as you want it and it will come off the CNC machine that size (as long as it is within the limits of what the machine can produce of course). Shape is no issue either, any shape you can draw can be machined. Part C shown below is an angle bracket with two indexing tabs, a lightening hole, and rounded corners for aesthetic and safety reasons. You would not even attempt to attain those features in a conventionally made shop-built piece.

The mechanical designer does not have to produce dimensioned shop drawings for the parts being fabricated on the CNC machine, or for the carpenters assembling the parts in the shop. Instead the CNC shops generally need only the full size two-dimensional outline of each part in closed polylines (using the jargon of AutoCAD) with notes on materials, quantity of each part needed, and some identifying part letter or number. Since properly designed parts will fit together in a logical way and hold themselves in alignment with minimal clamping, the shop staff welding these parts together should be able to work quickly and with few errors from just a few printed views of the CAD model. Since slots, tabs, and holes are all pre-cut, dimensioned drawings are not usually needed.

A
MAKE: 4

B
MAKE: 8

C
MAKE: 25

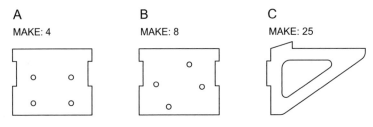

MATERIAL: 1/4" STEEL HRP&O

Bending – I-beams, channel, angle, or any other structural shape can be bent in very precsiely round radii by certain steel fabrication shops. Many commercial theatre shops own machines that can bend pipe and tube up to perhaps 4″, but for bigger sizes even they must outsource. When sending out a bending job, be sure to include a drawing—word descriptions can be too ambiguous. Specify a tolerance too, such as radius = 11′-2″ ±1/4″, as this will allow you to ask for the bends to be changed or redone if they do not meet the tolerance.±1/4″, as this will allow you to ask for the bends to be changed or redone if they do not meet the tolerance.

Extrusion – Aluminum extrusions can be manufactured to custom shapes at costs that are acceptable for some applications. There is a one-time die fabrication charge which will depend on the size and intricacy of the shape desired, and an extrusion charge which is based largely on the amount of aluminum used. Requirements for minimum runs are common too. The cost for all of this will run into the several thousands of dollars. Several scene shops have had extrusions made for them for framing stock speed-deck platforms, for a custom traveler track, and for linear guide rails for a zero-fleet winch design.

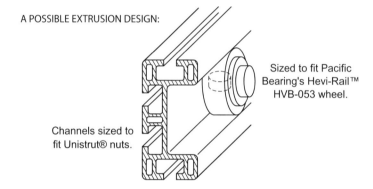

A POSSIBLE EXTRUSION DESIGN:

Sized to fit Pacific Bearing's Hevi-Rail™ HVB-053 wheel.

Channels sized to fit Unistrut® nuts.

Design for Assembly

Design for assembly, or DFA, is concerned with optimizing a machine's design in relation to how it will be assembled. For instance, can a heavy gearmotor be placed easily into its frame in one smooth motion, or does it have to be awkwardly snaked around framing to get it in place (or worse yet, it does not fit at all). Once in place, is installing the motor's mounting hardware easy or maddeningly difficult because of poor sightlines, tight access, and non-existent wrench clearance. As part of the design technique involving role playing, picture in your mind the steps needed if you were assembling the machine. Is there an order of assembly forced by the configuration of parts? How in the design could you minimize the number of tools needed for assembly? Always picture in your mind as you design the steps needed if you were to assemble the machine. Below are some suggestions relative to key DFA issues.

Sightlines – Just as the set designer should take into account audience sightlines in their designs, mechanical designers should insure that fastener holes are clearly visible for ease of assembly and maintenance. Three-dimensional CAD models rotated around on the screen will show you whether sightlines are good or not.

Standardize Hardware – Use as few different sizes and types of hardware as possible. Never mix Phillips and slotted screws, American and metric sizes, or bolt grades within the same sizes. If grade rated hardware is necessary somewhere, consider using that grade hardware everywhere. While this increases the cost of hardware for the whole machine, it reduces the chance of error during assembly.

Hardware callout on assembly drawings – If any specific hardware will be needed during assembly, notate it clearly on the shop drawings. For example, fully threaded bolts for those used as part of a chain tensioning adjustment mechanism, or grade 8 bolts to bolt down a flange block. The blind tapped mounting holes of reducers made by European companies, such as SEW-Eurodrive or Nord, are only available in metric sizes. Call these out clearly on the drawings so that someone does not jam in the closest U.S. size bolt thinking it's just a bit tight (... as has happened ...).

Wrench Clearance - Framing, and the placement of machine components, should not block tool or hand access to any threaded fasteners. This is a very important aspect of machine design, and too often ignored.

If a machine is being designed so that in use it sits on the floor or up against a wall, consider those surfaces in terms of wrench clearance during design (see illustration below). It is best if at least one end of each bolt and nut

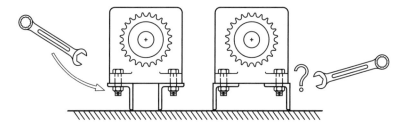

assembly is accessible with a socket wrench. Few things are more boring that using two open-end wrenches to undo a bolt and nylock nut. Also work to allow ample swing to the wrench. We have all cursed designs where access is so poor that a wrench can only be turned a fraction of a turn before it must be flipped over and then turned another fraction. During design, get a wrench or socket and measure it if you have doubts about fit, or draw up in CAD a block of different hex-key, socket, and open-end wrench sizes during a lull in your design work. It can be very useful to apply a virtual wrench to virtual hardware on your virtual machine design.

Wrench access should also be considered when selecting machine components too. The housings of gear reducers, mounting brackets for hydraulic cylinders, electrical disconnect switches, and other equipment may have very poorly designed access for the fasteners and tools needed to mount them onto support framing. You may not reject the use of a component solely on this issue, but your design of access to hardware on the framing side of the connection should be very clear to compensate for the part's poor clearance.

Beyond wrench clearance, human hands must place bolts, nuts, and washers. Machines must be designed so that there is enough room to make this possible. For example, assume that a thick block of plastic is being designed to bolt onto some framing, and that the bolt heads need to be recessed. A relatively long bolt can be easily placed into a shallow hole, but a shorter bolt cannot:

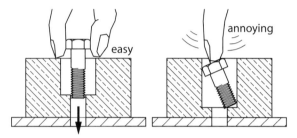

Oversize Holes – Typically holes for bolts should be at least 1/32″ oversized for easy fit and some misalliance tolerance. All holes should be chamfered on both sides with a countersink to eliminate burrs, and ease the edges for easier hardware insertion. Removing the burrs also eliminates a source of annoyance cuts on fingers placing hardware.

Nut Locking Techniques – Machines must tolerate the vibrations that will occur during transport and use. Every nut and bolt is susceptible to being loosened by vibration, and this must be prevented. Of all the techniques developed to prevent loosening, a four are common in theatre:

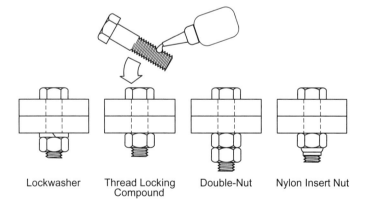

Lockwasher   Thread Locking   Double-Nut   Nylon Insert Nut
                 Compound

- **Split lock washers** – Barbs formed by an angled slice across a spring steel washer dig into both the nut and the mating workpiece, which resists nut loosening. The lock washer should be matched in hardness to the nut, else it will not dig in and hold it. The prime advantage of these washers is that the nut is free to spin down a long length of threads, if needed, and then a wrench is only necessary for tightening at the end. The main disadvantage is simply that they are an extra piece of hardware that must be put in place before the nut is threaded on, an occasionally awkward two-hand process.

- **Thread locking compounds** – Commonly referred to with the trade name Loctite®, these are basically anaerobic adhesives that cure only when both certain metals are present and air is absent. Available in liquid form, and now also in a semi-solid stick, a small amount is placed on the bolt threads where the nut will rest, and after assembly and a cure time, the nut is locked in place. There are over a dozen forms covering various bolt size ranges, threadlocking strengths, different metals, temperatures, and oil resistance. In a theatre shop, one or two general purpose types will cover the range of what is usually needed.

  Anaerobic thread locking compounds will not work on plastic hardware, they even attack some plastics causing them to fracture, so use more conventional adhesives if this hardware needs to be secured.

- **Double nuts** – A simple technique to hold nuts in place is to use two, jamming them against each other. Thin nuts, called jam nuts, are made just for this purpose, but surprisingly there is no consensus on which side of the conventional nut the thin nut should be used. Finding wrenches thin enough to enable the two nuts to be tightened is a common problem.

- **Nylon insert lock nut** – Usually called "nylocks," these nuts have a nylon ring retained onto the back side of a conventional nut. As they are installed, the bolt forms threads into the nylon which, because of the friction involved, holds the nut in place. Since the friction resists nut movement whenever the nylon is in contact with the threads, nylocks are a poor choice if they need to be run down a long length of threads before they tighten. Also, if there is any potential for a Nylok connection to get hot (above 120°F by some manufacturer's specs), it cannot be relied on to hold the nut in place. Nuts and lockwashers, or the use of a thread locking liquid, Loctite® for instance, will work better in both these cases.

Regardless of the locking technique used, it can be useful to run a paint marker line from the end of the bolt, across its threads, the nut, and out onto the attached workpiece to provide a visual indicator of whether the nut or bolt has changed position or not. If the line no longer lines up, something has shifted and the connection should be checked.

Part Symmetry – If there are multiple identical parts that will be assembled together (as for sheave assemblies for instance) they should be designed as, in order of best to worst:

- perfectly symmetric - so that no thought has to go into part orientation during assembly, and no errors in orientation are possible.
- obviously asymmetric - the parts clearly work only one way, and they are therefore easy for someone to assemble correctly.
- subtlety asymmetric - confusing to assemble unless clearly marked. An example would be a 6″ square plate with a center hole intentionally just 1/16″ off center.

Part Labeling can greatly aid correct assembly, both during initial assembly and later during load-in. A paint pen will mark steel in a durable and easily seen way, or stencils can be cut and pieces marked with spray paint. Color coding can be used to indicate paired mating points of parts to be assembled together with bolts. CNC machined parts can have letters or numbers cut into them during the cutting process, and these indelible marks will not be easily missed. Even just a simple V-shaped notch placed somewhere on a piece, which is then also clearly denoted on a drawing of the piece in its assembly, will keep confusion to a minimum.

Part Reorientation – The design of a machine should minimize the number of times it needs to be moved or rotated as it is being assembled. On a production line, the two seconds it might take for each flip of a small assembly could accumulate to an hour or two in a week, enough time over a year-long production run to make it worth considering how to eliminate those moves. In theatre, the typically infrequent assembly of one unique machine will not usually justify any time spent during design to save a few seconds during assembly. However, if an assembly is beyond what a single person can safely and comfortably move, then even in theatre it is worth considering the design in light of minimizing these moves during assembly.

Roller chain sprockets are available in three main mounting configurations: fixed bore with a setscrew on the key, taper-lock bushing with setscrews on the side, and QD (or Browning's very similar proprietary design) with hex bolts on the side. These use shaft space very differently both during and after assembly. A forth mounting style uses a keyless bushing (frequently known as a Trantorque® bushing from Fenner Drives, though other companies make similar products). Do not blindly put just any sprocket block into a drafting without a thought concerning wrench access.

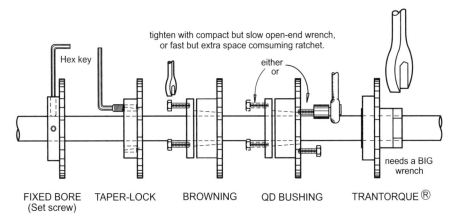

tighten with compact but slow open-end wrench, or fast but extra space comsuming ratchet.

Hex key

either or

needs a BIG wrench

FIXED BORE   TAPER-LOCK   BROWNING   QD BUSHING   TRANTORQUE ®
(Set screw)

Dimensioned Assembly Drawings – When draftings are being produced, don't forget dimensioned assembly information. Placement of a drum, sprockets, and pillow blocks on a shaft, for instance, would be set in the design of a winch, but that information is all too often not dimensioned on any drawing, as it's not seen as something that is fabricated. The assembly portion of construction is just as important as part fabrication.

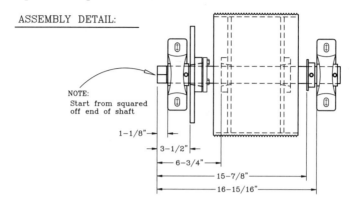

ASSEMBLY DETAIL:

NOTE:
Start from squared
off end of shaft

Welds – Notes on shop drawings should include where welds should be placed, and perhaps more importantly, where they should not be placed. This could take the form of standard welding notation, though this may require some training of shop staff, or simple obvious notes indicating "Don't weld on this face." Be especially aware of weld locations that will interfere with parts that bolt on later.

Assembly at Load-in – Theatre has that final assembly time called load-in. Usually time is at a premium then so machines should be designed to load in extremely easily. This is often best accomplished by making the machinery a complete stand alone module that needs little more than the floor to support it. If, on the other hand, lots of separate parts have to be attached to the building before being interconnected, then trial setup and running probably did not occur in the shop. What benefit is there to a machine design that both takes longer to load in, and it has never been tested?

Think (for those of you old enough to remember this ancient analog technology) of the difference between loading a tape onto a reel-to-reel tape deck, and loading a cassette. Make all your machines the equivalent of a cassette, so they can just pop into place.

Conclusion

Theatre mechanical designers have usually worked extensively in shops and onstage and know intimately the practical issues involved in the construction and use of scenery, rigging, and at least some machinery, and this is much to their benefit. The capabilities of a theatre shop, both in terms of equipment and personnel, and the demands posed by loading-in, teching, and running a show should never leave a mechanical designer's mind. But during the final stages of the design process, the drafting of construction drawings, and manufacturing issues such as those presented here should be at the forefront.

Part IV: A Compendium of Stage Machinery

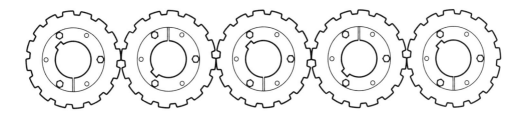

The final chapters of this book are intended to be a source of ideas for mechanical designers seeking inspiration about machines useful for some of the more common scenery movements: turntables, lifts, and deck tracked effects. Nothing contained here is new or innovative, but since, as far as I am aware, nothing like this has been published before, it should prove a useful record of existing designs and techniques.

The illustrations are intended to represent the majority of the information presented here. They are generally drawn as representing real components rather than as schematic symbols, a choice you may or may not agree with. This allows them to be both understood at a glance, and, unfortunately, to mislead into implying that one specific set of parts must be used, when combinations of others may work as well or better. Always attempt to draw the concept from the images, not just the literal version of what is shown.

As has been true for so many of the topics covered in this book, this section could be much larger. There are a number of stage machine types that unfortunately, due to lack of space, will not be covered other than a brief mention: turtles (units that both follow a deck track and spin), telescoping lifts, automating counterweight linesets, and traveler track for instance.

29

A Compendium of Stage Machinery

Overview

One important aspect of the early stages of the mechanical design of any new machine is to gather together and study the designs of machines that have already been built to solve a problem similar to the one at hand. No company would proceed with a new product, say a can opener, without buying, using, evaluating, and then disassembling every can opener they could find on the market. The information obtained from this exercise would provide an invaluable snapshot of the state of the art of can opening, and this, in conjunction with patent searches and a review of all published literature, would create the base upon which an informed design effort could begin.

Unfortunately, when it comes to stage machinery, there is little to research, and this is especially true of the type of machines that are the topic of this book—those that are specifically designed for a unique effect in a given production, or for a common generic but temporary use, such as a deck winch or turntable drive. Many machines of these types are designed and used every year, but their designs are ephemeral, lasting only the run of one production after which they are disassembled back down to their components so that they may be reused in some future project. Given the pace of theatre production, the design sketches and construction drawings created during the design of these effects are often never cataloged and archived for easy research even within the producing organization, let alone making them available to a wider audience. Books containing any material on stage machinery are few, and they are scattered across both time and a variety of languages, which makes it nearly impossible for the average technician to assemble a collection. (An annotated bibliography does appear just after the final chapter.) It is in this context that this compendium has been assembled.

The illustrations range from schematic concept sketches to complete draftings, from depictions of small elements of a much larger machine to that machine itself. None of these are intended as construction drawings, and few dimensions are given. The goal here is to inject ideas into the design process, not to circumvent it.

Technical theatre has never developed a generally accepted language associated with the drawings that are produced as a project evolves from the first ideas to construction draftings. This is probably because technical designs are very rarely developed or formally evaluated by a team, but instead are the product of one person working alone. This is being said here because the illustrations that follow vary widely in what they are meant to convey, and so in order to avoid confusion two terms need to be defined.

- **Concept sketches** can range from napkin doodles to fully detailed work in CAD, but in all cases the goal is to investigate some aspect of an idea to see if it merits further work. This statement is admittedly vague, but concept sketches cover essentially every drawing made for a project from when a pencil is first put to paper (which even in this age of CAD is still essential early on) until construction drawings are begun. Concept sketches are to concept design what mathematical calculations are to detail design. A good concept sketch should provide proof of the success or failure of an idea to meet the needs of the effect just as convincingly as a formula states whether a given beam will hold a given load.

- A **configuration concept** is a specific type of concept sketch that is used to show the layout of the major components of a machine, and it can vary from a block diagram to detailed draftings of the parts involved, but in all cases the goal is to show the relative spacial relationships between parts. For example, the mechanical power transmission path of a typical cable drum winch will run from brake-motor, to a gear reducer, possibly through a roller chain reduction stage, and on out to a drum. These four parts can be arranged or configured in a number of ways, with one configuration often being best for a particular application.

The small size of these drawings prevents a presentation of all the details involved in a particular machine, but as was stated above and worth repeating for emphasis, the intent of these illustrations is not to give you construction draftings, but simply to provide ideas that can expedite the development of the machine you are designing.

A disclaimer is in order here too. The machines shown on the following pages are intended to be used for the ideas they represent, but none of them should be used without thought for a specific purpose. Mechanized stage effects are potentially hazardous, and it is the primary responsibility of the mechanical designer to insure that each effect is given rigorous attention to eliminate or minimize those hazards.

All of the following chapters are in the same format. After a brief introductory overview, there will be four sections: Typical Application, Design Concepts, Machine Details, and Specification Issues.

Machine Details Common to Many Machines

Sprocket Capturing:

There are a number of components—chain sprockets, shaft couplings, and toothed belt sheaves for instance—that must be locked to a shaft both to transmit torque and to stay aligned with a mating component. A key fitted into a keyway on the shaft and sprocket held in place with a set screw is the common way this is accomplished, but it is surprising how poorly this works in the typical theatre environment. Vibration during transport, load-in, and use, combined with scenic moves

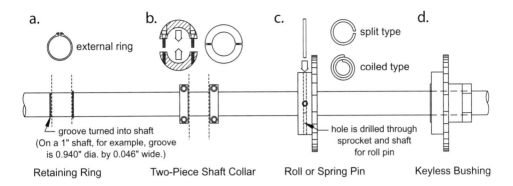

Figure 29.1   Four techniques to lock components in place along a shaft

that alternate forward then reverse, and keys typically not as precisely fitted as they could be all enable setscrew loosening. After this happens keys can fall out, sprockets can shift off the ends of shafts, belts jump off their sheaves, or shaft couplings uncouple—all very bad options. To reduce the likelihood of any of this happening, a few simple techniques can be used to keep keys and their mating components in place.

- Keyways can be milled into a shaft only where they are needed—at sprockets, drum hubs, or shaft couplings, for instance. A key is then captured in this defined position and cannot shift side-to-side. (This alone does nothing to hold the associated sprocket or sheave in place.)

- Shafts can be turned with a shallow groove to accept snap rings that confine a sprocket's hub to one location (Figure 29.1a). Making these grooves requires a metal lathe, or sending the shaft out to a machine shop that can do it for you. Obviously there is no flexibility in component placement once these grooves have been cut, therefore this is an approach worth doing only when the design is absolutely certain.

- Shaft collars can be installed on either side of a sprocket (Figure 29.1b). These collars will capture the key too, allowing the use of a shaft with one continuous keyway slot. Set screw shaft collars will work, but they mar the shaft with a dimple where the screw bites into it. A better though slightly more expensive choice is a two piece clamp-on collar. It has two parts, so it can be put onto a shaft even after a sprocket has been put in place, and the two screws simply clamp the collar sections together around the shaft, eliminating any damage to the shaft.

- Each component and the shaft can be drilled for a pin that locks both components securely together (Figure 29.1c).

- If there are multiple components on one shaft, as in the pillow blocks, drum, and drive and limit sprockets on a typical deck winch drum shaft, spacers can be made from pipe or tubing to be used between parts. Snap rings or shaft collars would be needed, in this case, only on the outboard side of each pillow block.

- Keyless bushings (a Fenner Drives® Trantorque® for example) work by gripping the shaft and component so tightly that no key is needed. Given this behavior, they eliminate the need for any of these techniques. They simply do not move (Figure 29.1d). Unfortunately these bushings are considerably more expensive than a few shaft collars.

Chain Installation and Tensioning:

All machines that use roller chain need to be designed to enable the installation and tensioning of these drives. A loop of roller chain, ideally made up without offset links, can be assembled to any size, but only in increments of two chain pitches. At least one of the sprockets that this loop goes around will need to adjust to tension of this setup, and so the mechanical design must allow for this. The ideal move-

Pillow block movement for tensioning adjustment:

Best   ⟵⟶   Useless

ment is for the adjusting shaft to move directly towards or away from the other shaft. Motion at angles of perhaps up to 45° off the ideal are acceptable, but adjustability in a direction perpendicular to the line formed by the two shaft centers is basically worthless. The geometry of that situation requires too much movement to take up even modest amounts of slack.

    To make chain tensioning an easy one person task, something is needed to hold the pillow of flange blocks in place while their bolts are being tightened. The addition of a T-slot nut welded to the bearing support framing allows a bolt to perform this function. T-slot nuts, designed for use with hold-down bolts on milling machines, have their tapped holes located high enough that the tensioning bolt head has clearance to spin. In place of the nut, a small plate could be cut, drilled, and tapped, but the labor cost for this would likely far exceed the cost of the nut.

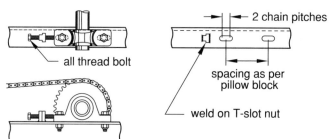

all thread bolt   2 chain pitches

spacing as per
pillow block

weld on T-slot nut

Backup Needs and Techniques

Any technique to move scenery can fail, and this is true across the full spectrum of technology from a push stick, to a fly system line set, to a servo motor drive. A failure doesn't have to mean a broken component, a failure can be caused by any of a number of causes: a batten snagging on lighting cables, a deck track dog jamming on a bolt dropped into its track, a power cord inadvertently kicked out of its outlet, or an operator error. The question here then is not will a failure occur, but rather what plans can be made to deal with a failure should it occur, what qualifications should run crew have attained to evaluate failures, and what form of backup, if any, is needed for this effect?

Some effects are not show stoppers if they should fail, say a motor driven snow drum, while if a center stage lift fails while down, it is doubtful that the show could continue with a gaping hole in the stage. Each effect will need to be assessed individually as to whether a backup technique is needed, whether one is possible, and what and where it is.

- Can a place to connect a handcrank be worked into the design of the machine's power transmission system? The traditional deck winch has a pull-pin device to disconnect a drum from its motor, which then allows the use of a handcrank as a backup. This has been a traditional feature of stock deck winches for years.

- Is the effect too large to be run via a hand driven backup? The average stagehand working reasonably hard can develop perhaps 1/3 HP from a hand crank. Is this power sufficient to clear the stage in an acceptable amount of time?

- Some machines are inherently un-backupable. A scissor lift run with hydraulic cylinders cannot be easily moved any other way. Dead haul winches, those that support a flown load without counterweight, may be difficult to back up safely.

- If the effect is a wagon on a flat deck, can stagehands just pull the knives and push the wagon off stage? This does not allow the show to progress as if nothing has happened, but it does remove a potentially awkward obstacle from the stage.

- Large hand drills have been used as backup motors for some effects. A socket or some other sort of driver can be clamped into the drill chuck, and then this connects somewhere into the drive train when needed. A large 1/2″ drill spins faster and has more power and more stamina than any stagehand could ever have.

- If the backup technique involves equipment not part of the normal operating setup, where will it be stored? Should there, for example, be a bracket on a deck winch frame to hold the backup hand crank when it's not in use?

Manual Backups:

Pull Pin Sprocket Release Device – Both deck winches and turntable drives typically power effects that involve no lifting force. Wagons cross flat level decks, and it is the rare turntable that is on a rake. If $F_{lifting} = 0$, then it is possible to disconnect the brake-gearmotor from the rest of the drive system without any risk of the scenery running away, driven by gravity. The wagon or turntable can then be directly pushed by hand, or a handcrank can be fitted onto a winch drum or turntable drive shaft, and the unit moved in that way. The disconnecting device used on Broadway for decades is a modified version of several manufacturer's models of overload slip clutches (Dalton model OSD for instance).

In the slip clutch as made, a very heavy force spring compresses two plates sandwiched around a flat plate sprocket. A large nut is turned in to adjust the spring pressure, and hence the torque at which the sprocket will slip. For use as a drive disconnect, the spring is removed and discarded, and holes are drilled through both plates and the sprocket to accept ball-catch quick-release pins. The pins are sized so that their ability to resist shear is considerably greater than the shear force that develops due to the torque flowing through the setup when driven by the motor. Two or three pins are typically used. The layout of holes for the pins should be in some asymmetric pattern that makes aligning the sprocket and reinserting the pins an obvious process. Attempting to locate the pins in a perfectly symmetric pattern can work with very precise layout, but too often hole locations are off by a few thousandths of an inch, and only one position of the sprocket works, while others look like they will, but do not.

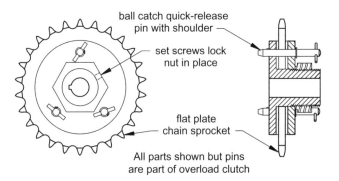

ball catch quick-release pin with shoulder

set screws lock nut in place

flat plate chain sprocket

All parts shown but pins are part of overload clutch

Hand Cranks – Human muscles have powered the movement of scenery for centuries, but this source has its limitations. A person can both actuate and control one effect quite well, but their power is quite low. A world class sprinter peaks at 1600 watts (2.1 hp) in the first few seconds after the gun, but a stagehand should not be expected to provide more than perhaps 1/4 hp.

The power developed by a spinning hand crank is no different than any other source of rotational power:

$$P = T\omega = rF\omega$$

A handcrank's power comes from hand and arm forces, F, acting at the radius from shaft to handle, r, all acting at some rotational speed, ω. There is a complex interaction between many factors that determines the potential power possible out of a given setup and individual: handle size, crank diameter, orientation of axis of rotation to the stance of the person, cranking speed, duration of the move, and the size and fitness of the person are some of the more obvious variables.

Finding scientifically quantified values for human power via handcranks is difficult—it's just not a power source that has been used in power critical applications (unlike bicycle-like pedal cranks, for which there is a large quantity of information available). One set of documented tests does provide the following information which is usable as a starting point guideline for hand crank design: a power of 150 watts (0.2 hp) can be efficiently produced by using a hand crank with a radius of 40 cm (16 in) spinning at a speed of 45 rpm, when it is mounted so that its axis of rotation is horizontal and at a height of 1 m (3 ft 3 in) off the floor.[1] Design the hand grip so both hands can fit on it comfortably, 8″ long minimum, and with a freely rotating grip surface roughly 1-1/4″ in diameter.

1. Mellerowicz, *Ergometrie*, 1962.

30

Winches

Overview

Grooved drum cable winches are the most common machines built for moving scenery. They find use everywhere on stage: moving wagons guided in deck tracks, spinning turntables (albeit not endlessly), powering counterweighted flying effects, and, with special consideration to single failure proof design, they can be made for dead hauling loads on lifts and in the flies. The benefits they offer arise mainly out of the wire rope they pull, which is relatively inexpensive, strong for its size, easily muled nearly anywhere via sheaves, requires tools for cutting and assembly that most theatres already own, and it is commonly used and well understood by many. On the other hand, wire rope is far from perfect. It stretches and twists under load more than we would all like, and it is only usable in tension, requiring loops of rope in order to pull both onstage and then off.

There are a limited number of basic parts that are used to construct virtually any cable drum winch: an electric motor, almost always with an attached brake, a gear reducer, the winch drum and its associated shaft and support bearings, and in some designs, a stage of roller chain speed reduction. Other components will often be needed within a winch frame, such as limit boxes to feed scenery position back to a control system, a motor power disconnect switch, and perhaps some form of cable tensioning mechanism. Given this short list of components, a great variety of winch designs have been created for use on stage. Winches with one sufficiently thin dimension can power a wagon from within a stage deck, or be laid out like books on a shelf to run counterweighted line sets on as narrow as 6″ centers. Long winches that are small in their width and height can fit into trusses to fly drops on touring shows, or just plain big winches can be built to dead haul a thousand pounds at high speeds.

Typical Applications

By far the two most common cable drum winch applications are to move wagons guided in deck tracks across a stage, and lifting winches used to power lifts running in the trap room or flown scenery that cannot be counterweighted. A typical deck winch has a somewhat dated, but still useful, conventional design that has been around with minor variations for at least the past 40 years.

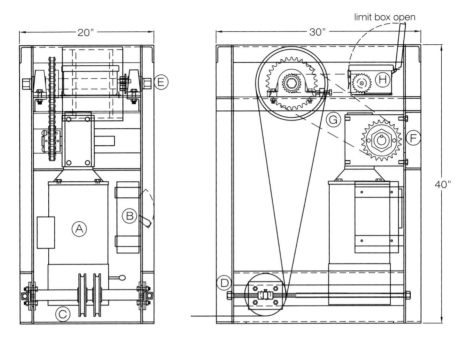

Figure 30.1   A typical deck winch

Figure 30.1 shows a generic design for the classic deck winch (guards removed for clarity). A brake-motor, **A**, couples to a c-face worm gear reducer just above it. The motor is the power source for the machine, and it is sized to deliver the force and speed the scenery being moved requires through the inefficiencies of the speed reduction stages.

$$P_{motor} \times efficiency = (\textbf{\textit{F}}_{accel} + \textbf{\textit{F}}_{frict} + \textbf{\textit{F}}_{lift}) \textbf{\textit{v}}_{max}$$

The traditional deck winch uses the relatively inefficient worm gear reducer that is shown here, and so the power available at the scenery may be 10% to 40% less than the power the motor is producing (with the exact loss being dependent on many factors, but primarily on the worm gear's ratio, and its input shaft speed). Price reductions of helical-bevel gear reducers, which often lose only 2% or 3% of the power flowing through them, have made the integrated helical-bevel gearmotor with brake a common deck winch power source today. The brake, mounted opposite to the shaft end of the motor, is used to hold the load in place when the motor is off, and plays no role in slowing down movement. A disconnect switch, **B**, allows power to be cut to the motor so that during maintenance you can be certain the winch will not power up. (NFPA Article 79, *Electrical Standard for Industrial Machinery*, gives some exceptions to this requirement, so the power connector can be the disconnect for some smaller power motors.)

The output shaft of the gear reducer drives a roller chain stage, **G**, that serves two functions. One, the use of chain allows the drum to be easily disconnected from the motor drive system to both ease cable installation during load-in, and allow for a manual backup during the run of a show. This is accomplished by the use of a pull-pin disconnect, F, that decouples the reducer output from the chain stage, and a hand crank that can be fitted on to the hex-shaped ends of the drum shaft, E. The drum is mounted in the frame at a height that makes the hand crank comfortable and ergonomically efficient to operate. With the increased reliability of all control and winch components, manual backups are not seen as absolutely essential as they once were in the past, and many newer winch designs do not include them. The second function of the chain stage is flexibility. The total reduction ratio between motor and drum can be changed relatively inexpensively by just changing a sprocket. Winches with different top speeds can be set up without having to change out the far more expensive reducer. A bonus of the chain stage is that since it reduces speed and increases torque between reducer output and drum shafts, a significantly less expensive lower output torque, yet higher efficiency, worm gear reducer can be used.

Wire rope usually runs down from the drum through sheaves in a tensioning assembly, D, and on out through a deck track to a scenic wagon. Flat plates, C, let the cable pass out close to the floor. Two acme threaded rods, one on either side of the frame, enable the whole tensioning assembly to be pulled back, taking up cable slack, and setting it to the proper tension. The two sheaves ride on a shaft sized to resist the considerable resultant bending force this cable tension provides.

In operation, the two cables running on and off the drum will track from side to side as the wagon being moved tracks across the stage. The fleet angle that consequently develops between the drum and the sheaves forces the sheaves to move sideways on the tensioner shaft. This is a technique that works, but just barely. The sheaves must have bronze bushed bearings, as other bearing types will not move sideways as reliably in response to side forces. The shaft should not rotate because each of the sheaves, which rotate in opposite directions, need to move relative to the shaft in order to experience the generally lower values of kinetic friction that are in play between the bronze bearings and shaft. A liberal coating of grease on the shaft never hurts either.

A limit box, H, is often mounted onto the winch. This provides position feedback to the control system, and ultimate limit switches that sense travel beyond some settable bounds. As shown, the limit box is driven by a roller chain stage from the drum. This preserves correct position information even if the drum is hand cranked. Other designs have used the reducer output shaft or even a motor shaft extension to run the limits.

The frame is constructed conventionally from steel angle and bar, and it encloses all the parts so that nothing protrudes beyond the planes of its shape. The frame dimensions of 20″ × 30″ × 40″ were set to values that can be easily remembered just for convenience. Access to the limit box, and wrench clearances were considered.

This conventional design has a long record of use, but many newer designs have eliminated the hand crank, the pull-pin assembly, and the chain stage, they use water-jet-cut flat-plate framing, and in some they have a zero-fleet mechanism built in to eliminate the walking sheaves. These changes can result in a smaller winch that assembles quickly and feeds cable off it from one unchanging position. In short those machines appear totally different.

Cable Drum Winch Concepts

On the following pages there are a number of configuration designs for cable drum winches. To simplify the images no framing, limit boxes or disconnects are shown. In most cases the gear reducers shown could be replaced by at least one other type without changing the basic configuration, a worm gear to helical bevel for example, and so do not take the illustrated reducers as the only choice.

Chain Drive Winch Concepts

Traditional Deck Winch

The illustration below shows the configuration of major components for a traditional deck winch. The speed reduction is comprised of a right angle worm or helical bevel reducer coupled to a roller chain stage that drives the drum. The drum is oriented over a tensioning sheave assembly that mules two cables off the drum down to the height of a typical deck track. A spring set brake on the motor shaft holds the driven loads in place whenever the winch is not running.

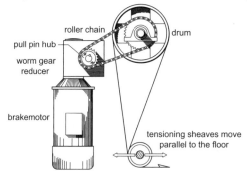

Advantages:
- Disconnecting the drum from the motor for a hand crank manual backup is easy using a pull-pin sprocket assembly on the reducer output shaft.
- This arrangement of parts puts the drum at an ergonometrically efficient height for hand cranking, and provides a space directly below the drum for sheaves that both tension the cable, and mule it to the correct height for a deck track.
- If a worm gear reducer is to be used, the chain reduction stage enables the reducer to have a more efficient lower reduction ratio, and a less expensive lower output torque rating.
- The top speed of the cable can be changed up or down (with a change in the pull force down or up respectively) by changing the ratio of the chain sprockets. This is much less expensive than the total replacement of the gear reducer which is the only recourse available in a direct drive winch.

Disadvantages:
- Many manufacturers of roller chain specifically state that it is not to be used for lifting. Therefore any winch with a roller chain stage should only be used in situ-

ations where lifting force equals zero, hence its major use pulling wagons across a level stage deck.

- This layout gets little use out of the relatively large empty space between the drum and the tensioning sheaves.
- There are more parts in this design of winch—more parts to design, to order, and to assemble—than in other designs. If no manual backup is needed, a simpler design is probably better, and a more compact winch will result.

"Mini Winch" Concept

This minor variation on the deck winch arranges the winch components more compactly, and that alone in the all too often tight confines backstage gives it a sufficient reason to be listed here as its own concept. In order to keep the package as small as possible, cable tensioning sheaves are not usually included as part of this machine, but they can be added on by designing a separate bolt-on tensioning frame. This design, in the form of the "mini winch" by Scenic Technologies, has been used over the years to automate hundreds of counterweighted line sets on Broadway.

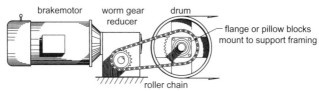

Advantages:

- The layout of parts, aligned along a line defined by the motor's shaft, is long, but compact in width and height. An application for this concept might be for a winch built into a truss to run a traveller track. For such use, 3/16″ or even 1/8″ wire rope would be acceptable, and this allows a given size drum to hold much more cable than it would if grooved for 1/4″ cable.
- The same speed changing possibilities, potential efficiencies, and cost benefits as stated for the deck winch above occur here too.

Disadvantages:

- Same as for the deck winch above regarding the roller chain stage.

Foldback Chain Drive Winch

The configuration concept shows a chain driven winch drum folded back over the motor and reducer. A long, small diameter drum is shown as an option, but this is not required.

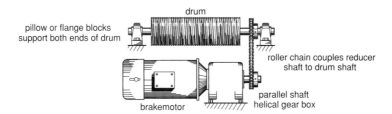

Advantages:

- The helical reducer delivers motor power efficiently to the load.
- Brake gearmotors in this configuration, are often much less expensive than other configurations.
- Same speed changing possibilities as was listed for the deck winch above.

Disadvantages:

- Same as for the deck winch above.

Direct Drive Winch Concepts

The term direct drive here refers to the gear reducer coupling directly to the drum shaft, with no intervening roller chain stage, usually by using a hollow output shaft.

Winches following these concepts are often used as the starting point for the design of dead haul, or lifting winches, an application that is potentially amongst the most hazardous for stage machinery. Conservative design factors are used throughout, relatively high gear reducer service factors are used, there are redundant brakes, sometimes purely mechanical overspeed brakes, and the control systems for the motor and brakes must be designed with the lifting application in mind. This book does not provide you with all the information needed to design a lifting winch and control system. Do so only under the guidance of someone qualified for that work.

Foldback Direct Drive Winch

This winch design relies on a gear reducer with sufficient input to output shaft distance to allow the drum to fold back next to the motor. The reducer's hollow output shaft allows a simple strong direct coupling of the gear box to the drum shaft.

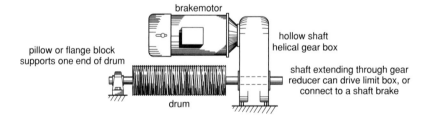

Advantages:

- This design, with the addition of a secondary brake on the drum shaft, can be made acceptable for lifting applications.
- This is a low part count concept, which should lead to a more rapid design and assembly.
- The efficiency of the helical reducer delivers more motor power to the load.

Disadvantages:

- Stock reducers of this type too often have input to output shaft distances that severely restrict the diameter of the drum. For example, if the minimum recommended D/d for 7×19 aircraft cable of 26 is used, a 3/16″ cable would need a drum 4-7/8″ diameter, and gearmotors accommodating this small a diameter drum are available. Many types of servo motors are considerably smaller in diameter than general purpose 3-phase AC motors, and their use allows more space for the drum, but at a considerably higher cost for the motor. This design can also be assembled with the drum out the other side of the reducer, and while then drum size is not limited, the compactness of the winch is sacrificed.

- The bearing on the opposite end of the drum shaft from the reducer must be aligned quite precisely to the line formed by the two bearings supporting the reducer's hollow output shaft. If this is not done, the reducer bearings could fail prematurely, or the drum shaft could suffer a fatigue crack.

- As with all direct drive machines, the top speed is set by the motor and reducer, and cannot be changed without a major change out of components.

- A manual backup is difficult.

Right Angle Direct Drive Winch

A very common design, this configuration does not have the drum diameter limitations of the previous concept. A hollow shaft gear reducer is used so that the drum shaft extends into and often through the reducer. This shaft, on the opposite side from the drum, may drive a limit box, or connect to a shaft brake.

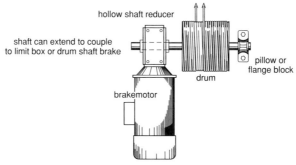

Advantages:

- The dimensions of the reducer and drum do not interfere with each other significantly, making large D/d ratio sized drums easy to accommodate.

- This design, with the addition of a second brake on the drum shaft, can be made acceptable for lifting applications.

- This is a low part count concept, which should lead to a more rapid design, and assembly.

Disadvantages:

- The bearing on the opposite end of the drum shaft from the reducer must be aligned quite precisely to the line formed by the two bearings supporting the reducer's hollow output shaft.

- As with all direct drive machines, the top speed is set by the motor and reducer, and cannot be changed without a major change out of components.
- A manual backup is difficult.

Short Travel Direct Drive Winch

Gear reducers with double ended output shafts commonly have overhanging load ratings high enough to allow them to support modest loads on a narrow drum without the need for any additional bearings. The shaft opposite the drum can be used to drive a limit box or to connect to an output shaft brake. The drums on this type of winch would typically have only one spoke locked to the shaft with a QD bushing fit into a weld-on hub, or by the use of a keyless bushing. (Taper-lock bushings tend to be narrow, and less suited for the loading condition posed by this drum.) The use of a yo-yo drum is another option.

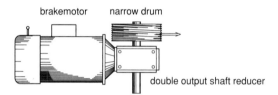

Advantages:
- Extreme simplicity. Motor, reducer, drum, done.
- This design, with the addition of a secondary brake on the other output shaft, can be made acceptable for lifting applications.

Disadvantages:
- The cable capacity of this design is quite limited.
- A manual backup is impractical.
- As with all direct drive machines, the top speed is set by the motor and reducer, and cannot be changed without a major change out of components.

Line Shaft Winch

Line shaft winches have one drum per cable in place of a single much larger drum holding multiple cables. In a batten winch application, the batten pipe hangs freely on cables dropping directly off each drum. If the drums are identically threaded, the batten will move sideways as the cable pays on and off the drums. If each pair of drums is set up with one right-hand and one left-hand threaded and only even numbers of drums are used, then the opposing movements of the cables will average out to no net side-to-side movement.

Given the multiple bearings involved, universal joints, as shown in the illustration, or shaft couplings can be used to allow for the inevitable misalignment between the bearings. An alternative approach would be to design a substantial support frame that would resist any significant deflection under load, install all the drum support bearings precisely along one line, and then use one long length of shaft to connect all the drums.

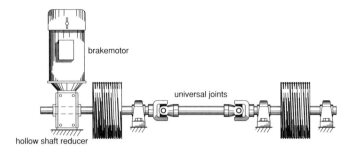

hollow shaft reducer

brakemotor

universal joints

Advantages:

- Cables may not have to be muled around at all, because the line shaft's drums are placed directly where a cable is needed.
- This design, with the addition of a secondary brake on the drum shaft, can be made acceptable for lifting applications. (Though since there are a number of potential failure points along a coupling-connected line shaft, a brake per drum may be design choice.)
- In motorized batten applications, all loads are vertical, eliminating horizontal loading of support structures.

Disadvantages:

- Line shafts are the very definition of a long power transmission shaft application, and to avoid excessive torsional deflection, a relatively large diameter shaft is needed. Hollow shafts can reduce weight while still preserving much of their torsional stiffness. A rule-of-thumb guide to an appropriate shaft size would be to combine the hollow shaft factor formula with the 0.08° torsional deflection rule-of-thumb formula:

$$D = \sqrt[3]{\frac{1}{1 - (d_{id}/d_{od})^4}} \times 0.29 \sqrt[4]{T}$$

A hollow steel shaft with the dimensions of, for example, a 2″ Sch 40 pipe (2.375″ od × 2.067″ id) would, following this criteria, be acceptable up to 120 ft-lb of torque. This same torque, applied to a solid shaft, would require a diameter of only 1.79″. But the solid shaft would weigh 8.56 lb/ft, and the pipe only 3.65 lb/ft. A huge weight reduction is possible if a relatively small increase in diameter is acceptable. These long shafts, hollow or not, must also be checked for the effects of bending stress due to their own weight, another area where the slightly larger but lighter hollow shaft will excel. This check would be accomplished by using the combined load shaft formula given in Chapter 16.

- A manual backup is impractical.

Thin Large Cable Capacity Direct Drive Winch

A rare and expensive design, this winch uses a large diameter turntable bearing or slew ring to support and drive an equally large diameter drum. The upper illustration shows a motor and reducer driving an external gear slew ring simply to clearly present the concept. A more useful compact design would use an internal gear bearing, allowing the motor and reducer to fit inside the drum, as shown in cross section in the lower sketch. With the motor inside, a winch could easily be built in the form of a cylinder roughly 3′ in diameter and a mere 8″ thick, with a cable capacity of 200′ of 1/4″ cable.

large diameter narrow drum attached to outer ring of bearing

pinion on reducer output
shaft spins bearing   external teeth crane bearing (slewing ring)

Advantages:

- A unique, essentially frameless winch with a high cable holding capacity for its size.
- This design, with the addition of perhaps a caliper brake clamping on another ring welded onto the inside of the drum, could be made acceptable for lifting applications.

Disadvantages:

- Slew ring bearings are expensive, and a drum of this diameter would be relatively expensive to make. This design could easily cost two to four times what any other design shown in this chapter would cost.
- A manual backup is virtually impossible.
- This winch would be considerably heavier than other concepts.

Zero Fleet Angle Winch Concepts

The fleet angle of a cable entering a sheave is defined as the angle between a line straight off the sheave, and the line formed by the cable:

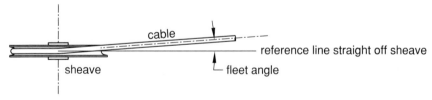

cable

reference line straight off sheave

sheave   fleet angle

The fleet angle for a threaded drum should use as its zero reference a line at the helix angle of the grooves, with fleet angle measurements being taken either side off of that. For a 12 inch diameter drum threaded at 3.25 TPI, the helix angle is:

$$\tan\theta_{helix} = \frac{1}{\pi(TPI)D} = \frac{1}{\pi(3.25)(12)} \qquad \theta_{helix} = 0.467°$$

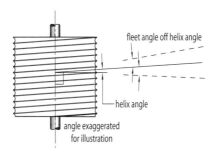

fleet angle off helix angle

helix angle

angle exaggerated
for illustration

At any fleet angle other than zero, the cable will rub on the side walls of the groove causing wear to both cable and drum. More importantly, the greater the fleet angle, the greater the friction between cable and groove, and the greater the tendency for the cable to ride the wall up and out of its groove. Once this happens, cables can wind over each other binding up the system, different speeds and travel distances will occur between cables still in and those out of their grooves, and in a closed loop rig, like a deck track, tension can build high enough to break the weakest component in the loop. None of this is acceptable.

Drums always have inherent fleet angle issues because, unlike what happens in a sheave, the point at which the cable leaves the drum moves as the cable pays onto and off of the drum. The rule of thumb maximum acceptable fleet angle is 2° on a grooved drum, and so this defines the distance to the closest fixed sheave for a cable traveling across a drum a given distance.

EXAMPLE: A 10″ diameter drum has been turned at 3.25 TPI for 1/4″ aircraft cable. An effect calls for 35′ of travel. Assuming a maximum fleet angle of 2°, calculate the minimum distance between the drum and the first fixed sheave.

SOLUTION: The circumference of the drum in feet is:

$$circumference = \pi d = \pi(10/12) = 2.62 \; ft$$

The 35′ travel will require some number of wraps around this drum:

$$wraps = \frac{35}{2.62} = 13.4$$

Since the drum has been cut with a pitch of 3.25 TPI, these wraps occupy a length of:

$$drum \; length \; used = \frac{13.4}{3.25} = 4.12 \; in$$

Now finally the distance to the nearest fixed sheave can be determined. Since a fleet angle of 2° either side of 0° is acceptable (the helix angle will be ignored as its effect here is small), a triangle is formed with a side length of 4.12/2 = 2.06″ opposite the 2° angle. By trig:

$$\tan 2° = \frac{2.06}{\Delta x_{sheave}} \qquad \Delta x_{sheave} = 59.0 \; in = 4.92 \; ft$$

Therefore, the closest fixed sheave should be no closer than roughly 5 ft from the drum, and aligned so that the cable runs straight off the drum at the helix angle in the middle of the effect's 35 foot travel.

Since it is unlikely during load-in that the cable and sheave will be aligned with a surveyor's precision, a more forgiving plan might be to assume a drum to sheave distance of 8′ or 10′, knowing that with this nearly any cable set up will work.

In situations where this amount of space is simply not available, a winch with a mechanism to ensure a constant zero fleet angle of the cable off the drum may be used. Additional benefits of zero fleet winches include that the cable will wind flawlessly onto the drum if it is always fed into the exact center of a drum groove, and, in some designs, the cable leaving the winch does not move side to side at all, allowing stationary muling sheaves to be very close to the drum.

Zero Fleet Angle by Moving the Winch

One way a fleet angle of zero can be maintained between a winch and a fixed sheave is to move the whole winch along the axis of the drum at a pace of one drum pitch per revolution of the drum. One common way this is accomplished is by attaching a length of threaded rod, cut with the same threads per inch as the drum, to the drum shaft. A fixed nut on this rod will draw the winch side to side as the drum rotates, always with the exact synchronization needed to maintain a zero fleet angle. As is true of all of the concepts shown in these chapters, not all configurations can be shown, and in this design in particular, several variations on what is illustrated are common. The inverse of the nut and threaded rod can be used, by holding the rod stationary, and spinning the nut. The motor can be next to the drum, with the fixed sheaves moved to under the drum. Stage Technologies Ltd., of London champions both of these variations under the name *BigTow*. If position feedback is taken off the motor shaft, the threaded rod can be moved to under the motor, and this design has been used by SBS Bühnentechnik of Dresden, Germany. The gear reducer shown in the illustration is not critical to the zero fleet angle concept, and other styles could be used. Some of the features of this design could fall under the claims of U.S. patent 6520485.

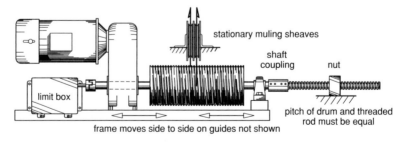

stationary muling sheaves

shaft coupling   nut

limit box

pitch of drum and threaded rod must be equal

frame moves side to side on guides not shown

Advantages:

- A closed loop of cable rigged to this winch, as for running a wagon in a deck track, is accommodated inherently by this design.

- The tension or compression that the threaded rod and nut experience is mainly a function of the friction of the guides enabling the winch to move from side to side. Tension on the cables does not translate in a one-to-one manner onto the rod, and so this mechanism is relatively efficient.

Disadvantages:

- This is a more complex mechanism than a conventional winch, an so there is more to design, fabricate, assemble, and maintain than in a conventional winch.
- Many different parts need to be precisely aligned relative to each other.

Zero Fleet by Moving the Drum

In George Izenour's book *Theater Technology*, he shows a number of variations on a zero fleet angle winch where just the drum moves. These winches were designed starting in the late 1950s and run to this day in some theatres as part of a permanently installed spot line rigging system. The winch depicted here updates the design by using low friction ball spline bearings. (Only one is shown through the cutaway of the drum, but there would be one at the other end of the drum too.) These transmit torque from shaft to drum, but allow free travel side-to-side along the splined shaft. A chain or gear driven threaded rod moves the drum via an arm assembly that has within it a nut traveling on the rod. Thrust bearings would be inserted between the arms and the drum.

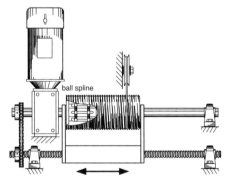

Advantages:

- The tension or compression that the threaded rod and nut experience is mainly a function of the very low friction of the splined nuts that enable the winch drum to move from side to side.
- Since only the drum and arm assembly move from side to side, all other components can be bolted onto a simple stationary frame.
- This design, with the addition of a secondary brake on the output shaft, can be made acceptable for lifting applications.

Disadvantages:

- The expense and dirt sensitivity of the ball splines may be negative factors.
- This is a more complex mechanism than a conventional winch, so there is more to design, fabricate, assemble, and maintain than in a conventional winch.
- The drum shaft's bending is accentuated by its long length between supports.

- As with all direct drive machines, the top speed is set by the motor and reducer, and cannot be changed without a major change out of components.

Zero Fleet by Moving Sheaves

Leaving the major components of the winch stationary and moving just muling sheaves is another possible zero fleet angle technique.

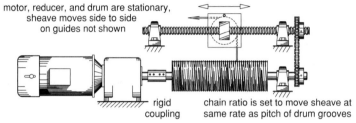

motor, reducer, and drum are stationary,
sheave moves side to side
on guides not shown

rigid
coupling

chain ratio is set to move sheave at
same rate as pitch of drum grooves

Advantages:

- The moving components are significantly smaller and lighter than moving the whole winch.

Disadvantages:

- Tension on the cables will place significant loads onto the sheave guides and threaded rod. The low friction of a ball nut and screw will reduce the power lost to friction in this assembly.

- A closed loop of cable, as for a wagon in a deck track, needs the arrangement shown in A below. Since the sheaves track from side to side, one cable needs to become longer as the other becomes shorter to maintain the fixed length of a cable loop. If the load is not a closed loop, such as if the winch were flying a batten, multiple cables can all mule in the same direction, as in B.

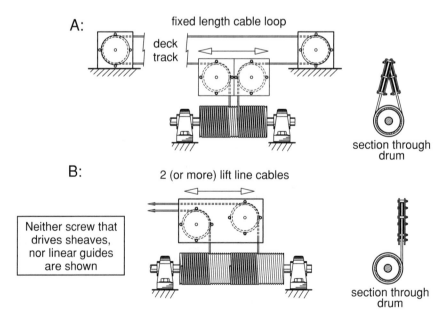

A:

fixed length cable loop

deck
track

section through
drum

B:

2 (or more) lift line cables

Neither screw that
drives sheaves,
nor linear guides
are shown

section through
drum

Machine Details

Cable Keepers, or Retainers

Wire rope will stay seated in the grooves of a drum provided there is sufficient tension to keep it there. If the cables coming onto the drum go slack though, wraps will unwind, jam, or fall off the drum. Two forms of cable retainers are common. One is simply a stationary bar, usually of plastic (UHMW-PE, or nylon) that is positioned close to but just not touching the cables on the drum. This bar prevents the cables from leaving their groove, but it does not hold the cable firmly in place. The other technique is a pinch roller. A free-spinning roller is pressed lightly onto the cables, and since all cables are in contact with the roller, no one can easily move independent of the others. The rollers can be made with materials like thick-walled neoprene tubing slipped over steel shafts (for example, tubing at 1-3/8″ o.d. × 1/2″ i.d. sells for roughly $10 per ft), or with extremely rugged but expensive cast polyurethane wheel stock (1-1/2″ o.d. × 1/2″ i.d. at about $50 per ft). The shop-built neoprene roller's shaft rotates and so it must be fitted into bearings, but the polyurethane's inner core is already a bearing surface, so their shafts can be stationary.

The keeper's ideal location is at the point where the cable first makes contact with the drum. Here there is no chance of slack allowing the cable to jump out of its groove. A keeper nearby is nearly as good, but a keeper on the other side of the drum from the first contact point is useless in preventing a slack line from jumping. If cables leave the drum from different points, an everyday example of which would be the two cables running out to a deck wagon, then two cable retainers would be best.

The position of the keeper should be reconsidered for each reuse of a winch. Different setups will often have the cables leaving the drum at different positions than the last use, and the keepers therefore may need to move.

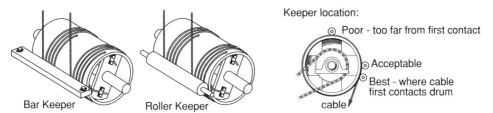

Bar Keeper   Roller Keeper

Keeper location:
⊙ Poor - too far from first contact
⊙ Acceptable
⊗ Best - where cable first contacts drum
cable

Winch Specification Issues

The essential first step in any mechanical design process is to identify a design specification for the machine being considered. The questions listed below can serve as a checklist to help streamline this step.

Effect Speed:

What is the maximum or top speed of the cable pulled by this winch?

- 3 to 4 ft/sec is typical value for the top speed of a variable speed deck effect, with 4 to 6 ft/sec typical for a fly effect. Special effect winches have used speeds exceeding 30 ft/sec.

- If multi-purchased rigging is involved, the speed of the cable pulled by the winch will be some number of time more than or less than the speed of the effect.

Does the speed need to be variable or is a single fixed speed acceptable? Is the position dependent variable speed characteristic of a yo-yo drum machine acceptable?

- Fixed speed winches generally run in the 0.5 to 1 ft/sec range—relatively slow to avoid excessive acceleration forces. A slow speed is also useful for accurate position of the load if the winch control will just be a handheld forward/reverse switch button box (like the so-called "pickle" used to control a chain motor).

What is the minimum speed needed?

- Speeds below roughly 2% of the top speed may require motor drives specifically capable of running a motor at these low speeds. An encoder may be needed on the motor to provide the motor drive with a motor speed feedback signal.

Pull Force:

What is the maximum total pull force the winch will exert on the cables off its drum?

- This number can either be related to the sum of acceleration, friction, and lifting forces if the winch is being designed to run a specific effect, or just a number chosen somewhat arbitrarily if a stock general purpose winch is the goal. Values for this latter choice would logically be some easily remembered number, such as 200 lb or 500 lb for instance.

Cable Capacity:

What is the travel of the piece being run by this winch? How will that piece be rigged to the drum?

- Sizing a drum to a known set of requirements is detailed in Chapter 19, but if a general purpose winch is desired, a rule of thumb would be to design a drum that can hold a single cable somewhere in the range of 70′ to 100′ long. A typical drum for a deck winch, for example, would be roughly 1 foot in diameter, and 8″ to 11″ inches wide.
- Always plan to leave a minimum of three wraps of cable on the drum between where a cable anchors to the drum and leaves it. The friction in these wraps greatly reduces the force the cable anchor experiences.

Drum Size Constraints:

Are there any special limitations of the size on the size of the drum? What factors will limit the diameter or length of the drum?

- Winches might be placed under decks, in trusses, on battens, and in other places where the space available for a winch is limited. Even if not especially constrained by specific application, backstage space is limited, and winches should be compact. Drums rarely need to go to these extremes, but a 4″ wide 2′ diameter drum will hold the same amount of cable as a drum 4″ in diameter that is 2′ long. Is one of these more suitable for your application than the other?

- A wire rope manufacturer's recommendations for the D/d ratio, or the ratio of drum diameter, D, to nominal cable diameter, d, will suggest the minimum diameter a drum could be with a still acceptably long cable life.
- The lathe used to cut the helical groove into a drum will place limits on maximum dimensions of the drum, especially diameter, but length also. Design a drum early in the design process and get advice from the machinist who will be making it as to its practicality.

Cable Management:

How many cables need to be anchored on the drum, and how many of these wrap one way versus the other? How will the cable ends be anchored at the drum? How much hand and wrench clearance will be needed at the anchor points?

Are cable keepers or rollers needed to retain cable on the drum?

Are cable slack or out-of-drum-groove sensors needed?

Is a zero-fleet angle mechanism needed?

Is a cable tensioning assembly needed on the winch?

- Traditional deck winch designs include a mechanism to tension the loop of cable that runs from the drum out to a deck track dog, but most other designs do not.

Brake(s):

Is a holding brake, used to keep loads in place when the winch is not powered, needed on this winch?

- It is quite rare to NOT need a holding brake. In most instances the brake will hold the motor shaft, as opposed to the drum shaft, because the speed reduction multiplies the brakes rated torque, allowing the use of a correspondingly smaller and less expensive size brake.

Are two brakes needed as part of a safety redundancy scheme?

- The use of a brakemotor provides one brake, and the second is placed at the opposite end of the power transmission system, on the drum shaft, or clamping on a drum flange. Some have however used two brakes on the motor shaft, and applied very conservative design factors to the gear reducer.

Is a purely mechanical overspeed brake or retarder needed, or is an electronic overspeed sensor acceptable?

Motor: electric, hydraulic

Is a particular type of motor required on this effect?

- Electric motors are nearly universal, but in rare instances a fluid power motor may be desireable (an underwater winch, for example, or a rope tensioning winch that normally works stalled and has an easily set maximum pull force).

Feedback device:

Does there need to be position feedback devices mounted on the machine?

- The motion control system will in large part set what is required—an encoder, a potentiometer, or limit switches, for instance.
- What drives these devices? The drum shaft? The motor shaft? The reducer shaft?

Disconnect:

Is a motor disconnect switch needed?

- NFPA Article 79 says, in part, that if motor is less than 2 HP and operates at voltages below 200 V to ground then the motor's plug can be a disconnect.
- The disconnect should allow for OSHA lock-out, tag-out.

How will brake power be involved with the disconnect?

- If a motor is disconnected, so too should be the ability to power up and release a brake. The wiring for electric brakes can be run through additional contacts on the motor disconnect switch.

Control Equipment:

Are any of the motion control or motor drive electronics mounted on the winch?

Backup:

What form of backup, if any, is needed for this winch?

- The ability to mechanically disconnect a drum from its motor and then use a handcrank as a backup has been a traditional feature of stock deck winches for years.
- Is the backup a hand crank? A backup motor that can be coupled in somehow quickly?

Frame:

What is the frame material and finish?
For this application should all the parts fit within the planes of the frame, or is it acceptable that some components protrude outside the frame?

Winch size and weight:

What are the limitations on the size allowed?

- Are there critical dimensions that will influence the design? Winches built to fit within trusses or within a deck face these often severe limitations.

Are there weight limitations?

- Should there be a castered dolly, handles, or chain hoist lifting points built for the winch?

31

Turntable Drives

Overview

Rotating scenery on a turntable, either for the dynamic visual effect they can provide, or to simply change scenes quickly in a blackout, is a relatively recent introduction into Western set design. The concept was imported into Germany in the late 19th century from Japan where turntables had been used in Kabuki theatre from the 1700s. In truth, turning platforms are documented in some Medieval and early Renaissance events, but they were forgotten after the development of the chariot and pole scene changing system in the early 1600s. Most German opera houses built in the last century have permanently installed turntables. These most often take the form of either a massive steel structure installed during the building's construction that spins both the stage floor and the trap room, or as a turntable built within a full stage wagon that stores upstage and rolls downstage when needed. The Frankfurt Opera has an exceptional example of the former, with one immense turntable 37.4 m (123 ft) in diameter, that carries on it a smaller turntable (relatively at least) of 16 m (52.5 ft) in diameter.[1] The Metropolitan Opera in New York, the stage of which was built to German models, has a 60′ square, 1′ thick upstage wagon that contains within it a 58′ diameter turntable.

Turntables built for temporary use in one production are usually of a more modest scale. Drawing only on my own experience, turntables have ranged from a small 1′ diameter 1′ high cylinder that carried a skeleton on a themed restaurant exterior facade, to a production that featured two 30′ diameter turntables sitting onstage side by side, each of which carried 22′ diameter turntables mounted eccentrically so that the edge of the smaller was in one spot 6″ from the edge of the larger. In between in scale there have been turntables on lifts, and turntables with separately driven rings or doughnuts around them.

Turntables also feature prominently in Broadway shows. For the initial 16 year run of *Les Miserables*, the barriers of Paris drove themselves via friction drives along deck tracks from offstage onto mating tracks on a precisely positioned turntable. In *The Lion King*, Pride Rock seems to spiral up out of the stage as a lift built

---

1. Grösel, *Bühnentechnik*, 36.

into the turntable hoists the Rock up with careful coordination between lift and spinning speeds. And the short run of *Jane Eyre* does not diminish the technical accomplishment of a turntable, mounted on the grid, and filled with intricately tracking winches, that allowed flown pieces to rotate in sync with a turntable onstage.

Only the machinery needed to drive turntables will be covered in this chapter. This is because, while the table itself is an important part of the system, the problem is more one of structural rather than mechanical design. In addition, despite the fact that doors and drawbriges are rotating units, they have little else in common with traditional turntables, and so they will be excluded from consideration here.

A Typical Application

The classic turntable drive technique uses an endless loop of wire rope, called a grommet, wrapped around both the outer edge of the turntable and an assembly of sheaves at the drive to transfer power from a motor to the turntable (Figure 31.1). The loop of wire rope is made by using a so-called long splice, which marries together the ends of the cable over a distance of roughly 1200 times the nominal rope diameter. With 1/4″ cable, the long splice would therefore be about 25′ long. While this splice can be done by anyone with two marlin spikes and some patience, most splices are jobbed out. (One set of instructions for a long splice involves a 56 step procedure![2]) Making the splice also presupposes that the exact circumference of the loop is known. While this dimension is not hard to calculate from a ground plan of the whole system, once the cable is made, it is difficult to accommodate any changes in this layout if they become necessary.

In theory, this loop of rope could be rigged like a v-belt on its sheaves, with roughly one half a wrap around each sheave and tension in the belt set high enough to prevent slipping. In practice this is not possible. Since a wire rope is much more slippery than a rubber v-belt, the rope tension would need to be set too high. So

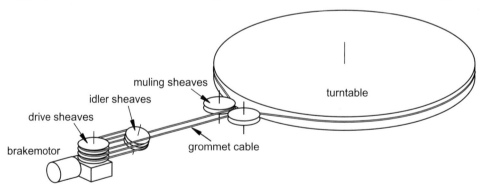

Figure 31.1 Basic layout of a grommet turntable drive

2. http://www.worksafebc.com/publications/health_and_safety/by_topic/assets/pdf/splicing.pdf

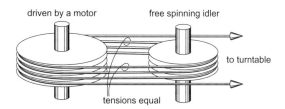

4 half wraps = 4 x 0.5 x 2π = 4π radians wrap angle

Figure 31.2   Grommet drive cable reeving

instead of just a half of wrap around a drive sheave, several wraps can be taken using the technique shown in Figure 31.2. Two multi-groove sheaves, one driven by a motor, the other a free-to-spin idler, enable the wire rope to make multiple passes around the drive sheave.

Driving this setup with a motor will create different tensions in the two cables running out around the turntable. There the difference in tensions creates a net torque that must equal $(T_{accel} + T_{friction} + T_{lifting})$ in order to spin the turntable as desired. For example:

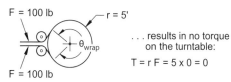

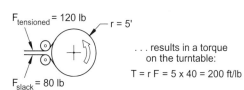

The situation at the turntable can be described mathematically by combining the formula for cable tensions in a cable wrapped around a cylinder and the formula for torque:

$$F_{slack} = \frac{F_{tensioned}}{e^{\mu\theta_{wrap}}} \qquad\qquad T = rF$$

The torque needed to spin a turntable by a cable wrapped around it is:

$$T_{accel} + T_{friction} + T_{lifting} = r\,(F_{tensioned} - F_{slack})$$

$$T_{accel} + T_{friction} + T_{lifting} = r\,F_{tensioned}\left(1 - \frac{1}{e^{\mu\theta_{wrap}}}\right)$$

All the torques would be obtained from an analysis of the scenery, actors and props in the conventional manner, r is the radius at which the wire rope acts on the turntable, and the rest of the variables are those of the cable friction formula.

EXAMPLE: Assume a given turntable requires 4250 ft-lb of torque during acceleration. The grommet drive cable will lie in a channel bent into a radius of 11′, and it wraps 320° around the turntable. The coefficient of friction between the wire rope and a rubber strip double stick taped onto the channel is estimated to be 0.2. What values of $F_{tensioned}$ and F_{slack} will be needed to run this turntable?

SOLUTION: Only the wrap angle needs conversion into different units to make it compatible with the formula.

$$2\pi \times \frac{320°}{360°} = 5.59 \; radians$$

Inserting the givens and solving for $F_{tensioned}$ yields:

$$T_{accel} + T_{friction} + T_{lifting} = r \, F_{tensioned}\left(1 - \frac{1}{e^{\mu\theta_{wrap}}}\right)$$

$$4250 = 11 F_{tensioned}\left(1 - \frac{1}{e^{(0.2)(5.59)}}\right)$$

$$F_{tensioned} = 574 \; lb$$

The value of F_{slack} can be found from:

$$F_{slack} = \frac{F_{tensioned}}{e^{\mu\theta_{wrap}}} = \frac{574}{e^{(0.2)(5.59)}} = 188 \; lb$$

The value of $F_{tensioned}$ informs the decision of what size wire rope should be used for the grommet. Given the result here, 1/4″ aircraft cable, with its breaking strength of 7000 lb would provide a 7000/574 = 12.2 safety factor. (Not accounting for any deratings due to the long splice, or the D/d ratio of the drive or muling sheaves.)

The calculations above are just for the turntable end of the system. At the drive the same basic situation exists—cables wrapped around sheaves. There, if the drive sheave setup providing 4 half wraps is used, the wrap angle is much greater than that around the turntable (12.56 rad versus 5.59 rad). Provided that the coefficient of friction between cable and sheave is anywhere near what is around the turntable, then slipping would occur first at the turntable and therefore the results of those calculations represent the worst case.

The initial tension of the cables must equal at least the average of $F_{tensioned}$ and F_{slack}. Here that is 381 lb of tension on each cable. When the motor rotates the drive sheave, one cable's tension will go up by 193 lb to 574 lb, and the other cable will drop 193 lb to 188 lb, and this develops the tensions needed to generate the torque required to run the turntable.

One last point about these cable tensions is that they have a significant consequence on the drive and idler shaft sizes. $F_{tensioned}$ and F_{slack} are not the only cable tensions in a grommet drive setup, there are the six other runs of the cable between the drive and idler sheaves. The same friction formula can be used to calculate these tensions, and if they are all summed together, they represent loads which can create large bending moments in the shafts:

Load due to cable tensions:

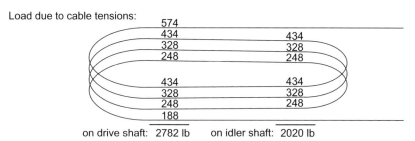

on drive shaft: 2782 lb   on idler shaft: 2020 lb

The drive shaft must be designed to withstand these side forces (partly negated by the chain tension in the opposite direction) and to transmit the torque from sprocket to sheave. This is definitely an instance where the combined moment and torque shaft formula must be used.

Amongst the effect design specifications for a typical grommet drive machine might be:

- Provisions for a hand cranked manual backup.
- A cable tensioning mechanism capable of developing the forces needed, and with several inches of travel to accommodate reeving the cable and then tensioning it.
- The ability to reeve the grommet easily, without having to temporarily unbolt bearings, or remove any framing.
- A substantial frame to resist the significant forces involved in cable tensioning.

The machine shown in Figure 31.3 meets these requirements. There is a standard type pull-pin release device that disconnects the gear reducer from the rest of the drive system, and a hex-shaped shaft onto which a hand crank will fit. The roughly 2:1 chain reduction ratio between that hand crank shaft and the drive sheave reduces the force needed on the crank handle.

To tension the cables, the whole drive machine, mounted on a separate frame inside the main box-like frame, is pulled back away from the turntable. This is enabled by sliding guides, detailed in Figure 31.4, made out of a stack of UHMW-PE (ultra-high molecular weight polyethylene, an inexpensive plastic with a relatively low coefficient of friction). These simple linear guides are inherently overconstrained, so the frames need to be welded together with care to insure the angle irons remain coplanar, and the UHMW guides are cut to leave plenty of clearance. Cable tensioning is accomplished by spinning nuts along threaded rods placed on either side of the motor which pulls the inner frame along its guides. Die springs are used to provide some resilience to the tensioning setup to account for slight eccentricity of the cable wrap around the turntable. Since the tension needs to be set to

TOP VIEW:

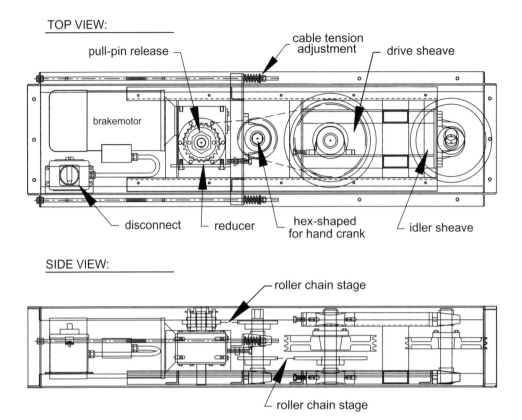

Figure 31.3   Grommet turntable drive

around 400 lb on each cable (assuming the values from the example above), each threaded rod and die spring will be set to this tension. The springs appropriate for this must be extremely stiff, deflecting perhaps only an inch at 400 lb. Die springs are the only commonly available spring that can match this requirement.

The cable can be reeved around the sheaves easily because the location of the drive chain and the support framing for the drive and idler sheave pillow blocks

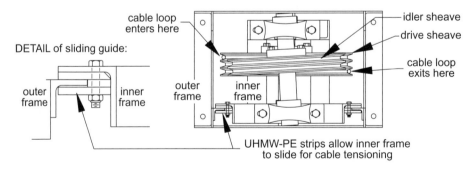

Figure 31.4   End view of grommet drive

leaves the top of the sheaves open. During load-in, two loops are made in the grommet cable, just as you might do while coiling up an extension cord, and they are passed through the end framing and up, over, and down onto the drive and idler sheaves. Easy and fast.

The outer frame of the drive must be substantial to withstand the roughly 800 lb load imposed by the sum of the tensions in the two cables. An additional frame, holding the two muling sheaves mounted out by the turntable, is often made long enough to connect back to the drive frame. That way the 800 lb tension does not have to be transferred through lag screws into the stage floor, and then through the floor on up through similar screws to the muling sheave frame.

The reduction ratio in this grommet drive consists of four stages, one gear, two chain stages, and the stage made up of the drive sheave and the turntable. Some parameters about the movement of the turntable must be known or assumed before these ratios can be determined. Typically these would be either the top edge speed of the turntable, or some move times and distances.

EXAMPLE: Assume that the top speed at the edge of a turntable 23′ in diameter is 4 ft/sec, and that the grommet cable runs at a radius of 11′. A standard 1750 rpm motor will drive this turntable. What is the total reduction ratio, and what is one possible set of gear, chain, and turntable reduction ratios?

SOLUTION: Linear edge speed can the converted into angular speed:

$$v = r\omega \qquad\qquad 4 = 11.5\omega \qquad\qquad \omega = 0.348 \; rad/sec$$

The motor spins at:

$$1750 \times \frac{2\pi}{60} = 183 \; rad/sec$$

The total reduction ratio is therefore:

$$n_{total} = \frac{\omega_{in}}{\omega_{out}} = \frac{183}{0.348} = 526$$

A rather large reduction ratio such as this is common in turntable setups. To find a set of ratios for the different parts of grommet drive, there is first a choice to be made in the diameter of the grommet cable as this influences the diameter of the drive sheave. Assume here 1/4″ aircraft cable is acceptable, and that the recommended D/d ratio of 35 for this cable type will be used. The minimum recommended diameter of the drive sheave is therefore:

$$35 \times 0.25 = 8.75''$$

At the drive machine there is no pressing need to make the sheaves as small as possible, and the idler sheave is often slightly smaller than the drive, so the task is to find an idler larger than 8.75″, and the drive sheave can then be some size up from that. Browning 5V sheaves are designed for use with V-belts, but with a very minor amount of machining on a lathe to round out the bottom of the sheave grooves they will seat a 1/4″ round cable. (They could probably be used as-is, but the cable wear would be somewhat higher.) In sizes over 8.75″, there are a number of possibilities,

Browning 5V sheave:

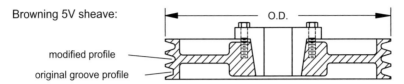

modified profile

original groove profile

and the choice is somewhat arbitrary. Assume a 12.5″ OD sheave, carrying the cable at a diameter of roughly 11.5″ is the drive sheave choice. This leaves ample room for a slightly smaller idler sheave. Given this, the reduction ratio between the diameter of the cable on the turntable and the drive sheave is:

$$n_{turntable\ stage} = \frac{d_{TT\ cable}}{d_{drive\ sheave}} = \frac{22}{11.5/12} = 23.0$$

With this ratio determined, the gear and chain stages need to make up the rest, so that:

$$n_{total} = n_{turntable\ stage} \times n_{gear\ \&\ chain} = 526 = 23.0 \times n_{gear\ \&\ chain}$$

$$n_{gear\ \&\ chain} = 22.9$$

Worm gear reducers are commonly sold only with ratios of 5:1, 10:1, 15:1, 20:1, etc. Any of these could be made to work if matched with a chain reduction stage such that:

$$n_{gear\ \&\ chain} = 22.9 = n_{gear} \times n_{chain} = 5 \times n_{chain} \qquad n_{chain} = 4.58$$

$$n_{gear\ \&\ chain} = 22.9 = n_{gear} \times n_{chain} = 10 \times n_{chain} \qquad n_{chain} = 2.29$$

$$n_{gear\ \&\ chain} = 22.9 = n_{gear} \times n_{chain} = 15 \times n_{chain} \qquad n_{chain} = 1.53$$

$$n_{gear\ \&\ chain} = 22.9 = n_{gear} \times n_{chain} = 20 \times n_{chain} \qquad n_{chain} = 1.15$$

Which of these might be best could depend on the force required at the hand crank shaft to manually move the turntable, the cost of the reducer (the higher chain ratios mean less output torque is needed at the reducer, which usually translates to a less expensive reducer), reducers you already have in stock, or a number of other choices. There is no unique correct answer, but instead many equally good possibilities.

There is no limit box on this machine because there is no positive connection between the grommet cable and the turntable. Even if cable tension is held high enough to prevent slippage, the cable will still slowly creep or shift position relative to the turntable as the moves occur. Variable loads and the vagaries of friction make this movement difficult to quantify or predict. So separate feedback setups, analogous to turntable drive techniques, are used to provide position feedback to a control system (Figure 31.5).

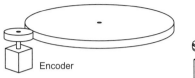

FRICTION DRIVE

- can slip
- easy, cheap
- needs relatively smooth round edge
  to ride on

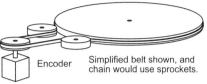

Simplified belt shown, and
chain would use sprockets.

TOOTHED BELT or CHAIN DRIVE

- slipping can occur if belt or chain is just wrapped
  around turntable
- awkward installation, belt or chain must be held
  in place as its being installed
- needs relatively smooth round edge to ride on
- potentially expensive

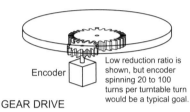

Low reduction ratio is
shown, but encoder
spinning 20 to 100
turns per turntable turn
would be a typical goal.

GEAR DRIVE

- will not slip
- will work on any shaped turntable with a
  center pivot
- potentially expensive
- must be mounted at the center, where cables
  may need to pass through
- backlash of gears can be an issue

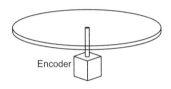

DIRECT DRIVE

- will not slip, and connections with no backlash
  are easy
- will work on any shaped turntable with a center pivot
- potential resolution problems (1 turn turntable =
  1 turn encoder)
- must be mounted at the center, where cables
  may need to pass through

Figure 31.5   Feedback device drive concepts

Finally, there are a few other points about this design worth brief mention. A disconnect for the motor and brake should always be included whenever the motor is above 2 hp. Roller chain always needs to be tensioned, and so adjustment of the gear reducer and drive sheave shaft have been included in this design to allow both chain loops to be tensioned separately. And a box, not shown, is built to surround the drive to help muffle sound, protect it during transport, and to act as a guard.

This machine, while perfectly functional, is somewhat old fashioned compared to what else might be designed today. A roller chain driven turntable using a water-jet-cut sprocket custom made to whatever diameter is needed replaces the long spliced grommet cable with a loop of easily spliced roller chain, and the drive becomes a gear-brakemotor with a sprocket on its output shaft (see page 369). Much simpler than the grommet.

Turntable Drive Concepts

A great variety of turntable drive concepts have been used over the last 100 years. Nine of these are shown here.

Endless Loop, or Grommet Drive

This is the classic turntable drive type described in detail in the Typical Application section above. A piece of wire rope is formed into an endless loop using a so-called long splice. This loop runs around both sheaves at the drive and the turntable.

Friction alone, between the cable and the surface it contacts, transfers the driving power from the motor to the turntable. The San Francisco cable cars, and most ski lifts operate using this basic principle.

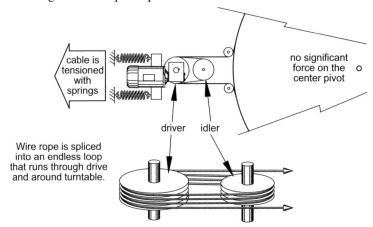

Advantages:
- The concept is proven.
- The components are standard and relatively inexpensive.
- The drive can be distant from the turntable, so that the noise of the motor and brake can be isolated.

Disadvantages:
- It can be difficult to find a company capable of making the long spliced cable. You can do-it-yourself with two marlin spikes and some instructions found off the web, but practice is needed to achieve even a passable splice.
- This concept cannot adapt to changes that affect the loop size short of making up another grommet.
- The cable will slip if cable tension is not maintained.

Typically there is only one wrap of cable around the turntable, but two will considerably reduce the tensions needed to prevent slipping. Unfortunately the cable cannot just be wrapped on twice, because eventually it will wrap over itself and jam. The arrangement of sheaves shown here will provide two passes of the cable around the turntable that will never allow the cables to overlap. The single sheave is mounted at an angle to transfer the cable between the upper sheave of one of the paired sheave sets to the lower sheave on the other,

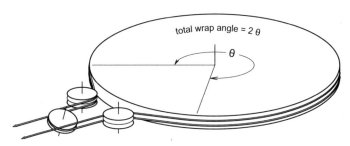

Chain Drive - Version 1

The turntable is connected to a large diameter roller chain sprocket that is driven by a gearmotor. The sprocket can be bolted to the turntable framing at its axis of rotation, which eliminates the need to size the shaft to withstand the full torque needed to spin the table.

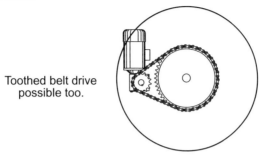

Toothed belt drive
possible too.

Advantages:
- The basic machine is very simple, being just a motor and some speed reduction components. All of these parts are off the shelf components.
- Chain drive is a positive, non-slip drive type.

Disadvantages:
- The large sprockets that bolt to the turntable are not generally stock items, and time to delivery may be unacceptably long.
- The largest commercially available stock sprockets have 112 teeth or so, resulting in sprockets too small in diameter to run large turntables.
- Even if a brakemotor is used, chain backlash will allow the turntable to freely rotate a fraction of a degree. A separate brake acting directly on the turntable may be needed.

Given the capabilities of CNC machining, sprockets of enormous sizes can be fabricated as segments, and then bolted or welded on to a turntable to form any size sprocket desired. The illustration below shows two mating ends of sprocket sweeps that would form a 1200 tooth #60 sprocket roughly 23′-10″ in diameter. These large sprockets can be drawn either by careful CAD work from scratch, or created in a few seconds by using a sprocket drawing program or macro (available on the web from several companies). Both nylatron and steel sweeps, cut from 4′ × 8′ sheets, have been used successfully. Before the segments are welded or bolted in place, a loop of chain should be masterlinked together around them, with that loop then used as a jig defining a perfect fit between chain and the huge sprocket.

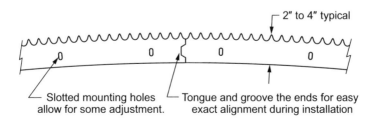

2″ to 4″ typical

Slotted mounting holes allow for some adjustment.

Tongue and groove the ends for easy exact alignment during installation

Chain Drive - Version 2

Since ANSI standard roller chain can be both easily formed into a loop of any size, and driven by sprockets, it can replace the grommet drive cable and simplify the drive machine considerably. At the turntable, the chain can either use the friction between the chain and turntable edge, just like a grommet cable would (often assisted with a strip of rubber having been attached to this edge), or an ANSI #40 chain can engage the teeth of a strip of size H toothed belt that has been attached to the turntable edge with double sided tape.

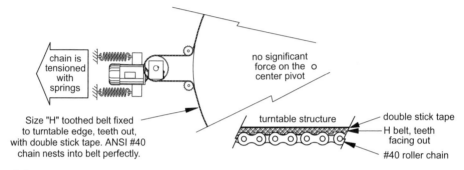

Advantages:

- This drive works on the same principle as the grommet drive, but the machine is less complex to design and build, and the endless loop of chain is trivial to assemble compared to long splicing wire rope into a loop.

- With the toothed belt, the drive is positive (non-slip) enough to allow a position feedback device to be run off the chain. That said, see the first point below.

Disadvantages:

- The chain can slip. With the toothed belt installed it is less likely to slip, but there is nothing like the true positive engagement of a chain into mating sprocket teeth.

- Both roller chain and toothed belts are relatively expensive, and this concept uses both.

- If the chain slacks at all, it will drop off the belt. A rim must be constructed to catch the chain should it go slack, so that it does not just drop off on to the floor. Both channel and angle iron, bent into the proper radius, and layers of plywood have been used successfully.

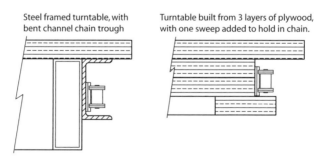

Chain Drive - Version 3

The turntable is wrapped with a complete loop of chain, and a sprocket driven by a gearmotor drives it in a gear-like manner. The chain loop around the turntable can either be made up tight by tensioning it and sinking it into some thick foam rubber tape, or by welding or bolting attachment chain onto the edge. In both cases, the outer edge of the turntable must be made as perfectly round as possible.

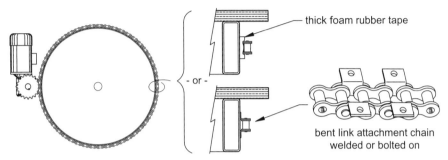

thick foam rubber tape

- or -

bent link attachment chain welded or bolted on

Advantages:

- The basic machine is very simple, being just a motor and some speed reduction components. All of these parts are off the shelf components.
- Chain drive is a positive, non-slip drive type (The chain can slip if just foam tape is used, but even one bolted on link of attachment chain can prevent this.)

Disadvantages:

- This concept does not easily accept a warped turntable edge or vertical deflection of that edge unless the drive is designed to float up and down.
- The full drive force appears on one tooth and one chain roller. Since this is not how roller chain was designed to be used, high design factors should be applied during chain size selection.

Toothed Belt Drive

With a toothed belt attached teeth out to the edge of the turntable, tank-tread-like toothed belt drive machines can drive the turntable around. A linear application of this technique is used in an extensive system of drives and wagons on the stage of Covent Garden in London.

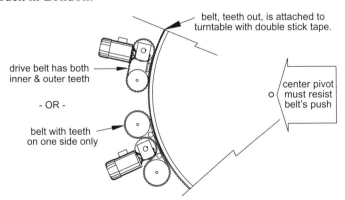

belt, teeth out, is attached to turntable with double stick tape.

drive belt has both inner & outer teeth

- OR -

belt with teeth on one side only

center pivot must resist belt's push

Advantages:

• A positive non-slip drive.

Disadvantages:

• Since toothed belts were never meant to be used this way, the pitch radius of a belt with its teeth facing out is different than the same belt with its teeth in. This limits the length of the engagement possible between the driver and turntable before the teeth interfere with each other. Only one pair of teeth are ever actually engaged, and they transfer all the force. Since none of these problems exist if both belts are straight, this technique works best if the turntable radius is large.

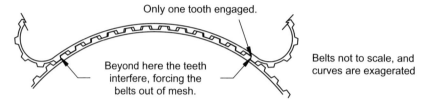

Only one tooth engaged.

Beyond here the teeth interfere, forcing the belts out of mesh.

Belts not to scale, and curves are exagerated

Friction Drives

A friction drive works very much like a small electric car. A soft synthetic rubber or urethane wheel, powered by an electric motor, pushes against the surface it contacts. The motor, a gear reducer, and the wheel may be stationary relative to the stage, and the wheel pushes the turntable around, or the motor, reducer, and wheel can be on the turntable, moving with it, as the wheel pushes on the floor beneath it. Since friction is the only connection between driven and driving components, slipping is a very real possibility, and the choice of the wheel, the contacted surface, and the contact pressure are important. The force that can be withstood by static friction, is a function of the coefficient of friction between the two materials in contact and the normal force:

$$F_{static\ friction} = \mu_s F_n$$

High values in both the coefficient and normal force will enable a high driving force.

Drive wheels are usually one of two types. Solid soft rubber or urethane wheels are made for general industry use as feed wheels to drive flat stock along a production line. These are fitted with hubs that take a conventional shaft and key. The other type is a pneumatic tire, like those used on go-karts. Buying one of these may involve the choice of four separate parts: tire, tube, wheel, and live-axle hub, to assemble a functional shaft driven wheel. The same pneumatic tire, tube, wheel, but with a chain drive hub and sprocket, will allow a roller chain to drive the wheel. Ball bearings in the hub allow the whole assembly to free-wheel around a fixed shaft. Traction tape, typically used on stair treads and looking little more than like tape with a sandpaper back, can be applied to surfaces the wheel contacts to greatly increase the friction between the two.

The normal force needed to prevent slippage can be developed with springs, pneumatic cylinders, threaded rod (which, though rigid itself, works well with the inherent springiness of pneumatic tires), and weights.

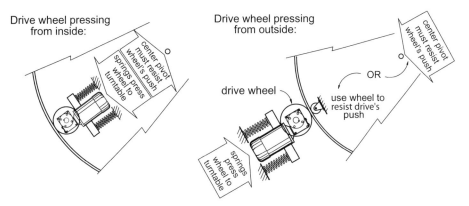

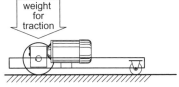

Advantages:

- A simple drive system involving a minimal set-up, and allowing rapid load-in.
- A friction drive with the motor and wheel mounted on the turntable works well for odd-shaped turntables, or turntables with their axes of rotation on or near an edge, for example a jack knife stage.

Disadvantages:

- Slipping. Design friction drives with considerable overhead, 50% would not be too much.

$$T = rF$$

$$T_{accel} + T_{friction} + T_{lifting} = r_{wheel\,to\,pivot}(\mu_s F_n)$$

where: the torques are as always

$r_{wheel\,to\,pivot}$ = the distance from wheel to turntable's axis of rotation

μ_s = coefficient of static friction between wheel and surface it contacts

F_n = the normal force between the wheel and the surface it contacts

The torques, radius and coefficient would typically be the knowns, and the normal force would be calculated. Design the machine so that this force can be increased well above what this formula says.

- Friction drives are not suitable for applications where the load will move by gravity if the drive slips. $T_{lifting}$ need not be zero, but it should only be a very small part, perhaps 10% maximum, of $T_{friction}$.
- The non-positive connection between the driving and driven parts means that position feedback must be taken off the turntable directly.

Bent Rack and Gear Drive

Driving a turntable entirely with gears guarantees that there will be none of the slipping that can occur in any of the friction based drives. One way to accomplish this is by bending rack, which is essentially a bar with gear teeth machined onto one side, and using those bent segments to form a large radius gear.

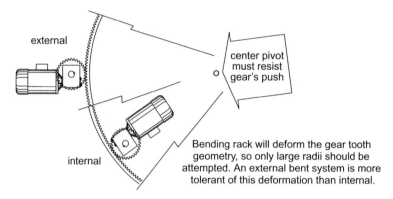

external

center pivot must resist gear's push

internal

Bending rack will deform the gear tooth geometry, so only large radii should be attempted. An external bent system is more tolerant of this deformation than internal.

Advantages:

- The basic machine is very simple, being just a motor and some speed reduction. All of these parts are off the shelf components.
- Direct drive is a positive, non-slip drive type.

Disadvantages:

- The rack must be bent only slightly else the tooth geometry will be so distorted that no pinion gear will mesh with the rack.
- The actual bending of the rack, and then forming those segments into a nearly perfect single gear is precise time consuming work. If the drive motor and pinion are spring loaded into mesh with the rack, then absolutely perfect roundness of the rack is not required since the motor could move in and out as needed.
- Noise can be difficult to suppress, and its pitch will vary with speed. Plastic pinions on the reducer have helped reduce this noise (but then concerns of the strength of the teeth become a bigger issue than when they are all steel).

Direct Drive

Driving a turntable through a shaft at its axis of rotation is, conceptually, very easy to do. In practice this is generally only worth considering for only relatively small turntables because of the expense, weight, and size of gear reducers and shafts that could supply the torques needed to run large turntables.

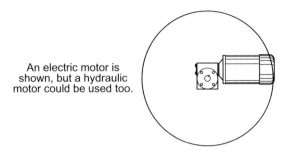

An electric motor is shown, but a hydraulic motor could be used too.

Advantages:

- The basic machine is very simple, being just a motor and some speed reduction. If a low speed, high torque hydraulic motor was used, then even the gear reducer could be eliminated. All of these parts are off the shelf components.
- Direct drive is a positive, non-slip drive type.

Disadvantages:

- Really only practical for smaller sized turntables, perhaps up to 4′ or 6′. The torque needed for large turntables could easily require reducers with 4″ or 6″ diameter output shafts. While these are available, they are both extremely expensive, enormous, and heavy.

Turntable Bearings, or Slew Ring Drive

Turntable bearings are designed exactly for the purpose of rotating large loads. In Germany, some theatres have huge permanently installed turntables, which include both stage and trap room levels, that spin on a single turntable bearing roughly 5′ in diameter. These bearings are designed for cranes, excavators, and rotating radar antennas—all long term very heavy duty uses.

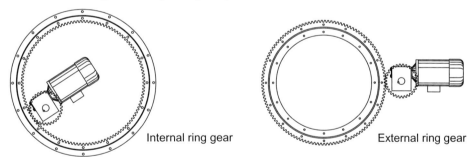

Internal ring gear   External ring gear

Advantages:

- An extremely robust machine with a huge load capacity is relatively easy and fast to design.
- Given a sufficiently sturdy mounting base for the bearing and structure in the turntable, no casters are needed. The entire load rests on the bearing. This greatly reduces $T_{friction}$, which may allow a smaller drive motor.
- The basic machine is quite simple.
- This is a positive, non-slip drive type.

Disadvantages:

- Cost. Cost. Cost. Slewing rings, even those of modest size, are very expensive, running several thousand dollars for the smaller sizes (16″) and prices go up from there.
- This is not a light weight drive system.

Limited Rotation Turntable Drive Concepts

If the turntable, or some other rotating unit, does not need to have the capability to spin endlessly, then several other drive concepts are available for use. These can be useful both for their simplicity, and the fact that exact increments of angular displacements are easily obtained without complex positioning control systems. For instance, a 180° hydraulic rotary actuator can only spin that exact amount, just run the actuator from one end stop to the other. If those two positions are all that is needed, then no sophisticated control is needed.

Rotary Actuator

There are a number of pneumatic or hydraulic rotary actuators manufactured just for this sort of application. Depending on the specific actuator, the angular displacements will range from one quarter up to several turns. Sizes of these actuator run from a small roughly 1″ cube with a 1/4″ shaft up to monsters with 3 *foot* diameter shafts!

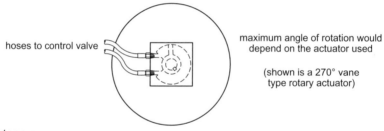

Advantages:

- Buy one part, install it, and its done.

Disadvantages:

- The cost or availability may be prohibitive.

Crank Arm Drive

Using a pneumatic or hydraulic cylinder to spin an object through 90° or so is a common simple straightforward technique.

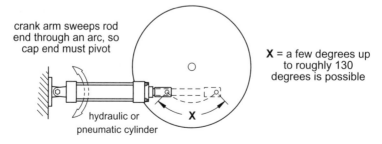

Advantages:

• Extremely simple system.

Disadvantages:

• Because $T = \mathbf{r} \times \mathbf{F} = rF\sin\theta$, there is no torque produced when the angle between the radius and force is 0° or 180°. This means rotation is always limited to less than half a turn, and how much less depends on the torque the spun load needs, and the values for the radius and force.

A quick non-mathematical way to determine crank arm length or radius can be done using CAD. (The terms in the following example use AutoCAD® jargon, but equivalent functions exist in other programs.)

EXAMPLE: Given a 6″ stroke pneumatic cylinder and the need to swing an arm through an angle of 75°, what radius arm is needed?

SOLUTION:

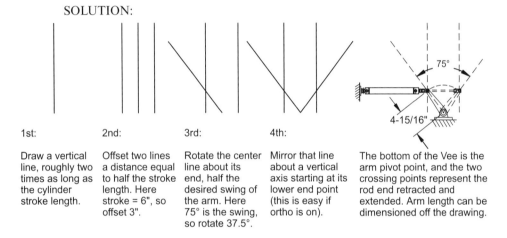

1st:	2nd:	3rd:	4th:	
Draw a vertical line, roughly two times as long as the cylinder stroke length.	Offset two lines a distance equal to half the stroke length. Here stroke = 6″, so offset 3″.	Rotate the center line about its end, half the desired swing of the arm. Here 75° is the swing, so rotate 37.5°.	Mirror that line about a vertical axis starting at its lower end point (this is easy if ortho is on).	The bottom of the Vee is the arm pivot point, and the two crossing points represent the rod end retracted and extended. Arm length can be dimensioned off the drawing.

Rack and Pinion

For angular displacements beyond what the simple crank arm setup can provide, a rack and pinion driven by a cylinder is a possible solution.

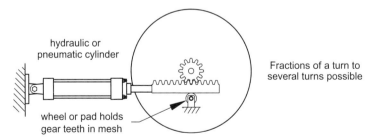

Advantages:

• Unlike a crank arm setup, the torque provided by this mechanism is constant.

- Rotations of up to several turns are possible. The angle of rotation can be determined from:

$$\theta = \frac{360 \times pitch \times l}{\pi \times n_{pinion}}$$

where: θ = the angle of rotation (degrees)
$pitch$ = the pitch of the gears used (unitless)
l = the cylinder stroke length (inches)
n_{pinion} = number of teeth on the pinion (unitless)

EXAMPLE: A 4″ stroke cylinder will be used to drive a 180° rotation. If 24 pitch gears are to be used, what size pinion is needed?

SOLUTION: No conversions are needed, so simply solve the formula for n_{pinion}.

$$\theta = \frac{360 \times pitch \times l}{\pi \times n_{pinion}} = 180 = \frac{360 \times 24 \times 4}{\pi \times n_{pinion}}$$

$$n_{pinion} = 61.12$$

Since gears will be available with only a integer number of teeth, round down to the next available size, here assumed to be 60 teeth, and calculate the needed stroke:

$$\theta = \frac{360 \times pitch \times l}{\pi \times n_{pinion}} = 180 = \frac{360 \times 24 \times l}{\pi \times 60}$$

$$l = 3.93 \; inches$$

The cylinder stroke, or the rotation of the spun unit, can be limited with hard stops to attain an exact 180° turn.

Disadvantages:

- Since this exact device is used inside one style of manufactured rotary actuator, why spend the time to re-design what can be bought already complete?

Cable Drum Winch Drive

Driving a turntable with a deck winch is little different than driving a wagon along a deck track. Just as the wagon's linear travel will be limited by the cable capacity of the winch drum, the rotational travel of a turntable is limited by how that drum capacity relates to the circumference of the cable as it wraps around the turntable.

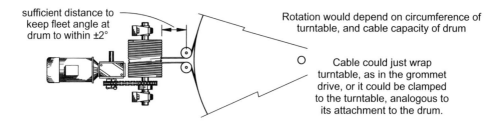

sufficient distance to keep fleet angle at drum to within ±2°

Rotation would depend on circumference of turntable, and cable capacity of drum

Cable could just wrap turntable, as in the grommet drive, or it could be clamped to the turntable, analogous to its attachment to the drum.

Advantages:

- If you have access to a deck winch, then the turntable drive is already built.
- The winch can be mounted at some distance from the turntable, potentially reducing noise, and removing the bulk of the machinery to less crowded areas off stage or in the trap room.

Disadvantages:

- Due to fleet angle issues, the drum cannot be mounted too close to the turntable.

Machine Details

Slip Rings

A lighting designer will frequently request that several dimming circuits be brought up onto the turntable. The sound designer may ask for speakers, or line level or microphone lines. Increasingly, video, DMX, Ethernet (or some other control network), hydraulic power, and even possibly a fiber optic cable are required be brought on also.

For travels of roughly 180° or less, a cable swag or a loop of cable chain out of sightlines upstage might suffice in getting cables onto the rotating unit. If the sum total of all the moves in a show does not exceed a few revolutions, and a trap room is present under the center pivot, it may be possible to run cable through a generous swag in the trap room that leads up through a hollow shaft at the pivot and onto the turntable. How many twists a cable bundle can withstand will have to be tested after it has be installed, and then it should be monitored during tech to insure it is never overturned. Once performances begin, the cables will have to be unwound after each performance the exact amount they were wound up during the last show.

For endless revolutions however, some form of slip ring will be needed to accomplish this. Slip rings consist of two main parts, circular conductive rings of brass, copper, or silver, and brushes that contact the rings. Either of these parts can

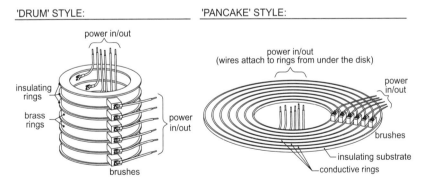

The brushes would be pushed against the rings by springs (not shown). An assembly would hold all the brushes in place, and usually this assembly is stationary, with the rings rotating with the spinning scenery.

Figure 31.6   Two main types of slip rings

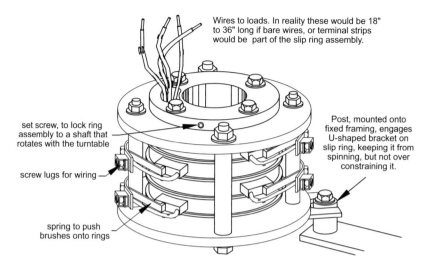

Wires to loads. In reality these would be 18"
to 36" long if bare wires, or terminal strips
would be part of the slip ring assembly.

set screw, to lock ring
assembly to a shaft that
rotates with the turntable

Post, mounted onto
fixed framing, engages
U-shaped bracket on
slip ring, keeping it from
spinning, but not over
constraining it.

screw lugs for wiring

spring to push
brushes onto rings

Figure 31.7   A typical drum type slip ring, with its housing removed

be the ones to revolve while the other remains stationary. Two main styles of slip rings exist, a drum style, that stacks the individual circuits vertically, or pancake style, where the conductive rings are arrayed horizontally (see Figure 31.6). The best style to use is mainly dictated by the space available at the turntable pivot.

The rings have maximum voltage and current ratings, and in some cases minimums too. If low level audio or network signals must pass through slip rings, ask the manufacturer their advise on how best to do this. Also inquire about shielding concerns, and distances between sensitive low-level signals and higher power ones feeding motors and lighting.

Since one ring is one wire, the slip ring assembly can grow quite large if a number of circuits needs to be passed through it. For just six lighting circuits, for instance, 18 rings for six sets of hots, neutrals, and grounds would be needed. (The six grounds and six neutrals can sometimes be commoned into a single ring each for ground and neutral wires, but that possibility depends on electrical issues beyond the topics that can be covered here.) Some Broadway shows have use slip ring assemblies passing over 100 wires, with these rings housed in an enclosure roughly 3' high, with a cost of approximately $10,000.

To avoid being overconstrained, slip rings usually attach rigidly to one part of a turntable mechanism, either to the fixed framing around the pivot point or to the turntable itself, and then a pin or arm simply forces the other half of the ring to rotate, but does not constrain it in any other way (see Figure 31.7).

If hydraulic or pneumatic power is needed on a turntable, the fluid power equivalent of an electrical slip ring is available (see Figure 31.8). Called rotary unions, rotary joints, or hydraulic swivels, these devices are rated for maximum pressure and rotational speed, but finding pressure drop versus flow information, so critical in hydraulic system design, will often require a direct call to the manufacturer.

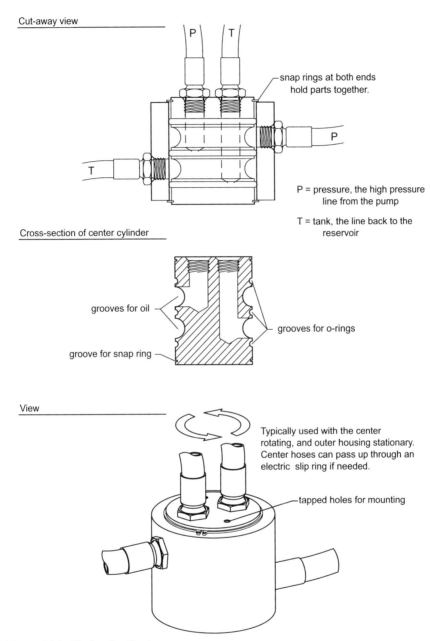

Cut-away view

snap rings at both ends hold parts together.

P = pressure, the high pressure line from the pump

T = tank, the line back to the reservoir

Cross-section of center cylinder

grooves for oil

grooves for o-rings

groove for snap ring

View

Typically used with the center rotating, and outer housing stationary. Center hoses can pass up through an electric slip ring if needed.

tapped holes for mounting

Figure 31.8 Hydraulic slip ring

Turntable Drive Specification

Before a turntable drive can be designed, a specification thoroughly detailing the effect should be made. Unlike most other mechanized effects, turntable drives and the scenery they move are often, in part, one and the same thing. A typical disk turntable is often both the scenic unit and the large sheave or sprocket of the final speed reduction stage. This means that the spec for the drive will involve the set design more so than occurs for most other effects. That said, this is not a serious complicating issue, but just something a bit different that must be dealt with.

The questions asked and points listed below should help streamline the development of a complete specification for a specific effect.

Physical Configuration: The designer's drawings or set model should clearly specify the major physical requirements of the rotating unit, such as:

- Shape: Is it a conventional round turntable, a doughnut, a jack-knife stage, an amorphous shape, etc. The location of the pivot point can change, for instance, what might appear to be a conventional disk turntable into an asymmetric unit incapable of being driven by any of the most common drive types. Always double check that the shape in the design can rotate as much as it needs to in the theatre without hitting obstructions. This applies three-dimensionally. Do not just check that the move in plan will work, but vertically too.

- Turntable support. Under a typical turntable disk is a forest of casters supporting the loads above, but turntables might be requested that are supported only within a few feet of their centers, necessitating both a different turntable structure to accommodate the overhang and a different drive type that works in towards the center and not by pushing or pulling out at the edge. Centering support is also different between a conventional disk and a doughnut turntable.

- Interrelated multiple effects: Turntables mounted on turntables are rare, but not unheard of (one short run Broadway show had a turntable on a turntable on a turntable, all eccentric to each other). Turntables have been build onto lifts, and into wagons. Space constraints often make these multi-effect units more challenging to design than multiple separate effects. Rarely also, turntables may contain lifts, have deck winches and tracks within their bounds, or need to align with deck tracks on a stationary surround to allow a piece to track onto and off of the table (most famously, the "barriers" on the original Broadway production of *Les Miserables*).

- Relationship of the unit to the building, and to other scenery around it. For instance, is there a trap room under the center pivot, is the table on a raked deck, is there a fixed deck surrounding it, or is there scenery under or behind it in which a drive machine could be hidden? Are there walls on both the turntable and a fixed surround that have to line up precisely after each move? This last question relates more to motion control than machinery, but those two topics are intertwined.

Travel distances: The production's set designer or director will ideally know exactly what moves the scenery will need to do, or, lacking this, worst case estimates will have to be made. Storyboarding scenes, or having the designer and director move set model pieces through the show's scenes can help pin down what the effect needs to do. Most important from a technical point of view is determining the extremes of rotation of the effect, that is what is the total number of turns or degrees between the furthest clockwise and furthest counter-clockwise the scenery moves.

- For a given production, a turntable may need to turn a nearly unlimited number of revolutions in one direction, or possibly just a half turn back and forth. A typical jackknife stage or a drawbridge can rarely turn more than 90°. This issue affects the drive type, and, if electrics or sound cables need to make it onto the turntable, whether a slip ring is essential or not.

- Some control systems with limited resolution trade off positioning accuracy for a greater travel distance, so for them 10 scenes of half turns alternating back and forth allows for more accurate positioning than the same 10 scenes each being a half turn the same direction (or 5 full turns).

Speed: Beyond the common concerns of identifying a maximum speed, and possibly the low speed requirements of any effect, a turntable's interactions with actors must be considered if moves happen *a vista* with actors stepping off of or onto the turntable gracefully. Since this totally subjective measure will affect turntable speed and scene change times, these moves will be difficult to estimate. A rule-of-thumb value for the maximum speed that actors could step onto or off of a turntable easily is an edge speed of 3 ft/sec (2 mph).

- Centripetal acceleration, which is proportional to a given radius and the turntable's speed:

$$a_{centripetal} = r\omega^2$$

is needed to keep an object moving in a circular path. A force directed inwards, towards the axis of rotation (the opposite of the so-called centrifugal force) creates this acceleration, keeping set pieces, props, and actors in position somewhere on the turntable.

$$F_{centripetal} = ma_{centripetal}$$

If the combined effect of speed and radial distance becomes great enough, scenery, props, and yes, even actors, may tip over or slide outward. While it is unusual for a turntable's size and speed to create any problems related to this, planning to get the table up and running as soon as possible during a show's load-in could allow actors more time to adapt the feel of a move.

Loading: What is the worst case load in terms of scenery, props, and actors on the unit. As was shown in a number of the rotational problems earlier in the book, actors on the turntable during a move can have a very significant impact on its moment of inertia, and therefore the power needed to drive it. Ask the director or stage manager how many of the cast might be on-board during a cue, or make a conservative estimate yourself from the play's script.

Noise: Not a criteria unique to turntables, but one deserving of special mention here. Turntables are often constructed with a large surface area covered in relatively lightweight materials. Dozens of casters telegraph any wheel or rolling surface imperfection on to this veritable speaker cone, and considerable noise is the result. So it is useful during the specification step in the mechanical design process to attempt to determine how quiet the turntable needs to be.

- Does it move during actor dialog, or only during scene changes, or, least critically, just within an intermission?
- Is the tone or feel of the production quiet, or will there be loud reinforced vocals and music?

Many factors will greatly influence what level of noise performance is attainable, but despite this, it is important to identify at the beginning of the technical design period what the goal is so that from the start, concepts consider noise issues.

Power on the turntable: Does electrics, sound, or automation need to get control or power wiring up onto the rotating unit? Is hydraulic or pneumatic power needed on the turntable? Video? DMX?

- For continuous rotation, or to eliminate the need to carefully monitor a cable swag, a slip ring assembly will have to be included into the design of the center pivot. There is no commonly available stock solution for this on doughnut or ring shaped turntables. Battery operated effects triggered wirelessly have been used in these situations.

Positioning accuracy: The position of turntables controlled by electronic means will need a position feedback device, a potentiometer on analog systems or an encoder for digital ones, somewhere in the drive system. The specification should state whether the positioning accuracy needed is more than typical. There are several situations that would require precise positioning:

- If walls rotating with the turntable need to align with stationary walls just off it,
- A trap on the turntable may spin over a lift
- If deck tracks run from a stationary surround onto the turntable, positioning accuracy would need to be particularly precise. A tolerance of only ±1/16″ between fixed and moving tracks would assure alignment.

Backup issues: A turntable is generally a major element in a show's set design. If the drive system were to fail, what options should be available in terms of backup? Whatever the plan is, it should be carefully communicated to stage management and the stage carpenter.

32

Lifts

Overview

Lifts have a long and continual history of use in places of entrainment. The Coliseum in ancient Rome had lifts used to raise animals into the arena for the bloody games played there, and in some Roman theatres there were apparently lifting mechanisms used to support a curtain that would be dropped at the start of a performance. Baroque theatres used lifts far more routinely than we do today. A free standing flat painted to represent a fountain, a sea monster, or a mountain was far more likely to be raised and lowered into an immensely deep space understage than flown. The understage at the Opera in the palace of Versailles (1770), for example, has five levels, and is nearly 50 feet deep.

Lifts, more than other types of machinery, routinely experience widely changing loads, and so until the advent of power sources beyond stagehands, lifts were severely limited in what they could do. Hydraulically run lifts, using water under pressure from tanks mounted high on a theatre's roof, were installed as a permanent part of the stage starting in the 1880s. This technology, with motor driven pumps soon replacing the elevated tanks, opened up the capability to lift hundreds of thousands of pounds. The Radio City Music Hall (1932) has a famous installation of lifts so advanced for their time that they were used as a model for World War II aircraft carrier lifts. Legend has it that guards were posted in the theatre for the duration of the war to prevent the secrets of these machines from being stolen.

Lifts built for use in specific productions cover a wide range of needs. At the Yale Rep alone, lifts have ranged from a 10″ square section of the stage floor that lifted an actor slowly up 6″ to menace those around him, to a 3-stage telescoping machine that transformed an 8′ diameter turntable at stage level into a spinning carnival-like thrill ride 12′ up in the air.

Arguably, lifts present a greater number of significant hazards to people around them than any other effect. A lift run to below stage level presents an open hole in the stage usually unguarded by a railing or any other barrier. Considering the many distractions on a stage during a load-in, or the darkness of a blackout during rehearsal or performance, it is unfortunately not surprising that deaths have occurred from people inadvertently stepping into the abyss. In addition, as a lift platform travels upward from trap room to stage, there are locations euphemistically called pinch points where the edge of the lift passes stationary structure. These locations can crush or shear off anything that overhangs the lift edge. Given that show specific lifts have been built with capacities at least up to 20,000 lb, someone's finger or foot will not even slow such a lift down. Also, lifts work against the unforgiving force due to gravity. In an improperly designed or poorly maintained lift system, a single part failure could drop the lift in a free fall to the bottom of its pit, or allow the lift platform to flip, dumping anything or anyone on it down into the hole. Finally, even small hand-crank-powered lifts are not devoid of hazard. In at least one instance I have heard of an operator's hands slipping off the hand crank and the lift started to free fall. The whirling handle broke the arm of the operator as he tried to regain control.

All these hazards can be minimized with good design, sound construction, and strictly implemented rules of use, but short of banning all access to the lift, they can never be eliminated. Therefore lift design deserves a thorough consideration of the issues of redundancy, conservative design factors, single failure proof design, and safety. And though not the topic of this book, all of this is absolutely true of a lift's control system also.

A Typical Application

Three key advantages of wire rope: its relatively low cost, high strength, and ability to be easily directed with sheaves, makes it just as useful for lifts as it is for other types of theatre machinery. In broad strokes, a cable run lift is little different from anything rigged to hang off cables. One of four cables can connect to each of the corners of a lift platform, and then run through sheaves to a winch specifically designed for lifting (other lifting machines are possible too, as will be shown later on in this section). Since the four cables keep the plane of the platform level, guides

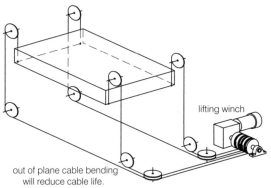

lifting winch

out of plane cable bending
will reduce cable life.

(not shown in the illustration) are needed only to prevent side to side sway. The distance between cable anchors and the upper surface of the platform must be large enough so that the lift can make it to stage level and still have those anchors be below where the cable enters the sheave.

This concept will work, but it has one significant single failure issue. If one of the cables breaks, slips free of its end connection, or otherwise stops supporting its corner, the platform can pivot about two of the remaining cable anchors, and

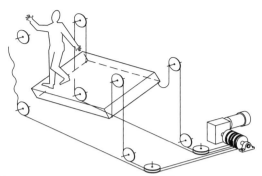

everything on the lift drops off it. The probability of this occurring can be reduced several ways. The lift's guides could be designed to prevent platform rotation. Redundant cables could be used, each capable of holding the full load, doubling the total to eight. The cables and cable anchor points could be sized using extremely conservative design factors, as high as perhaps 12, and in conjunction with this a frequent schedule of cable inspections and regular cable replacement could be instituted (as is routinely practiced in the world of performer flying).

The technique that will be shown here though is to provide both four lifting cables, as the lift already has, and four lowering cables, or cables that start at the same four corners of the platform, but travel down and through sheaves to the opposite side of the drum on the winch from the lifting cables. This prevents the platform from tipping because if a lifting cable were to break, the diagonally opposite lowering cable would go into tension, holding everything in place.

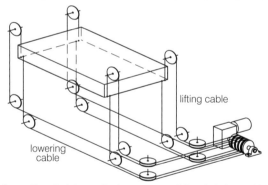

There is a side benefit of this technique. In a lift with just lifting cables, friction on guides, or binding between the fixed stage and moving platform might cause one edge of the platform to stay in place when the opposite edge was lowered by the winch. The resulting slacked cables could jump from sheaves or the winch drum (though both should be designed to prevent this), objects on the lift could begin to slide off it, or the tilt could relieve the binding and the platform would free fall to horizontal, exposing the lift cables to an impact stress. These problems are usually aggravated if the lift is lowered while empty, and the lift platform is of relatively light weight construction. Using both lifting and lowering cables eliminates the tipping, keeps cables firmly in their grooves, and all four corners of the platform moving in sync.

All lift platforms will need to be adjusted to level once they are loaded into the theatre, and tensions on the cables will need to be balanced so each carries their portion of the load. To accomplish this, the length of either end of each run of cable could be adjusted, but if a drum winch is used, adjusting the cables that anchor onto the drum is impractical. Given this, cable length adjustment can be built into the anchor points on the lift platform. Three techniques are shown below. (To simplify the illustration, only the lifting cables are shown. The lowering cables use exactly the same rigging, they just run down off the platform rather than up.)

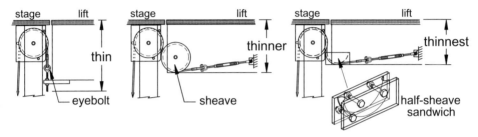

- A rated eyebolt double-nutted around a bar welded onto the lift framing will work, but it forces the lift platform to be thicker than it needs to be, reducing overall lift travel.

- A sheave can be used to turn the cable into the platform, where a turnbuckle enables cable length adjustment, but this too results in a platform thicker than it can be.

- Finally, since the sheave does not have to rotate (the cable through it only moves while the turnbuckle is being adjusted, and then only moving fractions of an inch), an inexpensive steel sheave can be sawn in half, and then bolted together with some plates that both hold a cable retaining pin, and are welded onto the lift framing.

If the trap room is shallow and the maximum lift travel possible is desired, this latter technique will prove useful.

Bending a stationary wire rope around a sheave will reduce its load capacity, but to a different extent than lines running back and forth over sheaves. This is because there is an uneven distribution of stress in the strands at any cross section of the rope on the sheave, but not the cyclically changing stresses that occur in running lines. The *Wire Rope Users Manual* describes that different D/d ratios affect the ropes efficiency, essentially a multiplier expressed as a percentage, that derates the cables working load.[1] For instance, a D/d ratio of 16 results in an efficiency of 90%, or a derating of working load by 0.9, and a D/d as low as 6 still preserves 80% of the working load. If this information can be applied to the 7×19 aircraft cable we commonly use, and that seems likely given the similar constructions of the 6×19

1. *Wire Rope Users Manual*, 3rd ed., pg 58. The information they give is for 6×19 and 6×37 fiber core and IWRC, not the 7×19 aircraft cable typically used in theatre.

IRWC specified in the *Users Manual* and 7×19 aircraft cable, then stationary sheaves at D/d of 6 need only be $6 \times 0.25 = 1.5''$ diameter—very space saving if an extra inch or two of space is needed. If a design factor of 8 is used, 1/4″ aircraft cable should in this case be loaded to no more than:

$$\frac{F_{breaking}}{n_{design\,factor}} \times n_{derating} = \frac{7000}{8} \times 0.8 = 700 \; lb$$

An example of a complete assembly of lifting and lowering cables, sheaves, and turnbuckles is shown in Figure 32.1, in both plan and section. In this example, travel distance did not need to be maximized, so sheaves are used to turn the cables

PLAN:

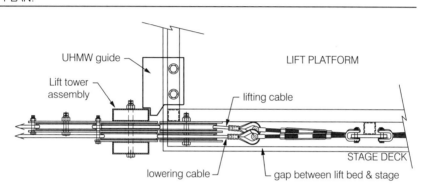

ELEVATION:

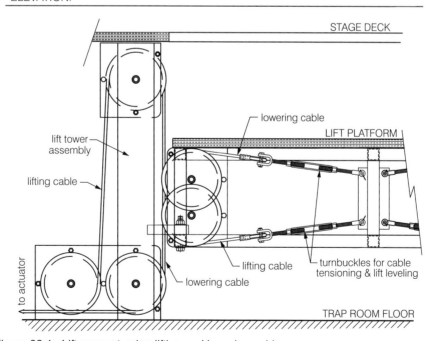

Figure 32.1   Lift concept using lifting and lowering cables

in towards the turnbuckles. Lift towers, made from two rectangular tubes, act both to support all the sheaves (and so also the platform and its load), and as guide rails.

A picture of the full roughly 5′ by 7′ lift, complete with a hydraulically operated lifting machine is shown in Figure 32.2. Since the intent here is to describe major design features rather than provide construction details, few dimensions and no component part numbers will be listed here. Instead, consider this a very detailed concept drawing and pull from it ideas of what you might use, or avoid, in your designs.

Four lift towers are held at the proper spacing by eight nearly identical frames, four running around the top, four around the bottom. The towers transfer the lift's load from sheaves carrying the lifting cables at the top, to the trap room floor upon which they stand. The towers also act as guide rails for notched UHMW blocks that prevent the platform from swaying. This assembly of towers and frames contains and holds in proper alignment all the rigging for the lift, and this enables a trial set up of the lift in the shop prior to load-in—an invaluable step that highlights any weaknesses in the design while there is still time to fix them easily.

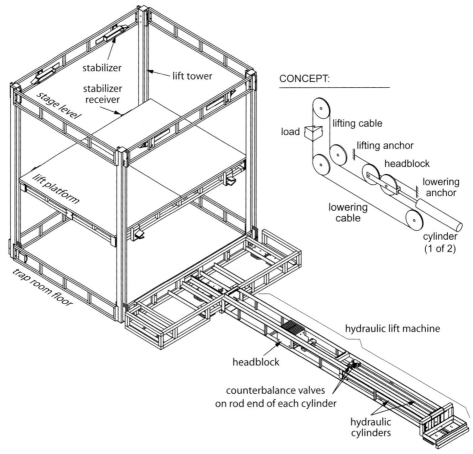

Figure 32.2   A cable run lift, using a double-purchased hydraulic lifting mechanism (with panels lining the lift shaft walls removed for clarity)

The hydraulic actuator for this design operates as shown in the concept sketch at the right of Figure 32.2. Each of the four pairs of lifting and lowering cables run over a headblock assembly that operates in a manner analogous to the arbor in a double purchase counterweight system. The headblock (like the arbor) moves half the distance of the lift platform (or handline). A pair of hydraulic cylinders pull on the headblock to raise the lift, and because of the double purchase of the headblock rigging, 1 foot of cylinder stroke equals 2 feet of lift travel. The pair of cylinders, each capable of supporting the full lift load, are part of the same safety related redunancy scheme as the lifting and lowering cables. For similiar reasons, an individual counterbalance valve is plumbed with steel fittings directly to the rod end of each cylinder port.

The rigging involved, an illustration of which is shown in Figure 32.1 below, might seem an example of excessive reverse and out of plane bending, but because no point on a cable ever travels any further than the lift platform travels, this problem only exists at points labeled a., b., and c. (which by symmetry exist on the right side also). If the rule of thumb stating that no sheaves imposing a reverse bend should be closer together than the distance the rope travels in 1/2 second at top speed, then the shortest distance between offending sheaves here, a., can be designed to exceed the minimum. Of course, frequent inspection for broken strands and discarding the cable even after use in just a run of a few weeks are steps that should be taken also.

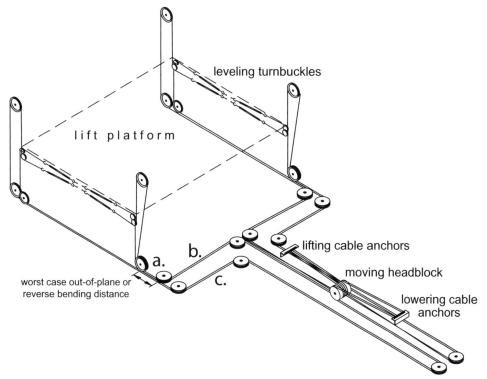

Figure 32.1   Cable lift cable rigging (lift towers shortened for this illustration)

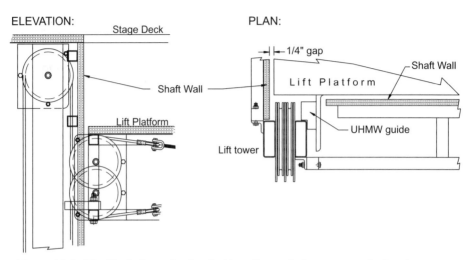

Figure 32.3 The lift shaft can be lined with walls to eliminate some pinch points

As mentioned earlier, lifts can present significant pinch, shear, and crushing hazards where the moving platform passes stationary structure, and the technical design must eliminate or mitigate all of these. Techniques vary from physical barriers that prevent anything from being within a shearing zone, to sensors that will trigger an emergency stop if they detect an object in harms way, to stagehands trained to watch for problems every time the lift moves, to requesting that the director block actors and props far from any hazard. The design and use of this lift involves all of these techniques.

Three sides of the lift shaft are lined with plywood sheets to eliminate pinch points. The plywood should run from stage level to just below the lowest point of lift platform travel (Figure 32.3). A few inches in each corner do need to be left open for the cables and guides, but these small slots can be avoided easily if actors and run crew are trained to stay away from them. All four sides of the lift shaft could be walled in, with a door leading onto the lift placed as needed. If this was done, the door should be fitted with a safety door interlock switch, a type designed for machine guarding. These switches enable two safety functions when encorporated into the lift control system. The lift should only be able to move if the door is closed, and the door should remain locked except when the lift is all the way down.

Fully walled in shafts with doors such as this are important if the lift runs quickly, or it travels a significant distance after an emergency stop occurs. If the lift both moves slowly, and does stop after only a short travel upon an E-stop, then other safety devices, such as light curtains or tape switches, could be used.

Light curtains typically have a long bar-shaped light beam transmitting component and an identically shaped receiver. These parts are placed to send a sheet of light across an area to be protected. A relay contact within the light curtain controller will be tripped if anything breaks the beams of light traveling from transmitter to receiver, and this signal would activate a lift E-stop. Integrating the two light curtain transmitter and receiver bars into a lift is often more difficult than it might first appear. This is simply because no part of the lift platform, its guides, or its cables can pass through the light beam or else every normal move would trip the curtain. The light can travel between the lift towers and the cables, as shown here, or the open side of the shaft could be along a side of the lift that is free of cables and guides.

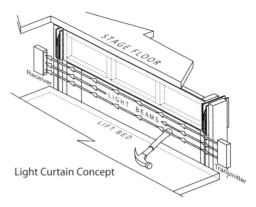

Light Curtain Concept

Tapeswitches, a tradename often used for these devices regardless of their manufacturer, are essentially long rubber bumper strips fitted along their whole length with a switch element. Pressing on the bumper trips the switch, and an associated controller monitoring it would trigger an emergency stop. The switches are available in different sensivities, different activation directions, and differing amounts of cushion distance between when contact with something is sensed, and when a hard aluminum frame is hit. This latter specification is important on a lift. If the lift will travel 2″ before stopping upon an E-stop, a switch with 1″ of cushion or "overtravel" is of no use—the object that tripped the switch may be sheared off by the time the lift is stopped.

Lift Concepts

Lift concept design is always bound by two key factors, the travel distance of the lift platform, and the space available in the theatre to accommodate this travel. Lifts that run from stage level down into a theatre's trap room are obviously limited to travel distances somewhat less than the trap room depth. Lifts that rise above the stage are also limited. If trap room space is available, a lift can be devised to push up from below. Broadway tours, though, usually assume there can be no penetration of the stage deck, so all lifting effects have to fit within a show deck only 8″ to 12″ thick – a severe limitation. In rare situations a lift platform can be supported off cables running up to the grid, which easily provides much more travel than any practical floor supported mechanism.

The concept illustrations generally show only the most common type of actuator used for that concept, but variations are of course possible. Lifts can be powered by cable drum winches that have been designed for lifting, or with a mechanism using hydraulic cylinders to pull cables, as was shown above. Electric motor driven screw jacks could be run with hydraulic motors. In rare applications, hydraulic cylinders could be replaced with pneumatic cylinders.

Cable Lifts

Whether they use only lifting lines, or both lifting and lowering, cable lifts are a staple of production specific stage machinery. This is primarily because the concept is so adaptable to a wide variety of uses, and the materials used are easily available, relatively inexpensive, and well understood by most theatre technicians.

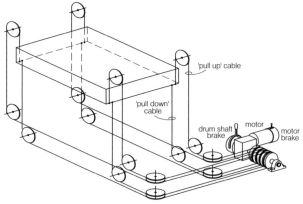

Advantages:

- The four cables typically used to support the platform keep it level, eliminating the need for a relatively long guide. Therefore lift platforms can be thin, maximizing travel.
- The actuating machine is remote from the lift, so vertical travel is not impeded by anything under it, and a lift can be fit in and around other things, and its cables just run to wherever the actuator will fit.
- Wire rope running over sheaves is a basic technology, typically already supported with wire rope cutting and swaging tools in a theatre's shop.
- Round or other non-rectangular lift platforms can be accommodated.

Disadvantages:

- The stretch of wire rope under varying tension means a cable supported lift is springy. It will drop when you step on it, and rise when you step off. This can be minimized by the use of rope diameters as large as practical, or through the use of a stabilizing device that clamps or holds the lift in place.
- A high load capacity lift would use larger diameter cables, with proportionally larger sheaves. These sheaves take up more vertical travel space, cost more, and are generally harder to obtain quickly than those for 1/4″ or smaller cables.

Scissor Lifts

A scissor lift combines an actuator, lift platform support structure, and leveling method all into one compact machine. At a minimum, a scissor lift mechanism consists two X-shaped pairs of arms that in their lowest height are nearly horizontal. An actuator, which is usually a hydraulic cylinder but any high force linear actuator will work, forces the scissors to open. In this simplest of scissors, one end of each arm has a pivot point, while the opposite end has a wheel. The pivots on all four arms are placed on one side of the X, and all the wheels on the other. As the lift rises, the upper and lower pair of pivots separate along a perfectly straight vertical line, while the wheels roll in towards the pivots. Multiple stage scissor lifts are analogous to stacking a number of these simple double-X lifts on top of each other.

The advantage they offer is a greater travel distance, and therefore greater height, for the same size scissor arm length. One or two stages is usually sufficient for scissor applications on stage, but some commercially available aerial lifts use up to 6 stages!

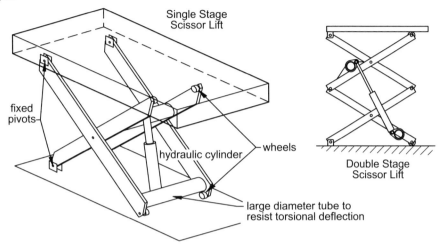

Advantages:

- Relatively thin when at their lowest height, scissor lifts extend 4 to 12 times their collapsed height (depending on the geometry of a specific machine). This is done without the need for anything above the platform pulling or guiding the lift.

- Little set-up is needed beyond placing them onto a level floor capable of supporting the weight of the lift and load. That said, guides should be used if a scissor lift extends up into an opening in a floor above it (as would be true if one was used in a trap room). This is to guarantee that the platform hits the opening, and does not catch on an edge of that opening.

- Commercially manufactured units are available in off-the-shelf and custom designs. Most of the stock lifts, made for industrial use, are in the 2′×4′ to 4′×8′ range of platform size, with modest travels up to around 4′. For examples of custom work, the Handling Speciality web site, www.handling.com, shows a number of custom lifts they have done for Broadway, theme park, and Las Vegas productions.

Disadvantages:

- Scissor lifts are invariably heavy. The structure needed to support a load and minimize deflection is considerable. Scissor arms are large solid or box steel shapes. The hydraulic cylinders that power the lifts are heavy too.

- With rare exceptions, scissor lifts are hydraulically actuated. An appropriately sized hydraulic power unit, HPU, and proportional valving will be needed to run typical velocity motion profiles. The HPU will need to be soundproofed.

- The total cost for materials is generally greater than for cable run lifts, due to the heavier structure.

There are several points of scissor lift design worth covering in some detail.

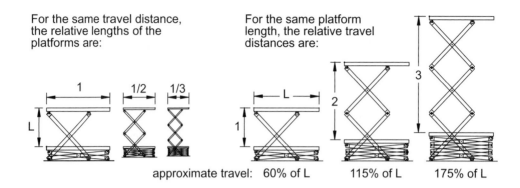

For the same travel distance, the relative lengths of the platforms are:

For the same platform length, the relative travel distances are:

approximate travel: 60% of L   115% of L   175% of L

Figure 32.4   Scissor arm length, travel, and scissor sections relationships

The geometry of the scissors mechanism forces an interrelationship between some of its dimensions in a way that simply does not exist for other lift types. A scissor lift in its lowest position has its arms nearly horizontal. The length of those arms define the minimum dimension of a platform placed on top of the lift, or conversely, the platform defines the maximum arm length. A 4′ square platform forces arm length to be slightly less than 4′. As the lift rises, the arms pivot up and, if carried to an extreme, they reach a point where the base of the X can no longer support the load, and the lift would just fall over—not useful. Also, the platform sees an ever increasing overhang as the lift rises, and so it too forces a limit on how far the X can rise. There are only rules of thumb for the top limit of a scissor mechanism, since there is no situation that defines an absolute one, but having the platform overhang be no more than 1/3 the platform length is what is used for the illustrations in Figure 32.4.

The structure that connects across from X to X acts to synchronize the movement of both scissors while providing a location to connect to the hydraulic cylinders. These cross members will be subject to torsional loading whenever the load on the lift platform is not distributed equally on both scissors. Closed shapes, such as a pipe or rectangular tube, resist deflection due to torque much better than any

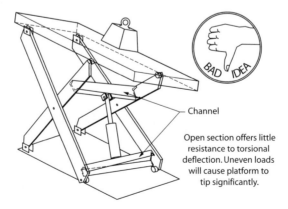

Channel

Open section offers little resistance to torsional deflection. Uneven loads will cause platform to tip significantly.

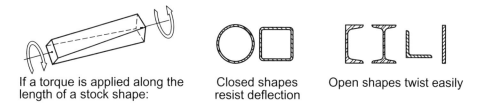

If a torque is applied along the length of a stock shape:

Closed shapes resist deflection

Open shapes twist easily

open shape of the same cross sectional area, such as angle, channel, or I-beams—on the order of 500 times better! Therefore cross members should never be open shapes.

The location of a cylinder, or cylinders, within the scissor mechanism has many variables, and there is no single correct answer for what cylinder bore, stroke, and placement to use for a given lift. Web searches for pictures of commercially made lifts will provide ideas, as will the small sample shown in Figure 32.5. Given that most cylinders used for these lifts are capable of pushing with tons of force, it is not only the cylinder that needs to fit within the lift, but also the sizable structures they press upon. The simple four step procedure shown in Figure 32.6 will, with some trial and error, provide a workable if not optomized cylinder location.

The number of cylinders to use in a given lift will depend on the force they must supply simply to lift the load, what size cylinders will physically fit within a given scissor frame, and any redundancy desired as part of a safety scheme. One cylinder is common in small commercially made lift tables, while some huge orchestra pit lifts have used eight cylinders.

Finally, one variant of typical scissor lift design is the lifting arm, essentially just half of a simple single-stage scissor. The lifting arm is useful for creating variable rakes, or, with the inclusion of the other half of the X, another way to actuate a scissor (see Figure 32.7).

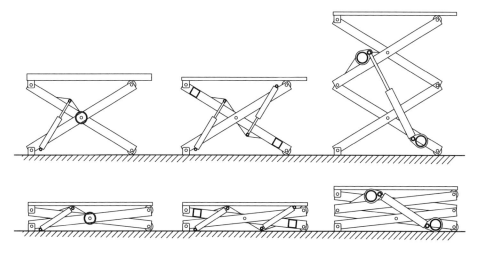

Figure 32.5 Cylinder placement and number variations

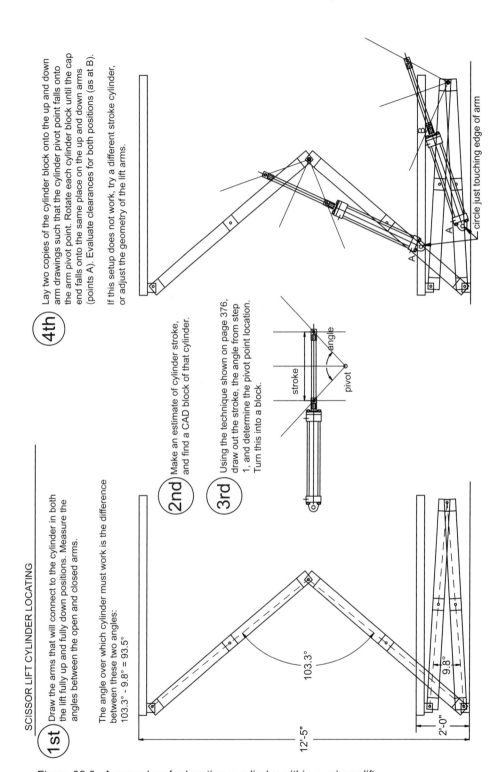

SCISSOR LIFT CYLINDER LOCATING

1st Draw the arms that will connect to the cylinder in both the lift fully up and fully down positions. Measure the angles between the open and closed arms.

The angle over which cylinder must work is the difference between these two angles:
103.3° - 9.8° = 93.5°

2nd Make an estimate of cylinder stroke, and find a CAD block of that cylinder.

3rd Using the technique shown on page 376, draw out the stroke, the angle from step 1, and determine the pivot point location. Turn this into a block.

4th Lay two copies of the cylinder block onto the up and down arm drawings such that the cylinder pivot point falls onto the arm pivot point. Rotate each cylinder block until the cap end falls onto the same place on the up and down arms (points A). Evaluate clearances for both positions (as at B).

If this setup does not work, try a different stroke cylinder, or adjust the geometry of the lift arms.

Figure 32.6   A procedure for locating a cylinder within a scissor lift

ELEVATION:

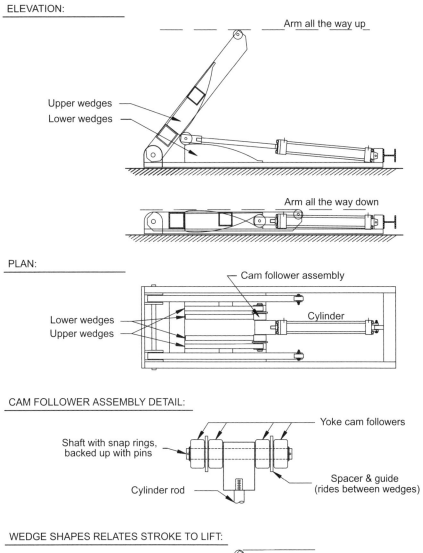

Arm all the way up

Upper wedges
Lower wedges

Arm all the way down

PLAN:

Cam follower assembly

Lower wedges
Upper wedges

Cylinder

CAM FOLLOWER ASSEMBLY DETAIL:

Yoke cam followers

Shaft with snap rings,
backed up with pins

Spacer & guide
(rides between wedges)

Cylinder rod

WEDGE SHAPES RELATES STROKE TO LIFT:

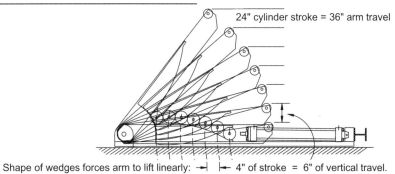

24" cylinder stroke = 36" arm travel

Shape of wedges forces arm to lift linearly: ⊢⊣ ⊢⊢ 4" of stroke = 6" of vertical travel.

Figure 32.7   A lifting arm

Screw Jack Run Lifts

There are three main screw jack lift concepts:

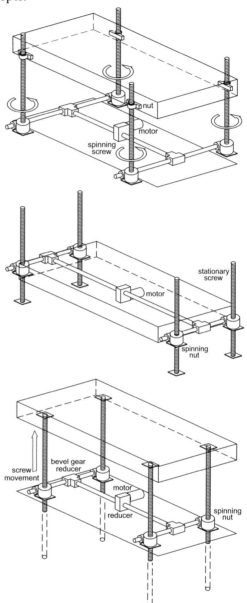

- Spin the rods with a motor and the nuts fixed to the lift platform will travel along them.

- Spin the nuts with a motor and they will travel up and down fixed rods. The motor, gearboxes and nuts ride the platform. The rods will be in compression and act as columns if they are anchored to the floor, or in tension if anchored at their top.

- The nuts housings are fixed to the floor, and when they are spun with a motor the rods drive the lift platform up and down.

Advantages:

There are only two significant advantages of screw jacks to counter the list of disadvantages, but they are both important enough to justify screw jacks in some instances:

- If the lift is designed with screw jack having an efficiency of less than 50%, the jacks will be self-locking (meaning the load will not be able to move the lift, even if the drive system fails).

- Rock solid rigidity, because the lift platform support is by steel columns.

Disadvantages:

- Generally more expensive, and slower than the other concepts.
- Mechanically involved. The installations shown in the concepts would have seven gear boxes, and possibly two universal joints on each of the six interconnecting shafts.
- The low efficiency, which was given as an advantage relative to self-locking, will require a motor with two to three times the power needed to actually lift the load.
- The inefficiency due to friction converts mechanical power to heat, and the corresponding temperature rise that results, which can destroy the jacks lubrication, limits the duty cycle of these devices. As always, consult a manufacturer for the ratings for their specific product.

Hydraulic Cylinder Run Lifts and Leveling Techniques

A hydraulic cylinder placed vertically under a lift platform enables it to directly push the platform up. The huge forces available from even modest sized cylinders, in conjunction with a proven ability of hydraulics to handle large loads, makes this an appealing idea. Add to that the near steel-column-like rigidity of a cylinder once stopped, and these lifts have greater stiffness than ones suspended off cables alone. Unfortunately, multiple hydraulic cylinders will ***never*** run in synchronization, the one requiring the least pressure will usually move its full stroke first, then the one with the next highest, and on until all have individually run in their turn. Therefore hydraulically run lifts must involve some sort of technique to force the cylinders, to run together. The stiff steel frame of a scissor lift will do this, and so too will the techniques shown below (many of the concept drawings show one cylinder, but two may be used as part of a safety through redundancy scheme).

Cable Leveling Techniques

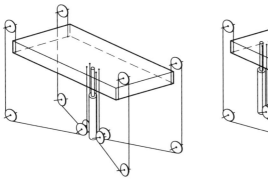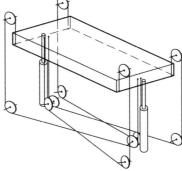

Advantages:

- Easy to implement if the length of the retracted cylinder can be accommodated in the space available.

- While oil is slightly compressible, and a cylinder will change length slightly with changes in load, lifts built this way still resist deflection far better than cable lifts.
- Hydraulic cylinders, with counterbalance valves steel-plumbed directly to the cylinder port pressurized by the load, are time-tested reliable lifting machines.
- More useful perhaps on a section of the stage floor that rises up to become a platform than as a lift dropping into the trap room.

Disadvantages:
- Since the length of a cylinder with the rod retracted is longer than its stroke, the lifting mechanism occupies a relatively large vertical space.

The Mayline

Named after the company that sold parallel rules for drafting tables (remember hand drafting?), a mayline consists of two mirror image runs of cable over sheaves that are mounted to the moving platform. All four ends of the cables are fixed to non-moving structure, though adjustability is needed during setup for cable tensioning and lift bed leveling. Depending on the layout and travel distance of the lift, a turnbuckle could be installed at one end of each of the two cables, or possibility in the run of the cable between the sheaves. Leveling is performed by loosening one cable while tightening the other. A typical mayline installation would use one mayline setup on each side of a rectangular lift platform. This keeps all four edges of the platform level, and provides redundancy should one mayline fail. This is mainly a technique useful for lifts pushed up by cylinders.

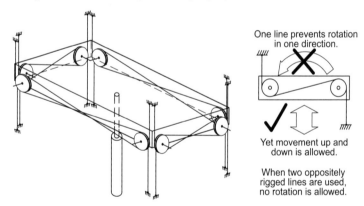

One line prevents rotation in one direction.

Yet movement up and down is allowed.

When two oppositely rigged lines are used, no rotation is allowed.

Advantages:
- A relatively thin leveling technique, so the lift platform has the potential for greater travel distance. Useful, for instance, if lift travel needs to be maximized in shallow trap rooms.

Disadvantages:
- This is not a technique worth considering if the lift is powered by cables, as they can be rigged as the leveling system.
- The stretch of wire rope under varying tension means a cable supported lift is springy. It will drop when you step on it, and rise when you step off. This can be minimized by the use of rope diameters as large as practical.

Sliding and Roller Lift Guides

Regardless of the lift actuator, lifts can be held level by various systems of sliding or roller guides. Issues of over or under constraint very easily arise here when the real lift differs from the ideal one drawn in CAD due to heat warping from welds, and imprecise construction. Beware.

A box frame guide relies on the lift platform being of sufficient depth relative to the width between guide rails to prevent the platform from tipping or jamming. The four guide columns here do need to be constructed carefully to ensure they all remain parallel and straight.

Manufactured linear bearings, or ones shop-built from cam followers can also be used to keep a platform level. Minimizing the number of guide rails simplifies the effort needed to insure that they are parallel.

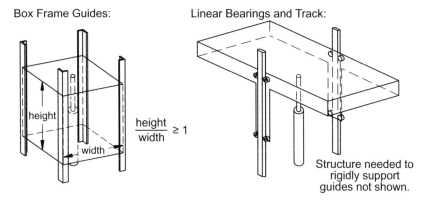

Box Frame Guides:

height

$$\frac{height}{width} \geq 1$$

width

Linear Bearings and Track:

Structure needed to rigidly support guides not shown.

Advantages:

• A simple way to get very solid leveling support.

Disadvantages:

• Vertical travel is reduced because of the space the guides must occupy.

Shop built guides should, as much as possible, rely on the parallelism of existing steel shapes rather than welding up a guide rail assembly:

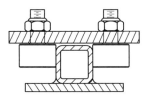

GOOD: The opposite walls of tube steel are manufactured parallel to within a few thousandths of an inch, so the slop needed to avoid overconstraint is very small.

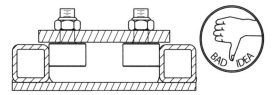

A BAD DESIGN: The parallelism of the tube walls here depends on shop tolerances, heat warping, twists in the tubes, or bends. It is difficult to make this work.

Rack and Pinion Leveling

Two or more pairs of a rack and pinion setup, with all the pinions coupled together with a shaft, is a time tested leveling system. The illustration shows the racks moving up and down with the lift platform, and the pinions and their shaft fixed. The inverse of this works too. Four racks could be mounted to the walls of the lift shaft, at the corners of the platform, and the associated four pinions would all be connected together (using shafts, universal joints, and 1:1 ratio mitre gear boxes) and mounted to the underside of the platform. Both of these variations are quite common in permanently installed orchestra and stage lifts here and in Europe.

One last variation on this mechanism is to power it with an electric motor instead of the hydraulic cylinders. A motor driven gear reducer would power the shaft connecting the pinions.

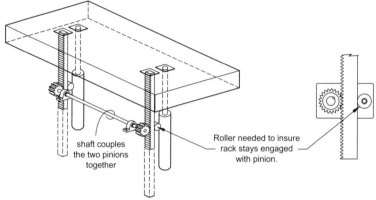

shaft couples
the two pinions
together

Roller needed to insure
rack stays engaged
with pinion.

Advantages:

• The synchronization is very good due to the stiffness of the solid steel components involved.

Disadvantages:

• Costs are high for the large heavy-duty size components typically needed for this technique.

• Space is needed for the racks as the lift drops.

• Relatively precise alignment between parts is required. This technique is no where near as forgiving as is mayline or other cable leveling schemes.

Proprietary Lift Mechanisms

There are at least two unique lifting mechanisms that appear more commonly in theatres as permanently installed orchestra pit lifts than for any show specific use, but they both have been used in special cases on Broadway shows. The Gala Spiralift® (galasystems.com) and Serapid's LinkLift™ (serapid.com) both push lifts up with steel columns from below. The Spiralift® ingeniously weaves together two steel components to create a round spiral tube of steel. The LinkLift™ can be thought of as a chain of stacked steel plates driven up by a sprocket.

Lift Specification

Dimensions: The designer's drawings or set model should clearly specify the major dimensions of the a lift, but:

- How does the lift's size, or its position, relate to permanent or difficult to move structure in the trap room?
- If the lift is being used to move furniture to the stage, has all that furniture been identified? Will anything the designer is likely to choose fit on the lift? This is an issue in three dimensions, length and width may be most obvious, but the height of a piece must be accommodated too.

Speed: The top speeds of lifts vary widely. A typical value is in the range of 1 to 2 ft/sec, but for special applications 10 ft/sec and more have been designed. Higher speeds imply longer stopping distances in an emergency stop situation, and this affects the lift safety systems. A completely walled in shaftway, with an entry door monitored with a switch that locks out movement if it is open, will eliminate pinch or crush points.

Loading: What is the worst case load in terms of scenery, props, and actors on the unit. Ask the director or stage manager how many of the cast might be on-board during a cue, or make a conservative estimate yourself based on the script.

Since many lifts form a part of the stage floor, they should be capable of supporting the typical code specified ratings of 150 psf live load. This however does not mean that a lift must be capable of running this load up and down.

Power on a lift: Does electrics, sound, or automation need to get control or power wiring up onto the lift? Is hydraulic or pneumatic power needed there too?

33

Tracked Scenery

Overview

Stage wagons, which are used to allow rapid and easy transport of scenery across the stage floor, date as far back as the ancient Greek *eccyclema*, a wagon described only briefly in some ancient texts. Roughly 100 years ago, German opera houses adopted wagons, as they had the turntable, for grand scale scene changes, and to this day huge full stage wagons are seen as essential for any proper opera house. At the Opera Bastille in Paris, a full stage wagon can be assembled from nine individual wagons that can all be coupled together in a 3 × 3 array. Each of these wagons is 6.5 m (21.3′) square, so if a particular set design requires it, the group of nine wagons forms a single mobile platform 19.5 m (64′) square![1] In the theatres with these types of wagons, large sidestage and upstage areas are needed to accommodate them as they shift around. For example, at the end of an act, the full set that is onstage might roll stage right to its storage position, while soon afterwards the complete set for the next act, already set up prior to the start of the show, rolls in from stage left to its place onstage. A third act set awaits its turn on the upstage center wagon. These wagons, acting in concert with equally elaborate lift and fly machinery, enable relatively fast blackout transformations, or visually stunning effects if viewed *a vista*. For use in the temporary setups being discussed here, the effects can be the same, the scale is usually just much smaller.

A castered platform that must move across the stage is nearly always guided by a track so that it closely follows a proscribed path and cannot veer off course, hitting building structure, scenery, props, or actors. The track fits within a system of platforms that form a show deck often covering the whole stage and wings. In large shows, these decks can be complex assemblies of effects including 6 to 10 deck tracks, cross stage slots for strip lights to up-light drops, fog effect outlet grills, sunroof mechanisms over lifts, pyrotechnic effects, inflatables, and any number of other effects. These decks tend to be 8″ to 10″ thick, often impairing audience sightlines from the first few rows of seats. At the opposite extreme, a regional theatre production may need just one deck track alone, and for this a track can be put into a thickness of 1″. This is a deck that is little more than two layers of sheetgoods.

---

1. Charlet, *L'Opera de la Bastille*, 162.

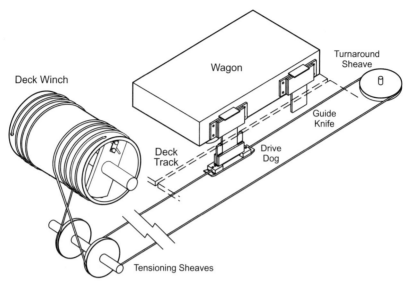

Figure 33.1   Basic components of a typical tracked wagon

Typical Applications

By far the majority of wagons are powered by deck winches pulling wire rope through deck platforming made specifically for a show. The deck has tracks or slots built into to it that allow the cable to be below the deck walking surface, hidden from sight, but its pull can be transferred up through the slot to a wagon rolling across the stage. Most of the advantages of this technique arise out the already familiar advantages of wire rope—it is strong for its size, relatively inexpensive, and easy to mule around in confined spaces with sheaves. Since the deck winch is already discussed as part of another chapter, the topic here concerns the cable as it leaves the winch and travels to and drives a wagon (see Figure 33.1).

The cable forms a fixed length loop, with both ends of the cable firmly anchored to the winch drum. A sheave defines the far end of the cable loop, and it, in conjunction with the deck winch tensioning sheaves and the drum allow the loop to be tensioned tightly, eliminating the slop a slack line would allow. At some place along one side of the taut loop of cable is a dog, basically a force transferring connecting point between the cable and a castered wagon. Most of the variations within cable driven deck track setups are variations on the design of this connecting point, and a number of those will be detailed below.

To ensure that the wagon follows the track, two points of constraint are needed, and so the driving dog is almost always paired up with a guide knife located on the wagon at a spot as far away as practical from the dog.

Four key components form the parts of the typical system: a drive dog and knife, a guide knife, a turnaround sheave, and the construction of the deck track and the deck that surrounds it. A section will be devoted to each of these topics below.

Drive Dogs and Knives

A drive dog is the connection point between a wagon moving across a stage deck, and the chain, belt, or, most commonly, cable that pulls it. A dog therefore involves two connections, one to whatever is pulling it along the track, and one to the wagon it pulls. Since wire rope is used so often, that connection will be discussed here, and the use of chains and belts will appear in the drive concepts section. The wagon connection, usually by way of a thin plate of steel called a knife, has only a few variations, and those will be discribed in the paragraphs below.

In the past, the loop of cable usually was cut where the dog was to go, and the two cable ends would then be anchored at either end of the dog with crimped stop sleeves or Crosby clips. Today most dogs clamp onto an uncut cable, either with several set screws directly bearing on the cable, or with two plates screwed together that sandwich around and grip the cable. The advantage of today's practice is simply that it is easier to set up a deck track without error than with the older method. The loop of cable can be run through the track, its ends attached at the drum, tensioned, and tested before the dog is clamped in place. No one now has to think about any of the issues involved with two individual cables, and installation errors are very much reduced.

If a wagon can stay permanently attached to the dog, then the connection from cable to wagon can be quite simple (see Figure 33.2). A short section of pipe, picked so that its inner diameter is only slightly larger than the diameter of the cable that will pass through it, is drilled and tapped for a number of cable-clamping set screws. The set screws, usually 4 to 6 of them, work best if they are the same size as the cable. A 1/4″ set screw will clamp down on a 1/4″ wire rope, while an 1/8″ screw would just pierce that cable's strands and not hold. The pipe is welded to a piece of bar stock so that the set screws will be accessible from through the deck track slot. This bar-stock knife is then just bolted to the wagon framing. A small hatch in the wagon provides access to allow bolting the knife to the wagon, and tightening the set screws onto the cable.

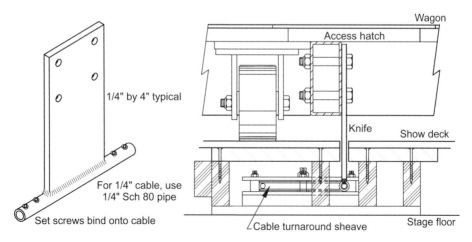

Figure 33.2 Simple dog and knife, bolted to a wagon.

This style of dog is supported entirely by the wagon, and it should never make contact with the bottom of the deck track, where it would take weight from the casters and bind. During design, leave sufficient clearance between the bottom of the dog and the track so that binding will not occur even if the track gets built slightly shorter than specified.

If a wagon needs to be disconnected from the drive cable, whether to exchange it for a different wagon, or just to clear out off-stage space, a setup using a removable knife is used (left side of Figure 33.4). Here the dog is designed with a slot capable of receiving a knife, typically made from 1/4" by 3" or 4" bar-stock. Bolted or welded to the wagon is a keeper with an identically sized slot. Connecting the wagon to the dog just involves moving the wagon keeper over the dog and dropping the knife through the keeper into the dog. (Which is easier said than done quietly in the darkness of backstage during performance. The top of the dog is often painted white to make it more visible.) To insure the knife fits easily into the dog and receiver slots, a few layers of paper or a length of small MIG welding wire should be clamped into the stack of parts prior to welding.

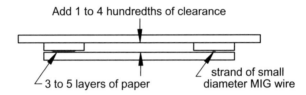

Unlike the permanently attached dog, this dog gets no support from the wagon it drives, so it constantly rides on the bottom of the deck track. The bottom plate is bent up or rounded on a grinder so as to act like a sled runner and easily ride across seams in the track and minor debris that falls into it. Some shops have attached a layer of UHMW or even Teflon onto the bottom of the dog to reduce friction, but it appears this is unnecessary.

Since large items—bolts, hair pins, screws—can fall into a track, the dogs can jam. Drive tracks should be inspected and vacuumed out frequently, but even this does not prevent something from dropping into the track during a show. The dog and track design shown in Figure 33.3 rides over debris in the track and jams do not occur.

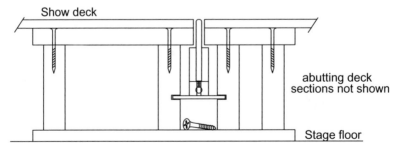

Figure 33.3 Dog that rides in slots, above debris in the track

Straight Track Knife, Keeper, and Dog:

Rotating Knife, Keeper, and Dog:

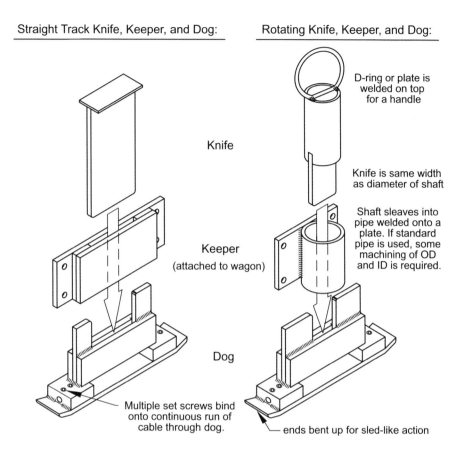

Knife

Keeper
(attached to wagon)

Dog

D-ring or plate is welded on top for a handle

Knife is same width as diameter of shaft

Shaft sleaves into pipe welded onto a plate. If standard pipe is used, some machining of OD and ID is required.

Multiple set screws bind onto continuous run of cable through dog.

ends bent up for sled-like action

Section of Wagon and Wooden Track:

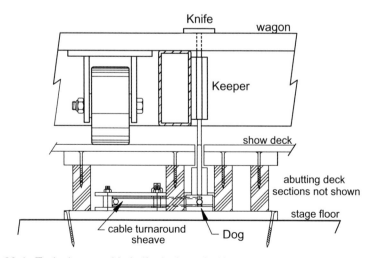

Knife

wagon

Keeper

show deck

abutting deck sections not shown

stage floor

cable turnaround sheave

Dog

Figure 33.4 Typical removable knife deck track drive components

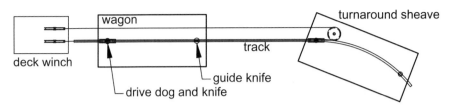

Figure 33.5   A curved guide track can turn a wagon as it approaches its position

Occasionally a wagon needs to track onstage in a straight line, and then turn as it completes its move (Figure 33.5). A conventional straight-track dog and cable rig can be used, but a guide knife, mounted at the leading edge of the wagon, will follow a curved portion of track that goes beyond the straight section of track where the dog can run. Since the platform must be able to rotate relative to the track, a rotating knife and keeper must be used for both the drive and guide knives (right side of Figure 33.4).

Guide Knives

Wagons driven along a single track generally use one drive knife, which sockets into the cable driven dog, and one guide knife. There is no need, nor any benefit from driving both knives, since nothing slips in a properly designed system. Plus an undriven guide knife just slotted into the deck track has no issues with overconstraint that two drive dogs and two welded-in-place receivers could very easily have. Three styles of commonly used guide knives are shown in Figure 33.6.

A removable guide uses exactly the same knife and receiver parts as the drive, there just is no dog beneath it in the deck track. Removable knives are useful if different wagons need to attach and detach from a track to allow different pieces to be moved on and off stage in different scenes. Removable knives also offer a crude but useful backup if the winch fails or the track jams – just walk out on stage, pull the knives, and push the unit back into the wings. Not pretty, but the show can probably keep going.

A fixed guide is just a piece of flat stock permanently bolted or welded to its wagon. These cost little, are easy to fabricate, and fast to install, but only acceptable if a wagon always stays in its track. They do not allow platforms to be rolled around the shop during build, or onstage during load-in since there is a large fin sticking out below the casters. This is not too bad if the unit is small enough to be lifted by a few hands, but fixed knives are a bad choice on large wagons.

The "pizza cutter" is a rolling fixed guide that resembles its round knife blade namesake. The guide disk has its outer edge carefully rounded and smoothed so that it resists snagging on anything in the track. Some people swear these work better because they can roll over some flaws in the track edge, rather than catch on them, but there is no conslusive proof that this is true.

In rare instances, a fixed caster is modified to include a "pizza cutter" guide next to the caster's wheel. The wheel is revoved from the caster frame and trimmed in width by 1/4." A 1/4" thick steel or aluminum disk roughly 1-1/2" larger in diameter

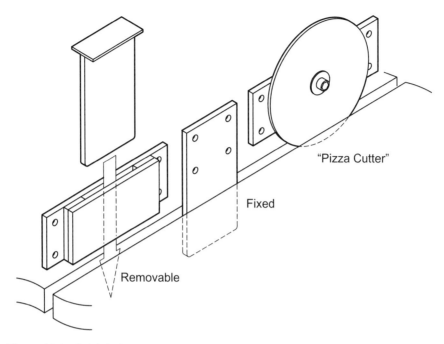

Figure 33.6   Guide knives

than the wheel (the space in the caster frame being the limiting element here) is screwed or bolted onto the trimmed side of the wheel, and the caster is reassembled. The compact combination of the weight supporting caster with a guide may be enough of a benefit to warrent the effort of making them.

Typical dogs and deck tracks are not presicion linear guides. Slop is intensionally left in the system to take into account fabrication tolerances, wood warping, uneven stage floors, etc. There is often enough slop that the distance between the drive and guide knives should be no less than 50% of the largest dimension of the wagon. Figure 33.7 illustrates this guideline.

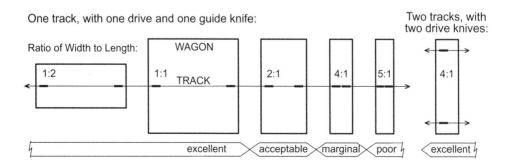

Figure 33.7   The shape of a wagon, its travel direction, and knife placement will
               determine how well the wagon is guided

Turnaround Sheaves

The turnaround sheave can be simply a single floor mounted sheave, and the out-going and return cables will be spaced apart a distance equal to the pitch diameter of this sheave (see bottom of Figure 33.4). A typical track section will have a structural member between these two cables that supports the decking above it. For a long run show, installing the cable and then installing the deck surface over it is no particular problem, but a touring show would not want to have to do this over and over. A "pinchback" turnaround sheave assembly, and a slight variation on the track design will solve this issue (Figure 33.8). The two sheaves in the "pinchback" bring the two cable loop lines to around 1-1/2" apart—a distance small enough that the decking can easily overhang. During load-in, an access panel over the turn-around is opened, both cables are dropped into the deck slot and wrapped around the turnaround, and the loop is then tensioned at the deck winch. The dog, which had been driven to beneath that access panel just before the last strike, simply drops back in that same place during the load-in. The whole cable loop is never undone from the winch, it is just spread out into the track and tensioned for use, or pulled up from the track, coiled up, and lashed to the side of its winch during transit.

Curved tracks

Curved tracks can add an extra visual dimension to *a vista* scene changes. With them, a single deck winch imparts both linear and rotary motion to the wagon. There are two major difference between straight and curved tracks. The cable is handled differently since it must be forced to follow a curve, and the dogs see side forces due to the tensioned cable pulling them around a curve.

For a gradual curved track, the concept shown at the top of Figure 33.9 can be used. The dog differs from a straight track version only in that it is constructed with a flat surface on one side. The cable tension will pull this side of the dog up against the side wall of the guide track. The track is lined with UHMW or nylon strips to reduce friction, and resist the wear of the dog and cable sliding along it.

For tighter radius curves, the cable would tend to saw through the platic lining the track, and the friction of dog against the track wall would be greater. The concept shown in the middle of Figure 33.9 has a dog with wheels that roll against the track wall, and sheaves are placed at 2 or 3 foot intervals along the track to support and guide the cable. The tabs on the dog up in the track slot will still be rub along the sides of this slot, but this has proven to be acceptable.

If the radius of the curver track is very tight—this technique has been used for a 2 foot radius corner on an L shaped track—the what is shown at the bottom of Figure 33.9 can be used. Here the dog has wheels both above and below the cable, so that all the side force on the dog is transferred through the wheels to the track wall.

In all three examples, the curved track wall is shown constructed from layers of plywood sweeps, ideally cut to all the exact same shape on a CNC router (an old fashioned band saw will work too ...).

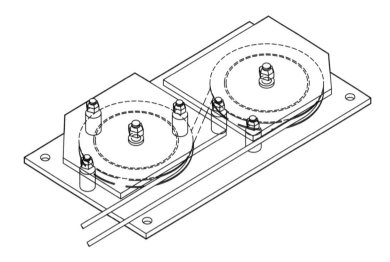

CABLE REEVING:

Slack loop of cable from deck winch is
dropped into slot between sheaves...

Dog

...and then the slack is taken up at
the tensioners on the deck winch.

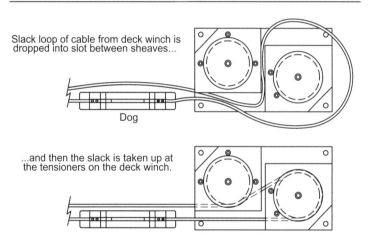

SECTION OF TRACK:

Both cables can be dropped into the deck track groove
without removing any deck section except at the turnaround.

Show deck

abutting deck
sections not shown

Stage

Pinch-back turnaround
sheave assembly

Drive cable

Return cable

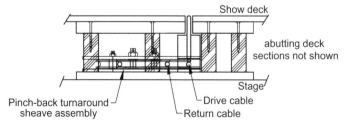

Figure 33.8   Pinchback turnaround sheave assembly

Very gradual sweep track dog:

Conventional dog built
with one flush face to
bear on curved track wall.

show deck

stage

Nylatron or MDS-filled nylon

Gradual sweep track dog:

show deck

stage

Identical sweeps of ply cut on a CNC router.

Sharp curve track dog:

Conveyer wheels from Palletflo.com

show deck

stage

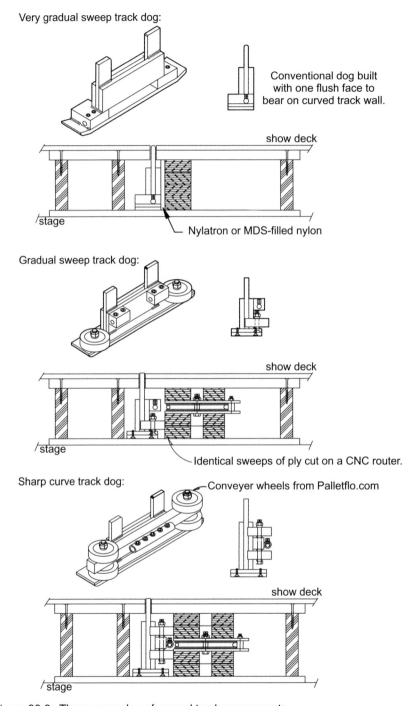

Figure 33.9   Three examples of curved track components

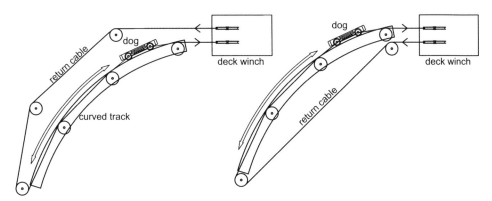

Figure 33.10   Two routes for the return run of cable in a curved track setup

The path the loop of cable takes always involves the curve of the track, but the return line can take two paths (Figure 33.10). It can run outside the curve through a series of muling sheaves, or it can return straight back along the inside of the curve. In either case, much more of the deck platforming is custom than in a straight track setup.

Deck Track Drive Concepts

Typical Deck Winch and Deck Track Drive Concept

A loop of cable is formed by anchoring both ends of a length of wire rope to a cable drum. The end of the loop farthest from the winch runs through a turnaround sheave. This is the same system already described in detail in the typical application section above.

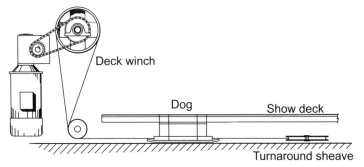

Advantages:

• Beyond the deck winch, the components are very inexpensive.

• Compact. A design, albeit not the one shown, has been built into a 1" high deck.

Disadvantages:

• While this setup works well most of the time, wire rope stretching under load can cause a surging motion, or enough slack on one side of the dog to drop the cable off the tensioning sheaves (Which are the only sheaves typically used without cable retaining pins).

Toothed Belt Drive Concept

Since a deck effect uses a fixed length loop to drive the dog, there is really no need for a drum. A loop of toothed belt, or the chains shown below, will drive a loop back and forth in much less space than a drum. Because the belt is relatively expensive (a ballpark of $2 per foot), half the loop can be belt, while the other half is wire rope. The setup is shown rigged with the dog above the return cable, but it will work with belt and cable side by side too. This latter arrangement would be required if a curved track is planned.

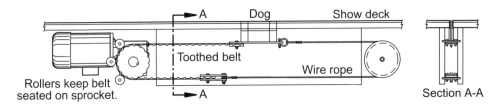

Advantages:

- The driving machine is little more than a brake-gearmotor with a toothed belt sprocket, all of which can be made compact enough to fit into a deck, rather than be set up outside it, as would be necessary for a traditional deck winch.

Disadvantages:

- Toothed belt is relatively expensive (but the lack of a drum should offset this expense).
- If the winch is in the deck, a manual backup is difficult.

Roller Chain Deck Track Drive Concept

A loop of roller chain is formed by anchoring both ends of a length of wire rope to a cable drum. The end of the loop farthest from the winch runs through a turnaround sprocket. The setup is shown rigged with the dog above the return run, but it will work with the chain loop sideways too. This latter arrangement would be required if a curved track is planned.

Advantages:

- The driving machine is little more than a brake-gearmotor with a sprocket, which can be made compact enough to fit into a deck, rather than be set up outside it, as would be necessary for a traditional deck winch.
- The components are commonly available.
- Chain is less springy or stretchy than wire rope.

Disadvantages:

- This drive could be too noisy. Padding chain paths with strips of carpet, and insuring that all seams between track sections are smooth will help minimize this noise.
- Chain is certainly more expensive than wire rope, but as was true for the toothed belt machine, the lack of a drum would offset much of this extra cost.

Serapid Push Chain Deck Track Drive Concept

A unique chain, manufactured to work in compression as well as tension, is capable of pushing a wagon as well as pulling it.

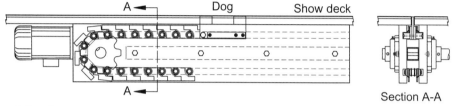

Advantages:

- The driving machine is little more than a brake-gearmotor with a sprocket, which can be made compact enough to fit into a deck, rather than be set up outside it, as would be necessary for a traditional deck winch.
- Certain crossing deck track arrangements can be implemented, something which is impossible with conventional cable loop setups.
- Since no turnaround is needed, and the chain can store compactly within a deck platform, a touring deck piece can contain winch, dog and chain all in one deck section. Just load in the deck and all the deck machinery it all set to go too.
- The chain is very rigid, so positioning is exact, and moved scenic pieces are not susceptible to any sort of surging motion as can happen on wire rope.
- The push and pull load rating is very high.

Disadvantages:

- The chain is designed for straight line motion only.
- While full setups of chain, drive sprockets, and guide rails are available from the manufacturer, shops often build their own chain guide tracks, and these are often rough enough that the many wheels on the chain create considerable noise. At least one shop has designed their own aluminum extrusion guide track to minimize noise. Using vibration isolation mounts to decouple the track from the surrounding deck platforms, and insuring that all track sections and seams are as smooth as possible will help minimize this noise.
- This technique is more expensive than any other shown here.

Friction Drive Concept

While a friction drive does not even need a track—there are no tracks in the street for your car for example—a tracked friction drive should be considered for some applications:

- Complex moves. A figure eight shaped track, for example, would be difficult to implement any other way. With pneumatic or hydraulic cylinders running railroad-track-like switches, passive guide tracks can be formed into any pattern.
- Actor or wirelessly driven devices are possible. A stage car, a motorcycle, or the boat in *Phantom of the Opera* are examples.
- Wagons that follow tracks onto and off of turntables or lifts, or that run along crossing tracks can be accommodated easily.

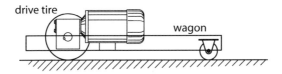

Advantages:
- The driving machine is quite simple.
- Performs some otherwise impossible moves.

Disadvantages:
- Exact position feedback is difficult. Since the drive wheel will slip or creep, by the drive wheel

Electric Dogs

Whenever electric power needs to be brought up onto a wagon, cables need to be run along the deck track, and on up through the track slot to the wagon. Commercially manufactered cable chain is made just for this sort of application. Typically made of snap together links of plastic, its square or rectangular hollow shape can be filled with wires, while its tough outer surface guides and slides along protecting the cables inside. The chain attaches to a special long dog (Figure 33.11) that has the typical receiver for a knife, an anchor platew for one end of the cable chain, and a bent sheet metal "chimney" that guides and protects the wires as they pass up through the deck track slot.

The deck track has a significant overhang covering the path of the chain, and these must be designed to support the worst case point load—perhaps a wagon's caster, or the ladder used during focus. On Broadway decks, it is not unusual that this overhang structure is 1/2″ steel plate.

PLAN VIEW SHOWING THE TWO TRAVEL EXTREMES:

(Shown at roughly one quarter the scale of the views below.)

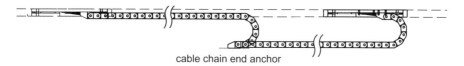

cable chain end anchor

SIDE VIEW:

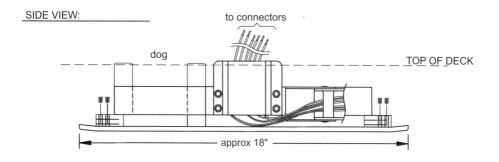

to connectors

dog

TOP OF DECK

approx 18"

TOP VIEW:

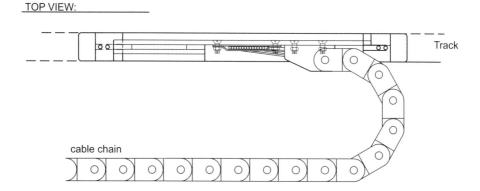

Track

cable chain

END VIEW:

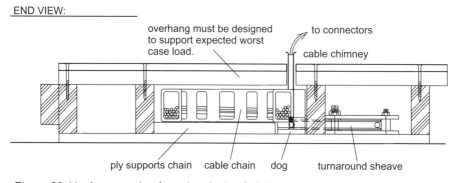

overhang must be designed to support expected worst case load.

to connectors

cable chimney

ply supports chain   cable chain   dog   turnaround sheave

Figure 33.11   An example of an electric dog fed via cable chain

ONE TRACK

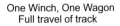

One Winch, One Wagon
Full travel of track

One Winch, Two Wagons
Travel only to center stage
Synchronized opposite motion

Two Winches, Two Wagons
Full travel, with limitations
Independent motion

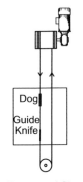

Dog

Guide
Knife

Turnaround Sheave

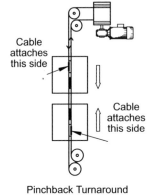

Cable
attaches
this side

Cable
attaches
this side

Pinchback Turnaround

Winch
runs this
wagon

Winch
runs this
wagon

TWO TRACKS, ONE WIDE WAGON

Line shaft type winch

Deck winch, 2 cable loops

Deck winch in trap room,
2 cable loops

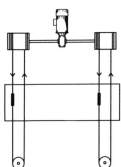

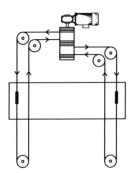

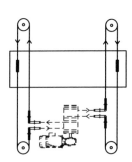

Deck winch, 1 cable loop

Deck winch, 2 cable loops

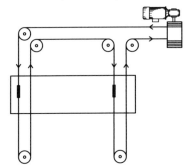

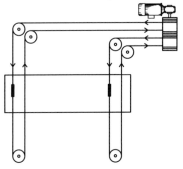

Bibliography

Overview

This bibliography is categorized by topic and annotated with brief descriptions pertaining to the relevance of the book to the current practice of mechanical design for the stage. Individual articles in serial publications (TD&P, Tech Briefs, Theatre Crafts, etc.) are numerous, but have not been included here.

The Internet has revolutionized the finding and ordering of new, used, and rare books. Typing an author and a few keywords of the title into a general search engine like Google, or going to used book dealer web sites, such as www.abe.com, can often find just about any book somewhere in the world in a fraction of a second. Used book costs vary widely, so search often if you do not at first find something affordable.

General Mechanical Engineering Books

Juvinall, Robert C., Kurt M. Marshek: *Fundamentals of Machine Component Design*, 2nd ed., New York, Wiley, 1991
> A good mechanical design text book. The book is divided into halves, with Fundamentals covering load and stress analysis, and materials issues, and Applications covering how this information applies to various machine components.

Oberg, Erik, et al.: *Machinery's Handbook*, New York, Industrial Press, Inc., over 40 editions starting 1914
> *THE* standard reference for the practical aspects of machine components, the *Handbook* contains 2500+ pages covering materials, measurement, machining, fasteners, threading, gears, shafting, etc. An essential reference.

Shigley, Joseph E., Charles R. Mischke: *Standard Handbook of Machine Design*, 2nd ed., New York, McGraw-Hill, 1996
> A reference work with accessible, readable sections on a machines components, not overwhelmed with math as some similar works are.

Young, Warren C., Richard G. Budynas: *Roark's Formula for Stress and Strain*, 7th ed., New York, McGraw-Hill, 2002
> *THE* standard for formulas covering nearly any conceivable structural situation. *Roark's* is quite daunting and dense with its information. Of limited use in typical stage machinery work, but it is useful to know it is there when needed.

The Mechanical Design Process

Boothroyd, Geoffrey, Peter Dewhurst, Winston Knight: *Product Design for Manufacture and Assembly*, 2nd ed., New York, Marcel Dekker, Inc., 2002
> An exhaustively thorough book on the topic, but since theatre does not use the majority of manufacturing processes detailed here, the book is for us of limited use.

Fogler, H. Scott, Steven E. LeBlanc: *Strategies for Creative Problem Solving*, Upper Saddle River, NJ, Prentice Hall, 1995
> An often amusing small book solely on problem solving techniques. Since it is written for a general technical audience, it is easily understood by anyone.

Pugh, Stuart: *Total Design, Integrated Methods for Successful Product Engineering*, Reading, MA, Addison-Wesley, 1990
> A classic on the subject, unfortunately out of print. Very readable, with many useful insights.

Pugh, Stuart, Don Clausing, Ron Andrade, Eds.: *Creating Innovative Products Using Total Design*, Reading, MA, Addison-Wesley, 1996
> A somewhat disjointed assemblage of the writings of the late Stuart Pugh, interesting mainly as a background to his design process, and for his plea to include engineering design into education.

Ulrich, Karl T, Steven D. Eppinger: *Product Design and Development*, 3rd ed. Boston, McGraw-Hill/Irwin, 2004
> A text book on design as done in general industry, with numerous examples, and problems. The first few pages contain eye opening information on the costs and design team sizes for five products ranging from a Stanley screwdriver to a Boeing 777.

Stage Machinery

Filipi, Joseph de, Clément Contant: *Parallèl des principaux théatres modernes de l'Europe et des machines théatrales françaises, allemandes et anglaises*, Paris, 1860, reissued, New York, Benjamin Bloom, Inc., 1968 (in French)
> Ninety percent of the book is on theatre architecture, showing plans and sections of the major theatres of the day, but the last roughly 40 pages show in considerable detail stage machinery and gas lighting equipment. The hardware shown: special hinges, joist hangers, and more hook and eyes than you can imagine they ever really needed, is long out of manufacture, but there are several lifts and trap opening mechanisms of interest. A book of interest mainly for the historian.

Grösel, Bruno: *Bühnentechnik*, Oldenbourg, Vienna, 2002 (in German)
> It is the many photographs of permanently installed stage machinery in Austrian and German theatres that make this book interesting. Installations featuring huge turntables, stage lifts, and motorized fly systems depicted in detail. The final third of the book functions roughly the same as the first half of this book.

Izenour, George C.: *Theater Technology*, New York, McGraw-Hill, 1988, 2nd edition: New Haven, Yale Univeristy Press, 1997
> A massive work covering areas of concern mainly for the theatre consultant and the historian. Beginning with a history of lighting, stage structure, and stage

machinery in western Europe and the United States, the book's major emphasis is on Izenour's long career as a consultant and inventor. There is little here for the day to day use of a technical director—that was never its intent—but this is a major book, and you should be familiar with it.

Kranich, Friedrich: *Bühnentechnik der Gegenwart*, Munich, Von R. Oldenbourg, 1929, 2 volumes (in German)

Volume 1 is of interest for its coverage of stage machinery, it has excellent illustrations of hydraulically operated lift leveling mechanisms (many of which were used as the basis for the illustrations here in Chapter 32).

Ogawa, Toshiro: *Theatre Engineering and Stage Machinery*, Japan, Ohmsha, 2000, English translation, Royston, U.K., Entertainment Technology Press, 2001

Written by a theatre consultant mainly for consultants, it therefore naturally concerns large scale permanently installed stage machinery. It covers the world in its examples, it documents machines in numerous photos and drawings, and it covers all relevant effects from lifts to flying. That said, it is not a "how to" book. It offers concepts for machines, but does not detail their mechanical design. A highly recommended book.

Rees, Terence, David Wilmore: *British Theatrical Patents*, 1801-1900, London, The Society for Theatre Research, 1996

A unique premise for a theatre technology book, the title says it all. Hundreds of patents on limelights, opera glasses, trick bicycles, and an electromagnetic flying effect, with copies of the illustrations that accompanied them. A fascinating book to flip through, but unfortunately little applicable to present day stage machinery.

Unruh, Walter: *Theatertechnik*, Berlin, Klasing & Co., 1969 (in German)

Another survey book, mainly for the users of equipment already designed and manufactured by others, it does offer a few tantalizing photos, unfortunately too small and too dark, of turntable drives, lifts, and winches. Not recommended, but if you can find an inexpensive copy, buy it.

Books Covering Mechanisms

Brown, Henry T.: *Five Hundred and Seven Mechanical Movements*, reprinted Mendham, NJ, The Astrigal Press, 1981, 1990, 1995

Originally published in 18 editions between 1868 and 1896, the pages of this book alternate between illustrations and text describing simple mechanisms: escapements, gearing of all types, linkages, cams, ratchets, pulleys, etc. The illustrations are small, nine to the page, and the text is brief but to the point. Despite its age, this is the best book for the money in this category.

Parmley, Robert O.: *Illustrated Sourcebook of Mechanical Components*, New York, McGraw-Hill, 2000

A roughly 600 page modern version of Brown's 19th century book. Great for concept generation on any mechanism out of the ordinary, and great to skim in your spare time to stoke your mind with ideas, but this said it is not a book you will consult often.

Other Cited Works

American Chain Association, *Chains for Power Transmission and Material Handling*, New York, Dekker, 1982

350+ pages on all things related to power transmission chains. Exhaustively thorough.

Bodine, Clay Editor: *Small Motor, Gearmotor, and Control Handbook*, Chicago, Bodine Electric Co.

A classic readable book on electric motors, now available for free download from the company's web site.

Educational Resources Committee: *Power Transmission Handbook*, Rosemont, IL, Power Transmission Distributors Association, 1993

An overview of machinery components from a non-mathematical point of view.

Parker Hannifin Corporation: *Design Engineers Handbook, Volume 1 Hydraulics, Bulletin 0292-B1-H*, Cleveland, Ohio, Parker Hannifin Corp., 2001

An excellent reference on all aspects of hydraulics. Highly recommended.

U.S. Tsubaki Inc.: *The Complete Guide to Chain*, Wheeling, IL, U.S. Tsubaki Inc., 1997

A very thorough presentation on all types of power transmission chains. A recommended source. Available online at: http://chain-guide.com/basics/index.html

Winsmith, *The Speed Reducer Book*, Springville, NY, 1980

An overview of gear reducers from a non-mathematical point of view.

Index

A

acceleration
    angular 63
    centripetal 64
    constant 13
    due to gravity 20
    linear 9, 13
acme screw 234
average caster radius 92

B

backups 336
ball screws 235
bearing
    friction 95
bearings 201–212
    cam followers 209
    linear 207
    mounted 205
        flange block 205
        pillow block 205
        self-aligning 206
    plain 96, 203
        PV factor 204
    rolling element
        friction 99
        types 202
    slewing rings 208
    thrust 98
belts
    toothed 186
    V 185
brakes 239–246
    caliper disk 239
    drum 240
    spring-set 239
bushings 199
    keyless 200
    QD 199
    split taper 199
    taper-lock 199

C

cable retainers 355
cam followers 209
    stud 209
    yoke 209
casters 212
    triple-swivel 214
center distance 174
center of mass 104
concept design 297
concept evaluation 304
concept evaluation matrix 305
concept generation techniques 298
concept sketches 334
Cone Drive 172
configuration concepts 301, 334
convertion
    angular to linear 63
    linear to angular 63
coordinates
    polar 59
coordinatesCartesian 59
counterbalance valve 167
counterweight 46
cross product 67
customary units 5, 24
cylinders 162
    clevis mount 164
    common sizes 164
    farm duty 162
    force 163
    K distance 165
    mounting configurations 164
    rod size 164
    selection 166
    stop tube 165
    tie rod 162

trunnion mount 164
welded end 162

D

D/d ratio 217
deck tracks 407–??
    dogs 409
    drive concepts 417
    specifications 422
degrees of freedom 306
design factor 148
design for assembly 325
design for fabrication 318
design for manufacture 317
DFA 325
DFM 317
disconnect 247
disconnects 251
displacement 4, 5
    angular 60
dot product 49
drawbridge 108
drums 223–231
    cable anchors 229
    diameter 227
    groove dimensions 226
    groove pitch 227
    wall thickness 224
    yo-yo 224

E

efficiency 169
emergency stop 150
    Category 0 150
encoders 250
equations
    constant acceleration 14–20
    constant angular accel 65
ESTA 151
E-Stop 150
extrusions 325

F

factor
    design 148
    safety 148
failure modes and effects analysis 313
FMEA 313
force 24
    acceleration 23–28
    friction 29–43
    lifting 45–48
    maximum 55
    normal 30

four quadrant diagram 114
frames 255–261
    corner details 257
    dolly 258
    water jet cut 256
freedom and constraint 306
friction
    bearing 95
    coefficients 34
        rolling 40
    kinetic 35
    measuring 36
    rolling 38
    rope on cylinders 40
    sliding 32–38
    static 33
fundamentals 3, 24

G

gear reducers 173
    backdriving 177
    mechanical horsepower 176
    parallel shaft 173
    service factor 178
    thermal horsepower 176
    worm 173
        efficiency 177
gearmotors 158
    selection 180
gears 171–180
    bevel 172
    helical 172
    miter 172
    rack and pinion 172
    spur 171
    worm 172
        center distance 174
Gravity 20
grommet drive 42
guarding 151
guards 147

H

hand cranks 338
hazards 146
    abatement 146
horsepower 49
hydraulic
    actuators 161

I

inspection
    scheduled 153
intensifier 244

International Electrotechnical
    Commission 158

J
jerk 9

K
K distance 165
keys and keyways 194

L
liability 145, 269
lifts 385–??
    concepts 393
    scissor lifts 394
    specification 404
    wire rope run 386
limit boxes 247
locked rotor torque 159
Loctite 328

M
maintenance 153
Mass 23
mass 24
Mathcad 313
mechanical design
    five key points 266
    individual's abilities 272
    teams 269, 270
mechanical design process
    concept design 297–310
    detail design 311–316
    manufacture 317–330
    overview 274
    specification 279–296
        elements 282
moment of inertia 72
    basic shapes 73
    reflected 138
        ratio 140
    transfer axis 75
motors
    electric 155
        AC 156
        C-face 158
        DC 156
        IEC 158
        NEMA 157
        servo 157
        speed torque curve 159

N
National Electrical Manufacturer's
    Association 157
National Fire Protection Association 150
Newton's Laws 23
NFPA
    Article 79 150, 251
normal force 30
nylocks 328

O
Osborn's checklist 302
oscillation reduction 127
OSHA 151, 152
overhung load 175

P
plane of contact 30
pneumatic
    actuators 161
polar section modulus 187
position sensing 248
power 49–55
    combined linear angular 129
    maximum angular 115
    rotation 113–123
Pugh, Stuart 282
pull pin release 337

R
radians 60
reduction ratio 170
reduction stage 171
reflected moment of inertia 138
risk assessment 146
roller chain 181–185
    ANSI standard numbering 182
    connecting link 181
    offset 181
    pitch 182
    sprockets 184
        A type 184
        B type 185
        chordal action 184
        wrench clearance 329
    strength 182
    tensioners 336
rolling objects 84
Roteks 208
rules of thumb 284

S
safety 145–154, 292

safety factor 148
scissor lifts 394
screw mechanisms 233–238
    acme 234
    ball 235
    screw jacks 236
service factor
    motor 160
shaft collars 335
shaft couplings 196
    jaw type 196
    roller chain 197
    universal joints 197
shafts 187–196
    combined torque and bending 191
    hollow shaft factor 191
    keys 194
        derating 188
    recommended diameters 196
    strength 187
    stress concentrations 193
    torsional stiffness 189
sheaves 219
SI 5
single failure proof design 147
slewing rings 208
slip rings 379
snap rings 335
specification 282
speed
    angular 62
    linear 7
    multiple in one system 136
    reduction 169
spreadsheets 312
springiness 126
stop tube 165
subscripts 5

T
tapped holes 321
TEAO 160
TEFC 160
TENV 160
Toothed belts 186
toothed belts 186
torque 66–68
    accereration 71–85

friction 87–100
    lifting 103–110
    maximum 124
treadmill 130
triple-swivel casters 214
turntable bearings 208
turntable drive 42
turntable drives 359–384
    concepts 367
    grommet 360
    position feedback drives 367
turntables
    average caster radius 92
    caster friction 89

U
universal joints 197

V
V-belts 185, 186
vector 4
    addition 61
    angular speed 113
    torque 113
velocity
    linear 7

W
watts 50
weight 26, 45
weld nuts 322
wheels 212
winches 341–358
    concepts 341, 344
    deck 341
        cable tensioner 238
    specification 355
    zero fleet angle 350
wire rope 215
    7 × 19 215
    D/d ratio 217
    galvanized aircraft cable 216
wrench clearance 326

X
XP 160

Franklin Pierce College Library

00170141